RADICAL PROTEST AND SOCIAL STRUCTURE

The Southern Farmers'
Alliance and Cotton Tenancy, 1880–1890

RADICAL PROTEST AND SOCIAL STRUCTURE

The Southern Farmers' Alliance and Cotton Tenancy, 1880–1890

Michael Schwartz

THE UNIVERSITY OF CHICAGO PRESS

Chicago & London

The University of Chicago Press, Chicago 60637
The University of Chicago Press, Ltd., London

97 96 95 94 93 92 91 90 89 88   5 4 3 2 1

Library of Congress Cataloging in Publication Data

Schwartz, Michael, 1942–
   Radical protest and social structure: the Southern Farmers'
Alliance and cotton tenancy, 1880–1890 / Michael Schwartz.
        p.   cm.
   Reprint. Originally published: New York: Academic Press,
1976. Originally published in series: Studies in social
discontinuity.
   Includes bibliographical references and index.
1. National Farmers' Alliance and Industrial Union.   2. Farmers—
Southern States—Political activity—History.   3. Southern States—
Social conditions.   I. Title.
HD1485.N35S37   1988   88-11919
338.1'06'075—dc19   CIP
ISBN 0-226-74235-0 (pbk.)

Contents

v

II AN ORGANIZATIONAL HISTORY OF THE SOUTHERN FARMERS' ALLIANCE

III THEORETICAL CONSIDERATIONS

IV THE PROCESS OF ALLIANCE PROTEST

Preface

My interest in protest groups as a subject of research was kindled by the almost total disjunction between academic literature on collective behavior and the reality I experienced as a participant in the Civil Rights, student, and antiwar movements of the 1960s. In my opinion, this failure derives from the refusal of sociologists to approach social movements as potentially successful and hence rational means of social reform. Academic researchers seldom ask if a movement could have succeeded. Instead, they assume the inevitability of failure; and this makes all protest in some sense pathological; the main issue becomes that of understanding why people join these failing enterprises. Hence the fascination with the "mentality" of social protest and the endless search for its "explanation" in the psychology of the participants. But such explanations are useless in answering any of the important issues revealed and raised by the 1960s: the effectiveness of protest as a reform strategy; the conditions of success and failure; the varying usefulness of centralized and decentralized structure; the question of how power is exercised and/or maintained by protestors; and the vexing issue of democracy and oligarchy.

A new departure is needed: a mode of analysis that can really explain and clarify how protest occurs and when it will grow or die. I have sought this insight in a study of the Southern Farmers' Alliance, the largest and most radical component of American Populism. The Populist movement had the broadest support of any post-Civil War insurgency, and it encompassed the entire range of reform strategy from counterinstitutions to armed violence. The Southern Alliance, until now relegated to the beginning chapters of monographs about the People's party, was particularly resourceful and creative in its attempts to dismantle the Southern tenant farming system.

This research has reaffirmed my conviction that many sociological questions can be answered only by approaching them historically. Historical analysis makes visible the process of social protest and brings into sharp focus the delicate and often complex interplay between a movement and the structure from which it derives. A movement survives and succeeds insofar as it anticipates and over-comes the resistance of the structure. It dies and fails insofar as it misunderstands or proves unable to counter this resistance. Likewise, the established structure can successfully resist change insofar as it is able to act flexibly; to anticipate, thwart, or redirect protest into less threatening channels; or to play upon divisions or weak-nesses within the protest group.

Thus, the dialectics of the relationship between movement and structure are crucial. By focusing upon the details of this interplay between the Alliance and the Southern tenant farming system, it is possible to discern the conditions of successful and unsuccessful protest. By analyzing the changes and developments in protest strategy—the new ideas and tactics that emerge as the movement de-velops—it is possible to uncover the potential and the limits of protest. And by studying the rationales that Southern farmers developed to explain their activities, it is possible to construct a theory of social protest that addresses the fundamental issues in the field of social movements. This movement-derived theory provides the foundation for the elaborate paradigm that forms the heart of this study and is the chief product of this research.

An interactive approach not only leads to a reinterpretation of protest move-ments, but also necessitates a reanalysis of the structures they seek to reform. Strictly economic analyses have failed to explain the apparent inefficiencies and irrationalities of the tenant farming system which developed in the postbellum South. What appears to the naked economic eye as inefficiency is uncovered by this interactive approach as essential to social control and is therefore—in a broader sense—both necessary and efficient. For me, this is important evidence of the fruitfulness of an interdisciplinary orientation. In this case and many others, the compartmentalization of research into economics, sociology, and history has limited our ability to understand even those phenomena that are apparently clearly within the purview of a single discipline.

For the most part, academic social movement literature has objectified its subjects and has therefore lost the insights gained by participants in protest. This book is in large part an attempt to retrieve the insights and experiences of Southern tenants and yeomen who resisted the development of cotton tenancy, a system that imposed hardship and misery on five generations of Southerners. This move-ment has, until now, been unappreciated either as a source of material about the process of social protest or as a creative and heroic effort by rank-and-file white and Black farmers to prevent the disastrous oppression that settled upon the South at the turn of the century.

I have no illusions about having conclusively proved anything. This monograph attempts to present a set of fresh historical and sociological facts, together with enough evidence to demonstrate their plausibility. I hope it is persuasive enough to encourage further research that will test, modify, and enrich the ideas developed here.

Acknowledgments

I owe particular thanks to three people. Harrison White helped me through the entire project. I am especially grateful for his willingness to sift through many bad ideas in search of the good ones. Laura Anker Schwartz kept a careful historian's eye on the line of argument, forcing me to treat my subject with respect while contributing crucial ideas which brought desparate elements together. Steven DeCanio made a substantive contribution to the analysis of tenancy. Though he has since abandoned this orientation, his work on its development was original and creative, and I feel I must acknowledge it.

I would also like to gratefully acknowledge the editorial assistance of Charles Tilly and Robert Marcus. They read and reread the manuscript, suggested sources, proposed reorganizations of the presentation, word edited, and provided needed encouragement. The quantitative sections of Part I were supported by NSF Grant GS 2689. Paul R. Levitt provided valuable assistance in the collection and analysis of this data.

Finally, I would like to thank a large number of people and organizations from whom I have borrowed ideas and insights, or received encouragement and help: Ad Hoc Committee to End Discrimination, Black Panther Party, Gary Blasi, Fredi Clark, Mark Comfort, Frederick Engels, James Forman, Free Speech Movement, Sandor Fuchs, Betty Garman, Alan Gilbert, Arthur Goldberg, Jacqueline Goldberg, Fannie Lou Hamer, The Harvard Movement, Joseph Helfgot, Carol Hendricks, Jared Israel, Mary Ellen Jenkins, M. L. King, Jr., Peter Knapp, Michael Kogen, Nancy Howell Lee, V. I. Lenin, Joel Levine, James C. Q. Loewen, Malcolm X, Wanda Mallen, Mao Tse Tung, Karl Marx, Michael Meyerson, Michael Miller, Huey Newton, Robert Moses Parris, Peace and Freedom Party, Charles Perrow, James Prickett, Progressive Labor Party, Mario Savio, Joseph Schwartz, Leon Schwartz, SDS, Bobby Seale, Paula Shatkin, Tracy Sims, SLATE, SNCC, Michael Useem, Eugene Weinstein, Barry Wellman.

INTRODUCTION

1

Tenancy, Southern Politics, and the Spiral of Agrarian Protest

For what avail our unexhausted stores,
Our bloomy mountain and our sunny shores,
With all the gifts that heaven and earth impart,
The smiles of nature and the charms of art,
While proud oppression in our valleys reigns,
And tyranny usurps our happy plains.
[Anonymous, *Raleigh Progressive Farmer*, April 2, 1889]

In the turbulence of the post–Civil War South, it was not easy to separate the truly significant developments from a wide selection of glittering irrelevancies. It was only when the dust settled in the early 1900s that the salient features of Southern society became visible. The subsequent 75 years have served to underscore the importance of three central institutions.

First, there emerged the most remarkable non-slave racial caste system developed up until that time. A system that can be accurately characterized as the parent of South African apartheid, the Southern segregation system was so complete and so fanatically enforced that huge budgetary and economic inefficiencies were required to support such minute institutions as separate bathrooms, separate schools, and even separate passenger cars on trains.[1]

Second, the Democratic party became the only viable political force in the South. The Republican party apparatus atrophied and no other political grouping arose to replace it. Despite considerable intraparty competition among Democrats, the South became the only region in which there was no consistent and important competition for elective and appointive office between two distinct and frequently very dissimilar party organizations.[2]

---

[1] Descriptions of the system can be found in C. Vann Woodward, *The Strange Career of Jim Crow* (New York, (1974); Allison Davis, Burleigh B. Gardner, and Mary R. Gardner, *Deep South* (Chicago, 1941).

[2] A good description of the workings of the one-party system can be found in V. O. Key, *Southern Politics in State and Nation* (New York, 1950).

Third, the South remained relentlessly rural, relentlessly agricultural, relentlessly cottonized, and relentlessly unmechanized. The rest of the country revolutionized agricultural methods or left farming altogether, but the South became more and more committed to a labor-intensive one-crop agriculture, with only minimal industrial development.

The one-crop farm tenancy system was the foundation upon which these anomalies of Southern social, economic, and political history rested. Yet this peculiar institution, in many ways as peculiar as the slave system which preceded it, has never received the attention it requires.[3]

[3]There is presently no satisfactory description of the Southern tenancy system. The only extensive economic effort, Matthew B. Hammond's *The Cotton Industry, An Essay in Economic History* (Ithaca, 1897), is very much out of date and filled with descriptions based upon racist assumptions about the behavior of tenants. Nevertheless, the book contains valuable figures and some important descriptive material. C. Vann Woodward, *Origins of the New South* (Baton Rouge, 1951), gives a more accurate, but very general, picture.

The most successful efforts have been more restricted works. Robert P. Brooks, *The Agrarian Revolution in Georgia 1865–1912,* Bulletin of the University of Wisconsin History Series, vol. 3 (Madison, 1914), has very good anecdotal material. It is probably the best single description of the operation of the system. However, it is distorted by racist assumptions and by its focus on one form of tenancy. Robert L. Brandfon, *Cotton Kingdom of the New South* (Cambridge, Mass., 1967), is much more modern, but this effort also restricts itself to one form of tenancy. Finally, Harold D. Woodman, *King Cotton and His Retainers* (Lexington, 1963), is an excellent reference for some aspects of the system. Though none of these works has a general analysis of the processes involved, much of the analysis contained in the present work rests on their descriptions. Robert Lee Hunt, *A History of Farmers' Movements in the Southwest, 1875–1925* (College Station, Tex., 1935), and Alex M. Arnett, *The Populist Movement in Georgia.* Columbia University Studies in History, Economics and Public Law vol. 104 (New York, 1922), both have additional anecdotal evidence.

There have also been a number of recent studies on aspects of tenancy. The two most impressive are Roger L. Ransom and Richard Sutch, "Debt Peonage in the South after the Civil War," *Journal of Economic History* 32 (September 1972), pp. 641–669, and Jonathan Weiner, *Past and Present* (August, 1975), pp. 73–44, "Planter-Merchant Conflict in Reconstruction Alabama". Others of interest are Joseph D. Reid, "Sharecropping as an Understandable Market Response: The Post Bellum South," *Journal of Economic History* 33 (March 1973), pp. 114–120; Robert Higgs, "Race Tenure and Resource Allocation in Southern Agriculture," *Journal of Economic History* 33 (March 1973), pp. 149–169; Stephen DeCanio, *Agricultural Production, Supply and Institutions in the Post Civil War South* (Cambridge, Mass., forthcoming); Stephen DeCanio, "Productivity and Income Distribution in the Post-Bellum South," *Journal of Economic History* 34 (June 1974), pp. 422–446; Roger L. Ransom and Richard Sutch, "The Ex-Slave in the Post-Bellum South: A Study of the Economic Impact of Racism in a Market Environment," *Journal of Economic History* 33 (March 1973), pp. 131–148; Robert Higgs, "Patterns of Farm Rental in the Georgia Cotton Belt, 1880–1900," *Journal of Economic History* 34 (June 1974), pp. 468–482.

Several other monographs deserve particular mention as sources for material on tenancy. Thomas D. Clark, *Pills, Petticoats and Plows: The Southern Country Store* (Indianapolis, 1944), has rich evidence about the day-to-day workings of the merchant–tenant relationship; Roger Shugg, *Origins of Class Struggle in Louisiana* (Baton Rouge, 1939), has particular evidence on landholding. Allen J. Going, *Bourbon Democracy in Alabama 1874–1890* (Montgomery, 1951), is a very informative discussion and of the legal and political tangles of tenancy; Frenise Logan, "The Movement of Negroes from North Carolina," *North Carolina Historical Review* 33 (January 1956), pp. 45–65, throws much light on the breakdown of competitive conditions.

Careful reading of newspapers, especially those connected to the protest movements, yields much descriptive material on the system. Those especially useful for the discussion in this book have been the *National Economist* (1889–1893), the *Mobile Daily Register* (1892–1894), and the *Raleigh News and Observer* (1886–1889).

Government documents are important but usually unused sources which are now readily available. Of particular importance are *Report on the Condition of Cotton Growers in the United States,* 53rd Cong., 3d sess., 1895, S. Rept. 986, Senate Committee on Agriculture and Forestry, which contains both systematic and anecdotal evidence in immense quantities (hereafter cited as *George Report*); and *Report of the Industrial Commission on Agriculture and Agricultural Labor* (vol. X of the Commission's Reports. 1901), 57th Cong., 1st sess., 1901, H. R. Documents 179 (hereafter cited as *Agriculture Report*), which includes extended testimony of 29 Southern planters.

Two widespread misconceptions have contributed to this neglect. One is the myth of the "New South" as a rapidly industrializing region closing the economic distance between itself and the mechanized North, while at the same time modernizing its agricultural profile. This image had an important political force during the pre—World War I era[4] and seems to have guided historical attention until very recently. But it had little economic substance. In fact, between 1880 and 1920, the South fell far behind the rest of the country in economic development. While the rural population of the nation as a whole declined from 72% to 49%, the 1920 South remained 72% rural (compared to 88% in 1880) and a substantial percentage of the urban population engaged in agricultural supply and service.[5] Moreover, the dominance of cotton farming reached incredible proportions. At the turn of the century, cotton accounted for 46% of the cash income of Southern farmers, and as many as 66% of all farms were principally concerned with cotton cultivation. In the Midwest, wheat farming accounted for under 25% of the cash income and dominated fewer than one-quarter of the farms.[6] Thus the "New South" did not abandon agriculture, and it did not diversify its crops.

The second misconception is more subtle and more pervasive: It underestimates the centrality of the tenant farming system in this arrangement. Partly, this underestimation derives from census figures that indicate that more than half of Southern farms were owner operated in 1900, and therefore tenant farming was not predominant. However, these figures do not take into account the widespread debt peonage which transformed farmers who technically owned their land into economically exploitable tenants. When this phenomenon is adjusted for, the number of tenants can be estimated at between 60% and 90% in the 1890s, a figure which indicates the centrality of farm tenancy in the Southern economic scene.[7] Moreover, this tenancy had the same economic consequences as the earlier slave system. The largest tenant plantations equalled in size and power those under slavery. There was as much centralization of land ownership in 1900 as in 1860, and the largest planters in 1900 controlled as many tenants as their spiritual fathers had controlled slaves.[8]

Despite the contrary imagery, the Southern one-crop farm tenancy system exercised the same domination over the economic life of the "New South" as the slave system had exercised over the Old South. And yet this analogy between "Old" and "New" could be extended to an assertion of continuity that would do grave injus-

---

[4] The *Atlantia Constitution* and its editor, Henry Grady, were notable for having successfully convinced many people that the South (the "New South") was defined by its burgeoning industry. That industry developed after the Civil War cannot be denied. But C. Vann Woodward shows in *Origins of the New South* that this new development, while affecting politics substantially, did not lessen the dominance of agriculture in the region.

[5] Figures compiled from Leon E. Truesdell, *Farm Population of the United States*, Census Monograph no. IV (1920), p. 179.

[6] Cash crop figures are for 1908; farm domination figures are for 1899. Figures calculated from *Thirteenth Census of the United States* (1910), vol. 5, pp. 490–556, 542, 557; *Twelfth Census* (1900), vol. 5, pp. 62, 90, 206–228; vol. 6, pp. 122, 414–429. *Twelfth Census* (1900), Chapter 5 of this volume.

[7] See Schwartz, *op. cit.*

[8] *Ibid.* See also Chapter 5 of this volume.

tice to the realities of Southern history. Consider briefly the historical argument that describes the one-crop tenancy system, the racial caste system, and the one-party political system as natural consequences of the economic and social circumstances of the post–Civil War period: The Civil War was fought over slavery, and afterward the North made only halfhearted attempts to impose further reforms. These attempts were defeated by the chaos of Reconstruction governments and the urgent need to reestablish a stable supply of cotton for the North and England. The Redeemer governments, which represented the same forces who had carried the South into the Civil War, brought back the same attitudes that had prevailed before. The most notable of these attitudes was a deep and abiding hatred of Blacks, which found expression in the establishment of the Jim Crow system, the establishment of tenant farming to hold Blacks in their place, and the creation of a one-party system to prevent the development of Black power through the electoral system. This system of racist control was made all the more inevitable by the inability of the South to compete with Northern industry (except for a few areas like Birmingham) because of the South's extreme underdevelopment. Moreover, the previous enslavement of Blacks, combined with the profound immiseration of poor whites, made them unlikely candidates for anything but non-mechanized agricultural employment. Still further, the entire situation made Blacks politically manipulable by radical demagogues and the whites manipulable by racist demagogues. Racial tolerance, political democracy, and industrialization were doomed by the legacy of the pre–Civil War society. All these factors, in construction with the urgent road to return to normalcy, forced the South back into the pre–Civil War mold. Thereafter, internal forces acted to preserve this system intact until after World War II.

The problem with this portrait was most dramatically expressed by the dean of Southern historians, C. Vann Woodward, in *The Strange Career of Jim Crow*. In this short monograph, Woodward revealed the astonishing fact that the racial caste system did not come into existence until after 1890, and it was by no means consolidated until 1910 or so. This alone severely undermined the traditional theory, since there is no way to explain why the reestablishment of the antebellum social arrangement took so long. To complicate matters further, other inconsistencies, previously ignored or misunderstood, became apparent. Blacks had voted consistently in many areas of the South until formal disfranchisement began—again in the 1890s. In the same areas, a viable and sometimes successful Republican party apparatus existed until that same time. Indeed, the Republicans even won state-wide elections as late as 1896. The one-party system simply did not exist before 1890.[9]

Tenancy was also in flux until after 1900. The system continued to spread rapidly until the turn of the century, and stability arrived only after 1910. Connected to this were the agrarian protests that died in the 1890s, with only a weird and refracted version surviving until the early 1900s.

[9] Key, *op. cit.*; John D. Hicks, *The Populist Revolt* (Minneapolis, 1931); C. Vann Woodward, *Origins of the New South*.

These facts lead to a rather striking conclusion: The social order that dominated the American South after 1900 did not follow on the heels of the Civil War. It emerged in the 1890s, fully 25 years after the war and 15 years after Reconstruction had collapsed. This considerable gap requires explanation beyond the postulate that antebaellum attitudes and politics were simply carried over into the postwar world.

What happened between the end of Reconstruction and the beginning of Jim Crow? Bluntly stated, the tenant farming system developed and came to dominate Southern life. The end of Reconstruction was the enabling legislation for this process, and the establishment of the segregated one-party South was its denouement. In between lay a period of social disruption, intense political and economic struggle, and mass protest. The history of the South is surrounded by the history of tenancy.[10]

Barrington Moore offers an important and powerful reinterpretation of the Civil War.[11] In his estimation, and in that of many other Marxists, the Civil War established the hegemony of the Northern industrial elite over the nation's politics. Before the war, the Southern planter aristocracy had effectively competed for this leadership, but the Northern victory broke their power and removed its foundation. The Reconstruction period represented a confused and contradictory attempt by the Northern interests to consolidate that victory and to prevent the reemergence of the planter aristocracy.[12] However, these efforts were made ineffective by a large number of disparate factors. One was the lack of unity among Northerners about how drastic the solutions should be. Another was the surprising resistance that the Southern planters put up, including their successful attempts to corrupt many Reconstruction governments. Still another was the unruliness of the Southern Blacks and whites who had joined forces with Northern interests: They continued to press for very radical actions (like the redistribution of land), as well as to promote policies that hurt the Northerners directly (like the ban on giving Mississippi public land to railroads).

These political features of Reconstruction life formed the backdrop to the urgent economic problem faced by Northern industry: the return to normal supplies of plentiful and inexpensive cotton. The social and political disruption associated with Reconstruction certainly interfered with this return to normalcy, and it was not too long before Northern business interests were ready to accept the reversal of their more ambitious schemes in exchange for economic stability.

In the period from 1868 to 1876, the federal government removed its military

[10]The analysis presented in this chapter is not intended to be a careful historical study. It adds little to the primary research on this period and relies for its evidence on the important historical works already published. It is an attempt to reinterpret the history of this period and place it in a deeper societal context. Much work would be needed to document and prove many of these assertions and interpretations, but such evidence would be out of place here. This essay has the more modest goal of placing the Southern Farmers' Alliance in a political, economic, and historical context that will make its dynamics comprehensible and indicate its central role in the history of the period.

[11] *Social Origins of Dictatorship and Democracy* (Boston, 1966), ch. 3.

[12]Unless otherwise noted, material for this discussion derives from Kenneth Stampp, *The Era of Reconstruction, 1885–1871* (New York, 1965); John Hope Franklin, *Reconstruction: After the Civil War* (Chicago, 1961); W. E. B. Dubois, *Black Reconstruction in America* (New York, 1935).

presence from one Southern state after another. It left behind power struggle between the antebellum planters (and their allies) and the newly freed Black farmers (and their allies). The planters retained title to the richest and most productive farmland and enjoyed widespread credibility—a carry-over from their Civil War leadership. The Blacks derived power from their numbers, their essential economic role, and the appeal of their programs to a great many poor whites. The struggle operated at many levels. The most visible was the tremendous armed strife which swept through the region during the period, including virtual wars in several states, and reigns of terror initiated and carried out by planter groups like the Ku Klux Klan and the Knights of the White Camelia.[13] Only slightly less visible was the struggle for control of state governments. Eventually each Confederate state saw "Redeemers" supplant Reconstructionists under the banner of drastic changes in policy and a thorough elimination of corruption.[14] Somewhat more subtle was corruption itself. Elected representatives of Reconstructionists were bribed and coopted by representatives of wealthy Redeemer interests. This resulted in the betrayal of campaign promises made to Blacks and poor whites, and the institution of policies that were less dangerous to the old upper class. It also resulted in widespread scandals which undermined the credibility of Reconstruction in general and the leaders in particular.[15] Ultimately the Redeemers won the political struggle, but they could not reestablish the prewar situation. Northern interests would not abide a return to formal slavery; they feared the power of a rejuvenated slavocracy. Black Codes, which would legally enserf the former slaves, were also impractical. Such codes, enacted and then abrogated just after the Civil War, required Blacks to sign labor contracts by January each year, with forced labor the penalty for noncompliance. Such a system, properly enforced, would guarantee Black plantation labor at extremely low wages, but Southern Redeemer leaders were afraid to try it. The system was so similar to slavery that it might arouse renewed Northern opposition. Moreover, the planters had been weakened economically and politcally by the war and Reconstruction; they might lose their fragile control in an attempt to impose such a system on the Black communities which had put up fierce resistance to their capture of state governments.

Because of these problems it was impossible to operate large landholdings as a single unit. The owners were forced to divide their holdings into small farms and rent each to a single family. In principle, this arrangement could have been the basis for small farmer prosperity, but other factors intervened. The tenants—and also owners of small farms—rarely had the capital to finance seed, equipment,

---

[13]For some treatment of this, see sources cited in note 12 above. A congressional report, *The Ku Klux Conspiracy*, 42nd Cong., 2d sess., 1872, H.R. 41 and S.R. 22, contains 16 volumes of testimony relating to this violent struggle.

[14]The struggle for control of state governments became the cornerstone of the Compromise of 1876, which marked the end of all federal attempts to inhibit planter interests. C. Vann Woodward, *Reunion and Reaction* (Boston, 1951).

[15]Ironically, after bribing Reconstructionists, the Redeemers then used this corruption as a campaign issue to justify expelling the former from office. The process reached full circle when the new "Redeemer" governments proved just as dishonest. See Stampp, *op. cit.*

and food until the crop was picked. In order to survive the growing season, they needed credit. The unique feature of the Southern system was the use of crop liens instead of loans on real estate. Under the lien system the farmer mortgaged the growing crop in exchange for needed supplies. When the harvest arrived, the supplier had first claim to the proceeds of sale, enough to cover the accumulated debt. The threat that the debt might be greater in value than the crop brought the supplier into the cultivation process as a directly interested party.

Chapters 2–5 discuss the translation of these basic ingredients into a complicated set of economic and social tensions that occupied Southern society for nearly a century. The most important outcome of these tensions was the development of debt peonage. When a farmer gave a crop lien, he was obliged to buy exclusively from one supplier. Frequently the crop did not cover the debt, and this meant the lien carried over to the next year's crop. The tenant or yeoman was forced to buy from the same supplier year after year; he was dependent for his livelihood on the amount of credit his creditor granted, and he was prevented by the lien law from renting another farm.

In this circumstance, an enterprising and unscrupulous supplier could exploit tenants and yeomen mercilessly. Indebted farmers were allowed to buy only the bare essentials and the cheapest goods. They were unable to pay for doctors or other services. Their creditor-merchant could demand that they work for him to reduce their debt and that they plant and cultivate their farms to his advantage. In short, they could be forced into a kind of serfdom.

By the time "Redemption" occurred in most Southern states, farm tenancy had already begun to develop. Without the power to reestablish plantation farming, these governments contented themselves with passing and enforcing lien laws and other legislation that gave institutional force to the developing tenancy system, while removing once and for all the threat that the Southern governments would act decisively in favor of poor Black or white interests.

Even this minimal effort was sufficient to guarantee the development and consolidation of the one-crop tenancy system.[16] Just as long as the lien laws were enforced and the government did not intervene otherwise, the internal dynamic of debt peonage cranked out immiseration and tenancy on one side, and centralization of economic power and wealth on the other. "Redemption" did not bring a return to slavery, but it made inevitable the long-run enserfment of Southern farmers.

In the meantime, the question of race had become buried under one layer of legislative rhetoric. There were no explicitly racist laws, and hardly any laws that were overtly racist in intent. The lien law and the developing tenancy system had no immediate racial targets. Every tenant and yeoman and landlord would be treated equally before the law, whether they were Black or white. But this lack of discrimination was more apparent than real. Researchers are able, to be sure, to uncover hundreds of Black landlords and thousands of prosperous Black yeomen, but this group was the exception.

---

[16] The dynamics of tenancy is more fully discussed in Chapters 2–5.

Success under the crop lien system depended upon ownership of land and the accumulation of enough savings to finance a crop without significant debt. Because Reconstruction had failed to grant the former slaves land or any other sort of compensatory payment, most Black farmers were forced to rent farms and borrow heavily against their future crop. Under these circumstances, it was almost impossible to escape debt peonage.

While many struggled against the grain and reached yeoman status, in general, Blacks sunk quickest and became trapped first. White farmers with no resources also fell quickly and joined Blacks at the bottom. Others, who owned or acquired land, were better able to resist debt and tenantization; yet, by the 1890s, most of these farmers had also become insolvent tenants. Nevertheless, some did remain prosperous into the twentieth century, and a few rose above yeomanry into land-lordship. A few tenants also rose, and a small percentage of the newly created landlords were Black.

During this period, there was intense racial prejudice. Lynchings were common, discrimination abounded, and Blacks were excluded from much of white social life. But this discrimination, while interpersonally overt, was structurally more subtle. It was not the strict apartheid that segregation would later bring, and it did not explicitly allocate structural resources on a racial basis. Instead, the structured inequality which distinguished the races at the end of Reconstruction was replicated and entrenched in the newly developed tenancy system. The Redeemer governments and Southern leaders made no effort to treat Blacks equally, but even had they done so, the tenancy system would have maintained and amplified racial stratification, with Blacks making up the largest part of the bottom and being virtually excluded from the top.[17] In this sense, the racism of the antebellum period was the cause of the continued racism of this period, though one must be careful to note that such inequality is maintained only when political, economic, and social structures are created which build on already existing inequities.

In another way, the New South was quite unlike the antebellum South. The Reconstruction had seen the rapid, though hardly overwhelming, buildup of industrial interests, almost all of them tied to Northern capital. During this time, when Southern leaders were hailing "The New South" as a developing industrial region, there was only a minimal industrial presence. Yet the industrial interests, especially the railroads, were strategically located, and however small an economic contribution they made, the Southern economy was dependent upon them. This dependence meant that industry wielded far more power than their narrow area of direct influence would suggest. Furthermore, much of the South, especially the leadership, saw salvation in industrialization, and it was recognized that the inhospitable tratment of already present industry could deter further investment. Finally, most of Southern industry had strong ties with Northern capital and

[17] A powerful analysis of the general nature of structured racism in American life can be found in Stanley Wilhelm, "Equality, America's Racist Ideology," in *The Death of White Sociology*, ed. Joyce Ladner (New York, 1973).

federal power. The South was no longer vying for national power, and it was dependent upon Northern-controlled resources and policies. The South needed investment capital—which is fundamental to tenancy—and capital was centered in the North. The South was affected by the tariff policies of the federal government, the state of the cotton manufacture industry in New England, and so forth. Since the Southern industrial interests were intimately tied to these powerful forces, they could not be easily attacked or even ignored.

Industrial interests had a coherent economic and political orientation, vast resources to pursue their goals, and the organizational capability to realize them. They had vital interests in the emerging structures during the Redeemer period. Railroads, in particular, jealously guarded their own economic position by buying and selling legislators who protected them from various control schemes.[18] In the absence of organized opposition, industrial interests influenced and political and economic life of the South without developing a substantial electoral or social base.

Before the tenancy system matured, these forces exercised great influence. The antebellum aristocracy was in no position to resist. The shortage of capital, the refusal of freedmen to re-enter prewar arrangements, and the general disarray of the economy made cotton cultivation problematical for even the largest landlords. Many lost their land and fell into poverty. Those who survived did so by adjusting to the new situation, mastering the techniques of tenancy, and adopting the mercantile strategies made possible and necessary by the crop lien system. They were joined in due course by enterprising merchants who survived the extremely risky process of extending crop liens, inducing yeomen debt, and acquiring the control necessary to the extraction of large profit.

This process was incredibly disruptive, and it was marked from the outset by widespread discontent and protest. During Reconstruction, the future tenants resisted land rental and sought yeoman status. During the 1870s, when the effect of the crop liens became apparent, there were many protests against this practice, centered especially among yeoman farmers. The Readjuster movement in Virginia and the Granger movement, which swept into the South during this time, reflected and channeled the discontent generated by the beginning of the immiseration process. In the 1880s, the Farmers' Alliance grew to become the largest protest of farmers in United States history. In this period, the whole system was brought under attack. In the 1890s, the Populist party sought to accomplish the same reforms through electoral action. At no time in the entire period was the South without its protest movement.

Protest by poor farmers was not the only conflict created by the newly developed tenancy system. As the rich landlords began to become truly rich, they discovered a particularly vicious set of antagonisms with railroads and other industrial interests. Of central importance in this conflict was the Achilles heel of the tenancy system: the necessity of tying impoverished tenants to the land. The crop lien was the legal mechanism for this: An indebted tenant could not leave his farm, since

---

[18] See Woodward, *Origins of the New South.*

any crop he cultivated had to go to the original lienholder. This mechanism was vulnerable in two ways. First, if the tenant left the county and located far from his lienholder, a landlord or merchant would happily rent to him, since it was unlikely that the original creditor could find him. Second, and more important for the industrial—landlord conflict, there were no real sanctions against the tenant working in industry, since he then produced no crop that could be foreclosed.

This vulnerability, combined with the consistently higher wages paid by industry, created tremendous disruption in the tenant farming areas. Whenever railroads or mines or factories began hiring workers, they found they could attract an unlimited supply of labor from the neighboring farming communities. This gave them leverage over their work force and over the landlords. They could hire on a seasonal basis, lay off when they did not need labor, and find ample workers whenever they rehired. There emerged a pattern of migration back and forth between farm and industry and a general mobility of labor—Black and white—into and out of tenant situations.[19]

This mobility placed great pressure on landlords and merchants. The key to successful lienholding was the establishment and exploitation of permanent debt, and this exploitation could not occur if the tenant or yeoman left or could established a credible threat to leave. Therefore, labor recruitment by industry made it extremely difficult for landlords successfully to pursue their fortunes.

In the 1870s and 1880s, this conflict intensified as the landlords became stronger and as they found less central, but still important, points of conflict with industrial interests. Not the least of these was the struggle over railroad rates. The high rates charged by railroads were paid for out of planter profits, and as soon as planters could effectively band together they began agitating for various reforms in rate setting. Similarly, the planters sought to control the developing cotton mills, to achieve price adjustments from them, and to partake of the cost reductions made possible by Southern processing of Southern crops.

As the decade progressed, the landlords added to their power by the process of centralization that took place inside the tenancy system. This enhancement of their leverage resulted in more and more insistent demands on their part, and it made their credibility as political opponents even greater. Moreover, unlike the industrial interests, the planters had a political base upon which to draw in their quest for legislative control. They appealed to smaller farmers to join them in overthrowing the rule of corrupt industrialists, and they fraudulently mobilized the votes of their mostly Black tenants. (The disfranchisement of Blacks actually began in the 1870s and 1880s, when Black Belt planters, in the attempt to assure themselves political leverage over industrial interests, stole the votes of their Black tenants and used them to establish a firm presence in state and federal governments.) The industrial interests, on the other hand, had little chance to mobilize large voting blocs, so they used their vast fortunes to buy state legislators' votes and thereby deflect or

---

[19]For discussion of this process, see Sheldon Hackney, *Populism to Progressivism in Alabama* (Princeton, 1969); Going, *op. cit.*

defeat bills they found obnoxious.[20] But this expedient was not always a satisfactory one, since the planters often exposed this corruption and used it to generate extreme antagonism toward the railroads.

The situation worked its way into a stalemate. On the one hand, the planters had a very distinct advantage in the political arena and could use this advantage to attack the railroads and other industrial interests. The purchase of state and federal officeholders was not a successful response to this power. On the other hand, industrial interests could continue to offer higher wages to tenants and liened yeomen, and the political strength of the planters was not effective in countering this disruption.

In states where there was very little industry (notably Mississippi and South Carolina), the stalemate was resolved by the overwhelming strength of the landlord class. But in other states, this stalemate became intimately intertwined with the Farmers' Alliance and the Populist party. We shall deal with this situation in more detail later, but it is useful to establish this context before launching into a complex and detailed analysis of both tenancy and the Farmers' Alliance.

During the late 1870s and early 1880s, the conditions for yeoman and tenant protest had continued to mature. As an increasing proportion of Southern farmers fell under liens and felt the immiseration generated by debt, the possibility of a protest which united yeomen and tenants across state and racial lines also increased. As the Alliance movement began to grow, it presented itself as simultaneously a threat to, and a salvation for, planter interests. It was a threat insofar as it focused its activities against local elites—the landlords and merchants. It was a salvation insofar as it focused its attack on more distant elites—the railroads and other capitalist interests. Moreover, those who flocked to the Alliance were exactly the people upon whom the planters were depending for their continuing electoral advantage. Without the backing of yeomen and tenants (especially white yeomen and tenants), the political base which gave the planters their main strength in the continuing struggle would be eroded.

As a consequence, many planters were attracted to the developing Alliance, and gave it their warm support from the moment it became a political force in the South. The Alliance even held the promise of breaking the stalemate by introducing a powerful new weapon on the side of the planters. The appearance of landlords inside a protest movement against tenancy is therefore only an apparent paradox, since the landlords themselves were in part protesting an oppressive status quo.

The tenancy system was the parent of the Farmers' Alliance, but the planter–industrial conflict was the political midwife. The uncertainty created by the real and potential recruitment of tenants and yeomen into industrial pursuits kept the social control on the farms from intolerable levels and allowed for political organizing or the farms. The continuing political struggle forced the planters to mobilize yeomen and tenants and therefore maintained the latter's interest in, and

[20]James Fletcher Doster, *Railroads in Alabama Politics, 1875–1914* (University, Ala., 1957).

understanding of, politics. The scandals and corruption with which each side charged the other further educated poor farmers about the realities of the political and economic system. The nurturance and support offered the movement by those planters who saw it as a promising vehicle for their own struggle gave it important resources and strength.

The unresolved planter–industrial conflict might have spawned a series of agrarian revolts like the Populist movement. As each subsided, a new one could have arisen by exactly the same process as the last—with misery creating the discontent, and the political situation creating the opening into which the protest would flow. However, the Farmers' Alliance and the Populist party themselves removed this possibility, forced an end to the political stalemate, and became a link in the causal chain between the slave system and the racial caste system that emerged in the early 1900s.

The Southern Farmers' Alliance began in the early 1880s, reached its zenith in 1890, and died soon afterward. In its wake it left the Southern wing of the Populist party, which from 1892 to 1896 contested for power in every Southern state. In a sense, then, the history of the Alliance must extend into the history of the Populist party, its most important and illustrious offspring.

But Populism did not end with the Populist party. In 1896, half of the Populist leadership returned to the Democratic party to support William Jennings Bryan for president. The history of the Alliance therefore extended into the Democratic party at the same time that the movement continued into the early 1900s as an independent, but electorally inconsequential, left wing alternative.

This historical extension of the Southern Alliance has led most historians to mark off the history of the Farmers' Alliance from its origins in each state in the 1880s to the demise of the Populist party in the early 1900s.[21] Yet this approach has been at the same time too broad and too narrow. The concern with the entire history of Populism has had the inevitable effect of focusing historical attention on the most well publicized and easily researched aspects of this history: the electoral campaigns. Accounts of Southern Populism have neglected generally the history of local organizing and protest undertaken by the Farmers' Alliance; even the one exception is overly organizational in focus and fails to analyze the origins and development of Alliance economic activity.[22] The Great Jute Boycott, cer-

---

[21] The most important general histories are John D. Hicks, *The Populist Revolt* (Minneapolis, 1931); and C. Vann Woodward, *Tom Watson, Agrarian Rebel* (Baton Rouge, 1939). Sheldon Hackney, *From Populism to Progressivism in Alabama* (Princeton, 1969), is of general interest. Two superb state studies exist: William W. Rogers, *The One-Gallused Rebellion* (Baton Rouge, 1970); and Roscoe Martin, *The People's Party in Texas* (Austin, 1924). Other useful sources are Jack Abramowitz, "The Negro in the Populist Movement," *Journal of Negro History* 38 (July 1953), pp. 257–289; Alex M. Arnett, *The Populist Movement in Georgia* (New York, 1922); John B. Clark, *Populism in Alabama* (Auburn, Ala., 1972); Lucius E. Daniel, "The Louisiana People's Party," *Louisiana Historical Quarterly* 26 (October 1943), pp. 1055–1149; Simeon Delap, "The Populist Party in North Carolina," *Papers of the Trinity College Historical Soceity* XIV (1922), pp. 40–72; Robert F. Durden, *The Climax of Populism* (Lexington, Ky., 1965); William Kirwin, *Revolt of the Rednecks*; Gloucester, Mass., 1964, Henry Lloyd, "The Populists at St. Louis," *Review of Reviews* 14 (September 1896), pp. 298–303; Frank L. McVey, *The Populist Movement* (New York, 1896); William D. Sheldon, *Populism in the Old Dominion* (Princeton, 1935); Francis B. Simkins, *Pitchfork Ben Tillman: South Carolinian* (Baton Rouge, 1944).

[22] Theodore Saloutos, *Farmer Movements in the South, 1865–1933* (Berkeley, 1960).

tainly one of the largest and most successful confrontations between consumers and suppliers in American history, has never been studied. The Alliance Exchange, the largest, most dramatic, and most nearly successful effort at counterinstitutional change ever attempted in this country, has received only cursory attention.[23]

More important than these gaps in historical knowledge has been the failure to analyze and understand the contrast between the Farmers' Alliance as a protest group and the Farmers' Alliance—Populist party as an instrument of electoral struggle. The transformation from the one to the other involved much more than a simple shift in strategy or tactics. The analysis presented in this monograph demonstrates that the two activities were deeply entangled and deeply contradictory at every level. Without the thoroughgoing mobilization and radicalization provided by Alliance economic struggle, the Populist party could never have been more than a tiny and inconsequential protest group. Yet the existence of the Populist party also depended upon the failure of these programs, the oligarchization of the Alliance, and the demobilization of its membership. Ironically, the Populist party was then destroyed precisely because of the economic powerlessness of its supporters, the undemocratic nature of its decisionmaking, and its inability to mobilize its rank and file to prevent fraud and corruption at the polls.

The mistaken focus on the Populist party has distorted our understanding of the post-Reconstruction South. It was the Farmers' Alliance, not the Populist party, which might have changed history. The Farmers' Alliance was the group that mobilized the agrarian revolt; the Populist party appealed to the already mobilized masses. The Farmers' Alliance attacked and disrupted the social fabric of the South; the Populist party only threatened to continue the disruption. The Farmers' Alliance created and built the insurgency which attacked the Southern Democrats; the Populist party channeled that insurgency into the electoral arena.

Refocusing attention on the Farmers' Alliance can also teach us a great deal about the nature of protest groups in the United States. Too often historians have fixed upon organizations like the Populist party:[24] a leadership group initiating and carrying through activities in the name of (and often with the support of) a large constituency. In contrast, the Alliance was a membership group that depended upon rank-and-file initiative and activities for its success; and this difference is of immense theoretical importance.

First, the study of the Alliance reveals that successful reform activity must derive from active rank-and-file participation. The focus upon disembodied leadership groups dooms the study of social movements to chronicles of failure, to analyses of why large numbers of individuals follow mistaken leaders, and psychologistic interpretations of leadership and followership. The Alliance offers a case study of a movement in which the membership made reasonable and sensible judgments about their lives, controlled their own activities, and utilized their reform organiz-

---

[23] Ralph Smith, "'Macuneism, or the Farmers of Texas in Business," *Journal of Southern History* 13 (May 1947), pp. 220–244; Homer Clevenger, "The Teaching Techniques of the Farmers' Alliance: An Experiment in Adult Education," *Journal of Southern History* 11 (November 1945), pp. 504–518.

[24] See especially Hicks, *op. cit.*; Woodward, *Origins of the New South*; Durden, *op. cit.*; Clark, *op. cit.*; Lloyd, *op. cit.*

ation to address real problems. In studying this process, we can understand the ingredients and conditions of successful social protest.

Second, this study allows us to understand the origins of groups like the Populist party itself. Such "leadership" groups derive from membership groups— in this case as the result of a complicated intraorganization process which is the substance of protest groups. Moreover, the seemingly irrational behavior of social movement membership, so long a point of major concern for social movement theorists, can be recast and understood within the framework of a process of organizational change. We perceive that social movements—even when their actions cannot redress their members' grievances—are rational attempts at social change complicated by the intrusion of intramovement difficulties and extra-movement opposition. This position is in marked contrast to a psychologistic interpretation.

Third, the possibility of studying *successful* reform activities as extensive as those undertaken by the Farmers' Alliance provides a window into the sociology of protest not afforded by either great failures like the Populist party or the smaller successes frequently studied. This leads us in two important directions simul-taneously. First, successful protest occurs when movement members develop and exercise power by using their positions within the established structure. In the Alliance, this phenomenon is revealed by the use of boycotts and counterinstitu-tions, both of which depended upon the withdrawal—either temporary or per-manent—of farmers from the economic routine of the tenancy system. Second, the development of these uses of structural power resulted in the mobilization of virtually the entire social structure in opposition to the Alliance. The fate of the Alliance and of the changes its members sought was therefore determined by the contest between the power latent in the tenant and yeoman roles, on the one hand, and the system's counterattack, on the other.

It seems, then, that a social movement is so intimately bound to the structure which gave it birth that we must begin the story of any such movement with an analysis of the established structure. Therefore, our analysis of the Southern Farmers' Alliance begins with an overview of the one-crop cotton tenancy system.

I

THE ONE-CROP COTTON TENANCY SYSTEM

2

Basic Tenancy Relationships

In the beginning of the year it is long time and long prices. In the end it is short crops and short prices, and the scene closes in bankruptcy and financial ruin.
[*Raleigh Progressive Farmer*, April 14, 1886]

In a farm tenancy system, the landowner divides his land into a number of farms and rents them to tenants who plant, cultivate, harvest, and market the crops. In the postbellum American South, farms were rented for cash or for a percentage of the crop. Rental rates varied according to the same principles that caused the price of farmland to vary: the quality of the land, the value of the buildings and improvements thereon, the proximity to markets, the price of cotton, the availability of other, similar farms at lower prices, and the number of potential renters.

Before we consider the peculiarities of Southern tenancy which affected rental arrangements, it is important to discuss certain concepts that are usually applied to tenancy situations. Most significant is the concept of "free competition," or a "competitive labor market," which is often invoked to describe or explain economic relationships. Under the hypothesis of free competition, any tenant who found charges too high would migrate to a better area; and any landlord who received too little rent could find a tenant who would pay higher rent. Tenants would gravitate to landlords who charged lower rents, leaving those who charged more with no labor, thus forcing a general lowering of rents. Through this process, an "equilibrium" market price would be reached. If such a free competition model applied to Southern tenancy, there would be no need to describe in detail the tenant—landlord relationship. The outcome of their interactions, the price of rent or the division of the crops, would be determined by market forces external to the conflict between individual landlords and tenants.

However, free competition did not always occur: Landlords were able to prevent tenants from seeking lower rentals. The most important mechanism for accomplishing this was the crop lien. We shall discuss this practice in detail later, but for now, we note one aspect of "lien law." If a tenant could not pay his rent, the landlord had the right to collect the harvested crop in payment. If the crop did not cover the debt, the landlord then had the right to the next year's harvest. If the tenant moved to a new farm, his former landlord could still collect the debt, and he had first mortgage on the new crop.

In short, an indebted tenant had little bargaining power with his or her landlord. He or she could not threaten to leave if the rental terms were below the market price because other landlords would not risk renting to a debtor whose crop could be confiscated. The indebted tenant did not, therefore, participate in competitive price setting for rental terms.

Even a solvent tenant might have difficulty finding and/or entering into a better rental arrangement. An entire legal system was erected to protect landlords from such an action. Events such as the 1889 "Negro Exodus" from North Carolina, in which over half the tenants left a single county in 2 months,[1] provided the impetus for the creation of this legal apparatus. Exodus movements occurred because local tenants heard from labor "drummers" of more advantageous rental arrangements in other states and left their homes to pursue these opportunities.[2] To prevent this movement, laws which prevented "drummers" from entering high tenancy areas were enacted and the penalties for "enticing" tenants were made extremely harsh.[3] Since the laws were most easily enforced in neighboring areas, tenants were frequently prevented from exploiting competition among neighboring landlords. They were generally better off fleeing the county entirely, hoping to escape "justice."[4]

These laws, together with the crop lien, meant that tenancy contracts were subject to various influences beyond competitive pricing. A "free labor market" did not exist in the postbellum South, and while competitive processes were a part of the tenancy system—in some cases, the dominant mechanisms—they were distorted and misshapen by these other institutions.

A second mistaken assumption about Southern farm tenancy designates the tenant as an "entrepreneur." An entrepreneur invests in a commodity, transforms it, and then attempts to sell it for a profit. An entrepreneur's livelihood depends upon low costs and high prices, and this is the image of the farmer which we all carry with us, an "ideal image." However, the unique aspect of the Southern system was that it sorted farmers into two separate groups, one that retained its entrepreneurial character and one that lost it. The first group, the planters or landlords,

---

[1]Frenise A. Logan, "The Movement of the Negroes from North Carolina," *North Carolina Historical Review* 33 (January 1956), pp. 45–65; *Raleigh News and Observer*, March 13, 1889–October 12, 1889.

[2]See, for example, *Proceedings of the Select Committee of the United States Senate to Investigate the Causes of the Removal of the Negroes from the Southern States to the Northern States*, 46th Cong., 2d sess., 1880, S. Rept. 693 (*Exodus Committee Report*); Joseph H. Taylor, "The Great Migration from North Carolina in 1879," *North Carolina Historical Review* 31 (January 1954), pp. 18–33.

[3]Allen Going, *Bourbon Democracy in Alabama, 1874–1890* (Montgomery, 1951), pp. 96 f; Logan, *op. cit.*

[4]Significantly, the mass introduction of automobiles in the 1920s undermined and destroyed many features of the tenant farming system precisely because it increased the mobility of tenants, who could take both their crops and their labor far away from the landlord and merchant. See Thomas Clark, *Pills, Petticoats and Plows* (New York, 1944), pp. 333–334; H. C. Nixon, *Lower Piedmont Country* (New York, 1944), pp. 66–68.

became businessmen who made large investments and hoped for large profits. The other, the small yeomen and tenants, gradually or rapidly lost contact with the market and became laborers on the land. Their livelihood came to depend on how much they could wrest from the landlord rather than their success at lowering production costs and selling at higher prices.

In order to make this distinction sharper, consider three ways of marketing a crop. In the first, the producer brings his or her crop to market and sells to the highest bidder. There are many means of accomplishing this, but in all cases, the seller has entered the market and participated in the setting of the price. His or her profit (or loss) depends on the cost of production, the size of the crop, and the price he or she is able to obtain. An increase in income depends upon reduced costs, increased output, or bargaining for a higher price.

In a second model, the producer must sell his or her crop to a single buyer who somehow has gained sole buying privileges. In this case, the transaction is basically outside the market, even if the selling price in some way depends upon the market price. The producer's profit (or loss) depends on the cost of production, the size of the crop, and the price. However, he or she has no role in the price setting process. If he or she wants to increase his or her income, then costs must be cut or production increased.

In the third model, the producer delivers the entire crop to the buyer and is not paid for it. Instead he or she is paid for his or her labor. Here the producer's income depends on the wages obtained for the labor; it has little to do with the price of the crop, the size of the crop, or the cost of production. An increased income depends upon discovering a way to extract higher wages from the buyer.

It is the first example which represents the true entrepreneur, because the producer enters the market and bargains for a higher price. This entrepreneurial status is the goal of all farmers, but in the postbellum South, few were able to maintain it. Instead, most yeomen and tenants fell into the second category. They were forced to sell to a single customer and therefore sought their profits in low costs and high yield. We shall call this situation true tenancy. It is a limbo between entrepreneurial farming and farm labor.

The third category of crop marketing is farm labor. In the 1890s in the South, many people who were called tenants were actually laborers because they lived on whatever their creditors would give them over the year.

Much of the confusion about cotton farming has developed out of a failure to distinguish carefully between these three forms of farming. Frequently it was not easy to categorize a particular farmer or group of farmers. Part of the goal in detailing the workings of the tenancy system is to draw these distinctions carefully and to demonstrate the importance of these contrasts.

The Basic Tenant — Landlord Relationship

The root of all tenant–landlord conflict was a dispute over who would reap the benefits of the tenant's labor. For example, one conflict between landlord and tenant arose over the "plantation farm"—that is, a farm run by the landlord himself, not by a tenant. Many landlords demanded that tenants work several days a month on the plantation farm as part of their obligations. This work could conflict with work on "garden plots," a small area the tenant used to grow crops for eating. Here we see a conflict over who would reap the benefits of the tenant's labor—if he or she worked the plantation farm, the landlord profited; if he or she worked the garden plot, the tenant benefitted.

In what follows, the major points of conflict between the tenant and landlord are discussed. Though many areas of agreement existed—both parties wanted to maximize yield, for example—it is the conflict which creates the dynamic in tenancy, and therefore it is the conflict which must be discussed.

The Rental Agreement

At the beginning of the crop year, the prospective tenant had some freedom in choosing where to farm and for what rent. Planters with available land competed for his or her labor, and the tenant was able to gain a measure of choice over the kind of land to be farmed, the amount of rent, and the choice of crops. This competition was not useful to the considerable percentage of tenants who ended the year in debt and were therefore obliged to rent from the same landowner again. In many places, tenants could not leave a farm without risking arrest for vagrancy or flight. As a result, tenants had some bargaining power, but by no means the power of an open market.

There were two basic considerations in establishing the rent:

1. *The productivity of the land.* This included both the size of the farm and the fertility of the soil. If the land was highly productive, the landlord demanded a higher rent. (That is, he would demand that the tenant work a larger proportion of his or her time on the landlord's share.
2. *Who provided the supplies.* If a tenant could supply his or her own plow, mule, and seed, the rent was lower. If he or she could not supply these and other staples of production, the rent was higher.

The rental fee was the result of the negotations on these two considerations. But the fee was not a function of these factors only. If there was a shortage of labor in the area, the landlord was forced to offer a prospective tenant much better terms. As it turned out, there was a real shortage of labor throughout this period, and rental agreements commonly reflected this situation. Unfortunately, as we shall see, the landlord could frequently make up for a poor agreement by winning other battles during the crop season. For example, he might force the tenant to purchase supplies at inflated prices or sell the crop at below-market prices.

Alternately, the tenant was often forced by circumstance to rent from a given landlord. In this situation, he or she had little leverage and might be forced to accept a bad rental agreement.

The resolution of this negotiation fell into two categories—sharecropping and cash rental.[5] In sharecropping, the tenant worked for a proportion of the crop. This setup was usually—though not always—tied to an agreement that the planter provide the mule and plow, the seed, the house, the fertilizer, and often the day-to-day supplies the tenant needed. The planter might also be granted the right to supervise closely the tenant's work and to hire additional laborers—out of the tenant's share—if he deemed it necessary. The share system could, and often did, mean that the tenant was little more than an agricultural laborer.

The cash tenant generally agreed to give the landlord a fixed price for the use of the land. This rent was paid at harvesttime: sometimes in cash, more often in crops. In this arrangement the tenant usually supplied the mule, plow, seed, as well as other supplies.

Much has been made of the distinction between cash and share tenancy.[6] The reasoning has been that the fixed rent meant the landlord did not need to oversee the land, since his portion was guaranteed. Therefore, he did not play an active role in the farming. The share landlord, on the other hand, sought to increase the crop yield in order to increase his share; that is, he had an incentive to supervise the work. However, in the real world, this distinction faded; the entrance of the merchant forced the landlord to attempt to maximize his share no matter what the formal rental arrangement was. In the Southern tenancy system, a wealthy entrepreneur could formally be a share tenant, while a penniless laborer might be a cash tenant (or even an "owner").

Selection of Crops

Crop selection was very frequently written into rental agreements,[7] and it was a matter of considerable struggle. In the 1890s, many people blamed the desperate condition of Southern farmers on "overproduction of cotton," which supposedly drove the price of this crop so low that few could survive by farming it.[8] Many modern analyses of Southern misery focus on irrational overproduction.[9] Recently, however, econometricians have suggested that cotton may have been the best choice of Southern farmers. The results of one such analysis point to the following conclusions:

1. During the period 1880–1910, cotton brought more return, *as a market crop*, than any of the other agricultural activities in which Southern farmers engaged.

[5] See Robert Brooks, *The Agrarian Revolution in Georgia* (Madison, 1914), especially pp. 52–53, on the theoretical differences between these two forms.

[6] *Ibid.*, Robert Higgs, "Patterns of Farm Rental in the Georgia Cotton Belt, 1880–1900," *Journal of Economic History* 34 (June 1974), pp. 468–482.

[7] Joseph D. Reid, "Sharecropping as an Understandable Market Response: The Post Bellum South," *Journal of Economic History* 33 (March 1973), pp. 114–120.

[8] *George Report*, pt. 1, pp. 275–401. Almost every witness mentions this *Agriculture Report*, pp. 60–61, 466, 915. (A full citation of these works appears in note 3, Chapter 1 of this volume.)

[9] William Ivy Hair, *Bourbonism and Agrarian Protest* (Baton Rouge, 1969), pp. 43–46. For a review of these theories see Stephen DeCanio, "Agricultural Production, Supply and Institutions in the Post Civil War South" (Ph.D. diss., MIT, 1972), pp. 242–247, 331–371.

2. From the point of view of its entering the market, cotton was *underproduced*. Indeed, "rational farmers would have been motivated to concentrate even more heavily in cotton production," except for some unknown "bottleneck."

3. There was no consistent trend toward increased cotton production between 1880 and 1910.

4. The South was not "locked in" to cotton farming. When prices went down, so did production, and vice versa.[10]

These results, however, are based upon a comparison between cotton and other crops as *market* items. Therefore, they reflect the suitability of cotton from the point of view of landlords who desired that their tenants produce a crop with the highest selling price.[11]

But tenants (and small yeomen) had very good reasons to favor food crops and livestock. The tenant could not take advantage of cotton's improved marketability. He or she could not afford to hold the crop for a good price, and by 1890, at least 60% of small farmers were forced by their debts to sell to the landlord or merchant at below market prices. More important, the tenant wanted to grow food crops so that his or her family could eat them, instead of being forced to buy food at extremely high prices. Corn, which farmers sold for 15¢ per bushel, might cost as much as $1.25 per bushel to buy.[12] At this price, even the best cotton acreage was worth planting in corn. Clearly, tenants were always better off it they grew their own food.

The landlord's preference for cotton was increased mightily when the landlord sold the tenant his or her supplies. In this case, increased cotton production meant that the tenants needed to buy more at the landlord's store; and food could be sold on credit at 50–100% above *retail* prices.[13] The landlord could make a double profit on cotton. First, cotton brought a better price on the market. Second, cotton production brought the tenant into the landlord's store to buy food, and the landlord made a profit on each sale.

Thus, cotton "overproduction" was a reflection of the success of the landlords in their day-to-day struggle with tenants. And the fact that it was not even more widely cultivated—that it was "underproduced" compared to its market value— indicates that tenant resistance was not wholly unsuccessful. Nevertheless, as the tenancy system took root in an area and as debt gave the landlord increasing power, cotton domination did increase. Because of this trend, the period between 1880 and 1890 saw increased proportions of cotton in every cotton state except Alabama.[14] In areas of firm landlord (or merchant) control, land lay unused or was

[10]DeCanio, *op. cit.*, pp. 244–247.

[11]*George Report*, pt. 1, pp. 318, 321, 341, 348, 415; *Raleigh Progressive Farmer*, August 7, 1888; Clark, *op. cit.*, p. 325. See Roger L. Ransom and Richard Sutch, "Debt Peonage in the South after the Civil War," *Journal of Economic History* 32 (September 1972), pp. 641–669, for a discussion of the many advantages of cotton cultivation for landlords and merchants.

[12]Clark, *op. cit.*, p. 162.

[13]See pp. 36–38.

[14]DeCanio, *op. cit.*, pp. 246, 341–372. DeCanio claims that this trend could be explained by expanding world demand for cotton, but he has no explanation for the lack of further expansion, which the world market could have supported (p. 297).

planted in cotton, while food was purchased at retail prices far above the cost of production.[15] In 1891, Laurens, South Carolina, farmers imported 60% of their food despite the capacity for self-sufficiency;[16] in 1893, Alabama Cotton Belt farmers had to purchase meat and meal from March until October because they "overplanted" cotton.[17]

Landlords did not benefit from unlimited expansion of cotton production. They found that growing food crops to sell to tenants was a profitable—perhaps essential—part of their business. Imported food cost landlords a great deal even at wholesale prices. The assertion of a Lowndes County, Mississippi, merchant that "the solvent planters are those who raise their own supplies"[18] was echoed by planters all over the South,[19] including one Jefferson County, Arkansas, landlord who asserted:

> Those who raise their own supplies, such as corn forage, meat and stock, are generally out of debt and have mortgages on their neighbors.[20]

But growing supplies was a different process when the landlord was in charge. His goal was to lessen his cost without reducing his sales. This was accomplished best through the plantation farm. While his tenants were forced to plant only cotton, the landlord set aside land upon which to grow food crops. He then sold this food at credit prices.[21] W. H. Morgan, a Greenwood, Mississippi, planter, asserted that this policy was the key to success:

> I would say it only pays to raise cotton in order to have a market at home for what you raise other than cotton. Your tenants or farm laborers are your patrons, and just so far as you can make them so, you are successful.[22]

In many cases, the landlord forced his tenants to cultivate the plantation farm as part of their contract or to pay their debts,[23] thus reducing his cost of growing food to almost nothing. If the landlord were not sufficiently dominant to use a plantation farm system effectively, he could allow the tenants to grow a specified amount of food crop and claim this harvest, along with the cotton.[24] In either case, he would attempt to maintain his profitable supply monopoly while reducing his

[15] *George Report*, pt. 1, pp. 275—438, especially pp. 314—315, 316, 318—319, 321, 323, 324, 327, 335, 341, 348, 352, 360, 369, 415; *Agriculture Report*, pp. 833—920.

[16] *George Report*, pt. 1. p. 290.

[17] Clark, *op. cit.*, p. 155.

[18] *George Report*, pt. 1, p. 325.

[19] *Ibid.*, pt. 1, pp. 327, 332, 335, 340, 348, 352, 366, 381, 383, 386; *Agriculture Report*, pp. 61, 121, 453, 500—501.

[20] *George Report*, pt. 1, pp. 371—372.

[21] Albert Bushnell Hart, *The Southern South* (new York, 1912), p. 264; Brooks, *op. cit.*, pp. 52—53; *Agriculture Report*, pp. 121, 453, 500—501.

[22] *George Report*, pt. 1, p. 347.

[23] Brooks, *op. cit.*, pp. 52—53.

[24] Reid, *op. cit.*, pp. 114—120.

own costs. Unfortunately he was very often successful, since in most large enterprises, the crop choice was determined unilaterally by the planter.[25]

Thus, even when the proportion of cotton was too great for tenant welfare, the
landlord found it profitable. However, if further expansion of cotton production did
not increase returns, or if price fluctuations called for reduction in acreage, landlords switched to other crops, provided that their cultivation did not interfere with
their supply profits.[26]

One Tennessee planter got out of cotton altogether on his own farm, but continued to hire tenants to grow cotton:

> Well, I do not plant cotton for my own crop; I am running a stock farm out there,
> and my surplus land, what I don't want to cultivate in corn and hay and grass, I rent
> out to tenants, and the bulk of that is planted in cotton.[27]

In Macon, Georgia, on the other hand, very low prices in 1891–1893 convinced
even the most committed cotton planters to allow their tenants to switch to the
cultivation of other crops.[28]

Overproduction was a matter of perspective. For the tenant, cotton was "overproduced" as soon as it meant he or she needed to purchase food which the tenant
might otherwise have grown. When cotton prices were low, the "overproduction"
was more severe, and it was made even worse when debt forced the payment of
credit prices. For the landlord, cotton was not overproduced unless its selling
price fell below that of some alternative crop.

In the conflict over choice of crops, the landlord benefited from high proportions
of cotton, while the tenant benefited from food crops. "Overproduction" was in fact
highly profitable to landlords, though it devastated tenants and small yeomen.

Fertilizers

As the land in the South became more depleted, the use of fertilizer became more
and more important in raising crops. However, it was not uncommon for the cost of
fertilizer to eat up the profits from an entire crop:

> A farmer from Stokes County [North Carolina] brought 1400 pounds of tobacco to
> market last week [all he raised] and sold it. He then went to pay his guano [fertilizer]
> bill: paid all he got for his tobacco, five dollars more, and still owes $1.30.[29]

[25] Roger Ramson and Richard Sutch, "The Ex-Slave in the Post-Bellum South," *Journal of Economic History* 33 (March 1973), p. 138; Reid, *op. cit.*, pp. 114–120. Hart, *op. cit.*, p. 264, asserts flatly that the landlord "settles what the crop will be," but he was observing the very largest holdings.

[26] DeCanio, *op. cit.*, pp. 364–365, 450–451, claims that the price responsiveness of cotton during this period demonstrates that landlords and merchants were not forcing tenants to grow cotton unprofitably. In fact, it simply demonstrates that when cotton became unprofitable for landlords, they were willing to shift their focus.

[27] *Agriculture Report*, p. 474.

[28] *George Report*, pt. 1, p. 415.

[29] *Raleigh News and Observer*, March 23, 1887.

TABLE 2.1
Why Tenants and Landlords Might Differ on Use of Fertilizer

Overall figures[a]	
Cost of fertilizer at wholesale price	160
Increased return due to use of fertilizer	180
Profit	20
Tenant's figures[a]	
Cost of tenant's share of fertilizer at retail price	100
Tenant's share of increased return due to use of fertilizer (50%)	90
Profit	10
Landlord's figures[a]	
Cost of entire supply of fertilizer at wholesale price	160
Return from selling half the supply of fertilizer to tenant at retail price (cost + 25%)	100
Net cost of half the supply of fertilizer	60
Landlord's share of return due to use of fertilizer	90
Net profit	30

[a] In dollars.

This example involves a small owner and not a tenant. The tenant had a worse problem: He had to pay his rent before he paid his fertilizer bill.

There were two conflicts over fertilizer: whether to use it and who was to pay. Both of these questions involved real divisions of interests. Sometimes, the increased yield was not enough to offset the cost of fertilizer. In this situation, the landlord might still demand its use because he did not want to see his or her soil depleted. The tenant would, of course, resist the use in this case because it involved investing his or her labor (and/or money) for something from which he or she did not benefit. A Georgia planter found this resistance inexcusable, but his complaint makes the tenant seem perfectly rational:

> The tenant and renter has no interest in your landed estate whatever. He therefore goes in to get the best crops he possibly can out the land with the least expense, and as fast as the land goes to where it is not remunerative to him he abandons it.[30]

Needless to say, planters tried to prevent this sort of farming.

Even when the value of an increased yield was greater than the cost of fertilizer, there could be conflict over its use, as Table 2.1 demonstrates. If fertilizer cost $160 at wholesale and produced a $180 increase in crop yield, it was certainly worth using. If the landlord and tenant split both costs and returns, each one might spend $80 and receive back $90 when the crop was sold. However, if the landlord were the supplier, he would purchase the entire fertilizer supply at wholesale, then sell the tenant his half of the fertilizer at retail, a markup of about 25% or $20. That is, the tenant would spend $100 on fertilizer and get back $90, hardly a profitable investment. The landlord, on the other hand, would invest $160 in fertilizer and sell

[30] *Agriculture Report*, p. 907.

half the supply to the tenant for $100; the landlord's investment thus was $60. If he received $90 from an increased crop, he would make substantial profit of $30. In this situation, the intervention of the landlord as a supplier to the tenant would mean that investment in fertilizer was a losing proposition for the tenant and a highly profitable one for the landlord. On the question of fertilizers, then, as in the case of rental arrangements and choice of crops, the landlord and the tenant had real differences in interest; when one gained the other lost.

Supplies

Landlord and tenant also fought over the day-to-day expenses of the farm. Two types of struggle were of considerable significance.

First, the landlord wanted his land and whatever equipment he had supplied to be maintained. He wanted the tenant to feed the mule well, keep the house up, and generally treat the farm as if the tenant himself owned it.[31] To accomplish this, some landlords stipulated in the rental contract that *they* could buy supplies for the upkeep of the farm and charge them against the tenant's share of the crop.[32] Many others made no such stipulation, but did this anyway.

Second, the landlords often ran supply stores of their own. They were especially interested in selling as much merchandise as they could to their tenants—enough, they hoped, to allow them to seize the tenant's share of the crop. This created yet another tension in landlord–tenant relations: a conflict over the price and quantity of needed supplies.

Planting and Harvesting

During planting and harvest, cotton farming required more labor than a farm family could supply. It was very much in the interest of the landlord to control these operations, if he could, and it was just as important for the tenant to remain free of landlord control.

At one extreme, a landlord would demand—sometimes as part of the contract— that tenants be available as cotton planters and pickers. Thus, tenant autonomy would disappear during planting and harvesting. Tenants and their families would work in great gangs on all the farms in the plantation. The landlord had a free hand.

> If the tenants get into a tight place with their cotton, the manager sends wage hands to their aid, and at picking time all available help of all ages is scraped together and sent out according to the needs of the plantation.[33]

The tenants were not paid for their labor, but the landlord charged them for the labor performed by others on their plots. "On some plantations tenants pay on an average nearly a hundred dollars a year for this extra help."[34]

[31] Clark, *op. cit.*, p. 326.
[32] Reid, *op. cit.*, pp. 115–118. 129.
[33] Hart, *op. cit.*, p. 266; also p. 258; Nixon, *op. cit.*, p. 60; Reid, *op. cit.*, p. 118.
[34] Hart, *op. cit.*, p. 266.

At the other extreme, the tenant could maintain total autonomy. In order to plant or pick his crop, he could organize exchanges with other tenants, hire labor if he could afford it, or negotiate short-term loans to pay the costs. He maintained his position as an independent entrepreneur.[35]

These two ways of arranging planting and harvesting had differing results for the fortunes of tenants and landlords. When the landlord supervised gang labor, he gave primary emphasis to the proper and extensive care of the cotton crop, assigning the other crops a secondary priority. This emphasis reflected his financial stake in cotton. When the tenants controlled the harvesting and planting, they attended to their garden plots and food areas with more care, leaving the cotton crop to a less central (but, of course, not minor) position.[36]

Thus, if the landlord controlled the labor, he could use it to enhance his profit. If tenants controlled their own labor, they could increase their own income. In this situation, when the landlord's profit went up, tenants' income went down, and vice versa. Like the tenancy contract, the choice of crops, the use of fertilizer, and the purchase of supplies, the choices around sowing and harvesting the crop were sources of tenant–landlord conflict.

Supervision

O. B. Stevens, Georgia commissioner of agriculture and a prominent cotton landlord, described the essence of the supervision conflict. The tenant, he declared, preferred rental to wage labor because

> *he is under the control of nobody; then he comes and goes when he gets ready; he works when he wants to and quits when he wants to.*[37]

On the other hand, the landlord preferred wage labor:

> *In my judgment and in the judgment of all farmers down there [Georgia Black Belt], we think that it is best to hire these laborers for so much wages per month. You can control the labor better and manage it better, and a man can take care of his land and take care of his stock better.*[38]

Stevens conceded the impossibility of recruiting wage labor, and for that reason, rentals became the predominant form of tenure in his region. But the landlords did not give up their ambition to "control" the labor of the tenants. Such a concession would be disastrous in many ways, leading to land exhaustion, destruction of houses and improvements, bad cultivation and so forth.

According to Philip Bruce, real tenant autonomy—at least for Black tenants—was an unmitigated disaster:

---

[35] Brooks, *op. cit.*, pp. 52–53.
[36] *George Report*, pt. 1, pp. 143–146.
[37] *Agriculture Report*, p. 909.
[38] *Ibid.*

The quality of the soil begins at once to depreciate from improper usage and careless cultivation, the buildings and fences soon fall out of order from natural decay or the depredations of pilferers; the teams decline to the poorest condition, the crops produced are of an inferior quality.[39]

"But this is not all," he declaimed;

Such an estate soon becomes the safe harbor of all the depraved Negroes in the vicinity; the vicious habits of the women and men alike increase owing to their removal from the control of the proprietor; thievish and superstitious practices are more common and open, and brawls and quarrels arise more often than elsewhere.[40]

And so on. This quote, and many more "scientific" works, cast the supervision question as deriving from the innate tendencies of Blacks or tenants—they could not exercise the self-discipline necessary to farm.[41] However, this "explanation" is hardly an accurate one. Beyond its racism lies its failure to account for the large numbers of Black landowners and tenants who worked diligently without supervision.[42] More important, the acceptance of such assertions diverts attention from the real *economic* conflict which was the backdrop of the supervision issue. The underlying purpose of the "control" that O. B. Stevens sought was the ambition to run the farm to maximize the profit of the landlord. The underlying purpose of the freedom from control sought by tenants was the ambition to maximize their own return, comfort, and livelihood. These two ambitions conflicted in a great many ways, and it is because of this conflict that

the owner or his representative now rides from farm to farm, watching the state of the crop, deciding on the method of cultivation, requiring the tenant to keep up his property and above all enforcing the regularity of work.[43]

And, to the great misfortune of the tenant, "in most cases supervision is very close."[44] The landlord won more than his share of the battles.

Supervision was needed and effective only insofar as it was able to force the tenant to do things he or she would not otherwise have done. Thus, a tiny battle occurred each time a supervisor ordered the tenant to do something. When the landlord won, he used the farm to enhance his profits. When the tenant resisted supervision, he or she used the farm to increase his own income or comfort.

[39] Philip Bruce, *The Plantation Negro as a Freedman* (1885), p. 215.

[40] *Ibid.* This purports to describe tobacco tenants, but similar (though not nearly so outrageous) descriptions can be found for cotton growers. See *George Report*, pt. 1, p. 314; and *Agriculture Report*, p. 907, for two examples.

[41] See Matthew Hammond, *The Cotton Industry* (Ithaca, 1897); and Brooks, *op. cit.*, for such an analysis cast in more "scientific" terms.

[42] Ransom and Sutch, "Debt Peonage."

[43] Brooks, *op. cit.*, p. 458.

[44] T. J. Edwards, "The Tenant System and Some Changes Since Emancipation," *Annals of the American Academy of Political and Social Science* 49 (September 1913), p. 34; Reid, *op. cit.*, pp. 114–120.

The perfect example of this kind of conflict was that over "garden plots" and farm animals. Most tenants had the right to plant about an acre of their farms with vegetables and other crops they could eat themselves.[45] Various farm animals supplied food as well. If the tenant spent considerable time tending the animals and the garden, this cut into the care of the cash crop. The closely supervised tenant would not be allowed to spend "too much" time of this garden plot, and in some cases, the landlord managed to eliminate tenants' gardens altogether.[46] A group of Mississippi planters, who provided their tenants with unsightly one-room houses, "without a glass window, set in a barren and unfenced waste, with a few wretch outhouses . . . and chinks between the logs such that rain drives into them" prohibited gardens supposedly because "they will become weed spots."[47]

Garden plots and the plantation farms discussed above were two aspects of the struggle over apportioning the tenant's labor time. The tenant desired to maximize his or her own comfort and income; the landlord wanted attention focused on the common enterprise. Thus, in the absence of supervision, the tenant might take time off from the farm to work in a lumber camp or a nearby cotton mill.[48] When they could, landlords enforced contracts against this.[49] They also attempted to prevent other unprofitable (for them) activities like fishing.[50] Even leisure time became controversial. One planter blamed the agricultural depression partly on "the tendency of ignorant people to lose too much time discussing the affairs of state and listening to the tirades of would-be politicians."[51]

One solution for the landlord was starvation, which could be used to force the tenant to work much harder, produce more, and increase the landlord's return. The technique was brutal but effective:

> He gives the said Negro [sic] four pounds of bacon, one quarter bushel of meal, and tells him to go on plowing. Cuffy knows who has him and he goes, and next Monday he comes again. If he has three or four acres plowed he gets some rations, if not, nothing but a cussing.[52]

Supervision also forced the tenant to perform a multitude of tasks around the farm that were unrelated to the tenant's own farm. Some tenants were obliged in the winter to make the fertilizer they would buy (at credit prices) the following spring.[53] Tenants planted and harvested other people's crops to work off their own debt.[54] Farmers' wives were put to work sewing clothes to be sold in the land-

[45] Edwards, op. cit., p. 40; Agriculture Report, pp. 416–417, 803.
[46] A black congressman from North Carolina told a congressional investigation that he knew of "plenty of cases where no vegetables were grown at all and they had to purchase them." Agriculture Report, p. 417.
[47] Hart, op. cit., pp. 115–116.
[48] Nixon, op. cit., pp. 133–134.
[49] Reid, op. cit., p. 129.
[50] Clark, op. cit., p. 304.
[51] George Report, pt. 1, p. 346.
[52] Clark, op. cit., p. 324.
[53] Clark, op. cit., p. 326.
[54] Brooks, op. cit., pp. 52–53.

lord's store.[55] Planters even cultivated their own farms using unpaid tenant labor.[56] One particularly meticulous planter recorded in his contract some of the non-farm tasks he expected his tenants to perform:

1. staff his farm;
2. produce 1000 fence rails per mule, haul them, and place them;
3. repair bridges on and off their rented property at his request;
4. haul crops, their own and others;
5. clean the planter's stable at his request;
6. cut lumber at his request.[57]

A third way that supervision arose was in connection with the upkeep of the property the planter rented to the tenant, including the house, the plow, the mule, seeds, and fences. The problem, according to one planter, was that the tenant "never looks out for the interest of his employer."[58] This situation could be remedied with "constant care and attention."[59] Some planters managed to prevent tenants from using horses or mules for transportation, recreation, or personal use; the animals were to be devoted exclusively to crop related activities.[60] Others prohibited the consumption of food crops before the planter took his share.[61]

If these oppressive measures and overbearing supervision were not carried out, the planters asserted, chaos would ensue. Tenants are

> disposed to run the reaper against stump. . . . The negroes [sic] will burn up the dry rails of all the fences in their vicinity, or they will tear from their cabins, for the same purpose, all the boards that can be thus used without exposing themselves to the severity of the weather.[62]

In reality, the advantage was with the landlords. The contracts often specified the exact upkeep of the property, and they also specified cash or crop penalties against offenders.[63] And while the contracts were often violated, the close supervision and the threat of withholding supplies helped assure their enforcement.

Dividing the Crop

The contract, which was supposed to resolve these varied conflicts, was sometimes extremely complicated and sometimes extremely simple. One researcher, after a meticulous study of a great many such contracts, gave the following assessment:

---

[55] Clark, *op. cit.*, p. 207.
[56] Reid, *op. cit.*, p. 128.
[57] Reid, *op. cit.*, p. 129; see pp. 114–120 for numerous additional examples.
[58] *George Report*, pt. 1, p. 356; see also *Agriculture Report*, pp. 459, 504, 506.
[59] *George Report*, pt. 1, p. 356.
[60] Brooks, *op. cit.*, pp. 70–79, 92; Reid, *op. cit.*, p. 116.
[61] *George Report*, pt. 1, p. 356.
[62] Bruce, *op. cit.*, p. 147.
[63] Reid, *op. cit.*, pp. 115–120.

A typical share contract would require the tenant to diligently farm and perform specific non-crop related tasks, for example, fence clearing, or barn maintenance. Less frequently, the share contract would require the cropper to accept the advice given by the landlord, to plant specific areas, or apply a unilaterally determined amount of fertilizer. Ancillary expenses were most often shared....[64]

The actual share of the crop varied with each contract, the result of elaborate and subtle bargaining.[65] Alonzo Mial, a North Carolina merchant–landlord, negotiated the following contracts in 1886–1887:

1. N. Gonter was completely furnished and shared half the fertilizer costs. He paid half his crop plus built a fence.
2. J. Phipps and T. Earp chose their own crops, furnished their own horse, and were supplied feed and $30; in return, they built a fence and paid half their crops.
3. A. Blake received all his furnishings and paid 1000 pounds of cotton and $20. Ira Richardson had the identical contract.
4. C. Pearce, G. Mial, H. Ohal, A. Fostno, and F. Powell received all furnishings except they paid half the fertilizer costs. Their rent was 1000 pounds cotton, $20, and all the cottonseed.
5. J. Pool received all furnishings and was required to plant six acres of cotton and the rest is corn. He gave half his crop and also donated his labor and that of his family to building tobacco barns.[66]

The division of the crop at the end of harvesting was part of the original contract. But the agreement was often altered by the various conflicts which occurred during the crop year. For example, the landlord might demand payment for the tenant's "abuse" of his property.[67] If the crop was of poor quality, the landlord could ask for more. If the tenant planted too few acres of cash crop, the landlord might claim a larger share of what was harvested. Few of these conflicts were formally resolved; therefore, additional disagreements often arose over them at harvesttime and decisions were not uncommonly reversed. With all this uncertainty, it is not surprising that wherever it was possible, "the 'riders' or assistant managers are in the saddle all day long, and a prudent manager casts his eye on every plot of cultivated ground on his plantation every day."[68] And it is not surprising that, in practice, landlord control was even greater than the contracts specified.[69]

But the ultimate resolution of this constant struggle was conditioned by the complicated relationships involved in supplying the farming enterprise. To understand just how these disagreements were resolved and how the conglomerate of the tenant–landlord relationships interacted as a whole, it is necessary to turn to a discussion of the other principal actor in the tenancy system, the merchant.

[64]Reid, *op. cit.*, pp. 118–119.
[65]Reid, *op. cit.*, pp. 115–120; King, *op. cit.*, p. 273.
[66]Reid, *op. cit.*, pp. 116–117.
[67]Reid, *op. cit.*, pp. 115–120.
[68]Hart, *op. cit.*, p. 258.
[69]Reid, *op. cit.*, p. 120.

The Merchant and the Crop Lien

Before 1900, bank credit was difficult to obtain in the South.[70] As late as 1886, there were no national or state banks in Louisiana outside of New Orleans. A majority of parishes had no banks at all.[71] The few banks were extremely reluctant to lend to landlords and totally unwilling to lend to tenants.[72] Land was poor collateral, since it had little market value even in the richest areas.[73] Only in the late 1890s did Mississippi Delta land—the richest cotton area in the country—become attractive as loan collateral.[74] During the bad times of 1893, Columbus, Mississippi, planters found that "in the present depressed condition, the price of land [is] merely nominal with no purchasers."[75] The conditions—even for big farmers—were so uncertain, and defaults on mortgage payments so frequent, that banks demanded and received as high as 25% interest.[76] Landowners in Georgia were willing to pay a 20% commission to an agent who could negotiate even a usurious loan.[77]

It took several decades before Northern capital flowed smoothly into Southern agriculture.[78] By the time it did, the crop lien system had taken hold and molded the cotton culture in its image. Under the crop lien, the tenant (or landlord) mortgaged his or her crop as security against which to borrow for supplies. The crop was pledged instead of land because the cotton was always marketable. This practice was by no means an innovation,[79] but as the lien system developed in the post–Civil War South, it acquired two features of special significance.

First, the liens in the South were not acquired from banks, because they were secure only if the creditor had the facilities to enter the cotton market. Furthermore, the small amounts of money involved in the liens made them expensive to administer and collect. Finally, tenants who took out the crop liens had little credit backing with which to guarantee their reliability. Crop liens were unthinkable unless the creditor had the capacity to oversee the spending of the money, as well as the planting and cultivation of the crop. This required a special kind of presence in the farm area, which banks were not equipped to provide. The role of credit supplier fell to the country merchant.

Second, the loans were rarely made in cash. Since the merchant was the source of credit, he found it more convenient and certainly more profitable to offer credit

[70] Ransom and Sutch, "Debt Peonage."

[71] Hair, *op. cit.*, p. 54.

[72] *George Report*, pt. 1, pp. 36, 309, 329; Clark, *op. cit.*, pp. 99–100. Roger Shugg, "The Survival of the Plantation System in Louisians," *Journal of Southern History* 3 (August 1937), p. 313.

[73] *George Report*, pt. 1, pp. 291–297, 320, 329; B. B. Kendrick, "Agricultural Discontent in the South, 1880–1900," In *Annual Report of the American Historical Association* (Washington, D.C., 1920), p. 270; Hart, *op. cit.*, pp. 144–145.

[74] Robert Brandfon, *Cotton Kingdom of the New South* (Cambridge, Mass.; 1967), pp. 40–42, 52, 122; Hart, *op. cit.*, p. 200. The tax burden contributed to the riskiness of land investment in the Delta.

[75] *George Report*, pt. 1, p. 325.

[76] Shugg, *op. cit.*, pp. 63–64.

[77] Alex M. Arnett, *The Populist Movement in Georgia* (New York, 1922), pp. 63–64.

[78] The number of national banks tripled from 1890–1905. Hart, *op. cit.*, p. 225). For further discussion of the paucity of bank credit, see Robert Somers, *The Southern States Since the War* (New York, 1871), pp. 184, 209–211, 241–243; Hammond, *op. cit.*, pp. 121–125.

[79] Brandfon, *op. cit.*, pp. 39–64; *Raleigh Progressive Farmer*, August 7, 1888; Hammond, *op. cit.*, traces its origins to the antebellum plantation owners; see also Clark, *op. cit.*, pp. 315–316.

in the form of charge accounts at his store. In doing this, the merchant accomplished two important business deals in one operation: He gave a loan on which he could charge interest, and he guaranteed himself a certain amount of business during the crop year.

Thus, the crop lien system introduced a new force into the struggle between landlord and tenant over the division of the crop. In order to maximize his share of the crop, the merchant need to maximize the accrued debt. He could accomplish this in several ways.

First, it became the goal of the merchant to be the primary supplier of the tenant. Whereas the landlord could offer the tenant a mule, plow, and fertilizer as part of the contract (thus increasing the landlord's contractual share), the merchant could convince the tenant that it was more profitable for him to buy these items on credit and keep a larger portion of the crop. This created direct competition between lanlord and merchant, since each desired to supply the tenant with equipment. However, this competition was not inevitable. If the landlord and merchant were the same person, he did not care whether he supplied the plow and mule as part of the contract or whether he sold them on credit. Or, if the landlord did not have the equipment to supply the tenant, he could buy the equipment from the merchant by giving a crop lien of his own. In this way, the merchant could in fact become the creditor of both landlord and tenant: He would be able then to take a part of both the landlord's and the tenant's shares of the crop.

Second, the merchant increased his share of the crop by maximizing the interest he charged on crop liens. Though the legal interest rate was often 6%, the actual rate was frequently 20%, and sometimes it reached 10% per month—120% per year.[80] In addition, the tenant paid a service charge of $1 or more.[81] The interest was charged for a year, but the loan was only until harvesttime—nine or fewer months.[82] The loan was often paid in monthly installments, so the merchant was loaning the full amount for only a month, while charging interest for an entire year. A large planter with holdings in Louisiana and Alabama, when asked the interest on crop liens, responded:

> From 20% up. I do not know any less than 20%, I mean it. Frequently they will buy stuff in August, and may pay for it with picking of the first crop in September or October, and when you calculate the annual interest, it is 200 per cent.[83]

Naturally, the extent of the extra interest depended on the possibility of the tenant's choosing another source for crop liens. The greatest abuses took place where there was little competition or when the tenant was bound by debt to a single merchant.[84]

[80]Hart, op. cit., p. 269; Jacqueline Bull, "The General Merchant in the History of the South," Journal of Southern History 18 (February 1952), pp. 42, 46—50.
[81]Clark, op. cit., pp. 316, 315, 142; Hallie Farmer, "Economic Background to Southern Populism," South Atlantic Quarterly 29 (January 1930), p. 84; Brandfon, op. cit., p. 109.
[82]Clark, op. cit., p. 315.
[83]Agriculture Report, p. 776.

Third, the merchant could increase his share of the tenant's crop by getting the tenant to overextend his credit. Once a lien was executed, no other merchant would give credit, since the holder of the first lien might take the entire crop. If the mortgagee exhausted the first loan and was forced to execute another with the same merchant, the latter of course profited handsomely. This not only increased the debt and therefore increased the merchant's return when the crop was harvested, it also enabled the merchant to demand a much higher interest because the debtor could not move to another supplier. And the merchant, of course, was constantly trying to sell items that the tenant might not have bought.[85] The proliferation of patent medicines and other questionable products was fed by the enthusiasm of the local merchants. Merchants would try to persuade tenants to replace plows, harnesses, and other goods they owned. They also sold luxury items—fine cloth, for example—in an attempt to exhaust the tenant's account.

Fourth, the merchant established a "credit price" for each product. The customer who paid cash received goods for the ordinary retail price, but credit customers were forced to pay a higher price. The size of this markup varied widely from region to region, from merchant to merchant, from product to product, and even from customer to customer. It was one of the most exploitative and detested features of the crop lien system.

A great many first-hand accounts report that the average credit markup was at least 25% above the retail price and about double the wholesale cost to the merchant.[86] Typical was a South Carolina planter—merchant who told an investigatory committee in 1900 that "the instructions are to put a 50% profit on the goods sold."[87] But the margin was by no means stabilized. Hammond estimated that credit prices were 40–100% higher than retail prices. Morgan estimated such markups to be 20–40% in North Carolina and 50–75% in Alabama. In Georgia in 1900, the commissioner of agriculture (who was also a large planter and merchant) estimated the credit markup at 25%, while the director of the Agricultural Experiment Station (and also a planter) gave a 30–50% estimate.[88] Clearly, there was much variety across and within states. Indeed, many merchants had different prices for different customers.[89] One observer commented, "they charge from 25% to grand larceny."[90]

---

[84]Hammond, *op. cit.*, pp. 150–155.

[85]*George Report*, pt. 1, p. 383; Edward King, *The Great South* (1875), p. 53, said that they "always manage to retain a profit, rarely allowing a freedman to find that his season's toil has done more than square his accounts with the acute trader who has meantime supplied him and his family with provisions, clothing, and such articles of luxury as the negro's [sic] mind and body crave."

[86]Matthew Hammond, "The Southern Farmer and the Cotton Question," *Political Science Review* 12 (September 1897), p. 462; W. Scott Morgan, *History of the Wheel and Alliance* (Fort Scott, Kans., 1889); Clark, *op. cit.*, pp. 158, 162, 165, 207, 210, 237, 279, 281, 285, 316–318; *George Report*, pt. 1, pp. 368, 376, 415, and *passim*; Hammond, *The Cotton Industry* (Ithaca, 1897), p. 153; H. C. Nixon, *Lower Piedmont Country* (New York, 1944), p. 58; *Agriculture Report*, pp. 47, 77, 112–119, 437, 445, 470–477, 776, 907–909; Hart, *op. cit.*, p. 264; Bull, *op. cit.*, pp. 46–50; Hair, *op. cit.*, p. 51.

[87]*Agriculture Report*, p. 118; see also Clark, *op. cit.*, p. 318.

[88]*Agriculture Report*, pp. 77, 445, 909.

[89]*Ibid.*, p. 77.

[90]Bull, *op. cit.*, p. 47.

TABLE 2.2
Chart of Actual Interests Charged on Crop Liens

Loan situation	Interest rate[a]	Sample figures for $150, 6-month loan[b]	
		Principal	Interest
Listed interest rate	8	150	12
Actual *annual* interest rate	16	150	12
Annual interest rate if interest is deducted at outset with service charge	21	136	14
Annual interest rate if interest is deducted and tenant pays credit price for goods 25% above cash price	76	109	41
Annual interest rate if interest is deducted, credit price is charged, and tenant purchases on credit over 6-month period	130	63.58[c]	6.83[d]

[a] These figures are percentages.
[b] In dollars.
[c] Average monthly balance.
[d] Average monthly interest.

The justifications for these policies were frail. Some merchants claimed the markups covered the cost of supervising the debtors' farms.[91] Others claimed that successful farmers were paying to cover the losses merchants suffered because of unsuccessful ones.[92] The typical justification was that high prices were charged to prevent default by borrowers from driving the merchant into bankruptcy. Certainly merchandising was a risky business, but even those in no danger of business failure charge high prices to credit customers.

One Mississippi planter told federal investigators that at least a little duplicity was needed for the system to work smoothly.[93] Few merchants in the South posted prices. Instead, they wrote down the cost of an item in secret code, so the customer could not read it, and announced as high a price as they could when the customer placed an order.[94]

> The great discrepancy was the sliding level in prices and the poor quality of goods carried in stock. They were bought at the cheapest wholesale prices and sold at maximum retail prices.[95]

The "credit price" meant that the tenant paid twice for his or her loan. The interest was the first payment, the credit price was the second.

Table 2.2 demonstrates how crop lien credit worked. A tenant did not have the money to pay for his day-to-day supplies so he executed a crop lien with a local merchant. He mortgaged his crop for $150 (a common mortgage) at 8% interest (the legal maximum in many states). However, the loan was due when the crop

[91] Clark, *op. cit.*, p. 318.
[92] *Ibid.*, p. 316.
[93] *Agriculture Report*, pp. 470–471.
[94] Clark, *op. cit.*, p. 317.
[95] *Ibid.*, pp. 316–317.

was picked, about 6 months away. Therefore, the loan was at 16% annual interest. Furthermore, the merchant deducted the interest immediately from the balance. The interest was $12 (8%), so the tenant had only $138 credited to his account. Deduct from this a $2 service charge, and we find the tenant was receiving a loan of $136 dollars upon which he would pay back $150. The tenant was paying $14 interest on $136, or about 10% in 6 months. The actual annual rate of interest was 21%.

The tenant had $136 to spend at credit prices. If the average price paid was 25% above the cash price (a modest figure), then the tenant was getting only about $109 worth of goods. He or she would repay the merchant for these goods with $150. The tenant actually received a loan of $109 for 6 months and paid $41 interest—an annual rate of 76%. However, most tenants could not spend all their credit at once. They received an account at the store and withdrew their goods in monthly installments. If a tenant used this credit uniformly throughout the 6 months of the loan, he or she was actually receiving a loan of $18 each month and paying $7 interest on each of these loans. In September, the tenant received a loan of about $18 and paid back $25 a month later. This represented an annual interest rate of 467%! The average annual interest rate was 130%

The figures in this example are not exaggerated. The basic interest was rarely less than 8%, and rates of 25% were not uncommon.[96] Rates of 10% per month—120% per year!—were not unheard of.[97] Credit markups could reach extraordinary levels. The *Atlanta Constitution* and the *New Orleans Louisianan* claimed the credit markup ranged as high as 200%.[98] In short, the credit system could soak up all the crop, and it did. The *Greensboro Herald* (Georgia) estimated that a farmer who borrowed $800 each year would actually pay $2800 in interest over a 5-year period.[99] In parts of Louisiana interest rates actually reached 500%[100] In the postbellum South, a farmer who incurred a $150 debt in order to obtain $100 worth of goods at the retail price was doing very well.

One contemporary described the crop lien thus:

> When one of these mortgages has been recorded against the Southern farmer, he has usually passed into a state of helpless peonage to the merchant who has become his creditor. With the surrender of this evidence of indebtness, he has also surrendered his freedom of action and his industrial autonomy. From this time until he has paid the last dollar of his indebtedness, he is subject to the constant oversight and direction of the merchant. Every mouthful of food that he purchases; every implement that he requires on the farm, his mules, cattle, the clothing for himself and family, the fertilizers for his land, must all be brought of

---

[96] Bull, *op. cit.*, p. 47, quotes an observer: "They charge from 25% to grand larceny."

[97] *Ibid.*, pp. 42, 47—49; Hart, *op. cit.*, p. 269.

[98] *Atlanta Constitution*, March, 3, 1885; *Ibid*, January 10, 1889, quoted in Bull, *op. cit.*, p. 49; *Louisianan*, April 5, 1879, quoted in Hair, *op. cit.*, p. 51.

[99] Clark, *op. cit.*, p. 322.

[100] Hair, *op. cit.*, p. 51.

the merchant who holds the crop lien, and in such amounts, as the latter is willing to allow. . . . The latter dictates what crops shall be grown, and how much of each. . . .[101]

Debt peonage usually developed over several years. And although it was not inevitable, it was the day-to-day spector of Southern life.

The country merchant's business was a precarious venture which offered the promise of fabulous success against the probability of total failure. The country merchants who were not destroyed by the competition of other merchants and landlords, who survived the years when they advanced far too much on a short crop, who avoided the squeeze of the wholesaler, and who learned to maximize their own share of the crop without driving the tenants from the land, built a secure and stable fortune. The vast majority, however, went bankrupt. Because of the risks involved, banks were reluctant to lend to merchants, though they were far more likely to loan money on the merchant's business than on the landlord's land. Well-entrenched merchants with a stable clientele and a profitable business were, of course, able to get loans fairly easily.[102]

The crop lien therefore brought the tenant into a second battle over the division of the crop, this time with the merchant. In many ways, the two struggles were identical. Both landlord and merchant were committed to maximum planting of cotton.[103] (One farmer testified that "ten acres of cotton will get you more credit than 50 acres of corn.")[104] Both were interested in supervising as closely as possible.[105] (In fact, some merchants justified their exorbitant credit charges as the cost of supervision.)[106] And both were committed to controlling labor in their own interest.[107]

Indeed, there was hardly room for both to function at the same time, and this created a third struggle—that between the landlord and the merchant. In order to understand that battle, however, it is necessary to investigate the structure of the larger system which was built upon the two basic relationships we have just discussed. To do this, we must look at the system in two pieces:

1. the system of credit and supply;
2. the system of marketing.

---

[101] Hammond, *The Cotton Industry*, pp. 149–150.

[102] Clark, *op. cit.*, pp. 99–100; See U.S. Bureau of Statistics, *Monthly Summary of Commerce and Finance of the United States* (Washington DC., 1896–1900), for bankruptcy figures demonstrate that retail merchants had one of the highest failure rates of any business.

[103] Hammond, "The Southern Farmer and the Cotton Question," p. 463; Clark, *op. cit.*, pp. 162–165, 325; *George Report*, pt. 1, pp. 275–438, especially pp. 321, 341, 348, 383, 415; Kendrick, *op. cit.*, p. 271. *Agriculture Report*, pp. 60–61, 833.

[104] *Agriculture Report*, p. 436.

[105] Clark, *op. cit.*, p. 52, noted that merchants "were always informed as to the crop of every customer and as to its general cultivation week to week": see also pp. 314–325. *George Report*, pt. 1, pp. 314, 334, 356.

[106] Clark, *op. cit.*, p. 318.

[107] "Merchants, once they granted a customer credit, were forced to keep track of what he was doing." Clark, *op. cit.*, p. 312; see also pp. 304–305, 313–334.

3

The Tenancy System

Then work for our order
  Day and night,
While hopes are good,
  And prospects bright.

Then times will be better
  When we sustain our rights;
And merchants and monopolies
  Shall cease to fight.

And may the Heavens shine on us
  And give us light,
To suppress our wrongs
  And defend our rights.

[J. P. Rogers, Wolf Pond (North Carolina) Farmers'
Alliance, *Raleigh Progressive Farmer* May 1, 1888]

The System of Supply and Credit

Figure 3.1 schematically indicates the supply system under tenant farming. For the tenant, the critical problem was to obtain credit, since he or she had little cash. Because bank loans were unavailable, the tenant either bought on credit through the merchant or was supplied by his or her landlord (who took a crop lien and became a merchant). Landlords became suppliers by obtaining credit from one of three sources: Bank loans were preferred since they did not involve liens and they had a fixed, though high, interest; credit could also be obtained from wholesale distributors, payable at harvesttime; and if all else failed, the landlord could mortgage his share of the crop to the merchant, purchase the supplies on credit, and sell them on credit to the tenant.

The merchant also sought credit from the same bank or wholesaler as the landlord. The competition between merchant and landlord was significantly affected by who obtained a loan. And that depended upon the capabilities of the individuals involved:

41

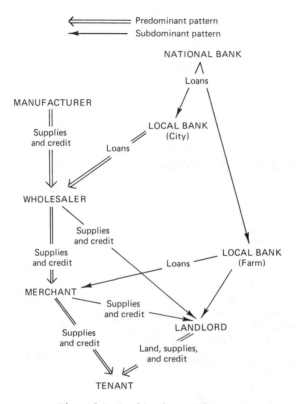

Figure 3.1   *Supplying the tenant farmer.*

Country storekeeping was one-half orthodox merchandising and the other half sizing up the capabilities and honesty of customers. It was a highly personal sort of enterprise which required a generous amount of giving and taking, and a keen sense of humor and understanding of all the frailties of mankind.[1]

The banks' practice of lending money to "the man" and not "the business" explains certain peculiarities in the Southern system of bank loans and wholesale credit.

Interest rates, despite usury laws, were very high. In Louisiana, for example, the rates were as high as 25% per annum on land, and in Georgia the landowner might be forced to pay a 20% commission to an agent for finding him a loan.[2] Merchants paid 18% per year despite a legal maximum of 8%.[3] In 1891, Tennessee cotton farmers paid 10—16% for 6-month loans, even with a picked crop as collateral.[4] The actual interest was probably over twice the legal limit.[5]

[1] Thomas D. Clark, *Pills, Petticoats and Plows* (New York, 1944), p. 52.
[2] Robert Shugg, "The Survival of the Plantation System in Louisiana," *Journal of Southern History.* 3 (August 1937), p. 313; Alex Arnett, *The Populist Movement in Georgia* (New York, 1922), p. 64.
[3] Arnett, *op. cit.*, p. 61. H. C. Nixon, *Lower Piedmont Country* (New York, 1946), p. 58.
[4] *George Report*, pt. 1, pp. 20, 24. A full citation of this work appears in note 3, Chapter 1 of this volume.
[5] *Agriculture Report*, pp. 47—48, 57, 61, 65, 73, 381, 432, 436, 444, 464, 926. A full citation of this work appears in note 3, Chapter 1 of this volume.

It was very important to the bank that the mortgagee repay the loan and not force foreclosure. A bank that foreclosed on a merchant was left with a store full of goods and crop liens. Neither the goods nor the liens were worth their face value unless the merchant was present to charge credit prices on the goods and make the liens collectable. Similarly, foreclosed land was little unless it could be profitably farmed. The hiring and handling of tenants and tenant contracts required the skill of the landlord. Consequently, a great many banks demanded crop liens for collateral even when ample land was offered. This pushed interest rates on real estate loans even higher[6] and created a powerful incentive for landlords to enter the supply business so that they could collect the entire crop. This situation, in turn, created another contradiction between merchant and landlord.

Because the bank wanted to avoid foreclosure, it closely supervised the operation of its debtors in an attempt to discover problems before they became too large. To ensure effective supervision, the banks enlisted a well-established landlord or merchant to oversee their stake in a business. This created a symbiosis between banks and their favored planter-merchants: Each one needed and protected the other. In many places, banks loaned only to the dominant landlord or merchant;[7] in others, the bank was owned or dominated by the local planter and merchant.[8] The unity thus created affected the functioning of the system in myriad ways. Banks refused to loan to actual or potential competition;[9] they would never loan directly to a tenant.[10] Banks helped to coordinate planter attempts at reducing their own costs. Sometimes this was done by squeezing the tenants mercilessly. One banker boasted to a congressional investigation that his bank had been instrumental in reducing the living standard of Marianna, Arkansas, farmers by 45–70% by reducing their credit accounts to as little as $50 for the year.[11]

Once stable relationships were established between banks and their client planters, money became available. The landlords could "judge" good risks, supervise the loans, and were eager customers for foreclosed property.[12] By 1900 in Louisiana, few large planters were deprived of bank loans. One cotton county that had one bank in 1890 saw five new ones open in the next decade.[13]

In Mississippi, the "deed of trust" was the inevitable means of land loans. This contract allowed the bank to appoint a trustee who had supervisorial power over the land and the right to take over the land after default. Furthermore, Mississippi law gave these mortgages first lien on the crops as well. Finally, the trustees were usually the largest planters in the area. The land officer

[6] *Agriculture Report*, pp. 78, 119, 433, 436; *George Report*, pt. 1, p. 294.

[7] *George Report*, pt. 1, p. 309; Jacqueline Bull, "The General Merchant in the Economic History of the New South," *Journal of Southern History* 28 (February 1952), p. 42.

[8] Clark, *op. cit.*, p. 331; *George Report*, pt. 1, p. 36 and *passim*; *Agriculture Report*, pp. 438, 822; Robert Brandfon. *Cotton Kingdom of the New South* (Cambridge, Mass., 1967), pp. 111–112.

[9] Clark, *op. cit.*, p. 331.

[10] Clark, *op. cit.*, p. 331; *George Report*, pt. 1, p. 36.

[11] *George Report*, pt. 1, pp. 36–37.

[12] Clark, *op. cit.*, pp. 92, 99–100 and *passim*.

[13] *Agriculture Report*, pp. 776–777, 926.

of the Illinois Central Railroad commented, "The chances are nine to one that the party who loans the money will own the land eventually."[14]

Since supervision was required and loans were not given unless the proprietor was trusted, most loans to country merchants and landlords came from banks within the county. Long distance loans were rare because outside banks had no way of deciding whether such a loan was a "good risk."

> I can't go to New York and borrow money. I can not go to Augusta to get money. I went there to make the experiment and I said to the President of the bank: "I want to borrow money." "What security do you propose to give." "Real estate." "I won't take that, any bonds?" "No." "We do not loan money on real estate." That throws me back to the country banks, where I can borrow, but I have to pay 13%.[15]

Above the local banks stood the national banks. Since capital was scarce in the South, most local banks were heavily indebted to the large Northern banks that funded them.[16] The day-to-day operation of Southern banks was not influenced by this, but major crises, like the 1893 panic, could dry up Southern credit by cutting its lifeline to the North.[17]

Wholesale merchants were in a favorable position to obtain bank loans. First, their business was more easily evaluated than that of landlords or country merchants because their books were more indicative of financial state, and the value of stock was a good indicator of the viability of the business. The wholesaler's profits depended more on measurable quantities than on the day-to-day vagaries of the tenant farm. Second, wholesalers generally had a local monopoly. Due to exclusive contracts, competition among wholesalers was hard to maintain over long periods. One soon drove the others out of business, and consequently a wholesale merchant who was the sole distributor in a county or region could guarantee himself a certain market whether or not his retail outlets survived. Third, the wholesale merchant's city location placed him nearer to the banks. The city banks, which refused retail merchants and landlords loans because they were unable to supervise these customers, were willing to loan money to the nearby wholesaler who was easy to oversee.

Thus, the wholesaler was often able to finance his enterpise wihout resorting to disadvantageous credit buying which placed him at the mercy of the supplier. He ordered directly from the manufacturer; and he bought the cheapest supplies because his location at the railroad allowed him to order from anywhere. Most convenient, when he did need credit he could get it from a supplier without an exclusive contract. A plow manufacturer might demand that his plow be the only

[14] Brandfon, *op cit.*, pp. 111–112.

[15] *Agriculture Report*, p. 119.

[16] B. B. Kendrick, "Agricultural Discontent in the South, 1880–1900," in *Annual Report of the American Historical Association* (Washington, D.C., 1920), p. 270; *George Report*, pt. 1, p. 309; Nixon, *op. cit.*, p. 57; *Agriculture Report*, p. 78.

[17] *George Report*, pt. 1, p. 357.

one carried by the wholesaler, but he could not demand that the wholesaler buy everything from him, since he had only plows to offer.

The system of supply and credit that served the tenant farming system pushed the task of finding cash further and further up the economic ladder.

> Q. *Farmers really do not borrow money as a rule?*
> A. *No.*
> Q. *How do they get supplies?*
> A. *Through merchants.*
> Q. *And the merchants?*
> A. *Through the banks.*
> Q. *And where do the local banks get their money?*
> A. *New York.*[18]

This credit ladder put a tremendous economic squeeze on everyone without cash:

> Cotton farmers must have ample cash to run themselves for a year, or else credit, because the returns for their investment and labor of the entire year could not be collected until the short selling season in the fall of the year. Naturally the banking and mercantile interests fell heir to the responsibility of supplying the credit needs. . . . The merchants who supplied the farmers on credit for the entire year were forced to carry all the different lines of credit the farmer might need. In order to be reasonably safe, the merchant took a mortgage at the beginning of the crop season on the entire crop to be planted (crop lien), and also upon the horses, cows, hogs, plows, wagons and agricultural implements the farmer might have.
>
> The merchant was loaded with a heavy burden that he was unable to bear, and he in turn frequently tied himself to some big, strong wholesale agency that would fill his order for all the different kinds of goods he might need. . . . This was a convenient and apparently logical and efficient method for the time being, but in the end it became expensive for all concerned. Farmers often bought blindly from the merchant, and the merchant did likewise in buying from the wholesaler. The wholesaler soon discovered the enormous risks involved, and necessarily charged greater margins to cover the risks.
>
> Neither the merchants nor the farmers were in a very good position to protest in regard to prices they paid. . . . Banks were carrying the wholesale merchants and when the farmers' cotton was ginned, there was no alternative for the farmer other than to sell his cotton in order to pay the retailer, so that the retailers might pay the wholesaler who in turn had to meet his obligations at the bank.[19]

In this account, the chances for survival appear to be equally slim for everyone in the system. This was not entirely true, for while the bankruptcy rate for merchants was very high indeed, the largest part of the new riches in the South were made by country merchants. The risks in that business were high, but so were the profits. The clever and unscrupulous merchant could make a fortune.[20]

---

[18] *Agriculture Report*, p. 78.

[19] Robert Lee Hunt, *A History of Farmers' Movements in the Southwest, 1873–1925* (College Station, Tex., 1935), pp. 29–30.

[20] Clark, *op. cit.*, pp. 330–340 and *passim*.

The System of Marketing

The tenant ran a gauntlet in his effort to bring the cotton to market. The first problem was picking the crop. Even if the tenant maintained the right to pick, he or she had difficulty hiring laborers. The tenant had little or no cash on hand and prospective workers had no guarantee that there would be any money left from crop with which to pay them. Therefore the tenant had to rely on his or her landlord or the merchant to get labor. Even if neither landlord nor merchant had the cash to hire labor, the former could demand that his other tenants work to repay their accumulated debt, the latter could so order his debtors.

Since the merchant (or landlord) could threaten to cut off credit, he could force people to work for very low wages. At the same time, he could sell their labor to other tenants for a much higher price. In sum, the lienholders controlled the picking process.

Once the cotton was picked, it had to be elaborately processed. This involved ginning, compressing into a standardized bale, and wrapping in a standardized way with a standardized wrapping material. Processing cost money which the tenant did not have. He or she once again turned to the lienholder for credit on wrapping costs, and in doing so gave him control of the processing.

In areas where tenants and/or small yeomen were heavily in debt, merchants and landlords became brokers for gigantic lots of cotton (or tobacco or whatever crop was grown). They could control who got the local processing business and this offered them an almost certain investment opportunity. Frequently a merchant or landlord owned the local cotton gin and compress. Sometimes, consortia of the largest landlords and merchants would combine to build and run a large gin or compress.[21] "Nearly every storekeeper was likewise a ginner."[22]

The processed crop was then sold. Since this was the time when debts fell due, the sale was intimately connected to the redemption of the crop lien, and this led to further conflict between tenant and landlord. The landlord or merchant wanted payment in crops and not cash, since he was guaranteed a profit on the resale.[23] He also desired to purchase the remainder of the crop, since he could then make a profit on the resale of the tenant's half as well. On the other hand, if the merchant or landlord could sell the recently bought crop at a profit, the tenant could usually sell it directly for a higher price.

In this conflict, the tenant was at a great disadvantage. The law favored the creditor, as did the crop lien contract. Moreover, it was the merchant or landlord who kept a careful record of the debt:

[21] Albert Bushnell Hart, *The Southern South* (New York, 1912), p. 259; *Memorial Record of Alabama*, 2 vols. (Madison, 1893), vol. 1, pp. 487–488; vol. 2, pp. 433–434; Clark, *op. cit.*, p. 43; Mildred Brewer Russell, *Lowndes County Court House* (Montgomery, Ala., 1951), pp. 160, 166; Edward King, *The Great South* (1875; reprint ed., New York; Burt Franklin, 1969) (American Classics in History and Social Sciences, no. 46), vol. 1, pp. 306–307; Nixon, *op. cit.*, p. 56.

[22] Clark, *op. cit.*, p. 325.

[23] Brandfon, *op. cit.*, chs. 2 and 3; Clark, *op. cit.*, p. 325.

> If he [the tenant] makes 10 bales, give him 2; and if he makes 20 bales, you still
> give him 2! They all do it, I do it myself—some of these things. It's just the same
> everywhere. The tenant is helpless—so you know these landlords are going to take
> what they want. How can the tenant get his share? Most of them can't read or write.
> They can't sell their own cotton. They don't know what it brings. They can't dispute
> the landlord's word, if he's white, and they can't move if they owe him. Even if they
> don't owe him, another landlord won't take them unless the one they're renting from
> is willing for him to go. [24]

It was the tenant's desire to sell the crop and then pay his or her debts. Failing
that, the tenant wanted to market what remained of the crop after the debt was
paid. It is essential to understand under what circumstances he or she could accomplish one or the other of these goals. In order to do this, it is necessary to
describe the top of the distributional system first.

The principal crop in the South was cotton. It accounted for 46% of the cash income and dominated as many as 66% of the farms. The other major crops, corn,
livestock, and wheat, produced less cash income and were largely consumed on the
farm. Cotton (and, to a lesser extent, tobacco) represented the connection between
Southern agriculture and the country as a whole. Cotton was the crop that brought
a crop lien, and both merchants and landlords wanted it grown on their land. To
understand the marketing of Southern crops, one must understand the marketing
of cotton.

The cotton crop was sold through a series of exchanges. These were clearing-
houses which handled huge quantities of cotton each year. There were perhaps
20 exchanges in the United States, but 3 or 4 dominated the market. Cotton might
go through one, two, or even three exchanges on its way from producer to manufacturer. For example, despite the possibility of selling directly to foreign countries,
most exported cotton was sold on an American exchange and then resold on a
foreign exchange.

All the business of a cotton exchange was carried on by brokers, who handled
the purchase or sale of cotton for a flat rate (usually $.50–1.00 per bale). A cotton
buyer hired a broker to purchase cotton for him. The buyer specified the grade (or
grades), the quantity, and the price (or range). At the same time, the seller hired
his own broker to handle his crop. The broker knew the grade and quantity of the
cotton, and the price (or range) the seller would take. Bargaining took place, and
the resultant transactions were each an element of the process that set the all-
important "price" of cotton.

The buyer in this initial transaction could be a manufacturer, a speculator, or a
cotton merchant. The manufacturer transported the cotton to a mill where it was

---

[24] Statement by landlord, quoted in Allison Davis, Burleight B. Gardner, and Mary R. Gardner, *Deep South*
(Chicago, 1941), p. 356. This book is an excellent description of tenancy in the 1930s, when the institution
was more rigid and structured mainly according to race. In the 1890s, the battles that ended in this kind of sub-
jugation were still being contested in most areas.

consumed. The speculator was prepared to wait and resell the cotton at a higher price. The merchant would transport the cotton to a more advantageous market and attempt to resell it at a higher price.

These last two buyers dominated the Southern market. The Northern manufacturers could and did (more and more as time went on) buy through the large Southern exchanges, but they could not and did not want to buy all their cotton for one year at harvesttime. Therefore, speculators often bought much of the crop and held it until the manufacturers needed it. In the meantime, they transported the crop to the North and made the sale through one of the Northern exchanges.

The British mills—where at least one-third of American cotton went each year—bought through the Liverpool exchange. The job of buying American cotton fell to the brokers at Liverpool, who bought the cotton at an American exchange and sold it in Liverpool.

In the early days of cotton growing, the new harvest glutted the market and prices dropped markedly. Huge quantities of cotton arrived at the ports in November, December, and January and sold at low prices. By May, the scarcity of cotton had driven the price far above the harvesttime levels. This seasonality encouraged speculators to buy when the price was low and sell when it was high. Together with the development of the futures market, the presence of these speculators stabilized cotton prices considerably.[25] By the 1890s, the price fluctuations during the crop year were usually much less than the variations of price from year to year.

Cotton futures developed because manufacturers needed to guarantee themselves a supply of cotton throughout the year.[26] In its simplest form, a "futures contract" was simply an agreement that a speculator would deliver cotton to a consumer at a certain time in the future. The price for delivery was determined by mutual consent. The management was usually profitable for both sides: The consumer guaranteed himself that he would have cotton when he needed it, and he could bargain his price at a time when the commodity was not too expensive. The speculator could buy during the glut at a low price and deliver to the consumer at a higher price, thus guaranteeing himself a profit.

The "futures market" developed out of these futures contracts. Just as the small transactions built themselves up into a cotton price each day, these futures transactions built themselves up into a price of cotton for future delivery. Thus, there would be a price for "March cotton," meaning the price that people were paying for cotton to be delivered the following March. In the futures market, there was a separate price for cotton to be delivered any month in the future. The futures market became (and still is) a speculative affair. Cotton was bought and sold in futures with no intention of delivery. Every *day* in New York (the principal U.S. futures exchange) saw as much cotton sold in futures as actually came through the exchange in an entire year.

Behind the merchants and speculators was the financial establishment. Like

---

[25] *George Report*, pt. 1, pp. 1–275, especially pp. 17, 85, 132, 232.
[26] *George Report*, pt. 1, pp. 1–275, especially pp. 27, 48, 53, 100, 117, 126–127, 176–178, 191.

all big business, cotton required a great deal of investment and finance capital. The organization of this flow of capital from the big banks to the markets is both important and interesting, but it is not critical to understanding the problems of the producer.

The export of about 50% of American cotton in the post—Civil War years[27] left brokers and speculators with large amounts of foreign currencies. The credit and trade arrangements which resulted were a critical part of the controversy over tariffs, but their main impact was on the big cotton merchants and a few very large planters. Only indirectly did any of this relate to the majority of farmers in the South.[28]

The producer had four options in selling the crop. First, he or she could sell on the futures market *before it was harvested*, thus guaranteeing a fair price, even if the price at harvesttime was above the futures price. This was a "sure," conservative approach to cotton marketing. Second, the farmer could sell the crop on the futures market *after it was harvested*. This was different from the first option in that the farmer now held the cotton until the delivery date. Since the sale had already been made, he or she could borrow on the stored crop. Third, the farmer could hold the crop off the market and wait for a higher price. This would be acting just as the speculators did, and it obviously required sufficient capital to wait out the market. Finally, the farmer could bring the crop to market when it was harvested and sell it at the current price. While this left him or her at the mercy of the market, the stabilizing influence of the futures market made this less disastrous in the postbellum period. It had the obvious advantage of giving the farmer cash at the time his or her bills fell due.

Large planters and merchants could profitably utilize the first option (selling before harvest) and many did so:

> Cotton futures in the fall of 1880 advanced to nearly 15 cents in New York. At that time I was running four or five plantations, upon all of which I made cotton. I immediately sold all my crops to be delivered in the spring. The crop proved to be a very large one, as I thought, the largest on record, and in the spring prices declined 4 cents a pound from the price at which I sold, and I realized $20 per bale profit over and above what I would have gotten on my crops had I not been able to sell the contracts against them.[29]

This strategy could be utilized only by producers who could credibly guarantee delivery. Large operators could establish their reliability over a period of years— the small farmer could not. The merchant and landlord could offer hundreds of crop liens as collateral for the futures contracts, the tenant had no such guarantees. The merchant—landlord might have savings to cover bad crops or bad contracts; tenants and yeomen had no such backing.

The second possibility, harvesting and then selling for futures, would seem to

[27] Figures for cotton export for each year can be found in the *Monthly Survey of Commerce and Finance*.

[28] This discussion of the upper structure of cotton marketing leaves out a great deal. However, since our concern is with the producer, we need only sketch those elements of the marketing system which relate tangentially to the circumstances on the farm.

[29] *George Report*, pt. 1, p. 101.

offer the best chances for the small farmer. The futures price was likely to be high compared to the market price, making it profitable to pay storage fees for future delivery. The futures contract was a guarantee that the crop lien would eventually be redeemed, and it could be collateral on a short-term loan. Moreover, a small farmer could guarantee delivery to a suspicious buyer because the crop had already been picked. This option offered the chance of selling first and paying debts with cash.

Despite its attractive aspects, this tactic was rarely used. No merchant or landlord was willing to allow a tenant to hold cotton when he himself could sell it in the same way. Merchants and landlords therefore demanded immediate redemption of the crop lien. When farmers tried to exercise this option, "they could not control their own crops for the reason that they were heavily indebted to the merchants, and, consequently, no matter what the price of cotton might be, they were forced to market it." [30] Whenever they could, lienholders forced their tenants to sell to them in October when the price was lowest, and in a great many cases the power of the crop lien was sufficient to force this sale.[31] Moreover, the small farmer could not obtain loans, even on a picked cotton crop. The few local banks were unwilling to lend money to tenants without the approval of the merchants or the landlords (see pp. 42–44). Thus, there was little chance for the indebted farmer to obtain credit while he held the crop, and without cash he would be unable to pay off his debts, live through the winter, and finance spring planting.

These two factors eliminated the encumbered farmers from the futures market. But even unencumbered farmers who could obtain loans found it difficult to hold crops because they were competing with speculators. The speculators bought at the current price, entered the futures market, and held the crop until the futures contract matured. Since speculators could buy and sell huge amounts, they could afford to work with small margins. The farmer paid storage fees and interest on a loan against the picked crop. By the time he or she paid these fees, the anticipated profit was eaten up.

For example, during 1895, the price of cotton rose. On January 2, it was 5.06¢ per pound and on December 2 it was 8.31¢ per pound. (The price peaked in October at 9¢ and declined slightly when the crop came in.) During this rising market, the futures price never was more than .82¢ (four-fifths of a cent) above the selling price. The peak occurred in April, when the cash price was 5.69¢ and the January delivery would make a 10% profit of about $4.00 per bale. After subtracting for storage (about $.50 per bale) and interest on the loan (say, 6%, a modest estimate), the producer would realize a profit of about $1.50 per bale for selling on futures.

This example demonstrates that it was possible to make a profit in futures. However, the small yeoman did not get loans at 6% and did not usually have cotton in April. The futures market during the harvest months rarely showed a dif-

[30] *George Report*, pt. 1, p. 90, see also pp. 144, 167–168.
[31] *Agriculture Report*, pp. 49, 419, 433, 444, 445, 454, 458, 461, 474; Hallie Farmer, "The Economic Background to Frontier Populism," *South Atlantic Quarterly* 29 (January 1930), p. 87.

ference of more than one-fourth of a cent per pound, yielding a gross profit of $1.25 per bale. Fifty cents in storage fees and $2.00 in interest meant a $1.25 loss per bale in the futures market.[32]

The prospects for high profit in the futures market were nil, and the small farmer was frequently victimized when he or she attempted to exploit futures.[33] A Memphis cotton buyer reported that "scarcely one merchant or banker in this town would extend credit to a man dealing in futures.[34] This problem did not affect the large operators, since they could hold their crop cheaply and invest wisely. Another broker remarked, "I have advocated, for a number of years, and have been able to get a certain number of planters to use the future market in this way, and they have nearly always found it a great protection to them.[35]

The third alternative, holding the crop until the price went up, was the traditional solution to low cotton prices. It presented the same problems as selling for future delivery at harvesttime. It was possible only if the farmer had enough capital to wait out the price or if he or she could borrow enough to get through this waiting period. Once again, such a tactic required the solvency or a credit rating that very few small farmers—tenants or yeomen—enjoyed. Once again, only the largest landlords and merchants could take advantage of this possibility.[36]

The structure of the cotton market excluded the tenant and small owner, while encouraging merchants and landlords to amass large blocks of cotton. These two effects were the nub of the tenant–lienholder competition. The small producer could not exploit profitable marketing opportunities, and he or she became the target for the merchants and landlords who could. Thus, in order to take advantage of the market, the merchants and landlords had to take advantage of the tenants and yeomen. Nothing demonstrates this situation more conclusively than the inability of the small producer to utilize even the one remaining chance to enter the cotton market—selling immediately at harvesttime. If the tenant wanted to avoid selling the entire crop to the merchant (or landlord) at a price set by him, he or she needed to sell as soon as the crop was picked. This possibility created the cotton factor, who sought to buy from small producers and then resell after amassing large quantities of cotton.

There were actually two types of cotton factors. One was a carry-over from pre–Civil War days. He did his business with a large planter who gave his entire crop to the factor. Sometimes the factor bought the crop, sometimes he was simply the agent of its sale. Whether by brokers' fees or by speculative profit, the factor made his money selling cotton. Before the Civil War, these factors had been the suppliers and wholesalers for the plantation,[37] but afterward, they were displaced by country and wholesale merchants. Better transportation contributed to this development,

---

[32] All figures from the *New York Times*, various dates throughout 1895–1896; see also *George Report*, 1, pp. 20–26.

[33] *George Report*, pt. 1 pp. 1–275, *passim*, especially pp. 26, 60–76.

[34] *George Report*, pt. 1 p. 74; see also p. 156.

[35] *George Report*, pt. 1 p. 207.

[36] *George Report*, pt. 1 p. 105.

[37] In fact, prewar cotton factors were the first to give crop liens. Hammond, *The Cotton Industry*, (Ithaca, 1847) p. 141.

as did the breakup of the slave system. In any case, these, brokers survived by providing large amounts of money and becoming, in effect, the financiers of cotton buying.[38]

> Selling cotton, buying supplies, and providing credit were the most important functions of the factor before and after the Civil War, but as the planter's representative in the market place, the factor was called upon to handle other business as well. The familiar ante-bellum service continued after the Civil War. Factors aided the movement of funds by collecting bills of exchange; they added their endorsements to planters' and merchants' notes that these notes could be more easily discounted in the banks, and they attended to other business and personal matters of their customers.[39]

But large cotton factors who operated in market cities could survive only in areas where they had a few large merchants or landlords to service. In other areas, no factor could operate without the capacity to check the performance of the small producer. Therefore, a second kind of factor developed (many of these formerly belonged to the first category of factors), who realized that he could outbid the merchant for the tenant's crop and then sell at the city market for a profit. These enterprising factors sent agents to the farms to buy the crop. In this way, the farmer did not have to travel to market to sell his cotton. He sold directly to the factor without leaving the farm, thus sparing himself the expenses of shipping and marketing. The factor bought for much less at the farm than in the city, thus guaranteeing himself a profit. Indeed, the development of factors' agents saved the factors from extinction, since otherwise all buying would have taken place at the farm by merchants or landlords and then sold directly through the exchange.[40] As we shall see, just the possibility of direct buying was enough to assure the factor a continued role in the marketing process.

The largest factors sent "field men" to the local harvest. The buyers set up "bucket shops" in a small town—temporary stores where for several days they purchased cotton from local farmers, then arranged for its shipment and moved quickly to the next town.[41] A large firm might employ as many as 10 field agents[42] who had an expert knowledge of the quality of cotton and up-to-date information on market prices. They bought the crop wherever they could get a good deal (from merchants as well as tenants and landlords), stored the cotton nearby, and sent the price information to the factor. The factor, because of his city location, could sell the cotton to a customer and then ship directly, thus eliminating the expense of shipping to the exchange and then reshipping. (This was made possible by the postwar railroad boom.)[43]

Factors' agents went mainly to areas where they could avoid the competition

---

[38] They were one source of capital for large planters and merchants. *George Report*, p. 223.

[39] Harold Woodman, *King Cotton and His Retainers* (Lexington, Ky., 1968), p. 266.

[40] *Ibid.*; see pp. 269–270 for a detailed exposition of this process.

[41] *George Report*, pt. 1 p. 182.

[42] *Ibid.*, pt. 1 pp. 16, 131.

[43] King, *op. cit.*, p. 54; *George Report*, pt. 1 p. 166.

of landlords or merchants.[44] They found it easier to buy in atomized and not yet tenantized areas, where they could bring their competitive advantage and the ignorance of the small farmer into play. However, the factors' agents went anywhere they could make a profit, and this could bring them into direct conflict with merchants and landlords. The conflict, however, was largely muted by the circumstances faced by encumbered yeomen and tenants.

The small owner or tenant farmer was forced by the marketing system to sell as soon as the crop was harvested. In doing this, he or she had three alternatives:

1. Sell in a city through a broker.
2. Sell at the farm to a factor's agent.
3. Sell all the crop to the merchant or landlord.

In 1890, the average bale of cotton sold for $35 on the farm and was bought by the foreign purchaser for $50 (excluding transport fees). Much of this difference was due to markups by merchants, landlords, factors, and others between producer and consumer. The small producer who sold in the market city was attempting to bypass certain of these "middlemen" and take their profits for himself. But few small farmers could successfully manage this.

Shipping cotton for sale in the cities became less and less prevalent in the post–Civil War period. The development of railroads, while making transportation cheaper, also led to the development of a local warehouse system. The large producer sent samples of his crop to town and his personal reputation guaranteed his honesty. The cotton was sold sight unseen. "Business is largely done between buyer and seller on the basis of a confidence which seems to the casual observer rather reckless, but which custom has made perfectly safe."[45] The same practice was followed by factors. They bought the crop at the farm, stored it locally, and then resold it at the exchanges. When delivery was requested, the railroads carried the crop directly to the customer.[46]

The small producer could not send samples of his cotton and sell at a distance, because he or she was not a "dependable" supplier. Therefore, he had to ship the crop to the market. This was an extra expense. Since he had no money, he had to pay in crops—at the railroad's price. Transport was not a trivial expense: For example, in 1888, charges for shipping from the interior of Louisiana to New Orleans (distances of less than 200 miles) ran about $1.50 per bale on bales that sold for $35–40 in New Orleans. This 3.5–5% charge could wipe out the profit of a marginal farmer.[47]

Only large crops could be sent and handled through the big exchanges. Since the brokers were the only ones who could work through the exchanges and since most buyers bought large stocks, the small tenant could hope to sell his crop only at some secondary point to a factor who would then resell it through the ex-

[44] George Report, pt. 1 pp. 8, 36–37, 110, 131, 207, 221, 222.
[45] King, op. cit., p. 53.
[46] George Report, pt. 1 pp. 38, 166; King, op. cit., p. 54.
[47] George Report, pt. 1 p. 415.

change[48] Therefore, there was still a middleman's charge, though not nearly so large as that involved in farm sale. Furthermore, there was a storage and sales charge connected to this process which also cut into the farmer's profit.

The farmer could not oversee the sale of his crop unless he followed his cotton to market. If he simply shipped his cotton to a factor, he did not have a chance to sell to the highest bidder. He would have to accept whatever price the factor offered. Therefore, in order to get some advantage from shipping his goods, the farmer had to go to the market town with his crop—and he incurred yet another expense, his own fare. And, every day without a sale added substantially to his expenses as he paid for meals and a room in town. The combination of uncertainty about selling price and the increased expense made shipment before sale a risky proposition for the small producer: Larger producers could better absorb the shipment expenses; the small farmer was usually forced to sell at his farm to his lien-holder or to the factor's agent.

The presence of a factor's agent created the kind of competition for the tenant's crop which should have led to a substantial increase in the offered price; if the forces of price competition had prevailed, the factor would have dominated the buying of cotton from the tenants. He had a much larger operation to begin with, and this allowed him to work with smaller margins of profit. He was able to hold the crop much longer than the landlord or merchant and thus gain a speculator's profit. The factor was more familiar with the market and knew when to buy and when to sell.

However, many reasons conspired to defeat factors' agents in almost every area where merchant-landlords were strong. First, any deeply indebted farmers were forced to sell to the landlord-merchant in order to cover their accumulated debt. By 1890, about 60% of all farmers were insolvent and they could not legally sell to anyone except their lienholder.[49] For these individuals, the only hope of getting a competitive price lay in "stealing" the crop. Landlords and merchants took "precautions to prevent tenants and customers from 'beating their accounts' in the fall. One share tenant, undertaking to dispose of cotton in a neighboring town without putting it to his debt was overtaken by a bailiff with attachment papers and saw his cotton unloaded by the side of the road."[50] One former district attorney commented, "I have prosecuted a good many men who were sent to the penitentiary for stealing a chicken worth 25 cents".[51] Needless to say, few factors found it worth their while to try to buy from this vast majority of tenants and yeomen. Furthermore, in heavily indebted areas—about 40% of all Southern counties were over 70% insolvent in 1893[52]—there was no reason for the factor's agent to appear at all.

---

[48] *Bradstreets*, XI (February 14, 1885), pp. 99–100, records 164 such interior markets. These could not have developed without the postwar railroad buildup. See Woodman, *op. cit.*, pp. 274–275.

[49] Michael Schwartz, "The Southern Farmers' Alleance: the Organizational Forms of Radical Protest" Ph.D. diss., Harvard University, 1971), ch. 3.

[50] Nixon, *op. cit.*, p. 59.

[51] *Agriculture Report*, p. 416.

[52] See Chapter 5 of this volume.

There would be only a few farmers from whom to buy, and their business could not make the undertaking profitable.

Thus, insolvency prevented effective competition by factors in many areas. Moreover, the power of the crop lien and its system—even when the farmer was not insolvent—defeated them in a great many other cases. Many lien contracts were like those written at Sunnyside Plantation, Arkansas: The landlord—merchant had the right to buy all the crop whether or not it covered the debt.[53] In most liens, the lienholder collected his share before any part of the crop was sold.[54] This right could be used to extraordinary advantage. The factor's agent could stay in one place only a couple of days, but the crops might be picked over a 3-month period. If the factor's agent was due to arrive early, the merchant could slow the harvesting (by failing to finance the hiring of extra laborers) so that the farmer would have no cotton to offer the buyer. If the buyer was to arrive late, the merchant could hasten the picking and the sale of the crop. Even a large planter—who did not have a lienholder pressuring him to sell—frequently faced uncertainty if he chose not to sell immediately.[55]

Merchants and landlords had tremendous leverage over their tenants. If the tenant sold to a factor, they could cut off credit the following year, cut off credit on the spot, or increase harassment through extra supervision of the tenant's work. The local processing and storage facilities—which were often owned or controlled by landlords and merchants—might raise their prices to exorbitant rates if the tenant did not sell to the local buyers.

Merchant—factor comptition was by no means consistent. It might appear one year and disappear the next. Since its existence depended on the presence of an outside buyer in the area during the harvest, the tenant could never tell whether to hold out on selling to the merchant or landlord. Furthermore, the advantages which accrued to large merchants or landlords in the competition led the factors to steer clear of counties wherein large enterprises operated. Since factors could more profitably operate in areas where no one had the operating scale to compete with them, they rarely appeared where they were needed the most—in counties with large merchant and landlord concerns.

When factor—merchant conflict developed, it was usually settled quickly. Since both merchant and factor were forced to pay higher prices because of their competition, there was a great incentive for them to cooperate. The typical arrangement allowed the merchant to buy as much cotton as he could afford, and be the factor's agent for the rest. The tenant was left to the tender mercies of the merchant, who became the factor's agent as well as the lienholder. It was in his (the merchant's) interest to buy the cotton for as low a price as possible, taking as large a cut for himself as possible (as his fee) and then essentially reselling the cotton to the factor. In this way, the factor played very much the same role that he had played before the Civil War—financial broker for the large plantations.

---

[53] Brandfon, *op. cit.*, p. 147.

[54] Charles S. Mangum, *The Legal Status of the Tenant in the Southwest* (Chapel Hill, 1952), pp. 289–291.

[55] *Agriculture Report*, pp. 473–474.

Ultimately, as the centralization of ownership and control developed in each county, the factor no longer found it profitable to compete with the local lien-holders. In 1893, A. N. May, a Memphis factor, told a congressional committee, "Our business is directly or indirectly with the planters in the river bottoms, the hill business being chiefly with and through the country merchants."[56] His statement was supported by the testimony of most of the merchants who appeared before the committee,[57] though one was careful to note that in some places the tenants were allowed by the planters to "handle their own cotton." In this situation, the factors dealt directly with the farmer.[58]

If the price that the merchant paid dropped too low, there was an incentive for a new factor to enter the market. However, once a linkage between one factor and the local lienholders was made, this was usually the end of any real price setting at the farm. The merchants as a rule could drive the tenants into permanent debt— thus guaranteeing control of the crop. Moreover, the backing of a city factor made it much easier for the local merchant to compete with a new factor, since he had the inside information and financial backing to compete. Finally, factors' businesses themselves became monopolistic and therefore did not encourage competition among the big concerns.

A large discrepancy between market and farm price would encourage a neighboring merchant to attempt to cut in on the market. This possibility was a particularly dangerous one. A nearby merchant might not stop with simply buying the tenant's crop. He could also try to gain the tenant's lien for the following year. This raised the spector of truly cutthroat competition among merchants. This very situation occurred occasionally, but not very often, and seldom more than once in one location. However, much of this process depended on the resolution of a previous conflict—that between the landlord and the merchant. It is that conflict to which we now turn.

---

[56] *George Report*, pt. 1 p. 221.
[57] *George Report*, pt. 1, pp. 25, 36–37, 110, 131, 207, 221, 222.
[58] *George Report*, pt. 1, p. 182; *Agriculture Report*, pp. 486–488, 492.

4

The Dynamics of Change in Southern Farm Tenancy

Ill fares the land, to hastening ills a prey,
When wealth accumulates, and men decay;
Princes and lords may flourish, or may fade,
A breath can make them, as a breath has made;
But a bold peasantry, as a breath has made;
When once destroyed, can never be supplied.
[Upton B. Gwynn, *Raleigh Progressive Farmer*, October 1889]

The Landlord and the Merchant

The landlord and the merchant were engaged in an intense competition over the division of the crop which only one could survive. Descriptions of cotton farming after 1880 rarely contained both landlord and merchant in stable, independent roles. They coexisted either for the duration of a power struggle between them or else in the context of one dominating the other.[1] Small landlords were often reduced to the status of debtors, executing crop liens for themselves as well as their tenants, and pleading for extra credit. In other situations, the merchant was owned by the landlord, or gave credit to tenants only insofar as the landlord permitted it.[2] Most frequently, however, the two roles were filled by a single individual. For example, *The Agricultural Revolution in Georgia* devotes more than half of its pages to first-hand descriptions of Georgia Black Belt plantations between 1905 and 1912,

---

[1] See, for example, on this, the struggle over the Landlord and Tenants Act in North Carolina described in *Proceedings of the Select Committee of the United States Senate to Investigate the Causes of the Removal of the Negroes from the Southern States to the Northern States*, 46th Cong. 2d sess, 1880, S. Rept. 693, pt. 2 (hereafter cited as *Exodus Committee Report*).

[2] For many examples see Thomas Clark, *Pills, Petticoats, and Plows* (New York, 1944), pp. 319–320 and *passim*; *George Report*, pt. 1 pp. 294, 298; *Agriculture Report*, pp. 49, 492, 926, and *passim*.

yet nowhere does it mention the coexistence of a planter and a merchant. In every instance in the Georgia Black Belt, the two roles were combined.[3]

Many sources of friction between the landlord and the merchant have already been noted. Each preferred to supply the tenant with plows, mules, and seed. Both wanted to provide extra labor. Both sought to become the tenant's principal creditor. And both wished to control the marketing of the crop. Yet despite these points of conflict, it is difficult to see why the loser of this compeition was inevitably driven into complete subordination or entirely out of the picture. It seems possible, for example, that a landlord could pass up the chance to make extra money and simply collect his rent. On the other hand, the merchant might restrict his business to selling day-to-day supplies and avoid competition over labor and other large expenses. In either case, one competitor would withdraw from the competition but would not be destroyed. To understand why such alternatives to total destruction were impossible, the development of the tenancy system must be reviewed.

Just after the Civil War, a large percentage of landlords found that they were unable to run their plantations by the system of labor gangs. The freedman (and white laborers as well) simply refused to work for the wages the planters were willing to offer. What amounted to a general strike in agricultural labor occurred. This crisis resulted from the "inability of the landlord to get him [Blacks] to do the labor he would contract to perform on the farm lands."[4] And when the infamous Black Codes were defeated,[5] the plantations collapsed. Farms were rented to tenants, who were financed by the new country merchants.[6] These merchants could control Black and white tenants through the leverage of the credit system. If they had enough capital or enough credit, they could expand their business to include all the expenses of the farm. The 43,000 merchants in the South in 1860 increased to 69,000 in 1870 and to 92,000 in 1880.[7]

In the late 1860s and early 1870s, many landlords withdrew from the countryside and hoped to live off flat rents from their holdings. This proved a cause of landlord impoverishment, not a guarantee of adequate income. With merchant encouragement and coercion, tenants built up supply bills so high that it took the entire cotton crop to cover them.[8] The landlord's share went to the merchant, and if the landlord refused to yield, the merchant refused to finance the crop.[9]

The landlord had little room to maneuver. In some instances, the merchant

[3]Robert P. Brooks, *The Agrarian Revolution in Georgia* 1865–1912, Bulletin of the University of Wisconsin History Series, vol. 3 (Madison, 1914).

[4]*George Report*, p. 314. (A full citation of this work appears in note 3, Chapter 1 of this volume.) For an extensive, nontechnical discussion of the immediate post–Civil War labor situation, see Stephen DeCanio, "Agricultural Production, Supply and Institutions in the Post Civil War South" (Ph. D. diss., MIT, 1972), pp. 32–104.

[5]Kenneth M. Stampp, *The Era of Reconstruction, 1865–1877* (New York, 1965), pp. 78–80.

[6]Roger W. Shugg, "Survival of the Plantation System in Louisiana," *Journal of Southern History* 3 (August 1937), pp. 311–313.

[7]All figures are from the U.S. census unless otherwise noted. The 1870 census is notoriously unreliable. Therefore, the only figures that can be trusted are those which are consistent with other, independent figures. In this case the 1880 figure suggests that the 1870 figure is within the proper range.

[8]Edward King,· *The Great South* (1879), p. 52.

[9]*George Report*, pt. 1 pp. 294, 310, 383.

could legally collect the landlord's share regardless of the contract between land-lord and tenant.[10] In most cases, he could take the crop and let the landlord sue. Very frequently, since the landlord and tenant had to depend on the merchant for credit and supplies, the absentee landlord welcomed the chance to countersign the lien rather than have the land lay fallow. In this case, the contract mandated merchant confiscation of the landlord's share.

Merchants could, by virtue of the joint liability of the tenant and landlord, collect the entire crop as payment for the various services (food, equipment, labor, and others) that they provided. Furthermore, the merchants soon discovered the Anaconda mortgage, which forced the owner to back up his crop lien with every-thing he owned—land, money, and personal property. If the crop did not cover the debt, the merchant could claim the landlord's bank account, home, and land to repay the debt.[11] A man could start as a rich planter with a large plantation and thousands of dollars but end up impoverished if he were forced to countersign his tenants' crop liens. Many of the largest prewar planters left their rural plantations and moved to town, expecting to live off their rents. Through the Anaconda mort-gage, they soon found themselves heavily indebted to the rural merchants who sup-plied their tenants.[12]

The tenants benefited from this friction between the merchant and the landlord. Since the merchant could expect to collect the entire crop and perhaps the land-lord's property if the tenant ran up a large enough bill, he was willing to sell on credit for more than the tenant's share. The tenant might therefore spend the owner's portion in addition to his own (although at exorbitant credit prices). The merchant, for his part, was anxious to extend this credit, since he made a profit on each sale and he could reach into the landlord's pocket to obtain his pay-ment.[13]

Thus, the landlord who failed to supervise his tenants who were supplied by the merchant could not survive. One Georgia planter was asked in 1900 about this strategy:

You mean to say, then, in the first place, the farmer, the landlord, the tenant, the cropper, or the laborer, if they have any advances made to them, are all in the hands

[10]For example, in Georgia between 1874 and 1875. Alex M. Arnett, *The Populist Movement in Georgia*, Columbia University Studies in History Economics and Public Law, vol. 104 (New York, 1922), p. 51.

[11]Hallie Farmer, "The Economic Background to Southern Populism," *South Atlantic Quarterly* 29 (January 1930), p. 84.

[12]This happened even to the prewar aristocrats. See, for example, Shugg, *op. cit.*, pp. 311–325; Matthew B. Hammond, *The Cotton Industry* (Ithaca, 1897); and especially the many dictionaries of biography of prominent Southerners, which seem to delight in mentioning not only those who succeeded but also their brothers who failed. However, the existence of impoverishment should not be confused with *redistribution of land*. As Shugg carefully shows, these huge ranges of land were usually transferred whole to the new owner: They were not sub-divided and sold.

[13]*George Report*, pt. 1, p. 383; King, *op. cit.*, p. 52. It is interesting to note that the image of the spendthrift tenant—especially the spendthrift black tenant—now takes on a new aspect. The tenant realized that if he did not spend on credit during the growing season, he was preserving the landlord's share, without helping himself at all. It is not surprising to find that tenants spent as much of the owner's share as they could get away with—and thus earned the hatred of the landlords and the designation "spendthrift."

of the money loaner?
Almost invariably, with a few exceptions.[14]

Landlords who did not act to preserve their holdings were soon foreclosed on. And since land values were low and taxes were high, neither selling nor leaving the land fallow was feasible.[15] In Louisiana, for example, land taxes doubled while land values halved in the period 1868–1877.[16] Some landlords, notably in Alabama during the 1880s, attempted a repeal of the lien laws, but such a repeal was both economically and politically unfeasible.[17]

In many states, landlords managed to obtain an automatic first lien on the crop,[18] but this leverage did not work by itself, since the merchant then demanded that the landlord waive his lien if he wanted the crop financed.[19] This waiver then forced the landlord to oversee the transactions—every credit purchase by the tenant needed approval of the landlord.[20] If the landlord failed to do this, the merchant would boost the sales and claim the entire crop.

But even this supervision did not work if the landlord had no alternative source of supplies. The merchant could still withhold credit if he felt the landlord was interfering with his profits. Therefore, the landlord needed at least the threat of alternative credit.

The logical solution was for the planter to supply the tenant himself. Since supplying equipment was not enough to protect the landlord fully, he would have to furnish all the tenant's supplies. This essentially made the landlord into a merchant—taking a lien from the tenant and moving back to the farm to spend his year as a merchant.

Certainly, the landlord could outbid the merchant for the tenant's lien: he could refuse to rent unless the tenant did business with him. However, he could not exercise this leverage without the wherewithal to finance the crop. So the resolution of the landlord—merchant competition turned on the competition for credit which we have already discussed. In this conflict, the small landholder had little chance of defeating the merchant, while the large owner was in a position of strength. Banks and wholesalers would not loan to small farmers, especially when they already had established ties to the merchants. Ultimately the small holders found themselves farming one part of their holdings and overseeing the tenants on the rest. They were called owners but they were hopelessly in debt to merchants and therefore might as well have been tenants. On the other hand, the solvent or

---

[14] *Agriculture Report*, p. 49. (A full citation of this work appears in note 3, Chapter 1 of this volume.) See also *George Report*, pt. 1 pp. 294, 298.

[15] Whether or not the land was planted, it was subject to taxation. The tax burden differed from state to state, but it represented about 80% of the government's revenue and was not insignificant. See comptrollers' reports for the states and Robert Brandfon, *Cotton Kingdom of the New South* (Cambridge, Mass., 1967), pp. 40–42.

[16] Roger W. Shugg. *The Origin of Class Struggle in Louisiana* (Banton Rouge, 1939), p. 244.

[17] William Warren Rogers, *The One-Gallused Rebellion* (Baton Rouge, 1970), pp. 15–21.

[18] *George Report*, p. 305; *Exodus Committee Report*, p. 209; *Agriculture Report*, pp. 47, 777, 805.

[19] *Agriculture Report*, p. 492.

[20] T. J. Edwards, "The Tenant System and Some Changes Since Emancipation," *Annals of the American Academy of Political and Social Science* 49 (September 1913), p. 42.

credit worthy landlord bought goods from the wholesaler and sold directly to his tenants. He had no reason to buy anything from the merchant and this eliminated the merchant altogether.

If the landlord could not adequately compete with the merchant, he was soon reduced to the status of a tenant himself—working on one farm to produce enough food to live. Otherwise he gave up his land to the merchant and went into other work. In this case, the merchant became the owner of the land—with or without the deed. He then collected both rent and lien from the tenants. If the landlord could and did compete, then the merchant was driven from the scene and the landlord became the merchant in fact. In either case, there emerged a combination merchant–planter who controlled the land, supplies, and labor.

The dilemma of the landlord is illustrated by J. R. Goodwin, a Memphis, Tennessee, planter. Goodwin, according to his own account, disliked overseeing and supervision, so during the 1880s, he rented his land at a flat rate, hoping simply to collect his cotton at harvesttime. However, it was extremely difficult to obtain tenants who did not need to give liens, and this led him to the choice of waving his own lien or furnishing the tenants himself. Goodwin would not waive his lien—he knew this courted disaster. This choice left him in the supply business and inevitably he found himself supervising his tenants: riding around the land and checking their work.[21] The logic of his circumstances led him to overseeing and supervising, even though he detested such work. Landlords who were not their own supply merchants were very vulnerable indeed, as the following testimony in 1900 illustrates:

Q. *You have been a successful planter?*
A. *Yes sir.*
Q. *You are one of the few, are you not?*
A. *Well, they could all be the same way I am.*
Q. *To what do you attribute your success?*
A. *Well, I expect I am because I attend to business.*
Q. *You are a merchant also?*
A. *Yes sir.*
Q. *And you furnish supplies to other farmers?*
A. *Yes sir, that is the way.*
Q. *An then you take their farms to pay their debts to you?*
A. *Yes sir, I had to take their farms to get something.*
Q. *Then the farmers whose plantations you got were unfortunate in their cultivation, were they not?*
A. *Yes sir, unfortunate because they did not tend to business.*
Q. *I asked you as a fact.*
A. *Yes sir, because instead of raising their own supplies, meat and corn, and every-thing, I had to furnish them.*

---

[21] *Agriculture Report*, pp. 474–475.

Q. How many places have you got?

A. Well I got, I suppose eight or ten different places in Tennessee, Arkansas and Kentucky.

Q. And got them all in the same way?

A. Yes sir, all except one.[22]

If one surveys the economic geography of the South in 1900, there emerges a clear pattern to the resolution of the landlord—merchant conflict. In the old plantation areas and the newly cultivated lands in the Black Belt, the landlords emerged victorious. Using mainly, but not exclusively, Black labor, these planters drove the merchants out, set up plantation stores, and oversaw huge holdings. Most descriptions of tenancy dwell on these plantations,[23] and see them as typical, though they actually produced only about half the cotton grown in the South.[24]

In the areas of the South that had been populated mostly by small white farmers before the Civil War, it was the merchant who emerged as the hegemonic force. Because of the small size of the holdings in these areas, the owners could not become their own suppliers, and sooner or later they became beholden to the merchant. The storekeeper might foreclose on the land when the debt was large, but even without foreclosure, he dominated the entire area he served with a certainty equal to that of the landlord in the Black Belt. These storekeepers could properly be called the lords of their domains:

> *Our fathers which art in Troy*
> *Wiley and Murphy by thy names,*
> *Thy kingdom of provisions come*
> *They will be done*
> *On my farm as it is at your store*
> *Give us this day our daily bread*
> *Forgive us our trespass on your barn*
> *As we forgive those who trespass upon ours,*
> *Lend us not into temptation, but deliver us from hungriness*
> *For thine shall be the crop, the mules and the land forever and ever*
> *If we don't pay.*[25]

The landlord—merchant competition was indeed unstable. But from the tenant's point of view, no matter how it was resolved, he or she dealt with only one man, a landlord—merchant combination. It mattered little whether the man who ran the store was the owner or his agent. It mattered little whether the merchant was originally the landlord, or vice versa. The day-to-day operation of the farm depended only on the fact that the tenant rented from the same man to whom he

[22] *George Report*, pp. 145—146.
[23] See, for example, King, *op. cit.*; Shugg, *op. cit.*; Albert Bushnell Hart, *The Southern South* (New York, 1912).
[24] Hart, *op. cit.*, p. 262.
[25] Clark, *op. cit.*, p. 155.

gave his lien and from whom he received his supplies. This arrangement ensured the tenant's inability to gain real economic leverage within the system.

Yeoman and Tenant

Small owners faced much the same problems as tenants. They had freedom from aggressive landlords but suffered from the general lack of capital and the instability of prices. This led first to entrapment by the crop lien and then reduction to tenancy. A man or woman could hold title to a farm while working as a subsistence laborer on it.[26]

In the last section, we discussed the technical possibility for a peaceful coexistence of landlords and merchants. For example, the landlord could supply his own tenants (and take liens) while buying his supplies from the local merchant. However, this arrangement was unstable because one or the other would "eliminate the middleman." The landlord would, if he could muster the money, trade directly with the wholesaler. The merchant would, if he could find a way, trade directly with the tenant.

The situation was different between yeomen and merchants: Neither could bypass the other. Yeomen would have profited from buying at wholesale, but the small scale of their operation made this economically unfeasible. And, since yeomen did not usually employ tenants (less than 25% of yeoman farms were subdivided), there was no reason for the merchant to bypass the small owner.

This lack of incentive to "cut out the middleman" on both sides suggests that an equilibrium could be reached between the yeoman farmers and merchants; it would seem that they had no choice but to deal with each other. However, circumstances and the tenancy system conspired against coexistence and made this situation unstable.

Yeomen expected to pay cash for supplies. They decided what crops to plant and grew many of their own supplies if possible. They could vary crops in response to the market. This decision-making control was a weapon with which to make a profit each year and to guarantee independence.

The initial snag arose in the marketing process. Chapter 3 detailed the difficulties that tenants faced in marketing crops. These difficulties flowed from two sources. First, the merchants and landlords used the crop lien to force tenants to sell to them instead of entering the market. Second, the tenant's small farming scale made it impossible for them to enter a market that favored large sellers.

The yeoman farmer was a small operator: In 1900, not more than 15% of owner-operated farms had 100 improved acres. Therefore, yeomen faced many of the same problems as tenants. They could not usually market crops in the big cities—expense was too great. They could not usually afford to hold the crop—the crop lien was due. Therefore, they were at the mercy of the market price at harvest-

[26]William Ivy Hair, *Bourbonism and Agrarian Protest* (Baton Rouge, 1969), p. 52

time. Even worse, they were doubly hurt by a marketing system designed to serve the tenancy system. In the West, where tenancy did not arise, there were a great many buyers in the field every year. In the South, the institution of tenancy reduced the number of buyers considerably. Yeomen often had no prospective buyer except the merchant, even when they were not subject to the coercion of a crop lien. Thus, even in the best of times, Southern yeomen found themselves injured tremendously by the tenant system and the lack of an open market.

The national economic situation also contributed to the economic failure of small farmers. The United States experienced several financial crises between 1870 and 1900. These crises, which dropped the prices of farm goods drastically, hit harder at cotton farmers than corn or wheat farmers. Whereas the general wholesale prices dropped 50% from 1870 to 1894 (the deepest depression year), cotton prices dropped 75%. While wheat and corn saw 10% price drops 5 times in the period, cotton prices dropped more than 10% during 10 different years.[27]

The sudden price drops and the continuing deflation hurt Southern farmers immensely. Since the prices dropped at harvesttime, just when they were forced to sell, this meant a sure loss for the year. Farmers who invested large sums of money at the precrisis prices found themselves getting paid with crop prices far below those of the previous year. Fewer than half of the cotton farmers showed a profit each year,[28] and many were therefore forced into debt in order to finance the following year's planting. When this happened, the continuing deflation made the debt loom larger and larger over time, while the continual drop in cotton price made it more and more difficult to repay.

Because of deflation, low prices, difficulty of marketing, and other factors, many yeomen ran out of money in the middle of the crop year. To complete the crop, the farmer had to obtain a crop lien. This meant that even the *possibility* of needing credit forced yeomen to grow cotton. They planted cotton to guarantee their credit at the country store, which did not give liens on other crops. And even a small loan could cause serious trouble. Besides changing exorbitant prices to credit customers, the lienholder could exact tremendous service charges for providing and paying the pickers. He could intervene at the processing and expropriate the rights to the sale of the farmer's share. All this might be made a condition for granting the lien in the first place.

Once a lien was given, a process of immiseration began. It might take many years, and it could be reversed. The frugal yeoman could resist the inducements and coercions to building up a large debt at the store and could carefully cultivate garden and food crops to reduce money needs. The holder of the lien, however, had countermoves. Merchants used their credit power and the threat of withholding the lien to force their debtors to plant more cotton and fewer food crops. Fewer food crops meant more business for the merchant. More cotton meant the

[27] U.S. Bureau of the Census, *Historical Statistics of the United States, Colonial Times to the Present; A Statistical Abstract Supplement* (Prepared with the Cooperation of the Social Science Research Council, Washington, D.C., 1960), pp. 115, 123–124, 296.

[28] See Chapter 5 of this volume.

farmer could sustain a large debt. (The merchant might also claim the food crops as part of the lien. Since there was not a large market for these commodities, the merchant could justify paying very low prices for them, then sell them back to the farmer for credit prices.)

The crop lien created a powerful dialectic between merchants and yeomen. The farmer spent all his cash one year and then gave a lien. When the crop was in, he or she paid the debt and converted the remainder into cash. However, for financing one-fourth of the expenses, the merchant might get one-half of the crop. Therefore, the farmer was likely to run out of money even sooner the next year. After selling the crop, he might have only one fourth of the return. Sooner or later, he fell into permanent debt—the crop simply did not cover his bill. When this happened, the merchant could take over the farmer's equipment, personal possessions, and land.

> The process of losing possession of farms in the South followed a regular credit routine. Accounts ran hopelessly behind for two or three years with unsettled balances piling up into such considerable sums that lien notes were no longer adequate coverage, then a mortgage was placed upon the land, and the annual deficit continued piling up until it consumed the full value of an unfortunate debtor's possessions. The customer "assigned" his land to the merchant, went through the fiction of making an independent settlement of his account and then moved his family away to begin anew as a tenant farmer.[29]

> Q. *You have been raising at a woeful loss for the past few years?*
> A. *Yes sir, so much so that nearly everybody has lost his home in the county. I have partly escaped, but the majority of people who farm are now homeless.*[30]

Merchants were usually reluctant to take land in foreclosure.[31] Since it was almost impossible to sell, they could not convert foreclosed land into money. If they did not foreclose, the bill for taxes went to the farmer. Since he or she could not pay, the merchant would "lend" the money and thus worsen the debt.

Because there was a labor shortage, it made sense for merchants to keep the yeomen on their farms. Rather than foreclose, merchants continued the debt from year to year. The yeomen were still the technical owners of the land, and they therefore kept working hard to regain clear title. If the merchant foreclosed, the yeomen would likely leave—going to another tenant farm or to the city and an industrial job. Since the merchant wanted to keep the farmer on the land, he found that he "frequently had to carry him ten years.[32]

This process of tenantization would not have been nearly so rapid nor nearly so devastating had there not been the rapid deflation discussed previously. Once a farmer fell into debt, it increased year to year, just by the force of deflation. With the ever greater drop in cotton prices, the farmer was doubly bound.

Nor would the tenantization process have been so severe had actual tenancy not

---

[29] Clark, *op. cit.*, pp. 321–322.
[30] *Agriculture Report*, p. 458.
[31] Clark, *op. cit.*, p. 32.
[32] *Agriculture Report*, p. 436.

been prevalent nearby. We have already seen that the existence of a tenant economy put yeomen at a tremendous disadvantage in the market. There was an even more compelling influence exerted by tenancy. Merchants who might otherwise have cautiously refused credit to a struggling farmer had great experience with crop liens, and confidence in the financial viability of the system. Rather than resist credit business—as they might otherwise have done—merchants encouraged it. They were protected by a legal system designed to safeguard the liens of large operators in the plantation areas, and further safeguarded by a government apparatus which was profoundly loyal to the whole tenancy system.

The insolvent yeoman was reduced to the status of tenant. Each year he or she needed larger loans to finance the crop. Soon the merchant successfully acquired the right to sell the cotton and removed the small owner from the market. Whether or not the land was seized, the yeoman became the merchant's tenant, working the land but not entering the market to sell the produce.

In 1905, one southerner gave the following account of the tenantization process:

> One neighbor said to another, in a sort of boastful way: "I have made arrangements, with a merchant, by which I can get whatever I need on my farm, all through the year, without paying any cash." "How do you do that?" asked the other neighbor. "Why, I just gave him a 'crap lien,'" answered the first neighbor. "What is a crap lien?" asked neighbor number two. "O, it's nothing but a promise to pay, at the end of the year, when the crop is gathered," said neighbor number one. "I believe," said neighbor number two, "I had rather pay the cash, for what I am obliged to have, and do without what I can't pay the cash for." "O, you are an old fogy," retorted neighbor number one. "My motto is, while we live let us live." "That's my motto, too," said neighbor number two, "and while I am living I had rather keep out of debt. That 'crap lien' you tell me about, may be a dangerous thing after all, instead of a blessing. At any rate, I wish you would let me know at the end of the year how it worked."

> As a matter of course, neighbor number one, who had taken the crap lien, traded extensively—and so did the family—they got such things as they severally wanted, all the time feeling highly elated over the fact that they had such good credit.

> At the winding up of the year, the crap lien began to draw, and it kept on drawing. It drew all the cotton and the corn, the wheat and the oats, the shucks, the hay and the fodder, the horses and the mules, the cows, the hogs and the poultry, the farm utensils and the wagons, the carriage and the buggy; and not being satisfied with its drawing outside, it drew the household and kitchen furniture, and, as neighbor number one in sadness explained to neighbor number two, it didn't quit drawing until it got the table, the plates and the dishes, the cups and the saucers, the knives and the forks, and, when it had gotten everything else, it reached for the dish rag, and wiped up the whole concern, not leaving even a grease spot.[33]

[33] Richard H. Whitaker, *Reminiscences, Incidents, and Anecdotes* (Raleigh, 1905), pp. 101–102.

Unfortunately, neighbor number two, the frugal one, was probably forced into the debt his friend leaped into. Perhaps it took several years longer, but the "crap lien" got to even the most careful farmers. In 1893, considerably fewer than one-third of the Southern farmers emerged from the harvest out of debt.[34]

A more poignant way of viewing the situation is provided by Southern folk music:

> *My husband came from town last night*
> *As sad as man could be,*
> *His wagon empty, cotton gone*
> *And not a dime had he.*
>
> *Huzzah! Huzzah!*
> *'Tis queer, I do declare*
> *We made the clothes for all the world*
> *But few we have to wear.*

From Tenant to Laborer

If the yeoman farmer could be transformed into a tenant, the tenant could be transformed into a laborer. For the yeoman, the key element in his or her degradation was debt which forced him to deal solely with his local merchant. For the tenant, the transformation involved his or her loss of autonomy with regard to any phase of cotton production.

Robert Brooks, writing in 1914, defined the difference between tenant and laborer as follows:

> Viewed in the proper light, only one form of tenantry exists . . . , namely renting. The share tenant is in reality a day laborer. Instead of receiving weekly or monthly wages, he is paid a share of the crop raised on the tract of land for which he is responsible. *Absolute control of the crop remains in the hands of the landlord.* He deducts all charges for support of the tenant, and turns over the balance to him. . . . Instead of standing over the gang of laborers constantly, the owner or his representative now rides from farm, to farm, watching the state of the crop, deciding on the method of cultivation, requiring the tenant to keep up the property, and above all enforcing regularity of work. . . . The wage hand was an uncertain factor in that he was liable to disappear on any pay day; the cropper is obliged to stay at least during an entire year, or forfeit his profits. This steadiness imparted to the tenant by self-interest doubtless compensates for the slight discipline. Indeed, the share system is not altogether incompatible with gang labor. Many planters hold that in large-scale production of the cotton, the really crucial point of difference between the share and renting systems is in connection with the preparation of the soil. When the plantation is organized on a share basis, the planter furnishes heavy plows and harrows and strong teams, and all the share farms are prepared just as if they were one farm, laborers and teams going in gangs straight over the plantation, regardless of the individual holdings. In this way every portion of the plantation receives similar treatment. Division into individual holdings is made after preparation and planting. Furthermore, as the croppers are under full control as to their time, they are sometimes worked in gangs during the cultivating season. For instance, if the manager sees that the crop of one of his share tenants is being neglected, he may send a

---

[34] *George Report*, pt. 1 pp. 275–403; and Chapter 5 of this volume.

gang of other croppers to put things to rights, charging the extra time against the negligent cropper's half of the crop. This sort of cooperation is not practicable with renters. In the first place the planter does not have control of their time. In the second place, renters' work-animals and tools are of varying degrees of efficiency, many tenants owning only the most wretched stock and implements. It would not be fair to combine poor animals with good ones and give the inefficient renter the benefit of the services of the equipment of the efficient men. A third difficulty is that renters are independent and differ in their ideas about farming, for example about the amount of fertilizers that may profitably be used.[35]

Brooks's distinction between "renters" and "sharecroppers" was correlated only loosely with the type of rental agreement. Whether the tenant was a "cash" tenant or a "share" tenant did not matter so much as the state of his or her debt. Brooks pointed out that after a successful year, many sharecroppers would demand a cash rental agreement instead of the previous share arrangement. The planter could then "sell" (on credit) to the tenant the same plow he had "supplied" the year before. The interest on this credit purchase would be about the same as the price charged for supplying it. Instead of supplying seed, the planter sold it. The farm animals were bought on credit, not supplied, and so on. The only difference betweeen this cash arrangement and the share system was that, instead of paying "rent," the tenant paid the same money as "interest."[36]

It can be seen that the key difference between the true tenant and the "day laborers receiving their pay at the end of the year"[37] was supervision. It was in the interest of the landlord (or merchant) to maintain maximum supervision over his tenants.[38] The reduction of the tenant to the status of laborer was completed when the landlord or merchant began exercising full control over all production and labor decisions.

There might be a vast difference between tenancy and ordinary wage labor. When a tenant (or yeoman) took out a lien with the merchant, the merchant tried to get the farmer to buy as much as he could and to plant cotton to cover the debt. The more the farmer bought, the more of the crop the merchant got. If the whole crop would not pay the bill, then the merchant could take possession of the equipment, personal property, and, finally, land (if there was any). However, if the tenant fell into debt beyond the value of his or her crops and possessions, the merchant would want to limit further buying. For example, if a farmer owed the merchant $150 for past purchases and had assets of $150, the merchant would be very reluctant to advance another $25 worth of goods, since he had no hope of repayment. At this point, the merchant would no longer be interested in encouraging farmer spending—in fact, he would want to discourage it. Of course, he was in an excellent position to do so, since the crop lien prevented the tenant from buying elsewhere.

Once he or she could no longer hope to cover the debt, the tenant could no longer spend freely. The merchant would refuse to sell anything that he (the

[35]Brooks, *op. cit.*, pp. 65–67.
[36]Brooks, *op. cit.*, pp. 60–61, 65.
[37]Brooks, *op. cit.*, p. 61.
[38]See pp. 29–32.

merchant) thought was unnecessary, and he would demand that the tenant explain where previously bought supplies had gone. This was the opening wedge of supervision—the merchant began overseeing every expense of the tenant's. The son of a Georgia merchant described the process succinctly:

> There was constant watching to make sure that tenants' accounts did not run ahead of their crop work and crop prospects. A tenant, getting in a risky situation, might be told to speed up his work or to cut down his buying. In certain cases, purchases would be limited to food, tobacco, and absolutely necessary work clothes.[39]

But this was not the end of the progression toward complete supervision. The wise merchant soon realized that he could supervise the actual work of the farmer and greatly increase cash yields. Furthermore, he knew that if he forced the farmer to plant only cotton, he might increase yield and debt simultaneously—by forcing the tenant to buy food at exorbitant prices at the store. As repayment for the debt, the merchant might demand that the tenant work extra time in the fields. Para-doxically, if the tenant were hopelessly in debt, the merchant might even demand that the tenant grow food crops which the merchant could appropriate.

The whole sequence was a neat cycle, perhaps overstated in this 1893 account:

> We think the tendency of provision and supply dealers to extend credit to farmers and largely to negroes [sic] unworthy of the same, charging time prices which will average over 50% interest, thereby taking great risks, said advance being made conditionally that cotton be planted and delivered against said debt, thereby forcing them to plant cotton is, in a measure, a cause of overproduction. The experience of the last few years has caused country merchants to greatly curtail the usual supply business, having lost heavily by failure of farmers to pay their debts with ruinously low prices for cotton. Consequently, for this reason largely, a moderate crop will be made.[40]

The tenant had little choice in the matter. The crop lien meant that no other supplier could sell supplies to the indebted farmer. If he or she refused to obey any command, the landlord (merchant) could refuse further supplies and food. The tenant would then be faced with starving to death or leaving the crop.

Being in debt was different from being hopelessly in debt. Some tenants fell into such large debt that they could never expect to recover, and once this happened, the crop lien carried over from year to year. Such an insolvent farmer—even if he or she retained title to the land—was bound to a landlord–merchant because of debt.[41] Obviously, the lienholder no longer needed to concern himself with courting the tenant in any way. He became a large entrepreneurial farmer with the same

---

[39] H. C. Nixon, *Lower Piedmont Country* (New York, 1944), p. 59.

[40] *George Report*, pt. 1 p. 415, also pp. 321, 322, 416.

[41] Because of this, it became possible for tenant labor to be sold by one planter to another. The contract of a tenant could be bought for something less than the size of the debt. "A regular trade of shiftless workers devel-oped." David Duncan Wallace, *The History of South Carolina* (New York, 1934), vol. 3, p. 395.

problems that every businessman faced: to maximize his yield and minimize his expenses. He had a captive labor force (the debtors), so he could cut their supplies to subsistence level with some assurance that he would not lose his workers. This reduced his expenses tremendously and guaranteed the merchant a much greater profit. He could also increase his yield by the close supervision of his laborers and and the emphasis on cash crops which he knew he could sell. All the advantages of "economy of scale" were applied and all production decisions were made in favor of the planter—merchant. It is not surprising that the largest Alabama landlord, who controlled 30,000 acres in the 1880s, announced that he "has no use for a nigger [sic] who pays out."[42] He wanted tenants who would remain in debt and therefore be vulnerable to maximum exploitation.

The hopelessly indebted yeoman or tenant was treated abominably.[43] Merchants and landlords literally refused food for the family unless the debtor's work met their standards.[44] Such debtors could not change landlords. A turn-of-the century tenant at Sunnyside Plantation tried to leave despite a $100 debt and was threatened with prison.[45] The lien law bound him to the land. Some landlords prohibited an indebted tenant from leaving the plantation for any reason, at any time. One such landlord had a simple policy: "If he goes away, I just go get him."[46] In the early 1900s, a landlord whipped a female tenant for not working fast. When repeated whippings did not succeed, she was hung by her wrists for 2 hours and she died. The culprit was not convicted.[47] In some places, planter control reach its logical extreme. M. L. Youmans, a Fairfax, South Carolina, landlord was asked in 1900 how he obtained laborer. "I raise them," he replied. "Their parents go there and stay, and they stay there."[48]

It is not surprising that planters could carry on a plausible (though ghoulish) argument about the relative "advantages" and "disadvantages" of slavery and tenancy. An observer in 1893 flatly stated that for a Black person, "As a slave, he was better fed and better housed than he is now."[49] A Memphis cotton broker and landlord elaborated on this theme to a 1900 congressional investigation.

> [Now] their rations are so much confined to bacon and corn meal. You know, when they were in slave times—they had a cow and they had milk, and they would get different kinds of vegetables and everything to eat. . . .
>
> Q. Did it cost the slave owner more under slavery to support the darky than he pays him under wages. . . ?
>
> A. It cost him more.[50]

[42]Hart, op. cit., pp. 373, 254. "Pay out" meant pay all debts.

[43]George K. Holmes, "The Peons of the South," Annals of the American Academy of Political and Social Sciences 4 (September 1893), pp. 265–274.

[44]Clark, op. cit., p. 324; George Report, pt. 1 p. 37; Agriculture Report, p. 497.

[45]Hart, op. cit., p. 281.

[46]Hart, op. cit., pp. 281–282.

[47]Hart, op. cit., p. 285.

[48]Agriculture Report, p. 121.

[49]Holmes, op. cit., p. 269.

[50]Agriculture Report, p. 505.

The next witness agreed in substance with the cotton broker but thought slavery a better system for the planter "when you take into consideration the much better control we had them under before the war."[51]

There were some checks on the degree to which merchant–landlords could oppress their tenants. Perhaps the most obvious was the general shortage of labor, which made it worthwhile to keep tenants in good health. Also, because of this shortage, a runaway tenant might not be returned—despite his or her having "broken the law"—because another landlord would welcome a new laborer. Therefore, merchant–landlords attempted to resolve some of the worst complaints in an effort to prevent mass migration. For example, after the crop was picked, the landlord might give his tenants a cash bonus even though their ledger showed them far in debt.[52]

Finally, the possibility existed that a tenant could escape debt. If the landlord began withholding supplies and closely supervising a tenant before the tenant was hopelessly in debt, he might in fact aid in the escape of that tenant from debt. Farming is a problematical business and the merchant could not always know whether the crop would cover the debt. If he began restricting credit before the entire crop was spent, he hurt himself by reducing his share of the crop.[53]

However, escape from debt was made all the more difficult because of extensive abuse and cheating on the part of landlords and merchants. Their local economic and political dominance allowed them almost unlimited freedom in altering the account books to guarantee continued debt, in adjusting prices to increase the debt, and in claiming debts that did not exist.[54] An unscrupulous merchant–landlord could keep his tenants in debt forever, and even an honest one could expect most of his tenants to remain in permanent debt.

The lienholder was the initiator of the tenant–laborer transition. He had to do this with care because a misfire might cause him to lose a tenant. However, he had much to gain from this transformation: increased production and decreased expenses. The system of farm labor—day laborers receiving their pay at the end of the year—could be very profitable indeed.

---

[51] *Agriculture Report*, p. 509.

[52] Hart, *op. cit.*, p. 272.

[53] Brooks, *op. cit.*, reports that tenants disliked supervision despite the fact that it could be proven that they were more productive and received more money at the end of the year. He explains this "strange paradox" as a "psychological phenomenon." However, as we saw in Chapter 1, such supervision meant that tenants could not budget their time during the year to their own advantage. It meant harder work, less leisure, and no opportunities for outside income.

[54] The Alabama commissioner of agriculture, himself a very large planter, said, "the merchant is human and he takes advantage of these things and gets all the profit he can." *Agriculture Report*, p. 926; see also *ibid.*, pp. 49, 925–926; William H. Skaggs, *The Southern Oligarchy* (New York, 1924), pp. 284–285; Hair, *op. cit.*, p. 54.

5

Cotton Tenancy, Farmer Immiseration, and the Reemergence of the Planter Aristocracy

Oh, the farmer comes to town with his wagon broken down
But the farmer is the man who feeds them all
If you'll only look and see I think you will agree
That the farmer is the man who feeds them all.

Chorus
The farmer is the man,
The farmer is the man,
Lives on credit till the fall
Then they take him by the hand and
They lead him from the land
And the merchant is the man who gets it all

When the banker says he's broke
and the merchant's up in smoke,
They forget that it's the farmer feeds them all.
It would put them to the test
If the farmer took a rest;
Then they'd know that it's the farmer feeds them all.

Last chorus
The farmer is the man,
The farmer is the man,
Lives on credit till the fall—
With the interest rate so high
It's a wonder he don't die,
For the mortgage man's the one who gets it all.
[Populist song from Edith Fowke and Joe Glazer,
Songs of Work and Protest (New York: Dover, 1973)]

Cotton Domination of Southern Agriculture

The conflicts between small farmers and their lienholding landlord—merchants were resolved in the course of seasons and decades of cotton cultivation after the

TABLE 5.1
Cotton Domination of Southern Agriculture

Year	Cotton as percentage of product sold	Cotton as percentage of total product	Dollar value of total product (× 1 million)	Dollar value of product sold (× 1 million)
1879	n.a.	38.6	666	—
1889	n.a.	29.5	773	—
1899	45.7	27.3	1354	833
1909	44.3	31.6	2578	1801

[a]n.a. = not available.

Sources: *11th Census* (1890), vol. 3, p. 90; *12th Census* (1900), vol. 5, pt. 1, pp. 326–327, 588–589, 630–631; *ibid.*, pt. 2; pp. 62–70, 213; *13th Census* (1910), vol. 5, pp. 490, 496, 507, 517, 522, 542–552, 557; U.S. Bureau of the Census. *Historical Statistics of the United States. Colonial Times to 1957: A Statistical Abstract Supplement* (prepared with the cooperation of the Social Science Research Council, Washington, D.C. 1960), p. 302.

Civil War. The individual outcomes added together into an evolving system which could be identified toward the end of the period 1870–1900 as the rightful heir of prewar slavery. The farmers' revolts of this period sought to alter or reverse this development, but the efforts of the Farmers' Alliance and its predecessor movements were largely in vain. The course of tenantization continued unabated and the South entered the twentieth century dominated by a set of economic arrangements which were to determine its fate until after World War II. This chapter offers a portrait of the system during the 1890s, after its basic shape had been determined but before it had become ossified into the twentieth-century precursor to apartheid.

Cotton farming dominated Southern agriculture to a degree unheard of in other parts of the country. Table 5.1 summarizes the available figures for the period 1879–1909. These figures indicate that cotton was the principal commercial crop, accounting for considerably over 40% of the farm income and well over 25% of the total value of farm products during the period.[1]

For our purposes, however, the monetary dominance of cotton is not so important as its numerical dominance. That is, we would like to know how many farmers in the South had cotton as their chief money crop and were therefore subject to the cotton tenancy system. Such figures are available only for the year 1899, when 1,413,000 Southern farms grew cotton and 1,207,000 did not. This amounts to 56% of all Southern farms.[2] In the bulk of these farms, cotton was the dominant crop. These "cotton dominated" farms represented 41% of all the farms in the South, and they produced over 60% of the commercial agricultural output of the South in 1899. Moreover, if we include in our total the farms that produced

[1]For a complete discussion of the derivation of these and other figures presented in this chapter see Michael Schwartz, "The Southern Farmers' Alliance: The Organizational Forms of Radical Protest" (Ph.D. diss., Harvard University, 1971), ch. 3.

[2]*Twelfth Census* (1900), vol. 6, pp. 414–415; *ibid.*, vol. 5, pp. 206–209.

crops in support of cotton farming, we conclude that as many as 60% of all Southern farms were dominated by the one-crop cotton system. A comparable analysis of the Midwest indicates that wheat areas were much less centralized: Wheat accounted for only 12% of the total crop value and dominated less than 30% of the farms.[3]

The Differential Profitability of Cotton Cultivation

The broad dominance of cotton farming in the South brought with it the peculiar logic attached to cotton production: the immiseration and debt peonage of small cotton farmers, together with the survival of a few large landlord—merchants who successfully exploited their debtors. This relationship is revealed by an investigation of cotton profitability, based upon an 1896 survey of Southern farms.[4] The year 1896 was one of 10 years in which there was a sudden drop in cotton prices. At year's end, therefore, a considerable proportion of farmers were unable to cover their costs. The figures reveal that at least 65% of financially independent small farmers—tenants or yeomen—could not cover their expenses that year. Moreover, there were very few financially independent farmers in 1896.[5] The overwhelming majority of small tenants and yeomen were already in debt and were forced to finance their crop through crop liens. For those among this group who were able to repay their debt at harvesttime, this meant only the added burden of high interest charges and a certain degree of credit pricing. Their ability to change merchants at year's end limited the degree of exploitation they experienced, and placed a ceiling on the extra charges that could be placed on their accounts. Even so, over 80% of these individuals lost money in 1896. Finally, among the hopelessly indebted farmers, those who were forced to buy their supplies and were subjected to the most excruciating forms of exploitation, only 5% showed a profit in 1896.

Merchant—landlords, on the other hand, were in a far better position to survive in 1896. Even in a bad year, they could squeeze a profit from their debtors. Their profits depended, of course, on the outcome of all the day-to-day conflicts described in preceding chapters. Those planters who failed to supervise their tenants could not do well in 1896. Those who were unsuccessful in reducing the standard of living of their tenants—and therefore the cost of maintaining tenants—increased their own costs and lessened or eliminated their profits. Those who failed to obtain control of the marketing process lost a crucial income-producing device and undermined their own financial well-being. Those who were unable to impress their tenants into intensive work during the planting and picking seasons were forced

[3] *Twelfth Census* (1900), vol. 5, pp. 62, 90; *ibid.*, vol. 6, pp. 206–209.
[4] James L. Watkins, *The Cost of Cotton Production*, U.S. Department of Agriculture, Division of Statistics, Miscellaneous Bulletin, no. 6 (1899). For a detailed discussion of this data, the calculations reported here, and the significance of the results see Michael Schwartz and Laura Schwartz, "Landlord Profit and Tenant Debt: The Differential Profitability of One Crop Cotton Tenancy in the Post-Reconstruction South" (forthcoming); see also Schwartz, *op. cit.*
[5] This situation is discussed later in the chapter.

to spend extra money on these tasks, thus destroying their chance to make a sizeable profit. In short, only those landlord—merchants who controlled and exploited their tenants made money in 1896. But those who successfully worked this system made a profit on well over 75% of their farms.

In 1896, as in many previous years, tenants and yeomen were driven into debt, while a few large and powerful landlords retained and expanded their economic empires. One-third of the crop years between 1870 and 1900 were as bad or worse than 1896, and these were the engines of the crop lien debt peonage. Once a farmer needed to borrow, a good year held out little chance of his retrieving his fortune. The lien system forced the tenant deeper and deeper into debt, while constantly increasing the economic leverage of the landlord—merchant.

The 1896 data suggest that even if the price of cotton had not dropped, approximately 50% of the average-sized farms would have lost money even if their operators were not indebted. Consider the consequences of this situation: In good years, the small unencumbered farmers barely survived, and every third year or so they were faced with a 10% drop in cotton prices which meant losing years for over two-thirds of them. If one assumes that most farmers began their operation with only enough money to finance a few losing years, simple probability analysis shows that after 15 years about two-thirds of them would be in hopeless debt.[6] Therefore, even those farmers who faced the postwar period with sufficient capital and equipment to produce a lien-free crop were forced into debt by the process cotton farming. They then joined the ranks of the many Southern yeomen and tenants who were without sufficient capital at the beginning of the postwar period: They financed their crop with liens, increased their costs dramatically, and faced the very improbable task of attempting to produce a cash profit. The initial indebtedness reduced their chance to make a profit even further, more or less guaranteeing a series of profitless years in which the farmer would fall deeper and deeper into debt.

Farmer Insolvency and the True Extent of Tenancy

The outcome of this process can be found in the results of a survey conducted by The George Committee in 1892.[7] This survey, part of a broader investigation into the condition of cotton farmers, recorded the responses of 58 "prominent" cotton growers about the financial condition of cotton farmers. The respondents

[6]We assume that for farmers who could finance their own crop, 50% will improve their position, 50% will lose. If a farmer improved his position enough, he reached landlord status and had an 85% probability of success. If he lost money several years in a row he fell into debt, with only a 33% chance of improving his position. If the debt became too large, the tenant then had only a minute chance of escaping. This is basically a Markov system, which can be analyzed according to routine analytic procedures. The results vary slightly according to how many intermediate stages are postulated and what beginning wealth distributions are assumed, but given these basic probabilities, the results always confirm 66% insolvency.

[7]*George Report*, pt. 1, pp. 275—403. (A full citation of this work appears in note 3, Chapter 1 of this volume.) For a fuller discussion of this survey and an assessment of its accuracy see Schwartz, *op. cit.*, ch. 3.

TABLE 5.2
Insolvency among Cotton Farmers

Percentage insolvent	Number of counties	Percentage of counties
≥ 90	27	13
75–89	48	23
51–74	32	15
50	44	21
30–49	18	9
10–29	12	6
≤ 9	26	13
Total	207	100

Source: George Report, pt. 1, pp. 275–403.

were asked to estimate the proportion "insolvent" in their area—meaning individuals whose "property . . . will not pay their debts."[8] This describes an individual whose entire crop was owned to the merchant—landlord, the hopelessly indebted small farmer. It is significant that no distinction was made by the George Committee between insolvent owners and insolvent tenants. The hopelessly indebted farmer was a single category, whether or not the individual held technical title to the land.

Table 5.2 is compiled from the George Report, and it confirms the bleak portrait suggested by the profitability data. In 72% of the counties surveyed, the majority of the farmers were insolvent. In 28% of the counties, over three-quarters of the farmers were in hopeless debt. The average insolvency rate across the 207 counties was an astonishing 60%. Another 30% of farmers were in debt and not insolvent, while a mere 10% were out of debt entirely. It is tempting to discount these figures as exaggerated, but they agree with other available estimates. The estimates based upon the 1896 profitability figures yeilded an insolvency estimate of about 66%, almost the same as that from the George Report. And this figure is confirmed by fragmentary estimates from contemporary sources. W. Scott Morgan, a Populist leader, reported in 1889 that 75% of Arkansas farmers and 33% of Texas farmers were insolvent.[9] The Alliance's national newspaper estimated 70% indebtedness among Louisiana hill farmers in 1889.[10] Matthew Hammond, the first academic analyst of Southern cotton tenancy, placed the figure at 90% for Georgia in the mid-1890s.[11]

The George Report also provides ample evidence that the immiseration of farmers was fundamentally connected to the nature of the one-crop cotton tenancy system. A comparison of the 27 most indebted counties (over 90% insolvent) with the

[8] George Report, pt. 1, p. 275.
[9] W. Scott Morgan, History of the Wheel and Alliance (Ft. Scott, Kans., 1889), p. 670.
[10] National Economist (Washington, D.C.), June 15, 1889.
[11] Matthew B. Hammond, The Cotton Industry (Ithaca, 1897), p. 155; see also Alex M. Arnett, The Populist Movement in Georgia (New York, 1922), p. 57.

TABLE 5.3
Tenancy in 1890 by Insolvency in 1893

Insolvency rate in 1893[a]	Tenancy rate in 1890[a]	
	Majority tenant	Majority yeoman
50–100	81.0	63.8
0–49	19.0	36.2
	$n = 78$	$n = 130$

[a]Expressed as a percentage.
Sources: George Report, pp. 275–401; 11th Census (1890), vol. 3, pp. 120–198.

26 least indebted counties (less than 10% insolvent) reveals that the immiserated counties planted almost twice as much cotton as their more prosperous neighbors. Moreover, only a few of the respondents reported economic fluctuations from year to year. The majority described the post–Civil War period as one of a steady deterioration of conditions for cotton growers; 1893 was the worst year up until the report. Hard times were built into the tenancy system; they extended from bad year to good, drawing more and more farmers into the web of debt and tenancy as the process of immiseration proceeded.

Finally, the *George Report* allows us to chart the connection between debt peonage and formal tenancy. A yeoman farmer could fall deeply into debt and ultimately be entirely subservient to the merchant, even while he held title to the farm. In this circumstance, the merchant could claim title to the land at any time, though many chose not to do so. At any given time, there was a large number of immiserated tenants who were still technically landowners, and for this reason, the count of tenant farms was always far below the actual number of insolvent farmers. Thus, in 1890, the census recorded 38% of Southern farms as tenant operated and in 1900 the figure had risen to only 47%. For Georgia, Mississippi, and South Carolina, the 1900 figures were over 60%, but even so, they were much lower than the comparable estimates arrived at through analysis of debt.[12]

Despite the discrepancies, the 1893 insolvency data and the census data on tenancy can be usefully compared. Table 5.3 demonstrates that tenant farmers were far more susceptible to debt than owners of land. Less than 20% of the high tenancy counties escaped massive debt, while the counties in which yeoman farmers predominated did almost twice as well. Of course, debt peonage was not unknown in yeoman counties: In the vast majority of these counties, the majority of the farmers were insolvent.

Table 5.4 charts the denouement of the immiseration process for yeoman

[12]*Thirteenth Census* (1910), vol. 5, pp. 122–127.

TABLE 5.4
Effect of Debt on Tenancy Rates[a]

	Insolvency rate in 1893	
	Counties with 50% or more of farms insolvent	Counties with under 50% of farms insolvent
Percentage of counties in which majority of farms were tenant operated		
1890	43.2	24.2
1900	59.2	32.3

[a]Sample sizes: For 1890, 50% and greater insolvency, $n = 146$; under 50% insolvency, $n = 62$. For 1900, 50% and greater insolvency, $n = 152$; under 50% insolvency, $n = 62$.
Sources: 11th Census (1890), vol. 3, pp. 120–198; 12th Census (1900), vol. 5, pp. 57–139; George Report, pt. 1, pp. 275–401.

farmers. Those counties with high insolvency levels became increasingly tenantized during the decade: Fully 16% became tenant dominated between 1890 and 1900. The low insolvency counties also showed a trend toward increased tenantization, but the rate was about half that of their highly indebted neighbors. Only 8.1% of these counties became tenant dominated in the decade 1890–1900.

Thus, debt was the bridge between yeoman farming and formal tenancy. Though merchants were reluctant to take possession, eventually the insolvent owners left or died and in this way the land changed hands. The merchant became the new landlord; and the newly created tenant farms began appearing in the 1900 census.

Tenantization through debt was the predominant economic experience in the South from 1876 to 1914. During this time, the cotton culture meant year after year of unprofitable farming for the small producer. Each year over 50% of cotton growers lost money and were forced to spend their savings and reduce their living standard in order to finance the next crop. As the losing years added up, the overwhelming majority were forced to execute crop liens to finance their farms, and these liens reduced their chances of making money even further. As the debt deepened, the landlord–merchant took control of the cultivation and oversaw the farm. The farmer had less than a 10% chance of showing a profit once the lienholder had figured in the cost of credit and had bought the crop at a price low enough to give himself a healthy markup. The chances of stringing together enough profitable years to escape debt were nil.

In the 1890s, over 60% of the cotton growers were insolvent. Another 30% were in debt and would become insolvent shortly. They functioned as tenants and laborers on land that was wholly controlled by the landlords and merchants. Their lives were miserable and their economic prospects bleak . In 1895, the conditions around Memphis typified those of the entire South: "The renting farmer is at the danger line of starvation, living from day to day with precarious and scanty supplies of food."[13]

---

[13]George Report, pt. 1 p. 200.

TABLE 5.5
Southern Farm Ownership in 1900

Total acreage	Farmers			Farms owned		
	Number	%	Cum. %	Number	%	Cum. %
0	1,179,329	37.1	37.1	0	0	0
1–99	1,139,857	35.4	72.5	1,233,679	48.1	48.1
100–500	800,277	25.1	97.6	1,064,923	41.5	89.6
501–1000	49,677	1.5	99.1	1,144,466	5.6	95.2
>1000	27,283	0.9	100.0	121,917	4.8	100.0
Total	3,106,423			2,564,985		

The "New" Landlord Class

On the other side of the crop lien were the landlord and merchant, the bene-
ficiaries of the tenants' and yeomen's hardships. The successful merchant or landlord "was a puppet master who made his community go through its peculiar
economic dance."[14] One-half of the tenantization process was the reduction of
farmers to tenants and then to laborers. The other half was the centralization of
land ownership and/or control in the hands of the merchants and landlords. Since
this process went on in part behind the statistics, it is even more difficult to
measure than the reduction to tenancy.

In 1900, the census reported ownership of tenant farms for the first and only
time.[15] These figures, in combination with those for owner-operated farms, allow
us to measure the degree of centralization. Farmers may be divided into three
groups: tenants, owner–operators, and nonoperating owners. There were 621,439
nonoperating owners, 1,385,656 owner–operators, and 1,179,329 tenants.[16] The
farms of nonoperating owners covered 24% of the total acreage, worth 25% of the
total value. We have seen, however, that the "owner–operator" category can mean
vastly different things. Therefore, Table 5.5 reports farm ownership by size of
holding. Some 72.5% of the farmers (those owning 100 acres or fewer) owned
48.1% of the farms, 15.1% of the acreage, worth 25.6% of the total value. Looking
from the other direction, we see that the top 2.4% of the farmers held 10.4% of the
farms, 45.3% of the acreage, worth 27.4% of the total value.

[14]Thomas Clark, Pills, Petticoats and Plows (New York, 1944), p. 53.
[15]Significantly, this occurred only after 10 years of Populist agitation; even census collection had very political
aspects. See National Economist (May 2, 1891).
[16]See Tables 5.5–5.8 for sources. These figures underestimate nonoperating owners in three ways. First, the
"owner-operator" category included a vast number of yeomen whose land was really owned by the merchant,
but whose land had not been seized. Second, we have no way of separating "manager-operated" farms—owned
by nonoperating owners—from the owner-operated farms. Therefore, they appear among owner-operators.
Third, the census figures exclude some 4% of tenant-operated farms because census takers could not identify the
owner. For the latter, see Twelfth Census 1900, vol. 5, pp. lxxxv–lxxxvi.

TABLE 5.5 (continued)

Acres			Value		
Number (× 1000)	%	Cum. %	Dollars (× 1000)	%	Cum. %
0	0	0	0	0	0
52,036	15.1	15.1	972,291	25.6	25.6
136,365	39.6	54.7	1,783,882	47.0	72.6
32,414	9.4	64.1	352,396	9.3	81.9
123,364	35.9	100.0	687,069	18.1	100.0
344,679			3,795,638		

Source: 12th Census 1906, vol. 5, pp. 4, 315.

We can see that centralization holds with equal force if we separate these statistics into tenant and owner-operated farms (see Tables 5.6 and 5.7). The richest 14.9% of the tenant operators owned 37.3% of the farms and 52.6% of the value. The top 3.6% of these owners, those with vast tenant farms over 500 acres in size, owned farms worth $250 million—26.2% of the total. Among owner–operators, over 50% owned farms of fewer than 100 acres, worth about $1000 on paper. But 3.9% of the owners had farms of over 500 acres, averaging over $15,000 in value— 19.6% of the total value.[17]

Another way to measure centralization of ownership and control is to look at the number of tenant farms each owner controlled. Since the competition among lienholders—given the low price of land—was much greater over tenants than over land, the number of tenant farms is as good, if not a better, measure of wealth than size of holding. What makes this measure weak is that it excludes those merchants who did not seize yeoman farms they treated as tenantholding. Therefore, the figures recorded in Table 5.8 underestimate the actual centralization. Even so, Table 5.8 reveals that some 70.4% of all tenantholders controlled only one tenant each. The top 5.8%—those who controlled five or more tenants each— controlled nearly one-third of the tenants (31.7%) on farms worth over one-quarter of the total value (26.7%).

Often figures such as those reported in Tables 5.5–5.8 cannot be fully analyzed without comparing them with other, better understood, statistics. Therefore, it is useful to compare these 1900 figures with those for landownership and slave-holding in 1860. It has often been asserted that land was very highly centralized in the South before the Civil War (as was slaveholding) and that this centralization was broken in the postwar years.[18] Figures 5.1 and 5.2 present two pairs of Lorenz

[17] This demonstrates that the owner-operated category included farms far too large to be anything but planta-tions—and it shows that the actual concealed tenantry was very great indeed.

[18] For a typical expression of this see Report of the Industrial Commission on Agriculture and Agricultural Labor, 57th Cong. 1st sess., 1901, H. Doc. No. 179, p. 465. Challenges to this idea appear in C. Van Woodward, Origins of the New South (Baton Rouge, 1952); Roger Shugg, "Survival of the Plantation System in Louisiana," Journal of Southern History 3 (August 1933), pp. 311–325.

TABLE 5.6
Ownership of Southern Farms Run by Tenants in 1900

Total acreage	Owners				Farms owned		
	Number	%	Cum. number	Cum. %	Number	%	Cum. %
<100	409,985	65.9	409,985	65.9	513,807	43.6	43.6
100–200	119,071	19.2	529,056	85.1	224,800	19.1	62.7
201–500	70,080	11.3	598,136	96.4	228,997	19.4	82.1
501–1000	15,906	2.6	615,042	99.0	110,695	9.4	91.5
1001–2500	5,259	.8	620,301	99.8	72,393	6.1	97.6
>2500	1,137	.2	621,438	100.0	28,637	2.4	100.0
Total	621,433				1,179,329		

(*Continued*)

TABLE 5.7
Ownership of Southern Farms Run by Owners or Managers in 1900

Total acreage	Owners			Acres^a (× 1000)			Value^a		
	Number	%	Cum. %	Number	%	Cum. %	Dollars (× 1000)	%	Cum. %
<100	719,872	52.0	52.0	36,153	13.8	13.8	728,706	25.7	25.7
100–175	376,554	27.2	79.2	37,319	14.2	28.0	514,087	18.1	43.8
176–260	133,459	9.6	88.8	27,979	10.6	38.6	379,768	13.4	57.2
261–500	101,113	7.3	96.1	34,389	13.1	51.7	425,082	15.0	72.2
501–1000	33,771	2.4	98.5	21,855	8.3	60.0	233,389	8.2	80.4
>1000	20,887	1.5	100.0	105,109^b	40.0	100.0	554,802	19.6	100.0
Total	1,385,656			262,804			2,335,834		

^{a} Estimate reached by taking average acreage and value of *all* farms in the size group (including rented farms) and multiplying by number of owned farms in the size group.
^{b} Includes gigantic cattle ranches.
Source: *12th Census* 1900, vol. p. 315.

curves which compare the degrees of inequality of 1900 and in 1860, the last year of the prewar South. The graphs show cumulative percentages on both axes; the diagonal lines represent "equality." The closer the graph line is to the equality line, the more "equal" the distribution of whatever is being measured. The further away the line is, the more unequal the distribution. The "Gini index" measures the average distance from the "equality" line; the more inequality there is, the larger the Gini index.[19]

In Figure 5.1, the 1860 figure is closer to equality than the 1900 line. This means that landholding was *more centralized* in 1900 than in 1860. However, note should

[19] For a detailed discussion of the procedures used to construct these curves see Schwartz, *op. cit.*, app. II.

TABLE 5.6 (continued)

Acres			Value		
Number (×1000)	%	Cum. %	Dollars (×1000)	%	Cum. %
15,883	19.4	19.4	243,585	25.4	25.4
16,206	19.8	39.2	211,821	22.1	47.4
20,472	25.0	64.2	253,124	26.4	73.8
10,559	12.9	77.1	119,007	12.4	86.2
7,435	9.1	86.2	83,676	8.7	94.9
11,320	13.8	100.0	48,591	5.1	100.0
81,875			959,804		

Source: *12th Census* 1900, vol. 5, p. 315.

TABLE 5.8
Control of Tenants in 1900

Number of tenant farms owned	Number of owners			Number of farms owned				Value		
	Number	%	Cum. %	Number	%	Cum. %	Acres (×1000)	Dollars (×1000)	%	Cum. %
1	437,144	70.4	70.4	437,144	37.1	37.1	38,621	430,288	44.8	44.8
2	94,747	15.2	85.6	189,494	16.1	53.2	12,161	146,607	15.3	60.1
3–4	53,401	8.6	94.2	177,677	15.1	68.3	10,677	126,833	13.2	73.3
5–9	24,892	4.0	98.2	162,195	13.7	82.0	9,178	105,518	11.0	84.3
10–19	8,218	1.3	99.5	106,484	9.0	91.0	6,065	71,664	7.5	91.8
20 and more	3,036	0.5	100.0	106,335	9.0	99.0	5,174	78,884	8.2	100.0
Total	621,438			1,179,329				959,794		

Source: *12th Census* 1900, vol. 5, p. 312.

be taken of the fact that the Gini indices are almost the same (.52 and .56); there-fore, the crudeness of the data makes it difficult to say that this proves anything more than that concentration was about the same. Since the 1900 figures exclude the extra concentration hidden by farms not taken possession of, it might well be that concentration was indeed greater in 1900.

Figure 5.2 compares tenantholding in 1900 with slaveholding in 1860. Here the 1860 figures show distinctly greater concentration. In this instance, the difference may be great enough to be called significant, except for the fact that once again the data for 1900 have underestimated the degree of concentration.[20]

These comparisons leave little doubt about the overwhelming concentration

[20]It is logical to expect that concentration of tenantholding would follow closely the pattern of concentration in land—though the existence of large cattle ranches in the data might perturb the figures. For 1860 the two Gini indices are very similar—0.52 and 0.56. In 1900, the comparative indices are 0.56 and 0.40. A possible explanation for this discrepancy may be that the tenancy data for 1900 ignores large plantations recorded as undivided owner-operated farms.

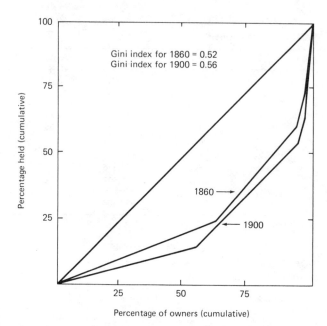

Gini index for 1860 = 0.52
Gini index for 1900 = 0.56

1860 →

← 1900

Percentage held (cumulative)

Percentage of owners (cumulative)

Figure 5.1 *Inequality among landowners.* [*Sources:* 8th Census *(1860), vol. 3, pp. 221, 224:* 12th Census *(1900), vol. 5, pp. 4, 312, 315.*]

of Southern agricultural wealth and power in 1900. The tenant farming system, through the operation of crop liens and debt peonage, resulted in the same steep hierarchy of ownership and control that its antebellum parent had produced. In a perverted sense, this fierce inequality is a tribute to the elegance of a system which could create and sustain the massive misery which was its foundation.

It is often supposed that in highly concentrated social systems the wealthy meet as equals. Table 5.9 demonstrates that this was not at all the case in the late nineteenth-century American South. Table 5.9 was constructed by considering the largest tenantholders in the South: those who controlled at least five tenants.

TABLE 5.9
Southern Plantation Ownership in 1900

Number of tenant farms owned	Number of owners			Number of farms owned		
	Number	%	Cum. %	Number	%	Cum. %
5–9	24,892	68.9	68.9	162,195	43.2	43.2
10–19	8,218	22.7	91.6	106,484	28.4	71.6
20 and more	3,036	8.4	100.0	106,335	28.4	100.0
Total	36,146			375,014		

(*Continued*)

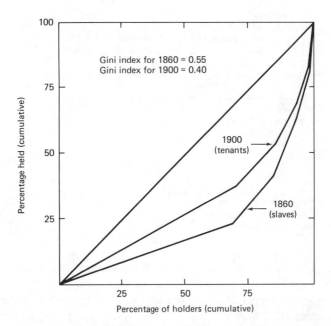

Figure 5.2 *Inequality among slaveholders and tenantholders.* [*Sources:* 8th Census *(1860), vol. 3, pp. 221, 224;* 12th Census *(1900), vol. 5, pp. 4, 312, 315.*]

Only 5.8% of the landlords were this large, but they held 31.7% of the farms, worth 26.7% of the total value of tenant farms. These men certainly look like the top of the heap, but Table 5.9 shows that, even within such an elite, there was much inequality. The largest of these landlords, the 8.4% who owned farms with 20 or more tenants working them, possessed 30.7% of the collective wealth. Table 5.10 is an explicit comparison between the concentration of wealth within the elite and the concentration of wealth in the whole of the Southern tenant farming system. The similarities are uncanny. For the whole system, richest group owned 32% of the farms; within the elite, the richest group owned 28% of the plantations. Among all farmers, the richest group controlled 27% of the wealth; within the elite,

TABLE 5.9 (continued)

Acres			Value		
Number (× 1000)	%	Cum. %	Dollars (× 1000)	%	Cum. %
9,178	45.0	45.0	105,518	41.4	41.4
6,065	29.7	74.7	71,664	27.9	79.3
5,174	25.3	100.0	78,884	30.7	100.0
375,014			256,006		

Source: 12th Census 1900, vol. 5, p. 312.

TABLE 5.10
Comparison of Centralization of Tenant-holding and Centralization of the Elite in 1900[a]

Status	Plantations	Acreage	Value
Poorest 70%			
All farmers	37	47	45
Elite[b]	43	45	41
Richest 8%			
All farmers	32	24	27
Elite	28	25	30

[a] Figures in this table are percentages.
[b] Farms with five or more tenants.
Source: Compiled from Tables 5.8 and 5.9.

the figure is 30%. The bottom 70% of tenantholders owned 47% of farm acreage; the bottom 69% of the elite controlled 45% of plantation acreage.

There was as much centralization and inequality *within the elite* as there was in the whole system. It is inaccurate to describe the system as one with a fixed dividing line which separated the relatively homogeneous elite from the relatively homogeneous tenants. Just as there were farmers at every level in the tenantization process, there were individuals at every level of wealth. In fact, the centralization among the elite suggests that the domination which the landlord class exercised over the rest of the system might well have been replicated as a domination which the big landlords exercised over small landlords. The mechanism for this domination was thrust upon the elite within the elite. Even a large planter ran the risk of debt unless he grew his own supplies and commanded a vast tenant labor force. In bad times, like the 1891–1893 depression, when debt levels were extremely high, even for landlords, "those who raised their own supplies . . . are generally out of debt and have mortgages on their neighbors."[21] With or without foreclosure, these mortgages became the mechanism of coordination and control *within* the planter class.

The degree of centralization which could be attained had definite limits. A plantation rarely became larger than the ability of its owner to coordinate the tasks of supply, supervision, credit management, and crop inspection. Beyond a certain size, expansion meant inefficiency and vulnerability, or else it necessitated a complete alteration in operating methods. More broadly, there is reason to expect that the steep gradient to ownership and control could not be easily made steeper. A dominance hierarchy among planters, like the one we have demonstrated, would seem to offer a method by which the very largest owners could exercise enough leverage to dictate to those just below, while the elite as a group could exercise enough leverage to coerce the large number of smaller farmers. It seems possible

[21] *George Report*, pt. 1 pp. 371–372.

that too steep a gradient at any level would create unmanageable control problems.

There is much evidence to suggest that such an upper bound existed for control and centralization of the cotton economy. We have already noted that centralization was almost the same in 1860 and 1900. This by itself suggests an upper bound in inequality which both systems reached and beyond which lay inefficiency and perhaps chaos. Further support for this assertion comes from a state-by-state survey of 1900 tenantholding that reveals no state with a Gini index greater than .60.

Our investigation of the elite within the elite demonstrated that the degree of centralization there was almost identical to that of the system as a whole. Once again, the upper bound on inequality lies at about .60. Moreover, despite all the forces for further centralization, this did not change at all between 1900 and 1910. The figures for the 2 years are so close (Table 5.11) that one suspects an "iron law" at work, suggesting very forcefully that the necessity of control placed a limit on the centralization process.

TABLE 5.11
Centralization within Southern Elite in 1900 and 1910[a]

Status	Plantations[b]	Acreage	Value
Richest 8.5%			
1910	28.0	23.0	26.0
1900	28.4	25.3	30.7
Bottom 68.5%			
1910	42.2	46.3	43,3
1900	43.2	45.0	41.4

[a] For 325 selected counties. See *13th Census* 1910, vol. 5. p. 879. Figures in this table are percentages.
[b] Farms with five or more tenants.
Source: 13th Census (1910), vol. 5. p. 881.

The tenant plantation, while not as elegant as its antebellum counterpart, was just as imposing. In 1910, the Sunnyside Plantation in Arkansas spanned 12,000 acres and 8.5 miles of Mississippi riverfront. Over 200 tenant families worked 4700 acres to produce 2500 bales of cotton worth about $1,250,000. To manage this vast enterprise required four assistant managers, each residing in a substantial home, immense supplies sold through the plantation stores, and 23 miles of track to accommodate the private railroad which hauled supplies and products.[22] The Bell Plantation in central Alabama covered 3000 acres. Other large owners possessed scattered plantations, sometimes as many as 30 different farms ranging up to 2000 acres.[23]

Joseph Norwood, who inherited 3000 acres from his father after the Civil War,

[22] Albert Bushnell Hart, *The Southern States*, (New York, 1912), pp. 254–255.
[23] *Ibid.*, pp. 254–255.

entered the 1890s with 8000 acres, a $100,000 per year mercantile business, a cotton gin, and a gristmill.[24] In 1884, T. J. Christian's merchandising business showed a $16,719.97 profit; in 1914, the profit was $222,040.43 and he owned 25,000 acres besides.[25] Robert Lawrence began as a merchant after the war, but by 1889 he had acquired 450 acres of choice cotton land, organized a mining and manufacturing firm, and bought the local newspaper, which he used to advance his political ambitions.[26] In the short period from 1865 to 1877, the Americus storekeepers in Americus, Georgia, became cotton warehousemen and insurance agents. By 1900, they had extended their interests into land, lumbering, and general building supplies.[27] The Braselton brothers in 1887 had only $5.00 in cash; in 1915, they owned 4000 acres, a cotton gin, a warehouse, a crosstie yard, a fertilizer factory, a gristmill, a post office, and a bank. Their income that year was over $1 million.[28]

The notion of Southern economic democratization after the Civil War is faulty and misleading. Joseph Norwood, T. J. Christian, Robert Lawrence, and the Braselton brothers were members of the planter class that dominated Southern agriculture in 1900 in the same way that their slaveholding predecessors had in 1860. They, like their predecessors, were a resident elite living on or near their enterprises and overseeing and protecting their investments by supervising the work of their tenants and debtors. And within this planter class, there was sharp inequality, producing a hierarchy among the prosperous which was just as marked as that between the elite and other farmers. This centralization, like that of the entire system, reached its practical limit.

With its immense concentration of wealth and power on one side, and poverty and fragility on the other, the tenancy system was by no means stable. Its instability was reflected in the repeated social upheavals of the 1880s and 1890s; in the racial caste system which was instituted at the end of the century; and in the continuing political differences that arose between the rural elite, with its basis in the tenancy systems, and the representatives of railroads and industry, who were tied to Northern economic interests. All these crucial political issues, and the smaller ones as well, were intimately tied to the structure and development of the tenant farming system.

[24] *Memorial Record of Alabama* (Madison, 1893), vol. 2, pp. 433–434.

[25] Clark, *op. cit.*, p. 331.

[26] *Memorial Record of Alabama*, vol. 1, p. 639.

[27] Harold Woodman, *King Cotton and His Retainers* (Lexington, Ky., 1968), p. 330.

[28] Clark, *op. cit.*, p. 331. For other examples see H. C. Nixon, *Lower Piedmont Country* (New York, 1944), pp. 57–59.

II

AN ORGANIZATIONAL HISTORY OF
THE SOUTHERN FARMERS' ALLIANCE

6

Growth and Merger

Rally, rally, gird on your armor,
O ye tillers of the soil,
Ye laborers in the workshop,
Ye horny-handed sons of toil.

Rally around the banner,
Of the great Alliance cause,
And let the work go bravely on
From Maine to the Rio Grande.

[L. J. S., *Raleigh Progressive Farmer*, October 15, 1889]

The Southern Farmers' Alliance flowed through the 1880s like a river on its way to the ocean. The tributaries began as small farmers' clubs in the early part of the decade, and each small stream grew as it gathered strength from the misery which the tenancy system created. As the clubs grew, they flowed into each other and contributed to the growth of the movement. As the decade progressed, clubs that had merged then recombined into larger and larger organizations, each one of these large groups was the summation of its many tributaries. Finally, in 1892, the Alliance, one million members strong,[1] lost itself in the Populist party, as a river into the sea.

But unlike a river, the Alliance absorbed two different kinds of streams as it proceeded. The main tributaries were large organizations of small yeomen and tenants who sought to use boycotts, form cooperatives, and engage in other locally based mass activities to reverse the process of tenantization and overcome the immiseration brought about by the crop lien system. The other tributaries were small organizations of large owners, which gathered together the leading farmers

---

[1]Unless otherwise noted, all membership figures are taken from Michael Schwartz, *"The Southern Farmers' Alliance: The Organizational Forms of Radical Protest"* (Ph.D. diss. Harvard University, 1971). app. I.

in a county or state to work out suitable solutions for the entire farming population and then attempted to use the power and prestige of the individual members to carry out the prescribed changes. The process of merger and absorption that occurred as the stream of Southern farmer protest grew is a good beginning focus for an analysis of its activities.

Early Growth and Merger

Historians of the Southern Farmers' Alliance trace its beginnings to Texas in the middle 1870s,[2] but the original group, which remained small and collapsed several times in its early years, bore almost no important relation to the later group which reached maturity in the 1880s.[3] Only in early 1882, with a substantial organization in Parker County, Texas, and a few members in neighboring areas, did the Alliance undertake its first attack on the tenancy system: a selective buying project aimed at reducing merchants' prices.[4] That fall, a state organization was formed and membership rose to 5000; 1883 saw it decline to 2000. A state official later diagnosed the decline as resulting from

> the want of Alliance literature, the means to employ active lecturers to visit and instruct, and encourage the sub-Alliances and institute new ones.... In their efforts to cooperate in buying and selling, in the past, they had almost always been treated with contempt by tradesmen and others, and *so far had failed to achieve practical benefits from their efforts.* Again, it had been a very sickly year throughout the counties where the Alliances had been formed, and the year previous being a political year, *a great many persons rushed into the order for the sole purpose of their own personal political aggrandizement;* therefore after the passage of the non-political resolution at Mineral Wells, they and their personal friends lost their primary interest in the Alliance, which caused the disorganization of several sub-Alliances during that year.[5]

The Alliance survived these early tribulations and it entered the middle 1880s as a healthy and growing organization of some 40,000 members, almost all of them in Texas. It was joined by the Louisiana Farmers' Union, the Agricultural Wheel, and the Brothers of Freedom, all of which had sprung up in much the same way and had developed into remarkably similar organizations. All four were membership groups which had local clubs as their basic building blocks. They directed their initial recruiting efforts at yeoman farmers, and their activities

[2]The principal Alliance-sponsored histories are F. G. Blood, ed., *Handbook and History of the National Farmers' Alliance and Industrial Union* (Washington, D.C., 1893); H. R. Chamberlain, *The Farmers' Alliance: What it Aims to Accomplish* (New York, 1891); Nelson A. Dunning, ed., *Farmers' Alliance History and Agricultural Digest* (Washington, D.C., 1891); and W. Scott Morgan, *History of the Wheel and Alliance and the Impending Revolution* (Fort Scott, Kans., 1889).

[3]C. W. Macune, "The Farmers' Alliance" (typescript on file at University of Texas Library), p. 4; Dunning, *op. cit.*, p. 18; Ralph Smith, "The Farmers' Alliance in Texas, 1875–1800," *Southwestern Historical Quarterly* 48 (January 1945), p. 349.

[4]Smith, *op. cit.*, p. 351; Dunning, *op. cit.*, pp. 35–37.

[5]Italics added; quoted in Dunning, *op. cit.*, p. 37.

centered around reforming or reconstructing supply and sales systems of Southern cotton farming.[6]

Since activities were generally centered around a county seat, where the farmers of a community bought supplies and sold crops, expansion within county limits was a natural outgrowth of any activity. But further growth was unwieldy and "unnatural," and at first cross-county expansion was haphazard at best, depending on the more or less problematical communication of the activities of small local clubs. Rapid statewide and interstate growth began only when the farmers' groups deliberately pursued it through the establishment of a statewide organizing apparatus capable of entering new areas and mobilizing potential members. In the case of the Alliance, this took place in 1882[7] and resulted in the expansion from 2000 to 38,000 members. The 1000-member Arkansas Agricultural Wheel formed a statewide organizing committee in 1883 and increased its membership to 25,000 in $2\frac{1}{2}$ years.[8] The Louisiana Farmers' Union and the Brothers of Freedom experienced similar growth for similar reasons, entering the middle of the decade with 10,000 and 15,000 members, respectively.

As these groups expanded, they began to run into each other. The Wheel and the Brothers of Freedom were the first to make contact, and their merger—voted in October 1885 and consummated in July 1886—was the first important merger among the groups that ultimately formed the Farmers' Alliance.[9] The second such merger united the Texas Alliance and the Louisiana Farmers' Union. Like the Wheel—Brothers juncture, it was managed with little difficulty, though unlike its predecessor, the prelude was tumultuous.

The Texas Alliance convened at Clebourne August 3, 1886, with membership at an all-time high of 110,000.[10] Nevertheless, the organization was in deep trouble. It was becoming clear that the initially successful county-level activities were failing, and the group needed new programs which could successfully ameliorate the oppressive conditions created by the cotton tenancy system. The convention decided to pressure the state legislature for "such legislation as shall secure our people freedom from the onerous abuses that the industrial classes are now suffering at the hands of arrogant capitalist and powerful corporations."[11] The list of demands included the opening of new farmlands through confiscation of large

[6]Theodore Saloutos, *Farmer Movements in the South, 1865–1933* (Berkeley, 1960), p. 62; Dunning, *op. cit.*, pp. 197–200; Morgan, *op. cit.*, p. 62; John Hugh Reynolds, ed., *Publications of the Arkansas Historical Association* 1 (1906), p. 224.

[7]Dunning, *op. cit.*, p. 37.

[8]Dunning, *op. cit.*, p. 200; Morgan, *op. cit.*, pp. 100 f.

[9]For information on this merger see Dunning, *op. cit.*, p. 201; Morgan, *op. cit.*, pp. 82–86; Reynolds, *op. cit.*, 222–224; Saloutos, *op. cit.*, p. 63.

[10]Information on the Clebourne convention and its aftermath, unless otherwise noted, was obtained from Fauk M. Drew. "The Present Farmers' Movement", *Political Science Quarterly*, VI (June 1891), p. 283; Dunning, *op. cit.*, pp. 40–56; John D. Hicks and John D. Barhart, "The Farmers' Alliance," *North Carolina Historical Review* 6 (July 1929), pp. 264 f; Robert Lee Hunt, *A History of Farmers' Movements in the Southwest, 1873–1925* (College Station, Tex., 1935), pp. 31–33; Smith, *op. cit.*, pp. 355–357; *National Economist*, December 14, 1889.

[11]"Preamble to the Clebourne Demands," in Dunning, *op. cit.*, pp. 41–43.

holdings and legislative attacks against railroads and other large enterprises affecting agriculture.[12] The new program was accompanied by the structural alteration necessary to convert a locally based economic pressure group into a statewide electoral action group. The Texas Alliance Constitution was altered to give greater strength and initiative to the state leadership, and a legislative lobbying committee was set up and began its work by monitoring the Democratic convention which was being held in Clebourne at the same time.

However, less than a week after the close of the convention, a group bolted the Alliance, called a rump convention, and elected new officers. This group claimed that the previous convention was void because it violated the constitutional stricture against partisan politics. Since this insurgent group contained local leaders who exerted great influence in the theretofore locally oriented Alliance, their protest threatened the very existence of the organization. As a consequence, C. W. Macune, the chairman of the executive committee, nullified the program of the August meeting and scheduled a unity convention in October. However, when Macune's efforts to negotiate a merger with the very large Western Farmers' Alliance foundered, he postponed the convention until he could offer a substantial program to the membership.

Such a program was ready by January, and the unity convention at Waco was greeted with three major proposals. The first was a new economic strategy built around an ambitious Farmers' Alliance Exchange. This exchange was intended to replace the retail and wholesale merchants by acting as supplier to the Alliance farmer during the crop growing season and as sales agent during harvest. (A detailed analysis of this remarkable enterprise can be found in Chapter 13.) The second was the institution of an ambitious organizing drive which involved a strengthened *national* organization with paid agitators in every Southern state. The third was the easily accomplished merger with the Louisiana Farmers' Union.[13]

The logic behind Macune's program was twofold. On the one hand, the exchange strategy headed off the move into electoral politics by offering plausible economic action for the immediate alleviation of the farmers' situation. At the same time, the expansion to a national organization held the promise of a vast pressure group; a huge farmers' organization to impress the government with the gravity of the farmers' plight and alter national policy. Thus, specific electoral action was replaced by a less particular strategy—the arousal of national public opinion.

Macune united the Waco convention with his proposals. The result was a new vibrancy in the organization and the beginning of the Farmers' Alliance as a major force for reform. By the next year, it had spread to five states and doubled its membership to over 250,000.

The Clebourne crisis in 1886, like the organizational crisis of 1882, is a widow into the internal dynamics of farmers' protest. The failure of local activities created

---

[12]Dunning, *op. cit.*, pp. 43–44.
[13]The text of Macune's address to the Waco convention appears in Dunning, *op. cit.*, pp. 48–56.

the pressure for change which found expression in two tendencies. The conflict between these tendencies was unresolvable through debate: Though the politically oriented group won the vote, the economically oriented group wielded the structural strength to emerge victorious. Finally, the key element in restoring the health of the organization was the institution of a program that offered the promise of successful reform, in this case locally oriented economic action together with the creation of a national organization potentially capable of affecting national politics.

The Farmers' Associations

During 1886 and 1887, the Farmers' Alliance and the Agricultural Wheel expanded rapidly on a course which carried them closer and closer together. As they grew toward each other, they absorbed smaller and larger groups which had sprung up in their paths. Among the groups they absorbed were the farmers' Associations, which based themselves among large planters. These groups, which sought to redress the grievances of the many landlords who felt the pressure of the Southern agricultural system, were destined to provide both the Alliance and the Populists with a substantial proportion of their leadership.

A good example of such a group is the North Carolina Farmers' Association, led by L. L. Polk, who later became the president of the national Alliance. Polk, a descendant of President Polk and formerly North Carolina commissioner of agriculture, founded what was to become the most important agrarian reform newspaper of the period, the *Raleigh Progressive Farmer*, in February 1886.[14] Soon afterward, he began organizing farmers' clubs to advance his reform programs: an expanded agricultural college, the reorganization of the North Carolina Department of Agriculture, and immigration to increase the supply of farm labor. The club movement met with some success, especially among the most prosperous farmers, who would have benefited from these programs.[15]

After nearly a year of existence, the club movement held its first statewide convention in January 1887. The call was so moderate that it won the endorsement of the governor. Despite some discontent among club members, this endorsement led to cosponsorship by the North Carolina Board of Agriculture and a list of prominent speakers, including a former governor and the president of the University of North Carolina. The attenders were primarily wealthy planters and the resolutions reflected their interests: a call for a national department of agriculture oriented toward research, and a host of legislative acts aimed at protecting large landlords.[16] These programs did not look at all like the calls for cooperatives, the

[14] Stuart Noblin, *Leonidas LaFayette Polk: Agrarian Crusader* (Chapel Hill, 1949), pp. 150 f.

[15] *Raleigh News and Observer*, January 5, 1887. For further evidence of the elite character of the group, *ibid.*, see *Raleigh Progressive Farmer*, March 24, 1886; *ibid.*, May 5, 1886; *ibid.*, June 9, 1886; *ibid.*, July 28, 1886; *ibid.*, December 1, 1886; *ibid.*, January 5, 12, 26, 1887; *ibid.*, February 2, 23, 1887. See also Chapter 15 of this volume.

[16] *Raleigh News and Observer*, January 20, 27, 1887; Noblen, *op. cit.*, pp. 175–180.

protests against landlords and merchants, and the challenges against the whole government which the Alliance and Wheel regularly approved at their conventions.

The convention formalized the club movement into the North Carolina Farmers' Association, which functioned until spring 1888, when it was absorbed by the Alliance.[17] The Farmers' Association concentrated on organizing large rallies whose purpose was to educate farmers about modern techniques.[18] This emphasis appealed to large farmers, who had the freedom to experiment and the resources to expand, but it had little relevance to the indebted small farmer, who needed to reduce supply costs or increase returns within the context of crop lien. Consequently, the organization did not prosper, and even the rallies owed their success in part of the publicity given them by the hardworking Farmers' Alliance, which had entered the state in January 1887, just after the Waco convention.[19]

In August 1887, Polk first met C. W. Macune; they both adressed the Interstate Convention of Farmers in Atlanta. (In some ways, their meeting was symbolic of the differences between them: Macune was a speaker because of his position at the head of the largest farmers' organization in the South; Polk was a speaker because of his individual prominence.) Upon his return to Raleigh, Polk fully endorsed the burgeoning Alliance, printed its organizational chart weekly in his paper, and began reporting its news on a regular basis.[20]

The dissolution of the North Carolina Farmers' Association into the North Carolina Farmers' Alliance during the ensuing 6 months created an influx of a large group of relatively prosperous tenantholding farmers who had decidedly different interests from those of the earlier Alliance members. "Where at first the leading and most influential men stood aloof," wrote one Allianceman, "they are now the most enthusiastic members."[21] The Long Branch Alliance in Paw Creek was made up of individuals who were "not only good citizens who mean to do well, they are well-to-do."[22]

These new members—large landholders and local politicians—were immediate candidates for leadership positions.[23] They were accustomed to prominence; many were expert public speakers; they had access to the press; they had the time and money to devote to organizational work. Polk became the new state Alliance secretary. S. B. Alexander, the new state president, was a college graduate, a high military officer in the Confederacy, a three-time state senator, and a candi-

[17]Noblen, op. cit., claims that it was absorbed by the Alliance in January 1888, at its second annual convention. But the Raleigh Progressive Farmer continued to display its officers into March, though no news of Association activities appeared. See, for example, Raleigh Progressive Farmer, February 7, 14, 21, 28, 1888.

[18]Raleigh Progressive Farmer, May 19, 26, 1887; ibid., June 2, 9, 1887; ibid., August 12, 1887; ibid., October 20, 1887; November 10, 1887.

[19]Raleigh News and Observer, October 30, 1887. See Chapter 15 of this volume for a full account of this period.

[20]Raleigh Progressive Farmer, September through December 1887 issues.

[21]Raleigh Progressive Farmer, June 12, 1888.

[22]Raleigh Progressive Farmer, April 24, 1888.

[23]Raleigh Progressive Farmer, June 5, 1888.

date for governor, as well as "one of the leading farmers" in Mecklenburg County.[24]

Dr. Reid Parker illustrates the process of infiltration well. Dr. Parker, a large and successful Randolph County farmer, had been an original organizer of the Association. He presided over the Trinity Farmers' Club, served on the state executive committee, and was a frequent speaker at Association picnics, where he repeatedly expressed his firm conviction that the farmer, through his own ignorance, was the cause of his mortgages and misery. Yet despite his disagreement with the Alliance program, which assumed merchant culpability for the plight of the farmer, Parker became the Randolph County Alliance organizer in April 1888. That summer, he acquired the title of state lecturer, and the following fall, he was appointed assistant state organizer. When the state organizer left that winter to return to his home in Texas, Reid became the combined lecturer— organizer.[25] Thus, the amalgamation resulted in leadership—membership divisions which were overlaid with class divisions, a process that occurred in many states.

This marriage of planter groups with yeoman and tenant groups produced latent or overt conflicts and contradictions. These conflicts had many facets, including a racial ambivalence which was introduced by the uncomfortable coalition of planters and yeomen inside the Farmers' Alliance. Consider, for example, the fact that the inclusion of landlords made it difficult for the organization to appeal to the tenants who rented from the planters. Since many of these tenants were Black, the Alliance was tempted to organize only white yeomen and along with landlords, and to develop a program that advanced the interest of these two groups. Unfortunately, this was extremely difficult for three reasons, none of which involved race. First, all successful landlords were also merchants; therefore, any antimerchant programs the group approved would at least in principle attack the landlords. Second, there were many white *tenants* inside and outside the Alliance; this meant that the exclusion of Blacks could not prevent tenant—landlord tensions from splitting Alliance membership. Third, the yeoman—tenant distinction was by no means clear, as we have already seen.

At first, the problem was minor. The Alliance began in "yeoman" areas, and it recruited planters from the Black Belt. The yeoman membership mounted struggles against local merchant—landlords in one part of the state, while the planter leadership in another part of the state excluded its black (and white) tenants from membership and focused energy on railroads and other purely mercantile interests. Racial exclusion was not obtrusive, and at the local level, Black yeomen might easily join in Alliance actions with or without being members.[26] Thus, in North

[24] *Raleigh Progressive Farmer*, October 27, 1887; *ibid.*, April 4, 1888; *ibid.*, August 14, 1888; *ibid.*, December 11, 1888.

[25] *Raleigh Progressive Farmer*, April 28, 1886; *ibid.*, May 26, 1886; *ibid.*, July 23, 1886; *ibid.*, December 22, 1886; *ibid.*, June 9, 1887; *ibid.*, August 18, 1887; *ibid.*, September 8, 1887; *ibid.*, October 20, 1887; *ibid.*, April 24, 1888; *ibid.*, August 28, 1888; *ibid.*, September 4, 1888.

[26] See, for example, *Raleigh Progressive Farmer*, April 30, 1889.

Carolina, L. L. Polk could call for the exclusion of Blacks from Southern agriculture yet not arouse visible opposition from the yeoman base of the Alliance.[27]

However, as soon as Alliance programs required support above the local level, real problems arose. In 1888, when North Carolina was still attending to local action and L. L. Polk was denouncing Blacks, the older state groups in Texas, Arkansas, and Louisiana had already begun organizing Black farmers to support various statewide projects.[28] The Texas Alliance supported the establishment of the Colored Alliance and gave resources and public endorsement to its efforts to establish a national organization parallel to the white Alliance.[29] When organizers for this group appeared in North Carolina, they caused grave problems for the planter leadership, who not only feared that the group would select them as a target, but that the association of the two groups would antagonize their planter constituency. Thus, when North Carolina Alliance President Alexander was asked about the Black Alliance's relationship to the white Alliance, he replied with a genuine lack of candor, "It is a separate and distinct group with which we have nothing to do."[30]

But this distance was hard to maintain, especially when the Alliance's national convention, held 2 weeks after President Alexander's statement, began to work toward the merger of the two groups.[31] Moreover, so powerful were the antiracist forces that the convention passed what may have been the most encompassing and economically radical resolution ever promulgated by a Southern white organization:

> Resolved, that it is detrimental to both white and colored to allow conditions to exist that force our colored farmers to sell their products for less, and pay more for supplies than the markets justify.[32]

Since it was these very conditions which allowed planters to grow cotton at a profit, action around the resolution would have seriously threatened the newly installed planter leadership of the North Carolina Alliance. However, the entire matter was delivered to the states for their action, and this guaranteed that the racial stance of the North Carolina Alliance would remain ambivalent.

Even the removal of the ban on Black membership the following year did little to alter the North Carolina situation.[33] In some areas, the Colored Alliance made

---

[27] Noblen, op. cit., p. 202.

[28] Saloutos, op. cit., pp. 63, 79.

[29] For further information on this understudied organization see Jack Abramowtiz, "Agrarian Reformers and the Negro Question," Negro History Bulletin 11 (March 1947), pp. 138–139; Jack Abramowitz "The Negro in the Agrarian Revolt," Agricultural History 24 (April 1950), pp. 88–95; Jack Abramowitz, "The Negro in the Populist Movement," Journal of Negro History 38 (July 1953), pp. 257–289.

[30] Raleigh Progressive Farmer, December 4, 1888; see also ibid., July 10, 1888, for a similar attempt to effect such a dissociation. See ibid., July 31, 1888, for a diplomatic but pointed response from the general superintendent for the North Carolina State Colored Alliance.

[31] "Proceedings of National Farmers' Alliance and Industrial Union of America, Meridian, Mississippi, December 5, 1888," reprinted in Raleigh Progressive Farmer, December 25, 1888; ibid., January 8, 1889.

[32] Ibid.

[33] "Proceedings of the Annual Session of the Farmers and Laborers Union, St. Louis, December 4–7, 1889," reprinted in Raleigh Progressive Farmer, December 24, 1889; ibid., January 7, 1890.

good progress, participated in parallel and joint protests with the white Alliance, and even coalesced with it.[34] However, this unity was balanced by the activities in the eastern half of the state, where the Alliance became an instrument of planter attacks upon Black tenants, a lobby for labor control legislation, and an object of Black tenant protest.[35]

In some states, there was little planter presence inside the Alliance: The interests of the large landlords found adequate expression through less problematical channels. South Carolina planters, for example, rallied behind the banner of Pitchfork Ben Tillman:

> *Captain Tillman married young and settled on a plantation of four hundred acres. He was successful until 1881, then enlarged his operation, and went into debt. He ran thirty plows—which means that he had thirty one-horse farms in his plantation and with all conditions favorable might have made two hundred and fifty to three hundred bales of cotton. Then set in a decline of prices and a succession of poor crops—in other words, after the manner of planters (and other people) he had speculated and suffered losses. He looked about for explanations and a remedy and saw, or thought he saw, them in state government and agricultural education.*[36]

Tillman formed a farmers' club and soon after, at the invitation of the state agricultural society, delivered a widely publicized and very abusive attack against the state government. This led to a column in the Charleston *News and Courier*, one of the principal daily newspapers in the state, through which he organized a statewide Farmers' Association. The founding convention in 1886 was attended by 12 state legislators, 2 lawyers, 12 doctors, 3 or 4 editors, and a good many merchants; the rest were prominent planters.

The program called for an agricultural college and other reforms similar to those demanded in North Carolina. But unlike the North Carolina group, the South Carolina Farmers' Association met with tremendous success. Tillman was publicized extensively by many newspapers, and he soon became a force in the South Carolina Democratic party. In less than a year, he was a leading candidate for governor. Lavishly financed in his campaign by many prominent farmers, and extensively supported by planter-oriented newspapers, he had a growing base among the less prosperous farmers. Tillman's ability to mount a serious challenge for state office in a short period of time gave credibility to his argument that meaningful reforms could be obtained through elections.[37]

During this period, the Alliance arrived in South Carolina and began to eat away at the poor farmer support of Tillman. Tillman, unlike Polk and despite his early friendship with the group, was unwilling to adopt a more directly yeoman

---

[34] *Raleigh Progressive Farmer*, July 8, 1890; *ibid.*, August 26, 1890; *ibid.*, October 28, 1890; *Raleigh News and Observer*, March 20, 1889.

[35] *Raleigh News and Observer*, April 27, 1889.

[36] William Watts Ball, *The State that Forgot* (Indianapolis, 1932), pp. 211–212.

[37] Francis Butler Simkins, *Pitchfork Ben Tillman: South Carolinian* (Baton Rough, 1944), pp. 90–105.

and tenant oriented program, and this earned him the opposition of the Alliance. As the Alliance began to take root, Tillman turned against it, and when he became governor, he did all he could to destroy this source of opposition to his rule. This attack in part explains the limited—50,000 members—size that the Alliance attained in the state.[38]

Here we see the strength of the planter class in South Carolina. Because an exclusively planter-oriented group could gain great strength and mobilize those segments of the press which allied with planters, and because planters had much greater strength in South Carolina than in less cottonized states like North Carolina, a planters' movement could sustain itself without significant accommodation to the less prosperous agricultural groups. Then, when the conflict among these groups arose, it did not arise as a battle *within* the Alliance, but rather as an *external* battle of two markedly opposite movements. In this situation, the tendencies within the movements were less ambiguous than in a combined group like the North Carolina Alliance. Thus, Tillman led South Carolina to disfranchisement of Blacks and Jim Crow legislation in 1896, many years before other, less planter dominated, states. The only state that enacted these laws earlier was Mississippi in 1890, another state where the conflict between the Alliance and the planter class was open and bitter, and the only state in which agriculture was as cottonized as in South Carolina.

The middle 1880s saw the absorption—or nonabsorption—of elite Farmers' Associations into the growing Alliance. Thereafter the activities and program reflected this tension, and the history of the Alliance reflects the organizational ambivalence such tension created.

The Merger of the Alliance and the Wheel

By 1888, the Agricultural Wheel, centered in Arkansas, had expanded into several neighboring states. Its membership of more than 100,000 made it the second largest agricultural organization in the South after the Alliance. Merger seemed inevitable, especially in light of the almost identical programs and structures of the two groups, but there was little impetus for such a unity. As late as October 1887, a leadership conference in Shreveport produced no conflict and no progress.

Along with the influx of elite leadership into both organizations came forces that sought to utilize the national strength of a united group to develop an articulated farmers' voice. Moreover, leaders with political ambitions realized that a single large group would better be able to publicize and promote them, bringing them to the broader public's notice.

While the merger was therefore highly likely, the developing class antagonisms created an uneasiness not present in previous amalgamations. As the December

---

[38] *Ibid.*, p. 133; Ball, *op. cit.*, p. 217.

1888 conventions drew near, the differences crystallized around the racial issue. The Wheel, even more so than the Alliance, had resisted the forces of racial exclusion. Whereas the Alliance had excluded Blacks while maintaining fraternal relations with the all-Black Colored Alliance, the Wheel accepted Black members—though in many areas, it maintained segregated locals clubs.[39] Correctly anticipating the merger proposal, the Mississippi Wheel attempted to prevent exclusionary policies from prevailing by passing an antimerger resolution at the state convention in fall 1888:

> Resolved: *That we do not think it advisable, prudent or just to go into a union with any organization [namely, the Farmer's Alliance] that requires us to exclude a part of our members. We having full assurance that the order has been of mutual benefit to us [i.e., both white and Black], we are opposed to excluding them from membership in the proposed organization, unless they prefer a separate organization with the same objects and aims.*[40]

However, this opposition was in vain. The two organizations met simultaneously in Meridian, Mississippi, in December and, despite considerable opposition, succumbed to the exclusionists. The newly merged organization was designated for whites only, with the understanding that close fraternal ties would be built with the Colored Alliance. After ratification by the states, the merger was completed the following October.[41]

Much is made of the racism of Southern white farmers and of the Farmers' Alliance, but even the policy of fraternal relations with a separate Colored Alliance stands in stark contrast to the policies of the Democratic party, the richer farmers' organizations, and the federal government, all of which advocated explicitly discriminatory policies. The Alliance and the Wheel undertook to create unity between Black and white farmers and to build a mutually beneficial relationship.

Rapid Expansion and Rapid Collapse

The 1888 merger created a new organization, formally entitled the National Farmers' Alliance and Laborers' Union, of about 300,000 members. By early 1890, membership was nearly 1 million. The organization, together with the Colored Alliance, could validly claim to speak for the mass of Southern farmers. The leadership's vision of a national farmers' voice was within reach, and this led to simultaneous national conventions of the four major farmers' groups in Ocala, Florida, in December 1890. In addition to the Southern Alliance and the Colored Alliance, the National Alliance, centered in the Great Plains, and the Farmers'

[39] Saloutos, *op. cit.*, pp. 79, 63.

[40] Morgan, *op. cit.*, p. 104.

[41] Dunning, *op. cit.*, p. 74; William Bliss, *The New Encyclopedia of Social Reform* (New York, 1908), p. 485; Blood, *op. cit.*, pp. 45–47; Reynolds, *op. cit.*, p. 227.

Mutual Benefit Association, centered in the Midwest, gathered to join forces. A A merger was not consummated, but a set of joint demands was passed. These demands lent credence to the claims of the leadership that they represented the united voice of American farmers.[42]

From this pinnacle, the organization disintegrated with startling rapidity. The 1891 national convention was canceled, and subsequent conventions were not even scheduled. By late 1891, the Alliance's enemies were writing obituaries,[43] and by 1892, its leadership began to desert it.[44]

This puzzling collapse is partly understood in the history of the Populist party. Alliance leaders and members created the Populist party in 1892 and built it with such energy and enthusiasm that it immediately became the largest and most threatening third party movement in the post–Civil War period. However, this is only part of the answer. People do not abandon large and vibrant organizations without cause. There was a push as well as a pull to this exodus, a push that was the culmination of Alliance activities in the 1880s. The discussion of this collapse is therefore properly placed with the discussion of these activities.

Organizational History, Organizational Structure, Social Class, and Oligarchy

The organizational history just reviewed can be threaded together into a causal pattern that reveals close connections among seemingly independent events. Figure 6.1 outlines the pattern of development associated with the early history in Texas, but it is also relevant to other states. This early period culminated in the crisis at Clebourne, brought on by the failure of local activities. This crisis was marked by an ideological debate, one side of which was defeated by the structural blocks inside the organization. The victory of the Macune plan committed the organization's resources to rapid expansion at the same time that it erected state bureaucracy. And from this flowed two important structural consequences. First, the Alliance entered a period of very rapid growth as it quickly reached an extremely receptive population. Second, the state organizations became important, visible centers of power and prominence, and this made them potentially independent of membership control.

These two outcomes were the enabling legislation for the influx of elite elements into Alliance leadership (Figure 6.2). In highly cottonized states like South Carolina and Mississippi, most large farmers and the politicians associated with them had little incentive to seek yeoman and tenant support. But in states like North Carolina, Texas, and Arkansas, where large farmers were not strong enough

---

[42] For a detailed but unanalytic description of this critical convention see Samuel Proctor, "The National Farmers' Alliance Convention of 1890 and the 'Ocala Demands,'" *Florida Historical Quarterly* 28 (January 1950), pp. 161–181.

[43] See, for example, "Crazes," *Nation* 53 (November 1891), p. 403.

[44] Haynes, *op. cit.*, p. 254.

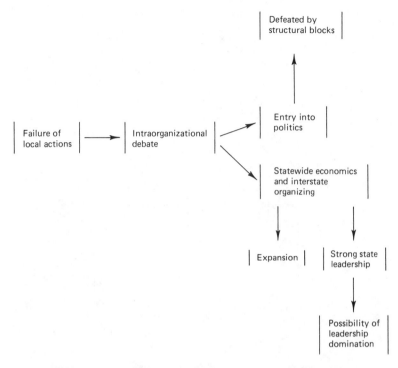

Figure 6.1   *The development of strong leadership in the Farmers' Alliance.*

to enforce their own political programs, the large and enthusiastic Alliance membership was a powerful incentive for elite participation.

Landlords and other elite individuals sought Alliance office, and the tenant and yeoman membership, recognizing the superior resources and skills which qualified the elites for leadership, endorsed this process, even if some policy disagreements had already begun to appear (Figure 6.2). Much of the later story remains to be told, but we can briefly sketch it here. The utlimate outcome of the failure of local actions was a sizable state apparatus controlled largely by elite elements whose class interests were different from those of the rank and file. As this division crystallized, the leadership pressed for independence from the membership, an independence which would free it to pursue policies that advanced its own distinct needs.

The collapse of the Alliance makes sense when viewed through the lense provided by this structural analysis. In the first instance, it was difficult for it to settle upon economic programs that could help the small farmer rank and file which did not attack the increasingly powerful planter-oriented leadership. For this reason, membership enthusiasm diminished even before large members began to leave. This created the "push" away from the Alliance. In the second instance, the elite leadership sought to affect state and national politics for precisely the same reasons

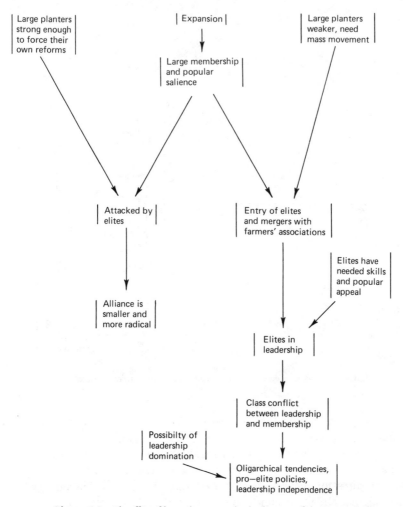

Figure 6.2   *The effect of large planters on the development of the Farmers' Alliance.*

that the Farmers' Associations had done so. They energetically built the new Populist party and they successfully rallied the Alliance rank and file to its banner. This plausible electoral strategy was the "pull" that reduced the Alliance structure to an empty shell by 1892.

It was the history and development of the Alliance which made it possible for the Populist party to become the largest third party movement in the history of the United States.[45] And it was the creation of the Populist party which ensured a rapid and unambivalent death for the moribund Alliance.

[45]See C. Vann Woodward, *Tom Watson: Agrarian Rebel* (Baton Rouge, 1939); John D. Hicks, *The Populist Revolt* (Minneapolis, 1951).

7

Structure and Structural Tension within the Alliance

> From the Rocky Mountains on our West
> Where the icy breezes blow,
> From the Rio Grande River
> Which borders Mexico,
> O'er the broad sweep of valley
> To the ocean on our East
> We hear the farmers rally
> From the greatest to the least.

[Linn Tanner, *Raleigh Progressive Farmer*, April 23, 1889]

Alliance Organization

The structure of the Alliance was responsive to both the structure of farm tenancy and the programs of the organization. While the changing programs meant continual changes in shape, the constancy of the tenancy system ensured a stable skeleton. Figure 7.1 offers a schematic view of the organization.[1]

A selective buying campaign or the creation of a cooperative store focused attention upon the large towns where purchases were made; the county Alliance was

---

[1] The formal properties of Alliance structure can be found in the following documents: "Constitution of the Farmers' and Laborers' Union" (adopted December 7, 1889), printed in "Proceedings of the Annual Session of the Farmers' and Laborers' Union, St. Louis, December 4–7, 1889"; this is reprinted in *Raleigh Progressive Farmer*, December 24, 1889; *ibid.*, January 7, 1890; "Constitution of the Farmers' State Alliance of North Carolina" (adopted at Rockingham, N.C., October 4, 1887), reprinted in *Raleigh Progressive Farmer*, December 1, 1887; "Proceedings of the National Farmers' Alliance and Co-operative Union of America, Shreveport, Louisiana, October 12–14, 1887," reprinted in *Raleigh Progressive Farmer*, November 3, 1887; "Proceedings of the National Farmers' Alliance and Industrial Union of America, Meridian, Mississippi, December 5–8, 1888," reprinted in *Raleigh Progressive Farmer*, December 25, 1888; *ibid.*, January 8, 1889; "Proceedings of the Annual Session of the Farmers' and Laborers' Union, St. Louis, December 4–7, 1889"; "By-laws of the Burleson County [Texas] Farmers' Alliance Co-operative Assciation," both reprinted in *Raleigh Progressive Farmer*, March 13, 1888.

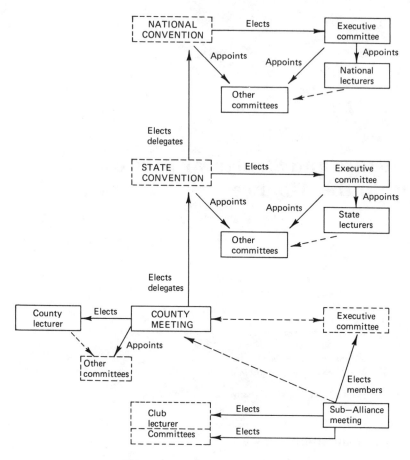

Figure 7.1   *Farmers' Alliance structure.*

therefore the main organizing vehicle for local economic action. This gave both power and prominence to county leaders, who presided over these central activities and made the day-to-day decisions which determined their success. Among county leaders, the most important was the lecturer (or organizer), usually the only full-time officer. The lecturer was the public face of the Alliance, responsible for forming new clubs, meeting with established clubs, and "talking up" the Alliance all over the county. Frequently, he also filled other positions: A North Carolina activist was simultaneously lecturer for several counties, county business agent for his home county, and president and lecturer for his local club.[2]

These county-level leaders were the unsung heroes of the spectacular growth of the Alliance during the late 1880s. One North Carolina lecturer, W. A. Austin, began his tenure of office in December 1887 by uniting the 10 existing clubs in his county into a county organization. Then he set about organizing new clubs. In 2 weeks, he

---

[2] *Raleigh Progressive Farmer*, December 15, 1887; *ibid.*, January 5, 12, 1888.

formed 12 groups in 12 locales. In subsequent weeks, Austin settled down to a pace of one new club a week, and turned his attention to bringing in new members. By the second county meeting 5 months after he bagan work, his county had 30 clubs and 1023 members.[3] V. N. Seawell, a lecturer in a nearby county, gave 16 speeches and organized 14 clubs in 1 month. In a single year, this extremely energetic worker organized nearly 200 clubs in a 5-county area.[4]

While most lecturers were not as devoted as Austin and Seawell, their wide contacts and heavy time commitment made them more visible and prestigious than the other officers. The president and executive committee were ordinarily full-time farmers and could not easily meet, especially when they lived in different parts of the county. This left much day-to-day responsibility in the hands of the lecturer, even when he was not formally responsible, and it almost guaranteed that the lecturer would exercise a disproportionate amount of power.

For example, during non-election years, the question of partisan politics was not current in the organization, but it might be a talking point for a lecturer trying to win people over to the Alliance. These new recruits might ultimately push the group into electoral activity. In Texas between 1880 and 1882, statewide lecturers were operating for the first time and they brought a large number of members into the organisation on just such a basis. When the group subsequently voted against participating in electoral politics, the resulting exodus of members created an organizational crisis.[5]

In this way, the lecturer could almost dictate policy, but even without this sort of explicit independence, he wielded preeminent influence. Since he was the outside representative, he came to the group meetings as the expert on what would appeal to those not yet organized. Since the Alliance was concerned with expanding membership, the informed opinion of the lecturer carried great weight in deciding what programs and positions should be adopted and what should be avoided.

The countywide focus of activities and the countywide power of the lecturer would seem to leave little need for the local club. However, the local club (or "subordinate Alliance") actually played a multifaceted integrative role which complemented the activist nature of the county group.

First, the locals were essential for recruiting membership. Alliance membership was secret and restricted to farmers who supported its principles and activities. Local clubs played an important role both in maintaining secrecy and in enforcing membership restrictions.

While much has been made of the role of secrecy in developing membership commitment, the Southern Alliance often utlized secrecy in a very practical, unspiritual manner. Since the opposition was usually a local merchant—landlord with formidable power, secret membership protected activists from reprisals which facili-

---

[3] *Raleigh Progressive Farmer*, December 15, 1887; *ibid.*, January 5, 1888; *ibid.*, January 12, 1888; *ibid.*, April 24, 1888.

[4] *Raleigh Progressive Farmer*, February 28, 1888; *ibid.*, December 9, 1888.

[5] Nelson A. Dunning, ed. *Farmers' Alliance History and Agricultural Digest* (Washington, D.C., 1891), pp. 37–38.

tated organizing. For example, one North Carolina county organization suspected that the cotton buyers to whom they sold were underpaying their customers:

> They proceeded very quietly and by a free use of the telegraph wire found that the prices at that hour in Concord, Monroe and other comparatively small markets were from a few cents to as much as 76¢ and $1.00 . . . lower than in Charlotte. . . . The cotton buyers tried to laugh it off and promised to pay better prices, and they have done so ever since. Now if these men had not belonged to a secret society, their plans would have been frustrated. The cotton buyers would have known the project was on hand and would have had prices booming, but as it was, they were caught napping.[6]

Membership restrictions also reflected the rural class struggle: The Alliance was meant to exclude all enemies of the working farmer. A representative membership limitation passed by the Wheel in 1887 read:

> The objects of the order shall be to unite fraternally all acceptable citizens, male and female, over the age of eighteen years, who are actually engaged in the occupation of farming; also all mechanics who are engaged in the pursuit of their respective traders; provided that no lawyer, merchant, banker, nor the proprietor of any manufacturing establishment who employs more than three hands, shall be eligible to membership; and provided further, that there shall be separate organizations for white and colored.[7]

These exclusions were meant to prevent the infiltration of individuals who would oppose the interests of yeomen and tenants, and the prohibition against merchants and nonoperating landlords was a statement of analysis: It said that these people had irreconcilable differences with farmers and that these differences flowed from their position in the social structure, and not from their opinions.

These were not mere formalities; constant attention was paid to refining and developing membership criteria. For example, the original Alliance clause focused on merchants:

> In North Carolina any person or persons, who may secure privilege license to conduct a mercantile business as a merchant shall be ineligible to membership. . . .[8]

While this excluded merchant–landlords, it was interpreted by North Carolina President Alexander (a planter) to allow a landlord–merchant into membership if he "sells provisions only to his hands or tenants and does not procure license to sell to the general public."[9] With the ambiguous licensing procedure and the

---

[6] *Raleigh Progressive Farmer*, April 17, 1888.

[7] Dunning, *op. cit.*, p. 209; for other membership restrictions see *ibid.*, p. 171, and *National Economist* (Washington, D.C.), November 2, 1889; see also note 1 above.

[8] "Proceedings of the National Farmers' Alliance and Co-operative Union of America," reprinted in *Raleigh Progressive Farmer*, November 3, 1887.

[9] Syd Alexander, president of the North Carolina Farmers' Alliance, writing in *Raleigh Progressive Farmer*, February 6, 1888.

developing contradictions between tenants and landlords, this criterion became a point of great difficulty for many clubs.[10] Leaders were caught up in frequent quarrels and deluged with queries about ambiguous cases. Ultimately, at the 1889 national convention, the question was resolved by the complete exclusion of land-lords. The new clause excluded any planter from membership if he was involved in any "mercantile pursuits as a means of profit."[11]

To enforce class exclusion and maintain secrecy, complicated membership pro-cedures were adopted. Prosepctive members were discussed and voted upon, and even one "no" vote could result in rejection.[12] Only the local clubs could oversee the process of selection and maintain secrecy, because the membership had friendly knowledge of possible members, as well as the time and mutual trust to evaluate candidates carefully. Moreover, when the club members knew their neighbors, such discussion was often unnecessary, and this added to the usefulness of local clubs.

Despite these restrictions and the secrecy which sometimes resulted in one club's not knowing of the existence of its neighbors,[13] exclusion was often in-effective. Landlords and merchants, as well as other wealthy and influential individuals, often gained admittance:

> One of the great dangers to its [the Alliance's] success and usefulness lies in the fact that unworthy men in no way directly connected with tilling the soil as a means of sustenance—seek membership in its ranks that their own ends may be accomplished, regardless of the welfare of the order.[14]

And even when they themselves were excluded, these outsiders made their pre-sence felt by coopting eligible individuals. The Georgia state President warned in 1890, "our only danger now is from within. Designing men on the outside are com-pelled to use inside men to accomplish their purposes...."[15] These dangers were minimized by an active club system and maximized when clubs did not function.

The second function of clubs was education. In the pre-1900 South, a farmer went to the county seat less than once a week, and this made frequent countywide mass meetings impractical. Moreover, the average county organization contained 700 members—far too many to sustain an educational discussion.[16] The clubs, there-fore, were called upon to build membership understanding and commitment to the

---

[10] In North Carolina, the controversy can be followed in the question and answer column written by state President Alexander in the *Raleigh Progressive Farmer*, January 12, 1888; *ibid.*, March 6, 1888; *ibid.*, April 20, 1888; *ibid.*, May 1, 1888; *ibid.*, June 12, 1888; *ibid.*, July 3, 10, 17, 24, 1888; *ibid.*, December 4, 1888.

[11] "Constitution of the Farmers' and Laborers' Union," reprinted in *Raleigh Progressive Farmer*, December 24, 1889.

[12] Dunning, *op. cit.*, p. 223; *Florida Dispatch* (Tallahassee), February 28, 1889.

[13] *Florida Dispatch* (Tallahassee), February 28, 1889.

[14] *Raleigh Progressive Farmer*, September 19, 1889.

[15] *National Economist*, January 17, 1891.

[16] Michael Schwartz, "The Southern Farmers' Alliance: The Organizational Forms of Radical Protest" (Ph.D. diss., Harvard University, 1971), app. I.

program of the organization. The following description suggests the degree to which these small groups could act in this manner:

> Along in the spring, a man came through organizing an order called the Brothers of Freedom. Sam and I joined as did almost every other farmer. We held out meetings in the schoolhouse and met every Saturday afternoon. While the object of the order, as well as I can remember, was to promote the welfare and best interests of farming people, I do not recall that any of us ever discussed any subject connected with better farming. We said nothing that would give any enlightenment on such subjects as how to reclaim worn out land, or how to cultivate the land so as to obtain a better yield of crops. We were supposed to know all about those things already.
>
> It would seem that our particular lodge developed into an order, the object of which was to oppose the town people, especially the merchant. The merchant, although necessary, was looked upon as a common enemy, and under the miserable system of business and farming which prevailed, the people had some grounds for complaint. The merchant sold supplies to the farmer, such as food, clothing and implements, in the spring of the year, to be paid for when the crops were gathered in the fall. As security for the payment for such supplies as were thus advanced, he took a mortgage on the homestead. Where the farmer was renting, as in the case of Sam and me, he took a mortgage on the stock and growing crop. We called this system buying and selling on credit.
>
> The credit price of goods was about one-half more than the cash price. If sidemeat sold for ten cents a pound cash, the credit price was fifteen cents. If a so-called ten dollar bucket of lard sold for cash at one dollar, the credit price was a dollar and a half. . . .
>
> As we held our meetings weekly we soon grew tired of lambasting the merchant and other people who wore store clothes, and we began holding our secret and business meetings once a month. However, we held open meetings on Saturday night and let our lodge drift into a kind of literary or debating society. At these open meetings all were invited, whether they belonged to the lodge or not. Women and children attended, and our programs consisted of readings, recitations, speeches and debates.[17]

Despite the author's disparagement, it is clear from his description that very active "education" took place. The extensive discussions clarified and enhanced members' understanding of their plight. And other chapters did not restrict their discussions to the merchant. Such objects as reclamations and bigger yields were indeed discussed.[18]

But this passage underscores the inadequacy of the local club that lacked the activist orientation usually provided by the county group. The local discussions had clearly laid a basis for action, but action could not be undertaken by a small club. When no countywide activities developed, the group was left with a purpose. It soon disposed of secrecy, which was useful only in protecting active groups. Then, when the debates became repetitive, the lodge dissolved entirely.[19]

[17] Wayman Hogue, *Back Yonder, An Ozark Chronicle* (New York, 1932), pp. 194–197.

[18] W. Scott Morgan, *History of the Wheel and Alliance and the Impending Revolution* (Fort Scott, Kans., 1889), pp. 202–207.

[19] Hogue, *op. cit.*, pp. 197–198.

It might be said that the county and subordinate Alliances gave the organization its heartbeat. The clubs filtered the membership and developed the understanding necessary for participation in protest activity. The county groups coordinated action and gave the group direction. Between them, they provided the organization with its prime resource—an active, committed, and disciplined membership.

State organizations often began as simple coordinators of local actions,[20] but their nature soon changed. In every case, the statewide organization replaced haphazard local expansion with systematic proselytizing across the state. This work was done by full-time state lecturers, individuals usually selected from the ranks of the most successful county organizers. The lecturers invaded new areas, formed new clubs, and inspired local actions. They sold Alliance literature to the new recruits, collected the first round of dues, and received commissions as high as $5 for each club organized.[21]

The impact of statewide organizing was manifold, and one of its major effects was to undermine the autonomy of county and local groups. Such organizing created statewide leaders with a mass following around the state. It brought people into the Alliance on the basis of the lecturer's appeal; more often than not, this involved statewide rather than local action. It undermined the filtering and education functions of the locals by recruiting large numbers of members in a way different from the slow deliberative process of club expansion. This allowed antagonistic elements into the organization and created less self-reliant local groups.

Thus, statewide organizing created both a pull and a push toward state coordinated activity. The pull derived from the formation of a full-time statewide leadership with a real base among the membership; the push came from newly recruited membership without the skill or the inclination to plan and promote local actions. This new force within the organization became the source of a wide variety of complicated interchanges between local groups and state leadership. We have already discussed the Clebourne convention, which reflected one facet of this contradiction, and the issue of Black exclusion, which reflected another of its facets. Later, we will return to these issues in greater detail, both as a theoretical point and as an axis around which the history of the Alliance turned.

The national organization remained weak throughout the history of the Alliance. It was never the locus of mass protest; even the national jute boycott was carried on outside the national structure (see Chapter 14). Its incipient role was to enable the Alliance to develop national political visibility,[22] but this role was prematurely aborted when the Populist party replaced the Alliance in 1892. The national organization could not acquire power in the way the states had. National lecturers were not day-to-day organizers who collected dues; they were famous personages who

---

[20] For example, the Arkansas Wheel began in this manner. Dunning, *op. cit.*, p. 206.

[21] *Florida Dispatch* (Tallahassee), October 10, 1887. This could be a tremendous amount. The lecturer might organize two or three clubs a week during periods of rapid expansion.

[22] See, for example, Robert Lee Hunt, *A History of Farmers' Movements in the Southwest, 1873–1935* (College Station, Tex., 1935), pp. 31–33; Dunning, *op. cit.*, pp. 48f; John D. Hicks and John D. Barhart, "The Farmers' Alliance," *North Carolina Historical Review* 6 (July 1929), p. 264.

arrived in the morning, spoke to the assembled masses in the afternoon, and moved on in the evening. Their successes were reaped by the states and the national Alliance organization always remained dependent upon the states. It was loaned $500 by the Texas Alliance when it was founded,[23] and 4 years later, it was still begging for money—this time in the form of uncollectable dues owed by over half the state organizations.[24] The history of the national Alliance was unfulfilled and uneventful. The locus of Alliance activities flowed from local to state but it did not progress further.

TABLE 7.1
Average Acreage in Cotton for Counties Organized by the Farmers' Alliance

State	Year of first state convention	Number of counties organized	Mean acreage in cotton for organized counties in 1889[a]
Texas[b]	1887	18	33,700
Tennessee	1885	5	21,000
Mississippi	1886	5	16,400
Alabama	1886	12	33,800
Florida	1887	17	8,400
North Carolina	1887	7	29,400
North Carolina[c]	1888	46	17,300

[a]Cotton acreage for Southern counties is not available for specific years. Figures for 1889 were compiled from the 1890 census (11th Census, vol. 5, pp. 393–397). There was no major variation from year to year, so these data are accurate enough for use in this analysis.

[b]Data were not available for the first Texas convention, held in 1882. Data reported here are from an incomplete list of the counties represented at Waco convention, January 1887.

[c]New counties organized between the first state convention (August 1887) and the second state convention (August 1888).

Sources: Membership figures for states are taken from the following:

Texas. W. Scott Morgan, *History of the Wheel and Alliance and the Impending Revolution* (Fort Scott, Kans., 1889), pp. 104, 288; Nelson Dunning, ed., *Farmers' Alliance History and Agricultural Digest* (Washington, D.C., 1891), pp. 17, 36; Ralph Smith, "The Farmers' Alliance in Texas, 1875–1900," *Southwestern Historical Quarterly* 48 (January 1945), pp. 348, 351, 355.

Tennesse. Morgan, *op. cit.,* p. 100.

Mississippi. Morgan, *op. cit.,* pp. 102–103.

Alabama. Thomas McAdory Owen, *History of Alabama and Dictionary of Alabama Biography* (Chicago, 1921), vol. I, pp. 564–565; William W. Rogers, "The Farmers' Alliance in Alabama," *Alabama Review* 15 (January 1962), pp. 5–6.

Florida. Jacksonville *Florida Dispatch,* Ocotber 10, 1887; *ibid.,* October 17, 1887.

North Carolina. National Economist, May 25, 1889; Simeon Alexander Delap, *The Populist Party in North Carolina,* Historical papers published by the Trinity College Historical Society, ser. xiv (1922), pp. 93–95; John D. Hicks, "The Farmers' Alliance in North Carolina," *North Carolina Historical Review* 2 (April 1925), p. 170.

[23] Dunning, *op. cit.,* p. 58.
[24] Dunning, *op. cit.,* p. 169.

The Social Origins of Leadership and Membership

The Farmers' Alliance began and grew strong in cottonized, white yeoman farmer regions in the South. Table 7.1 illustrates part of this pattern: The first counties organized in Texas, Tennessee, Mississippi, Alabama, Florida, and North Carolina were all heavy cotton growers. The figures for Mississippi and Alabama are hardly earthshaking, since almost all counties in those states were heavy cotton growers (over 10,000 bales per county). But the other entries are more significant. The 18 early Texas counties for which data are available planted about 600,000 acres of cotton, 15% of the state's total.[25] In Tennessee, the Alliance took root in a small five-county region that grew cotton, while the rest of the state was mainly devoted to other crops. In North Carolina, the Alliance began in seven very heavily cottonized counties; in 1887, all of them planted over 20,000 acres (Table 7.2). In 1888, it spread to 46 new counties, all but 5 of which produced cotton—an average of 17,300 acres per county. Only in 1889, after the vast majority of cotton counties had been organized, did the Alliance make substantial inroads among the 30 non-cotton counties.

Florida reveals this process even more clearly. In early 1887, two organizers from Texas arrived in Florida. One started in Jackson County, the principal cotton county, and the other in Citrus, a fruit growing county which raised no cotton at all.[26] In October 1887, the first state convention was held, and the Alliance had spread to 17 counties. Of these 17, 13 were cotton producers and 6 of the 9 heavy cotton producers were represented. In a bare 6 months, the Alliance had dug deep roots in the cotton areas of Florida. In the meantime, the organizer who had started in Citrus County has managed to organize only one other fruit county

TABLE 7.2
Alliance Organizing and Cotton Farming in North Carolina[a]

Year counties organized by Alliance	No. counties no acres cotton	No. counties < 10,000 acres cotton	No. counties ≥ 10,000 acres cotton
1887	0	0	7
1888	5	14	27
1889	18	0	4
Never organized	7	0	0
Total	30	28	38

[a]Counties are classified by the acres of cotton planted in 1890.

Sources: "Year organized" data from *National Economist*, May 25, 1889; Simeon Alexander Delap, "The Populist Party in North Carolina" Historical papers published by the Trinity College Historical Society, ser. xiv (1922), pp. 93–95; John D. Hicks, "The Farmers' Alliance in North Carolina," *North Carolina Historical Review* 2 (April 1925), p. 170. Cotton acreage data from *11th* Census, vol. 5, p. 395.

[25] For sources on which counties were organized see Table 7.1 Figures for cotton acreage were compiled from *Eleventh Census of the United States* (1890), vol. 5, pp. 393–397.

[26] James O. Knauss, "The Farmers' Alliance in Florida," *South Atlantic Quarterly* 25 (July 1926), p. 301.

TABLE 7.3
Average Percentage Yeoman and Average Percentage
Black in Counties Organized by the Farmers' Alliance

State	Mean percentage yeoman, 1890	Mean percentage Black, 1890	Year	Number of counties
Texas	60	5	1886	18
Tennessee	69	22	1885	5
Mississippi	66	18	1886	5
Alabama	58	34	1887	18
Florida	79	38	1887	17
North Carolina	63	38	1887	7
	62	39	1888	46

Sources: References on Alliance counties can be found in Table 7.1. Percentage yeoman in 1890 data compiled from *11th Census* (1890), vol. 5, pp. 120–192. Percentage black in 1890 data compiled from the U.S. Bureau of the Census, *Negro Population in the United States, 1790–1915* (Washington, D.C., 1915), pp. 776–793.

(Duval) and had moved into cotton areas, where he had had more success.[27] The Florida experience was almost a social experiment—two Alliancemen tried to organize two different areas and one was successful while the other was not.

Despite its emphasis on cotton, the Alliance did not locate at first in the most heavily cottonized areas of the South. These areas tended to be heavily tenantized and predominantly Black; the Alliance began in white yeoman areas (Table 7.3). In Mississippi, for example, 58% of the total population was Black, 53% of the farmers were tenants, and the majority of the counties planted well over 20,000 acres in cotton. The Alliance did not take root in the "typical" Mississippi cotton county. Instead, the first five counties each had less than 20% Black, fewer than 50% tenants, and an average of only 16,400 acres in cotton. In Texas, only 1 of the 26 most cottonized counties was among the first to be organized. These 26 counties were 29% Black and 60% tenant; the Alliance counties were 5% Black and 40% tenant.

The spread to the heavily tenantized Black Belt areas began after Clebourne. The new programs created a broader basis for the Alliance and provided the organizational resources to recruit tenants. Moreover, the rapid growth began attracting landlords in these areas. In Alabama, Florida, and North Carolina, the Alliance began in 1887, after Clebourne, and this is reflected in the earliest organization. The first counties in these states averaged over 33% Black, a much higher figure than the early counties in Mississippi or Texas. Similarly, the figures in Table 7.3 indicate the penetration into tenant areas. Nearly half of the farmers in the early Alabama counties were tenants, and neither Florida nor North Carolina had any really heavily tenantized areas. In Florida, there were only five cotton counties with

[27] Sources for organizing data are Knauss, *op. cit.*, pp. 301–302; and (for exact county names) *Florida Dispatch* (Jacksonville), October 10, 17, 1887; *ibid.*, February 14, 1889; *ibid.*, November 21, 1889; *ibid.*, January 2, 1890.

less than 60% yeomen, and the Alliance organized three of them in its first months. In North Carolina, there were 20 cotton counties with less than 60% yeomen, and 16 of them were organized by 1888. All 11 of the very heavily tenantized counties (over 50%) had been organized by 1888. Thus, by 1888 at least, the Alliance had broken through the resistance of the heavily tenantized counties of North Carolina.

The evidence presented here is by no means complete. It serves, however, as a backdrop to forming a picture of Alliance membership in its first years. This picture is confirmed by the one extant membership survey, conducted by the South Carolina State Alliance in early 1889. This survey, though very sloppily conducted, is still a moderately good indicator of Alliance membership. Clubs covering 12,500 Alliance members responded. Of the 8655 members who reported their occupations, 8021 (93%) were farmers; 64% of the farmers were yeomen and 36% were tenants. In a state that was over 50% tenant, these figures suggest that the Alliance, in South Carolina as in other states, made its early and most extensive appeal to yeomen. However, given the probability that the number of tenant members was underestimated in this survey, and that even so over one-third of the members were tenants, we see that the Alliance was by no means restricted to yeomen but made significant gains in bringing tenants into the organization.[28] We can conclude that the Alliance, predominantly yeomen and confined to over-whelmingly white cotton areas, later established itself in more heavily Black and more heavily tenantized areas.

Alliance leaders were not typical members: They were recruited from different social classes and they might very well act against the interests of the membership. This problem was of constant concern to a great many Alliancemen:

> One of our greatest faults is that we elect or promote men to prominent offices in our order who either hold or have held prominent political offices. I consider that a weak point in our organic law. Can you point out a single one at the present time elected to any political office who is not under the thumb and influence of either of the old political bosses?[29]

Underlying this opinion is the idea that a person's background made a great deal of difference in his leadership behavior. Another Alliance member stated this well: "I wish there was an article in our constitution prohibiting politicians from membership in the Alliance, and where a member turns politician to dismiss him from the order at once. Because they are welded to their idol, they will never be any more than a firebrand in our ranks."[30]

---

[28] Results of the survey were published in the *National Economist* (Washington, D.C.), May 29, 1889. The survey was conducted by sending questionnaires to each club; about 40% responded. The experience of modern polling suggests that such self-selecting questionnaires will overrepresent the higher social classes, the highly educated, and the larger clubs. Thus we can expect that the percentage of farmers was greater than 93% and that the percentage of tenants was greater than 36%.

[29] *Florida Dispatch*, July 4, 1889.

[30] *Ibid.*

TABLE 7.4
Farmers' Alliance Leadership[a]

Part A: Occupation of leaders				Part D: Previous political officeholders among leaders[i]		
Occupation	Number	Percentage		Occupation	Percentage held office[g]	Percentage no office
Farmers	27	53		Farmers	27	73
Farmers with other occupations[b]	17	34		Non-farmers	14	86
Non-farmers[c]	7	14		Total	26	74
Total	51[d]	100				

Part B: Wealth of leaders[e]				Part E: Combined index[j]		
Occupation	Percentage wealthy[g]	Percentage not wealthy		Occupation	Percentage elite	Percentage non-elite[g]
Farmers[f]	18	82		Farmers	59	41
Non-farmers	14	86		Non-farmers	100	0
Total	18	82		Total	65	35

Part C: Education of leaders[h]		
Occupation	Percentage high education[g]	Percentage low education
Farmers	32	68
Non-farmers	71	29
Total	38	62

[a]Derived from lists of officeholders in the Alliance and Wheel, elective and nonelective, at the state and national levels.

[b]Men whose principal occupation was farming but who also engaged in other jobs at one time or another or simultaneously with farming. The main such combinations were farmer-stockman and farmer-teacher, each with five members. The actual number in this category may be higher due to effects discussed in note g.

[c]Lawyer-editors (3); teachers (2); businessmen (1); and minister (1).

[d]The list included six leaders with no occupation given. These were excluded from the analysis.

[e]Men were considered wealthy if the description said they were wealthy or if they were known to own large tracts of land (say, 1000 acres); see also note g.

[f]Including "Farmers with other occupations" from Part A.

[g]According to the way the data were collected, attributes such as wealth were mentioned when they occur, but nothing was said if the person had little money or education or never held political office. Thus, if nothing was said, we must assume the attribute was not present. This underestimated the number of wealthy leaders since nothing would be said if the author had no information on wealth. Therefore, a correct reading of this table takes the first column as a minimum figure and the second as a maximum. A correct interpretation of the first row of Part B, for example, would be that "at least 18% of Alliance farmer leadership was wealthy."

[h]High education was considered to be any college training, with or without a degree, and/or training as a school teacher; see note g also.

[i]A man was considered to have had previous officeholding experience if he held elective office in some level of government *before* he became active in the Alliance or Wheel. Men elected to office through Alliance or Wheel endorsement and support were not included unless they also were elected without such support previously.

[j]Any leader who was either wealthy, had high education, or had held previous office (or more than one of these) was coded as "elite." All others were considered non-elite. See note g.

Sources: *National Economist Almanac* (January 1890), pp. 71–75; W. Scott Morgan, *The History of the Wheel and Alliance* (Fort Scott, Kans., 1891), pp. 353–376.

116

A great many planters and other elite agriculturalists entered and rose in the Alliance because of the absorption of farmers' clubs in such states as North Carolina, Alabama, Virginia, and even South Carolina.[31] This probably occurred in a less systematic way in the remaining states. The outcome of this differential recruitment can be found in an analysis of the social backgrounds of national Alliance leaders. The Alliance printed brief biographies of its leadership. A systematic look at these biographies offers one way to understand exactly who the leaders were.[32]

Table 7.4 presents a rough picture of the attributes of Alliance leadership. Perhaps most striking is Part A, which shows that only 14% of the Alliance leadership were not farmers. Fully 86% were agriculturalists, though a large proportion were "hyphenated" farmers—men who had other occupations besides farming.[33] Furthermore, the nature of their other occupations suggests that these may have had a great deal to do with their rise to leadership. Of the 17 hyphenated farmers, 12 had other occupations which involved intellectual training and special leadership skills.

Parts B—D of Table 7.4 specify more directly the exceptional attributes of the Alliance leaders. Data were available which measured the wealth, education, and previous political experience of the Alliance officeholders. More than one in six leaders was wealthy, and even one-quarter had held previous political office.[34] Over one-third had attended college. While these figures are certainly far above the comparable ones for the Alliance membership,[35] they are by no means as high as they could be.[36] If we were looking at Parts B—D only, our conclusion might well be that most of the Alliance leaders were not particularly elite in origin. However, when we recalculate our data to describe how many Alliance leaders either were well educated *or* were wealthy *or* were previous officeholders, the combined total is 65%. In other words, *no more* than one-third of the Alliance

[31] See Chapter 6 of this volume. William W. Rogers, "The Farmers' Alliance in Alabama," *Alabama Review* 15 (January 1962), p. 6, describes this process in some detail and points out the elite status of Alliance leaders in Marshall, Tuscaloosa, and Elmore counties; see also O. M. Bratten, "Elmore County Politics, 1890—1900" (M.A. thesis, Yale University, 1966), p. 25; William D. Sheldon, *Populism in the Old Dominion: Virginia Farm Politics, 1885—1900* (Princeton, 1935), pp. 23—25; Francis Simkins, *Pitchfork Ben Tillman: South Carolinian* (Baton Rouge, 1944), pp. 147—150.

[32] Biographies and social background in this section, unless otherwise noted, were found in *National Economist Almanac* (January 1890), pp. 71—75; Morgan, *op. cit.,* pp. 353—376.

[33] Because of the nature of the data, the 34% figure given in Part A of Table 7.4 may be considerably lower than actual percentage. See note to Tables 7.4.

[34] Actually, these are both underestimates, since the nature of the data makes these minimum figures. See note 9, Table 7.7.

[35] Fewer than 1% of Southern farmers were wealthy. See Chapter 3. The percentage of Americans who had gone to college in 1890 was considerably lower than 5%, and for Alliance farmers it was likely even lower. (The 5% figure was derived from data in the *Annual Report of the United States Commissioner of Education* (various dates), which are reprinted in U.S. Bureau of the Censury *Historical Statistics of the United States, Colonial Times to the Present, A Statistical Abstract Supplement* (Prepared with the cooperation of the Social Science Research Council, Washington, D.C., 1960), p. 211.

[36] For example, a survey of Populist officeholders in 1892—1896 in Alabama revealed that very few—less than one-quarter—were farmers and among these farmers almost all were wealthy, most were college educated, and over half had held previous office. (Figures are from unpublished data collected by the author.)

leaders had non-elite origins, as did the mass of Alliance membership (see Part E of Table 7.4).[37] This figure suggests that Alliance leadership was, by and large, recruited from a different pool than the membership itself.

The differences between leaders and members in the Alliance took on meaning only when the leadership had both the inclination and the possibility to act against the wishes or interests of the membership. These inclinations and possibilities were the emergent properties of Alliance structure and activities in the late 1880s and can only be assessed together with them.

Newspapers and the Leadership—Membership Contradiction

One purpose of Alliance newspapers was to present the organization's viewpoint to potential members and sympathizers, particularly in areas of minimal Alliance presence. This was especially crucial when the group could not rely on the regular newspapers to present its side. In late 1887, the Atlanta *Constitution* published a letter from Newman, Georgia, charging the Alliance with illegally attacking local merchants and fomenting discord throughout the South. The letter was republished by a substantial proportion of the papers in the Southeast, while Alliance replies were not printed.[38] It fell upon the *Raleigh Progressive Farmer*, the largest Alliance newspaper in the region, to rebut the charges; and it did so with a series of articles culminating in a letter from an Allianceman in Newman. The letter denounced the accuser as a "migratory bird, ... a lawyer who had failed as a newspaper editor." Moreover, said the rebuttal, "the merchants of Newman were more indignant about it than even the Alliance."[39]

The projection of the Alliance to the outside world was an important ingredient of Alliance journalism,[40] but it contradicted, at least in part, another function of the newspaper: membership-to-membership communication which allowed local groups to exchange organizing ideas and tactical ploys (see Figure 7.2). Membership articles also contained minutes of meetings, lists of new clubs, official policy

[37] Although the data used for these figures are imprecise and obviously inadequate in many respects, one feature of them strengthens confidence in them. Since they derive from two sources, we can treat the two samples of leadership separately, to see if the two groups of leaders have the same profile. Such a technique is a test of the reliability of the data. If the two samples are very similar, this suggests that the most important source of error (lack of information about wealth, education, or officeholding) may not be too severe. With that introduction, we can report the results when the simple is divided into its two constituent parts. The similarity is remarkable:

Sample	Sample size	Percentage farmers	Percentage hyphenated farmers	Percentage wealthy	Percentage high education	Percentage previous office	Percentage elite
Farmers' Alliance	29	51	34	21	38	21	73
Farmers' Wheel	22	55	32	14	36	32	55

[38] *Charlotte* (N.C.) *Democrat*, November 25, 1887; *Raleigh Progressive Farmer*, May 15, 1888.

[39] *Raleigh Progressive Farmer*, December 1, 12, 22, 1887.

[40] See, for example, *Raleigh Progressive Farmer*, February 2, 1888; *ibid.*, March 27, 1888; *ibid.*, June 16, 1888; *ibid.*, September 18, 1888.

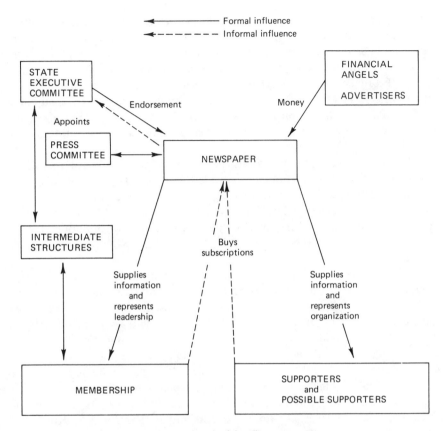

Figure 7.2 *The role of the Alliance newspaper.*

statements, and other material that outsiders often found dull or even offensively partisan. The incompatibility often led to the establishment of two newspapers, such as the internal *Florida Farmers' Alliance* and the publically oriented *Florida Dispatch*. However, this arrangement was financially impractical for many state organizations. Florida attempted to resolve this by printing the *Farmers' Alliance* as the four middle pages of the *Dispatch*; this allowed the internal bulletin to be removed when the paper was sold to uninterested outsiders.

Such solutions were not entirely satisfactory and the "inside—outside" contradiction often became overlaid upon leadership—membership contradictions. Most membership-to-membership communications took the form of poorly written articles penned by local Alliance secretaries. Even when these had wider interest, they were not appealing to the uncommitted outsider. Therefore, many newspapers followed the pattern established by the *National Economist*; as the newspaper gained readership and solvency, it replaced its crudely worded, membership-authored local news with broadly appealing polished prose composed by professional writers. As the quality improved, the content changed.

If such a process was accompanied by political cleavage, the migration of content did more than convert the paper from an internal communication device to an organizing vehicle. In North Carolina, it gave the paper a different political complexion by freeing the editor from dependence upon rank-and-file news sources. Between February and October 1888, the *Raleigh Progressive Farmer* filled its pages with a variety of stories, but it failed to publish a flurry of membership-authored articles calling for the establishment of a statewide cooperative. Indeed, it published a rebuttal to the idea without ever printing the rank-and-file arguments.[41]

The solution to these contradictions lay in the proliferation of Alliance newspapers, so that there were enough to serve all functions. The estimate of one researcher, that 1000 such papers were being published in 1890, suggests that all the needs may have been fulfilled.[42] Texas and Alabama had 100 papers each.[43] Georgia had three state organs, and Kentucky, with a small organization of fewer than 40,000, had two.[44] Texas had established two newspapers even before the first state convention.[45]

But the average life of these papers was less than a year, and they rarely were self-supporting. The *Raleigh Progressive Farmer*, the North Carolina state organ and the most famous Alliance paper, had only 915 subscribers as late as September 1887, and only 11,760 in January 1890.[46] Louisiana, with a state membership of 20,000, could not support a state organ at all and was forced to disseminate state news through the *National Economist*. In Florida, the internal *Florida Farmers' Alliance* was absorbed by the external *Florida Dispatch*, which immediately got into financial trouble.[47] Alabama changed state newspapers five times because of successive bankruptcies.[48] Only Texas's *Southern Mercury*, with 25,000 subscribers and at least one $10,000 subsidy from the state organization, was relatively untroubled.[49] The *National Economist*, drawing upon the entire organization, achieved a circulation of 125,000.[50]

The problem was mainly money:

> The major fact was that businessmen did not choose to advertise in what they considered radical journals. As a result, the reform editor was almost totally dependent on his subscribers for the support of the paper, and when they did not pay, the editor went bankrupt. The columns of Alliance papers were filled with appeals to delinquent subscribers.[51]

A paid-up subscription list was an unreachable goal. Kentucky, with a statewide

---

[41] *Raleigh Progressive Farmer*, February 9, 1888; *ibid.*, October 2, 1888.

[42] William Rogers, "Alabama's Reform Press," *Agricultural History* 34 (April 1960), p. 62.

[43] *Ibid.*; Roscoe Martin, *The People's Party in Texas* (Austin, 1924), pp. 194 f.

[44] *National Economist*, May 24, 1890.

[45] Dunning, *op. cit.*, pp. 32, 35. The first was the *Wetherford (Tex.) Herald*, established in February 1881; when it failed, it was replaced by the *Jacksboro* (Tex.) *Rural Citizen* in August.

[46] Stuart Noblen, *Leonidas Lafayette Polk: Agrarian Crusader* (Chapel Hill, 1949), p. 210; *Raleigh Progressive Farmer*, July 10, 1888.

[47] *Florida Dispatch* (Jacksonville), February 7, 1889.

[48] Rogers, "Alabama's Reform Press," pp. 62–66.

[49] *Progressive Farmer*, January 5, 1887.

[50] C. W. Macune. "The Farmers' Alliance" (typescript available at Library of University of Texas, 1920).

[51] Rogers, "Alabama's Reform Press," p. 66; see also *Raleigh Progressive Farmer*, April 24, 1888; *ibid.*, July 3, 1888.

membership of some 40,000, could muster a total of but 3500 paid-up subscriptions to its two state organs.[52] Pickens County, Alabama, had 800 Alliance members but only 70 paid for their newspapers.[53]

Most of the 1000 Populist newspapers were simply not viable.[54] Bankruptcy was close to inevitable, and the possibility of successful operation was linked to outside supplies of money.[55] The financial realities of the Alliance movement meant that the successful newspapers were privately owned and widely circulated; they could not cater to the particular needs of the rank and file because the rank and file could not support a newspaper. Thus, the *Jacksonville Florida Dispatch* and the *Raleigh Progressive Farmer* both predated the Alliance. Their affiliation with the group coincided with the elevation of their editors to positions of Alliance leadership.[56] In these cases and many others, the newspapers was not in any way controlled by the Alliance, because the owner—publisher was in no way dependent on the group for his existence. The editor's allegiance was voluntarily given and could be withdrawn without penalty. Moreover, these tenuous enterprises were often dependent upon their advertisers (who disliked "radical journals") or on politically unreliable financial angels.[57]

As a consequence, newspapers were most often interested in appealing to the broadest readership and in moderating the attacks on local elites who controlled advertising and other revenues. They became, de facto, a force for moderation, and they tended to side with the leadership, which pursued these same policies. The *Southern Mercury* did not necessarily speak for the membership when it declared that the Alliance did not desire to "injure the business" of anyone—not even the supply merchants.[58]

The high visibility of Alliance editors combined with the organizational dependence which quickly grew up around their papers to make them formidable forces within the organization. Their structural partisanship meant that their influence was most easily recruited by elite-oriented leadership groups. The tensions created by the difficulties of newspaper publication thus compounded the already existing leadership—membership tensions.

Financing the Alliance

The Farmers' Alliance, like other protest groups, depended upon the energy and commitment of its membership for its strength. Money was a secondary concern; it was useful, but not central, to the organization. Thus, the quickly expanding North Carolina State Alliance emerged from 1887 with only $877.15 (despite dues owed of

---

[52] *National Economist*, May 24, 1890.

[53] Rogers, "Alabama's Reform Press," p. 67.

[54] Even the *Progressive Farmer* was in constant trouble; see Noblen, *op. cit.*, p. 210.

[55] Rogers, "Alabama's Reform Press," p. 66.

[56] *Florida Dispatch*, March—October 1887, various issues; *ibid.*, October 10, 1887.

[57] See, for example, the *People's Weekly Tribune* (Montgomery) 1892—November 1896. This was financed by Reuben Kolb, Populist gubernatorial candidate and a wealthy planter.

[58] Reprinted in *Raleigh Progressive Farmer*, September 8, 1897.

nearly $13,000),[59] and the national Alliance spent only $19,651.65 in 1890—its peak year.[60] Of the national budget, $12,400 was devoted to salaries of officers, and all but a small proportion of the remainder was utilized in various internal functions such as payment of conventions bills.

Local Alliances had the fewest money problems. With at most one full-time officer, often unpaid, the needs of the locals could be met by taking collections when necessary. The visibility of the need made it all the easier to meet. The state organization, on the other hand, had several full-time officers and a variety of office expenses. It depended upon the $.25 quarterly dues,[61] and it was dependent upon the local clubs to collect dues. Their inability to collect as much as 10%[62] of the dues indicates the lack of coercive power that leadership had over membership. The national organization was even more vulnerable—it was wholly dependent upon states' sending 5% of their net receipts.[63] In 1889, only one state paid its entire bill, and in 1890, only 18 of 22 states paid anything at all.[64]

After Clebourne, especially when leadership–membership tensions began to develop, methods of raising money without the mediation of local groups were devised. The most consistent moneymaker was collection of initial dues by state organizers. Whereas early state groups had appropriated as little as $.65 from a new club,[65] in later years, they collected a $9.00 charter fee, initiation fees of $.50 per member, and $.25 per member dues, as well as whatever money was spent on literature.[66] Even in small states, such collections could net a tidy sum.[67]

---

[59] *Raleigh Progressive Farmer*, February 9, 16, 1888.

[60] Dunning, *op. cit.*, p. 157. Even a major political campaign cost less than $2000. *Dallas Morning News*, November 29, 1892.

[61] Dunning, *op. cit.*, p. 158.

[62] *Raleigh Progressive Farmer*, February 9, 16, 1888.

[63] The national policy varied. The general rule was that the state paid the National Alliance $.05 per member. This worked out to be more than 5% because despite the $1.00 dues, dues were paid quarterly and often members paid only $.25 and did not pay the rest of the year. This meant the $.05 sent to the national Alliance was 25% of the membership dues actually collected. This policy gave the national Alliance no share of any collections other than membership.

At other times the actual formula was 5% of the state budget. This gave the national Alliance only $1.25 on a payment of $.25 dues, but it cut the national in on all other collections. See Dunning, *op cit.*, pp. 60, 158; Morgan, *op. cit.*, pp. 147 f.

[64] *National Economist*, January 4, 1890; Dunning, *op. cit.*, pp. 158–159; *National Economist*, 20, 1890.

[65] *National Economist*, June 29, 1889.

[66] *Florida Dispatch*, October 10, 1887.

[67] While the states could prosper—given membership expansion—from this way of reaching members' pocketbooks, the national might still starve without the donations from the states. Despite the fact that the national orators drew huge crowds and inspired many new chapters, the payoff for these activities generally went to the state, which organized the meetings. The national orators never stayed around afterward to collect the dues. In one stretch, Harry Tracy, one of the most successful national organizers, made 180 speeches in 90 days—2 per day (*National Economist*, June 29, 1889). At this rate he had no time to help on organizational problems or collect dues, but this did not prevent the local groups from capitalizing on his presence. For example, using the drawing power of Harry Tracy's name, it was possible to attract nearly 1000 people to a rally in Wake County, North Carolina. Tracy spoke in the afternoon and then left to keep another engagement. That evening an organizing meeting took place at which state and local leaders spoke and helped set up various activities (*Raleigh News and Observer*, July 24, 1889).

Since national organizers were the most famous and demanded Alliance leaders, they could not afford the leisure of dues collection, organizing chapters, and selling literature. Thus, the nature of the national organization defeated its efforts to make direct contact with the membership. In 1890, the national organizers were able to collect $1380.33 in profits on national literature and $918.95 in dues from unorganized states. This represented less than one-fifth of the income of the national organization.

Once local clubs were established throughout the state, initiation fees were no longer reliable sources of state organization financing. Other methods of direct collection were usually unsatisfactory, and this meant that state organizations were under constant monetary pressure. One solution to their fiscal difficulties lay in obtaining funds from outside sources. It is difficult to determine how frequently this method was utilized, since it was almost always subject to interpretation as attempted bribery and therefore concealed. However, because of its potential as a source of both funds and corruption, we shall consider a few well-publicized examples. One notable contribution was made when it became known that the Alliance Exchange of Texas would attract farmers from great distances. Several cities began bidding for the exchange, and Dallas won by offering $10,000 cash, a rent waiver, a huge lot to build upon, 50 acres of water, and several other guarantees contingent upon long-time location in Dallas.[68]

Perhaps the most consistently reported outside donations were connected to Alliance conventions. In 1890, the national convention was held in out-of-the-way Ocala, Florida, because of the inducements the city had offered:

A short time before the meeting many delegates were gratefully surprised at receiving passes from their nearest point on the Louisville and Nashville, and some of the other Southern railroad lines, to Florida and return. While at Ocala no pains were spared, on the part of the citizens of that enterprising city, to make the stay of the delegates as pleasant as possible. Carriages were furnished for drives, receptions were held, public demonstrations of many kinds were furnished, hotel bills were paid, and orange and lemon groves were for the time given over to fruit-hungry people. Excursions were arranged to points of interest, notable among which was the "Silver Spring," the "Phosphate Quarries," and the "Cedar Mills" at Homassa. After the adjournment of the Supreme Council almost the entire delegation started on a two weeks pleasure trip, which covered the points of interest in the state. A special train was furnished free by the different lines of railroads.[69]

This description is a bit florid, but the official statements of the inducements indicate that it is not far off the mark. Some of the attractions are listed here:

1. The meeting hall was donated rent-free.
2. All Alliance members were entertained at local restaurants at half price and officers were entertained for nothing.
3. $7000 in cash was donated for convention expenses.
4. An exhibit was set by the local Alliances advertising the advantages of Florida agriculture.
5. 1000 boxes of five oranges were distributed.
6. Free transportation for the delegates was provided by the Lousville and Nashville Railroad.
7. Free carriages were supplied during the convention.

[68] Roger Smith, "Macuneism, or the Farmers of Texas in Business," *Journal of Southern History* 13 (May 1947), pp. 229–232.

[69] F. G. Blood, ed., *Handbook and History of the National Farmers' Alliance and Industrial Union* (Washington, D.C., 1893), p. 41.

8. A free excursion around Florida was provided for delegates after the convention was completed.[70]

The total value of these inducements—excluding the railroad fares—has been
estimated at well over $15,000.[71] This was considerably more than the national
Alliance's income from all other sources, which amounted to less than $14,000.[72]

Such inducements were a routine part of Alliance conventions. The Florida state
convention in 1889 had obtained a rent-free convention hall, half price on transportation to the convention, and a free excursion for delegates.[73] A large part of the
cost of the 1889 national convention was paid by the St. Louis Board of Trade; each
delegate received $3 a day for expenses.[74]

Whether or not such inducements were intended to corrupt, they restructured
leadership–membership relations in a number of ways. Without this outside
funding the state and national organizations would have been forced to undertake
fundraising among the membership. The success of these efforts depended upon
boosting membership commitment so that outside funding, which released the
leadership from these efforts, resulted in a "freeing" of the leadership from undertaking membership oriented activities. Moreover, the lavish, vacation atmosphere
of these conventions altered their appeal. Somber, austere conventions attract only
the most dedicated members, those with a deep commitment, a definite point of
view, or a major issue to raise. Alliance conventions attracted the vacationer as
well; even an uncommitted, marginal individual would attend if he could. This presented the leadership with a more agreeable group, less likely to raise contrary
ideas.

Outside funding—even in the absence of sinister motives—freed the leadership
from membership constraint. Combined with sinister motives, outside contributors
drove the wedge of class interest into the organization. In Georgia, the state leadership became involved in various deals with railroads and therefore sought to
prevent Alliance attacks on the industry. The leadership allowed the membership
to think that a railroad commission was actually working hard at controlling railroads. To the innocent eye, this seemed true, but to the informed eye of the leadership—who were entrusted with making sure that progress was made—it was
clear that the commission had been diverted from taking any real action. Because
the membership trusted the Alliance leadership, they believed it was moving
against the railroads. Thus, the personal interests of Alliance leadership in a few
railroads had led to concealment of important information about the railroad
commission.[75]

[70] Knauss, op. cit., p. 310; Samuel Proctor, "The National Farmers' Alliance Convention of 1890, and its 'Ocala
Demands,'" Florida Historical Quarterly 28 (July 1950), pp. 162, 180.

[71] Proctor, op. cit., p. 162.

[72] National Economist, December 20, 1890. Almost certainly the main motive for this lavish display was to advertise
Florida agriculture—both for future sales of fruit and for attracting farmers to the land-rich area.

[73] Florida Dispatch, September 26, 1889; ibid., October 3, 1889.

[74] Blood, op. cit., p. 39; National Economist, December 21, 1889.

[75] National Economist, November 9, 1889; Raleigh News and Observer, August 4, 7, 1888.

This phenomenon can be placed within our earlier discussion of the separation of membership from leadership. In this case, the class nature of the separation is particularly evident. When Alliance leadership had a stake in the advancement of railroads or other enterprises which the membership had a stake in attacking, the leadership—membership conflict hinged on class identification. It was in this situation that the most important forms of manipulation and other top—bottom antagonisms occurred. Unlike the other developments which resulted from the separation of upper organizations and locals, these "class" conflicts had a long-range potential and were resolved only with the liquidation of one or another of the "interests." That is, it is impossible for a protest organization to function if its leadership and membership have different class interests. Either the leadership is removed or the membership is diverted to useless activities.

The Farmers' Alliance and the Southern Tenant Farming System

The Alliance and the tenancy system faced each other as adversaries. Tenancy, with its awkward shape and inelegant style, was fueled by the overwhelming strength of its internal dynamics, and it created its own defenders among those at the top. At the same time, it antagonized the individuals upon whose labor it depended. The Alliance harnessed the discontent of this immiserated population and organized it into a coordinated counterforce to the tenancy system. But the Alliance itself contained the contradictions of the system from which it had sprung: Different groups were absorbed into the organization and the conflicting interests were built into its very structure.

The conflict between the Alliance and the tenant farming system therefore had two incarnations besides the overt contradiction between the protest group and the system. One was the day-to-day tenant—yeoman versus landlord—merchant struggle we have already discussed and which led to the creation of the Alliance. The other was the friction created within the Alliance, a refraction of the society-wide conflict which gave birth to farmers' protest. The entrance of elite elements into the organization meant that the same contradiction arose as a part of the internal life of the group. The organization history we have just reviewed reveals the manifold areas in which this contradiction was expressed. The process of expansion led to the absorption of planters Farmers' Association into a yeoman—tenant group. The pressures for expansion and political visibility led to the promotion of these same individuals. The ebb and flow of economic protest pushed the Alliance into an increasingly centralized structure which allowed for leadership autonomy. The exigencies of finance and communication fitted into this pattern by creating cooptative pressures. The history of the Alliance is partly the history of parallel changes: the class make-up of the leadership became more elite as the organization became more dependent upon the leadership.

At the same time, however, the crop lien system was working its inevitable havoc upon tenants and yeoman. As the Alliance grew, it became more and more the central institution to which the Southern farmer turned for relief. This continuous and increasing influx of angry debtors expanded and consolidated the basis for mass action and protest. By the late 1880s, the Alliance had grown to nearby 1 million members: It was the largest mass protest group ever assembled by American farmers.

The forces at work inside the Alliance reflected the forces at work on the outside. But the equation was different and outcome was not inevitably a replay of the larger game. The activities of the Alliance were determined by the complicated rules by which the behavior of protest organizations are governed, and therefore we turn now to those considerations.

III

THEORETICAL CONSIDERATIONS

8

Defining the Farmer's Alliance

The tenant system created problems for farmers and these problems aroused discontent. The discontent led to protest, but the protest was useless unless it was coordinated and channeled into actions that produced social change. A specialized organization designed for this task was needed.

The Farmers' Alliance was a "conflict" organization designed to aid its membership in fighting with other organizations over some rewards or gains. While many organizations are involved in conflict, certain organizations are designed to function primarily in conflict situations. Thus, while a business competes with other businesses, its principal function is to produce goods at low cost. This results in tremendous internal conflict between owner and employees, but this is an *intraorganizational* conflict and its structure reflects this fact. On the other hand, the workers in the business may form a union to give shape and direction in the conflict to their interests. The structure of the business contrasts sharply with the structure of the union (or the Farmers' Alliance), which is designed to give organizational articulation to the conflict between workers and management.

Protest organizations are designed to attack a given structure, and they are specially constructed for this task. Sometimes the opposition is well defined; a union easily focuses its attention on the corporation in which its members are employed. Other times, the target is not clearly perceivable; the Farmers' Alliance did not always perceive the boundaries of the cotton tenancy system it challenged. But in either case, the protest group *derives* from the parent structure, is indelibly influenced by that structure, and would have no purpose without it.

These two aspects—the basis in conflict and its derivative nature— distinguish the protest organization from other "mutual benefit associations."[1] Little attention has been paid to the structural consequences of these features,

[1]Peter Blau and W. Richard Scott, *Formal Organizations: A Comparative Approach* (San Francisco, 1962), pp 45–49, contains a full description of this more general type of group.

though they are crucial in determining the functioning of an organization.[2]

In order to effect change, an organization must have some leverage, or power, over the system it wishes to change. Power can derive from "institutional" or "noninstitutional" sources. Consider, for example, the contrast between landlord—merchant power and yeoman-tenant power. Once a tenant was indebted to his supplier, the supplier could, because of the lien law, grant or withhold food and supplies. This conferred upon the landlord vast power to make decisions about cultivation, to force the tenant to alter his behavior or change his farming policy to suit the landlord. On the other hand, the tenants under a landlord also had power. If they could organize and uniformly withhold their labor, they could force the landlord to change his policy or else lose the whole crop. This, of course, depended on the prevention of his farming other tenants to take the place of the strikers. In other words, a good organization was needed.

Landlords did exercise power over tenants and tenants *could* exercise power over landlords. However, there is a fundamental difference between the two types of power. The power of the landlord rested on the enforcement of the lien law. If there were no lien law, then the tenant could escape the landlord's power by buying or borrowing from some other merchant or supplier. He could even offer to pay back the new supplier first, if there were no lien law. Thus, he could escape the leverage of the landlord. The landlord's power rested on his having the force of the state behind him. If a tenant (or another merchant or supplier) did not abide by the lien law, then the whole force of the state could be brought to bear on the situation. If the force of the state were not available—for whatever reason—the power of the landlord dissolved.

The tenants, in contrast, exercised power without the aid of the state. Once their strike was organized, and for as long as it was maintained, they exerted a power independent of the state. Whereas the state could prevent the landlord from exercising any power at all simply by refusing to enforce the lien law, it could not affect the power of the tenants if their strike held—except through the use of police, and even this tactic did not always work.

It is clear from these considerations that we can distinguish between power that depends on the state and power that rests on sources outside the state. The former power can be called *institutional* power; the latter, *noninstitutional* power.

One might argue that the landlord could exercise power without the state if he could organize other landlords or suppliers to obey the lien law. That is, if the tenants could organize to exercise leverage over landlords, then landlords could organize to exercise leverage over their tenants. If all available suppliers organized, then they could enforce the lien law without any help from the state. If this were accomplished, then the landlords, too, would be exercising noninstitutional

---

[2]A notable and important exception is Ralf Dahrendorf, *Class and Class Conflict in Industrial Society* (Palo Alto, Calif., 1959), especially pp. 157–205. Dahrendorf treats protest groups as a unique category, and in that sense his book provides the theoretical background to the approach used here, though the conclusions I reach disagree in many ways. Dahrendorf focuses upon the conditions under which protest will arise, while this study investigates the functioning of an already existing protest group.

power. In fact, one can see an intimate connection between the two sorts of power by looking at this example a little more closely. Crop liens were given long before there were lien laws, and they were enforced by just such an organization of suppliers. However, eventually, landlords looked to the government for uniform and consistent enforcement of these contracts, and the lien laws were the result. After the enactment of lien laws, of course, the landlords no longer needed as tight an organization since the state was now in charge of enforcement.

This shift—from depending on formal or informal organizations of suppliers to depending on the state for enforcement—is the *institutionalization* of power. Institutionalization does not mean that the source of power has become institutionalized, it means that the *source of power has changed.* When lien laws were passed, the *source* of power of the lien shifted from the organized power of suppliers to the established police power of the government.

Consider another example. The Farmers' Alliance began by boycotting gougers and mass buying at those stores which agreed to give Alliance members a good price. The Alliance hoped to force all (surviving) merchants to lower their prices. This represented the use of noninstitutional power—power which flowed from the organized buying power of the farmers. Later, the Populist party tried to elect officials who would pass *laws* against price gouging. This was an attempt to get the state to enforce what previously had been attempted through the organization of farmers. The *source* of the power would be changed.

Moreover, we can see that the act of entering elections is itself a shift from the use of noninstitutional to institutional power. This is much like the contrast between landlords' power and tenants' power. By the use of the boycott, the tenants could win regardless of the stance the state took on the question. Elections, on the other hand, could be successful only if the government as a whole supported the rights of the insurgent forces. Elections could be declared "illegal" or fraud could be practiced by those in control of state apparatus, and thus an electoral majority could be deprived of its victory. The farmers would not have any recourse, however unjust the action, unless they could get the courts or the legislature to act for them. But these forces, the courts or the legislature, are once again the government. The power still lay with the government. Thus, unlike the tenants' boycott, which exercised power independent of the power holders and the state, the electoral insurgency could succeed only with the sufferance of those in control of the state apparatus. Electoral power is institutional in character.

The essence of all power is the ability to prevent someone from doing something he or she wants to do. To make this clear, let us return to the landlord–tenant example. On the one hand, the landlord in the tenant system had overt power as soon as he obtained a lien; the threat of refusing further supplies forced the tenant to obey the landlord in many realms. On the other hand, the tenant had a latent power; if he and the other tenants refused to grow the crops, the landlord would lose a great deal of money. (The power was latent because it depended on the organization of other people.)

Both tenant and landlord derived their power from the structure of their relationship. The landlord's power flowed from his ability to refuse to perform his role as supplier (along with the enforcement of the lien law, which prevented anyone else from performing it). The tenant's power lay in his ability to refuse to play his role as crop cultivator (along with his ability to organize other tenants to refuse). The entire history of the Farmers' Alliance can be seen as a series of attempts to harness the potential power which flowed from the position of the farmer in the economic and political structure. The Alliance boycotts, for example, were attempts to use the farmer's position in the economic supply structure (that of customer) to effect changes in that structure (reduction of prices, better merchandise).

The power relationship between landlord and tenant is called a *contradiction.* Each is dependent upon the other, but an advance of one is contingent upon damage to the interests of the other. Moreover, one is dominant, the other subordinate: On a day-to-day basis the tenant could not overcome the power of the landlord. One tenant acting alone could not influence the system to any degree. Only when all the tenants employed by a single landlord acted in unison, could they exert tremendous pressure.[3] This points to an essential ingredient of noninstitutional conflict groups—they require mass organization. Without the united efforts of most, if not all, of the people who are in similar circumstances, none of these people has much power. Thus, if one tenant quit, he was easily replaced. But if all quit, the landlord was in trouble. If one customer refused to buy at a merchant's store, there was little pressure on the owner. But if many boycotted, the storekeeper had to worry about the fate of his business.

We can designate this relationship as that of "the many to the few." In most situations where there is a contradiction between two groups of people, on one side, the dominant side, the service is provided by relatively few people to relatively many people. Thus, one merchant supplied many farmers and one landlord had many tenants. This is a large component of the ability to dominate because the small group can easily frame and execute a common policy to its mutual advantage. The other side, with many people involved, finds it harder to organize and therefore harder to exercise its potential power. The "many" must make strenuous efforts to organize, efforts which are often thwarted by the few, who see clearly that their dominance is threatened.

One further point must be made about conflict groups. We have seen that the power of the individual can be realized only by all acting in concert. This, of course, is the essence of organization. However, what must be underscored is that power implies not only coordinated action, but also a coordinated change of behavior. For example, in the Alliance boycotts of merchants, power was exercised by farmers' refusing to buy at the merchants' stores until prices were lowered. This strategy would not have been effective unless the Alliance ensured that the customers would return when the prices were lowered. (This example demon-

---

[3] This conforms with the classical Marxist use of the term. See Mao Tse Tung, *On Contradiction* (Peking: Foreign Language Press, 1970).

strates the weakness of a "spontaneous boycott" in which the victim has no guarantee that change will win back his customers.) Therefore, truly effective organization requires organizational discipline—the willingness of the bulk of members to agree to act in concert, to coordinate this activities, and then to change their behavior together. Only with such disciplines can a conflict group which depends on mass organization realize its potential power.

We have been discussing the attributes of noninstitutional conflict organizations. We can briefly review these attributes and then proceed to a discussion of the behavioral laws of these groups.

1. *Conflict groups* are designed to develop power in order to fight against some self-conscious adversary. Their task is to battle for certain commodities with other groups. There is a *contradiction* between themselves and their adversary—a relationship in which one side loses when the other gains.

2. Protest groups are *derivative*. They are generated by a certain parent social structure of organization and their main purpose is to effect change in that structure.

3. *Noninstitutional* power does not depend on laws and law enforcement. This power, and the power of groups which exercise it, is *alegal* (if not illegal).

4. *Institutionalization* of power means changing the source of power so that the government now enforces the same policies that were previously enforced by noninstitutional means. It does not mean that the *source* of power has been "recognized" or "integrated into the structure," but rather that a different power source is now enforcing the policies which the noninstitutional power source had previously enforced.

5. *Structural power* derives from the role an individual or group plays in a structure. Although all power flows from the ability to take away from the adversary his, or her ability to do something, structural power implies that the powerholder is an integral part of the system—that his or her day-to-day activities are necessary for the system to work. A strike is an exercise of structural power, while bombing a building is not.

6. *Mass organization* depends on bringing together large numbers of people in order to exercise power. None of the individuals could exercise power without the coordinated efforts of large numbers of those in similar circumstances.

7. *Organizational discipline* is the ability of an organization to get its membership to act in a coordinated fashion and to *change* its behavior according to organizational decisions.

9

The Parameters of Organizational Behavior

Underlying any analysis of protest organizations is a set of fundamental propositions about the forces that condition and limit these groups. In many ways, it is these propositions which are being tested both in the elaboration of theory and in the concrete descriptions of Alliance activities. To clarify and sharpen what follows, therefore, it is useful to make these propositions explicit and to discuss alternative approaches found in other discussions of mass protest.

Rationality and Irrationality

People who join protest organizations are at least as rational as those who study them. Each member is a hypothesis-testing social scientist who begins with ideas about how to accomplish certain explicit ends and quite routinely modifies (or does not modify) these ideas as events or new information provide him or her with data about their correctness. The original ideas derive from previous experiences, and the new ideas which arise to displace the old ones must "prove" themselves by better explaining old and new experiences.

Despite this rationality, individuals and groups of individuals can adopt and act upon totally erroneous and counterproductive theories and ideas. Furthermore, once an idea is empirically contradicted, there is no guarantee that it will be replaced by an accurate one—or even that it will be replaced! Finally, not everyone in an organization will have the same ideas or soon come to complete agreement.

Thus, although members of protest organizations are rational, they often do not possess all the facts they need to assess the situation accurately, and they frequently make judgments—individually or collectively—which are wrong.

This straightforward approach to human behavior has found little favor in the most prominent analyses of social movements. Instead, theorists like Lang and Lang, Turner and Killian, and Smelser, despite some structural concerns, have sought a social psychological explanation for protest behavior.[1] This social psychological approach posits that protesters do not undertake an action primarily because it is a reasonable solution to a well-defined problem. Rather, actions are chosen primarily because they suit the "personality" of the individual or fulfill some temporary psychic needs, whether or not they have a reasonable chance of success. Thus, while social movements may adopt tactics that could be the best way to achieve their stated ends, this is by no means the normal situation. Feuer, for example, asserts that student movements have "been largely dominated by unconscious drives" and that their activities are guided not at all by a rational pursuit of their stated goals.[2]

To underscore the dramatic contrast between the structural, "rational," view presented here and the social psychological, "irrational," approach, consider the apparently simple question: Why did people join the Farmers' Alliance? The theory of rationality offers the answer that most members saw the group as a promising mechanism for redressing grievances against the tenancy system. A few others saw it as a possible vehicle for personal aggrandizement. In either case, the motives were straightforward projections of roles played in the outside system.

But the issue is much more complicated. Why didn't every yeoman and tenant join the Alliance? If it is rational for one to join, wasn't it rational for another? Stated more generally, this question becomes the central issue in the study of mass movements. What causes two individuals to disagree over how to resolve their common problems? Every social movement has revealed such disagreements. Certainly no movement has mobilized everyone it proposed to serve. Furthermore, among the mobilized there are important disagreements in strategy. The Civil Rights movement of the early 1960s had many different tendencies, ranging from initiation of lawsuits by the NAACP (National Association for the Advancement of Colored People) to armed resistance practiced by the Deacons for Defense in Alabama, Louisiana, and Mississippi.[3] The antiwar movement of the late 1960s also divided over tactics: The SDS (Students for a Democratic Society) initiated militant action; the Mobilization Committee and various other groups undertook nonmilitant agitation; supporters of Eugene McCarthy and other "peace" candidates adopted electoral strategies. And beyond that, within each tendency, divisions occurred and reoccurred over tactical and strategic orientation. Sometimes these intraorganizational divisions were quite spectacular: the split in SDS led to three separate groups.[4] Other times, the divisions led to the expulsion of one tendency, as in the abandonment of the Monroe, North Carolina, chapter of the

---

[1] Kurt Lang and Gladys Lang, *Collective Dynamics* (New York, 1961); Ralph Turner and Lewis M. Killian, *Collective Behavior*, 2d ed. (Englewood Cliffs, N.J., 1972); Neil J. Smelser, *The Theory of Collective Behavior* (New York, 1962).

[2] Lewis Feuer, *The Conflict of Generations* (New York, 1969), quoted in Turner and Killian, *op. cit.*, p. 377. For a powerful refutation of this theory see Max Heirich, *The Spiral of Conflict: Berkeley, 1964* (New York, 1968), especially ch. 1.

[3] For information on this short-lived, but very significant, group see *New York Times*, June 6, 1965, p. 1; *ibid.*, July 9, 1965, p. 1; *ibid.*, August 15, 1965, sec. IV; *ibid.*, August 30, 1965, p. 18; *ibid.*, January 29, 1966, p. 9; *ibid.*, April 6, 1966, p. 29; *ibid.*, September 17, 1966, p. 26.

[4] Alan Adelson, *S.D.S., A Profile* (New York, 1971), contains a useful description of these divisions; see chs. 1–2.

NAACP when it began using guns to defend itself against Ku Klux Klan attacks.[5] Many times, internal conflicts are resolved without undue strife, but frequently a trace of the differences is found in changes of policy and ideology of the organization. The shift of the Congress of Racial Equality from an integrationist nonviolent militant action group to a nationalist Black capitalism group is a case in point.[6]

Certainly the explanation for these enormously complex phenomena involves a whole range of variables, but at the core of this complexity lies a relatively simple question: Why do two individuals with apparently the same problems find themselves advocating and pursuing entirely different and sometimes conflicting solutions?

There are four possibilities:

1. Both solutions are practical and will solve the problem. Pursuit of either one is rational.

2. One or both of the people are not behaving rationally. The cause of this may be "irrational" in that the individual tries to pursue his or her goals, but certain psychological problems present him or her from thinking clearly. Or the cause may be "arational" in that the individual is maximizing some emotional need like companionship instead of pursuing his or her stated goals.

3. There is only an apparent similarity in the problems of the two individuals. In fact, they have different goals, resources, and/or interests and each one is rationally pursuing his or her own goals. What is rational for one is not rational for the other.

4. One or both are wrong, but both are still behaving rationally. Much like a scientist doing research, a person with troubles tries to uncover the source and solution through the analysis of data. Most often neither the researcher nor the protester possesses all the data needed; often they possess incorrect, misleading, or prejudiced data, and therefore many incorrect hypotheses "fit" the existing data. The honest disputes which exist for many years in science do not necessarily imply that one side or the other is irrational. They often indicate that the information is simply not available to decide which view is correct. And even after the information becomes available, those adhering to the incorrect point of view may rationally maintain that perspective until they themselves see the data. Thus, an individual may quite rationally pursue incorrect and hopeless strategies to solve problems if one or another of two conditions exist: The information does not exist to demonstrate the hopelessness of the strategy, or the information exists but is not available to that person.

Let us discuss each of the four alternatives in turn. Consider the first possibility: Two individuals adopt two equally correct but different strategies to solve their common problems. This is certainly possible, but the evaluation of two differing tactics goes far beyond whether or not they will work. The two tactics are bound

[5] Robert F. Williams, *Negroes with Guns*, ed. Marc Schleifer (New York, 1962).
[6] Earl Ofari, *The Myth of Black Capitalism* (New York, 1970).

to differ in many important ways, among them the chances of rapid success, the expense involved, and the risks involved. These considerations are important to people who are trying to decide how to redress grievances. Therefore, when two individuals disagree it must be because of one of the following possibilities.

One or both is not thinking rationally about the comparison. For example, one may be so enamored of the possibility of rapid success that he or she does not see that he or she has not clearly evaluated the risks that make the given tactic less sure.

The two have different resources or goals which makes one solution better for one; the other better for the other. Their difference of opinion is rational. For example, one individual might have less time but more money and therefore advocate a more expensive but quicker solution.

Either one or both may lack the necessary information to see the inferiority of the proposals they have made. Given the amount of data available, both solutions are rational. For example it may not be possible to assess the relative costs or risks of two plans. Nonconclusive arguments could be made for either one.

We see, then, that the first possibility, when broken down, amounts to a re-definition of the next three. Of these, the first two (nos. 2 and 3 above) have received attention from theorists of social movements. The third has been un-justifiably ignored and will form the heart of the analysis presented here.

Consider, then, the second possibility: that one or both individuals is behaving irrationally. How frequently do individuals believe that they are pursuing one goal, but are actually unconsciously responding to some other psychological or emotional imperative? If we are to believe the bulk of social movement literature, this is the explanation for the overwhelming majority of social movements.[7] Mostly, this view is assumed, but not discussed, and the rationale for this approach cannot be evaluated. Neil Smelser expresses clearly the crucial logic underlying the irrationalist position. He begins by characterizing the ideas that motivate social movements (and all other forms of collective behavior) as "wish fulfillment."[8] "For instance," he writes,

> in the norm-oriented movement, we shall find extraordinary results promised if only certain reforms are adopted, and (on the negative side) gloomy predictions of decay and collapse if the sources of strain are not attacked quickly and vigorously. Adherents to such movements exaggerate reality because their action is based on beliefs which are both *generalized and short circuited.*[9]

Given this general description of the peculiar beliefs which motivate participation in collective behavior, Smelser can specify the type of "short circuit" involved in any particular mode of activity, from rumor to revolution. All are equally inadequate as reasoning processes, but they are significantly different in terms

---

[7] Anthony Oberschall, *Social Conflict and Social Movements* (Englewood Cliffs, N.J.: Prentice-Hall, 1973), pp. 3–5, 11–16, offers a succinct review of the intellectual roots of this orientation, though he overemphasizes the degree to which recent theories (Killian's and Gusfield's, in particular) have discarded these notions; see pp. 140–141 of this volume.

[8] Smelser, *op. cit.*, pp. 71–72.

[9] *Ibid.*, p. 72.

of the behavior they produce.[10] In other words, the assumption of irrationality (or arationality) is one foundation of Smelser's typology of collective action.

This approach implies a far-reaching conclusion about social movements: They are not useful mechanisms of social change. After all, if the reasoning behind them is shortcircuited and the results promised "extraordinary wishfulfillment," they can hardly be the appropriate mechanism for social change. Smelser assesses their role as follows: "Episodes of collective behavior often constitute an early stage of social change; they occur when conditions of strain have arisen, but before social resources have been mobilized for a specific and possibly effective attack on the sources of strain."[11] The logic here is brutally straightforward. If the basic ideas that motivate collective protest are not well reasoned, then it follows inevitably that the movement cannot be the best avenue to the changes being sought.

In one swoop, Smelser has argued away *any possibility* that social movements are reasonable, sensible methods of redressing grievances, and it is this logical jump which reveals the fallacy behind the "irrationalist" approach to social movements. We can see this if we scrutinize the method by which the thought process is proven to be irrational. There is no direct proof offered that the thinking is "exaggerated" or "short-circuited," that the radical ideas are not accurate assessments of the situation. Instead, the proof always rests on the prima facie assessment of the tactics used. Smelser, for example, assumes that any collective activity is irrational if it "disregards many existing moral and legal restrictions and violates the interests and integrity of many individuals and groups."[12] Smelser cannot apprehend the existence of a situation in which such disruptive behavior might be an unfortunate necessity or perhaps the only means of preventing major social disaster.

This argument is found in many contexts, and we need not belabor it here. The point is that the "individual irrationality" argument really depends upon an assumption that the social movement as a whole is irrational. This assumption is testable. The irrationality hypothesis predicts that any given movement will undertake activities that could not achieve the desired goals—the "short-circuited" logic leads the movement astray.

Obviously, not all social movements have been irrational, and this should, by itself, undermine the logic of Smelser's argument. But the dispute does not die that easily. Two issues remain.

First, even if some social movements behave rationally, how can one explain movements that pursue tactics incapable of producing desired results. One could posit that some social movements recruit rational individuals, while others recruit "short-circuited" thinkers. However, careful observation reveals that even the most irrational movements act rationally in various situations or at various times. The irrationality hypothesis therefore requires that the individuals in a movement

---

[10] *Ibid.,* pp. 80–130.
[11] *Ibid.,* p. 73.
[12] *Ibid.,* p. 72.

phase in and out of rational thought in unison. This is absurd. It is much more reasonable to assume that the mistakes of a social movement are produced by structural processes which do not depend upon identically irrational ideas in the bulk of the membership.

Second, it is clear that people behave irrationally much of the time. Social movements certainly cannot be immune to this endemic problem. To be sure, individuals are frequently irrational in their behavior, but large social movements involve many different individuals. For a great many people all to exhibit the same irrationality at the same time requires the existence of powerful and visible social forces. In the absence of these, it is reasonable to suppose that the small irrationalities will cancel each other out.

Many theorists search for exactly these visible social forces to explain certain mass activities. Oberschall, for example, declares that people will fight harder around symbolic issues than material ones because "the elimination of the personal element in conflict tends to make conflict sharper and more intense, tends to imbue the participants with self-righteousness and moral fervor that keeps being re-enforced through group support."[13] Thus, while for the most part participants in social movements are characterized by "rationality" and "selfishness,"[14] they abandon both of these traits in the emotional reaction to symbolic conflict: "Disrespect for symbols or an attempt to substitute different symbols will be perceived as an attack on the integrity, moral standing, sense of identity, and self-respect of the entire nation or group, threatening the basic consensus and principles of legitimacy upon which social order is founded."[15]

In this conceptualization, people mostly are rational, but certain things, like nationalism, are "arational"—agreed upon with faith and held as unchallengeable values. An appeal to these deeply held beliefs nets an emotional, not a rational, response. Furthermore, it is easy to spot the social forces generating these emotions because they are visible and important features of the socialization system.

This seems, therefore, to be a reasonable middle road. Unfortunately, under scrutiny it becomes just as monolithic and vulnerable as Smelser's: The theory assumes that these emotional attachments are permanent and pervasive. For example, consider the individuals who attack the underlying values and trigger the emotional response. They are not any less socialized than those who defend the values. So how does one explain their willingness to attack, except by asserting that socialization does not affect each person equally? Moreover, even the most extreme construction of this theory admits that individuals are sometimes caught up in symbolic conflict and sometimes they are unresponsive to it. That is, it is not true that "disrespect for symbols" will inevitably be "perceived as an attack." Sometimes it will be and sometimes it will not be so perceived.

---

[13] Oberschall, *op. cit.*, p. 50.

[14] *Ibid.*, p. 25.

[15] *Ibid.*, p. 50. In another context, Oberschall argues that participants in social conflict are characterized by "rationality with respect to means and ends and selfishness with respect to motives" (p. 25). These two arguments taken together lead to the paradox that people in social movements are basically motivated by selfish rationality, but they fight hardest when engaged in unselfish causes.

What then, determines who will be loyal to which values and when they will defend them? Oberschall's logic suggests that loyalty is a function of the degree of exposure to socialization. Those who are least exposed to the value-developing devices would be the first to abandon them and those most exposed would be the last to defend them. No evidence has ever been generated to demonstrate this. Instead, analysts have studied the conflict and simply *assumed* that those who attack the system are the least socialized and those who defend it are the most socialized.

This kind of argument is circular and it assumes away the possibility that the two sides are motivated by rational instead of emotional considerations. It is perfectly reasonable to posit that those who attack symbols do so out of self-interest—the benefits of a successful broad attack may be very great. Those who defend the system may benefit from its defense. For example, it is quite possible that "an attempt to substitute symbols" *really is* an attack on the integrity, etc., of a society and that it *really does* threaten "the basic consensus and principles of legitimacy upon which the social order is founded." Many individuals may (rationally and reluctantly) decide that such an attack is the only way they can redress their very deep grievances. Others may (rationally and enthusiastically) decide that such an attack is a powerful threat to their style of life and standard of living. Such a circumstance would result in deep and intense social conflict, but it would not represent any differential socialization whatever. Both sides might be behaving emotionally, but their emotions would be adjuncts of rational calculations, and the intensity would not be caused by emotions but by the very important issues at stake.

The irrationality approach and its "arational" derivative are actually assumptions about the cause of social movements. They offer little to help us in the understanding of protest groups, because they provide no way to predict protest activities. Instead they offer a post hoc "explanation" for the puzzling aspects of protest activities, and even this post hoc explanation crumbles under scrutiny.

The rationalist perspective suggests analyses that are subject to measurement, and it explains how individuals can be regularly involved in symbolic conflict without resorting to clumsy theories of competing values. Its apparent weakness is that it seems to assume "superrationality"—that individuals are always in complete command of their self-interest. However, this assumption is not necessary to the argument, as we shall presently discover.

Let us consider now the third possibility for explaining differences over tactics: that differences indicate contrasting goals, resources, or interests. A good way to illustrate the problems with this approach is to consider the pluralist theory of American government.[16] Pluralists argue that when a situation arises which causes difficulties for a group of citizens, they will ordinarily form an "interest group" which seeks to redress their grievances. This guarantees that the rights and desires of every grouping in the United States are represented.

[16] The main variants of this theory can be found in Robert Dahl, *A Preface to Democratic Theory* (Chicago, 1956); David Truman, *The Government Process: Political Interests and Public Opinion* (New York, 1957); and Arnold Rose, *The Power Structure* (New York, 1967).

According to the pluralists, therefore, when an individual has complaints, he or she will do the rational thing: form a group to pressure the government. But then why do some individuals in the aggrieved population join the group while others do not? And, within the group, what accounts for disagreements of strategy and tactics. The pluralists seek the answer to these questions in the analysis of "background" variables that subdivide any particular group according to sub-interests.[17] Thus, even with the same economic grievances, Catholics and Protestants are expected to respond to different proposals differently, in accordance with their contrasting moralities. Old people and young people disagree over what kinds of social welfare to support because of their differing welfare needs.

All this is very sensible if it is not assumed to be the only process at work. Certainly those who experience problems will seek to solve them, and people with different needs may pursue different ends. But to assume that one will always—or even frequently—see clearly what programs will satisfy both one's needs and desires is quite absurd. The "rationality" that the pluralists assert is really "superrationality." Social systems function to obscure and distort the sources of problems and to make individuals with similar grievances see them as different. Whether or not people with common grievances will perceive them as "common" is a serious question which depends upon a great many structural factors. The most rational and sensible individual is trapped by the information and perspectives bequeathed him or her by the social structure, and therefore the formation of pressure groups is always problematical. "Rationality" has its limits. Indeed, in many situations none of the "rational" solutions will work, and the "correct" solution cannot be found.

Because of the ambiguities that social structures create, the fourth possibility in the list given above is centrally important to understanding social movements. Information and understanding is scattered unevenly and to some degree randomly within a social structure. Those who seek to redress grievances have only imperfect knowledge of their plight and that of others. Since each person possesses a different set of facts and ideas, different people believe in different solutions.

In large part, the task of a protest group is to facilitate the exchange of information and initiate actions that test the practicality of the competing ideas. But this process is problematical, indeed, involving as it does so many other factors we have yet to discuss. The relationship between this "structured ignorance" and the question of rationality, irrationality, and arationality can now be clarified.

We have asked: What distinguished those who joined from those who did not join the Farmers' Alliance? There are two answers to this question.

First, not everyone occupied the same position in the tenancy system. In the beginning, the Alliance adopted programs that would benefit yeoman but not

[17] The most famous example of this sort of approach was a predictive analysis of the 1960 and 1964 presidential elections which attempted to predict the voting behavior of 420 different categories of individuals, then aggregate these figures into state-by-state scores. Ithiel de Sola Pool, Robert P. Abelson, and Samuel Popkin, *Candidates, Issues and Strategies* (Cambridge, Mass., 1964).

tenants, and therefore tenants with a clear understanding of the system quite logically rejected the Alliance while their yeoman neighbors were joining. Later, when Alliance programs offered the promise of serving tenants, tenants joined in greater numbers. As far as it goes, this "pluralist" argument is correct, but it does not answer the question completely. Despite this logic, a great many yeomen did not join, and more than a few tenants did join at first. The pluralist might seek to find subgroupings to explain this: In areas where there was prosperity, there would be less Alliance activity, religious interests might impinge, and so on. Certainly there is virtue in this procedure and no analysis of the Alliance could proceed without it. But it soon produces very much diminished returns without finally explaining why some rich farmers joined and many poor yeomen did not.

Ultimately the answer must be sought in an understanding of the ambiguities produced by life under the tenancy system. Cotton farmers in the 1880s were exposed to a great many different ideas about how to improve farming. Crop diversification, more intensive labor, waiting for a good year, political action within the Democratic party, and joining the Farmers' Alliance were only a few of the proposed solutions. Perhaps if every farmer had had the same experience or had as complete a view as 80 years of hindsight allows us to obtain, agreement as to the correct action might have been greater. But in 1880, different people had had widely different experiences in the tenancy system; some had tried crop diversification and failed while others had yet to try it; some had worked hard in the Democratic party without success while others had not or had had ambiguous experiences; some had seen the failure of the Grange and interpreted that failure as final evidence against protest while others had seen a glimmer of hope therein.

With hindsight, we may be able to say that certain strategies were doomed to fail, and even in the 1880s, it might have been possible to demonstrate conclusively that one or another option was superior or inferior. But given the lack of communication and the widely differing experiences that cotton farmers had had with tenancy, a great many different solutions could be articulately and persuasively defended.

Southern cotton farmers were "rational," but not superrational. Many different, but plausible, strategies presented themselves; different individuals therefore pursued different strategies—though most of these were doomed to failure. But what determined who chose what option? Given two equally plausible and certainly rational ideas, who will choose which one? In this context, we can see the role that irrational or arational motives can play. In an ambiguous situation, psychological and emotional predilections certainly will influence a person's choice.

But we must point out that this influence is small compared to that of differing experiences. Even in the same town, different individuals had had widely varying experiences with cotton farming. One person had experimented extensively; another had tried improving his application of a single method of cultivation; one person was new to farming; another had had great experience; one person had had both great success and great failure; another had seen steady immiseration; one tenant had had a strict landlord; another had had only lax ones. The sources of these different experiences are buried in the complexities of the tenancy system, but at least one consequence is clear: When different individuals seek to analyze their common problems (if indeed they are common), they will bring to the task entirely different bodies of data. These differences will make the same idea seem very promising to one person and meritless to another. One need not search for different personality types to explain differences in analysis between individuals, however much such personality differences exist. Different experiences produce different opinions.

The most important implication of this argument has to do with "attitude change." If differences of opinion reflect different information, then any process of information exchange should bring about convergences of opinion. Since protest groups bring together individuals around the particular purpose of redressing grievances, they generally produce arguments, research, and action directed toward the problems, which result in the exchange of information among members (and, to a lesser extent, non-members), the compiling of new data that speak to arguments and disputes, and activities that try to apply one or several theories on how to cure the troubles. This process serves to homogenize the information the members possess, to invalidate many opinions by newly uncovered evidence, and to bring about greater unanimity among the membership.

This portrait of the organizational process contrasts sharply with the views most often expressed about protest groups. Consider, for a moment, a change in an organization's demands. If one assumes that organizations inevitably express the interests of their membership, then any change in organizational behavior must represent a change in the membership or else a change in interests. If one looks at organizational activities as an expression of emotional needs, such shifts must indicate a change in these needs. Neither of these hypotheses is particularly appealing. But if we see change as the replacement of a failing strategy by a more promising one, such switches in program become comprehensible.

To summarize the discussion thus far, we can review the answers to the fundamental question posed earlier: Why did people join the Farmers' Alliance?

The social psychological theory seeks the answer to this question in the analysis of the emotional needs of the membership and the ways organizational activities fulfill these needs. Members *think* that they are pursuing reform, but they are wrong. In this sense, they are irrational—they blind themselves to their own true purposes; or they are "arational"—they are moved by emotion and not by logic. In this analysis, one person joins the group while another fails to join because each has different emotional needs.

The pluralist theory seeks the answer to our question in the refined analysis of the self-interest of each individual involved. A person joins an organization because it will help him or her reach a desired end, and refuses to join if it cannot help. Since there is much diversity among individuals, the reasons for joining can always be found by a close enough analysis of each individual. This type of analysis is "superrational" because it assumes that each member possesses enough information about the prospects of the organization, the actual outcomes of a proposed activity (before the activity is tried), and his or her own needs to make a judgment about joining or not joining. One person joins and another refuses because of different self-interest.

The rationalist theory seeks the answer to this question in an analysis of the "parent" social structure. Individuals join social movements because their experience with the system makes it plausible for them to try the tactics those movements propose. Large numbers join movements because they have similar grievances and similar experiences which lead to similar conclusions about how to change things. Many times, these conclusions are wrong, but they are not *irrational*—any more than a false scientific generalization based on inadequate data is irrational. One person may join an organization while another refuses because the available information is ambiguous. The different decision need not reflect different emotional needs and it need not reflect different self-interest. It will most likely reflect different bodies of information, with each decision being "rational" in its context.

Oberschall has summarized the rationalist perspective quite forcefully.

> The rational component in social conflict and collective behavior is present in much the same way as it is present in other choice and decisionmaking situations in everyday life.... This principle applies to the incumbents and the agents of social control as much as to their opponents. Both sides lack full and accurate information about each other; they have misconceptions about each other's strengths and weaknesses; and they respond to concrete problems and choices in complex ways, with a mixture of outrage, anger, puzzlement, and shrewd, informed calculation. The information and conceptions they possess can be found out by means of empirical study and can then be fed back into the model of man, the decisionmaker, whose main features are rationality with respect to means and selfishness with respect to goals.[18]

The Role of the Social Structure in the Behavior of Social Movements

There is a certain intimacy between a social structure and a protest group attempting to change it. The protest organization is derivative from this "parent" structure in so many ways that no such movement can be understood without constant reference to these crucial connections. In a way, the two structures are engaged in an elaborate dance with the motions of the one responding in subtle and overt ways to that of the other, and then triggering equally subtle and dramatic responses.

This point is almost completely neglected in even the most informed literature on protest organizations. One symptom of this is the failure to distinguish protest groups from other organizations which do not share their derivative nature.

---

[18] Oberschall, *op. cit.*, p. 25. Ironically, Oberschall himself does not consistently use his own model of man (see p. 140 of this volume).

Hirschman, in a generally thoughtful and sometimes extremely useful discussion of protest within organizations, describes his work as follows:

> The argument to be presented starts with the firm producing saleable outputs for customers; but it will be found to be largely—and, at times, principally—applicable to organizations (such as voluntary associations, trade unions, or political parties) that provide services to their members without direct monetary counterpart.[19]

Trade unions are protest groups whose members are employed in the very business the union is trying to change. The membership is individually and collectively subject to the power of the structure it is attacking. This is certainly a very different sort of situation from that of the *customers* of that company, who have a sporadic and uncoercive connection to it. A union provides a service to its members and a company provides a service to its customers. But the union provides its "service" by forcibly exacting concessions through mass action and the threat of violence, while the corporation provides its customers service through production of goods, advertising, and market competition. Certainly the structures necessary to facilitate these processes are very different, and whatever similarities exist are conditioned and delimited by this profound distinction. Failure to distinguish among "service" organizations in terms of their relations to outside structures makes broad generalizations either abstract or suspect.

The major works on social movements and social protest give only minimal and unsystematic attention to these connections. Each of the three major texts on collective behavior deals with the "sources" of protest in one short chapter and scattered comments in other chapters.[20]

The work that has been done on the role of outside structure falls into three broad categories. First, for the social psychological perspective, the understanding of social movements lies in the analysis of membership psyche. Extensive effort has been made to analyze the role of social structure in the creation of the emotional and ideological variations among prospective members of groups. It is not surprising, therefore, to find in McLaughlin's reader one section on "Motivational Factors and Personality Dispositions" and another on "Conversion and Entrance to Membership." These sections delve into the kinds of psychic states that conducive to protest activity and, *within that context*, analyze the social structures that may produce them.[21]

Second, analyses are made of malfunctions in a social system which cause discontent and protest to arise. Turner and Killian, for example, argue that collective behavior of all kinds is triggered by unanticipated events, disruption of normal social relations, or a clash in values within a society.[22] In this kind of analysis,

---

[19] Albert O. Hirschman, *Exit, Voice and Loyalty: Responses to Decline in Firms, Organizations and States* (Cambridge, Mass., 1970), p. 8.

[20] Lang and Lang, *op. cit.*, pp. 3—23; Turner and Killian, *op. cit.*, ch. 4; Smelser, *op. cit.*, ch. III.

[21] Barry McLaughlin, ed., *Studies in Social Movements: A Social Psychological Perspective*, (New York, 1969) pp. 69—202; see also Lang and Lang, *op. cit.*, pp. 507—516.

[22] Turner and Killian, *op. cit.*, pp. 64—75.

the movement is seen against the background of the social system from which it arose, and the researcher scrutinizes the social system for the precipitating malfunction which brought the movement into existence.

Third, considerable attention has been given to the question of "structural conduciveness" of social structures in permitting protest groups to exist. For example, Smelser contrasts the social structure of the United States, which permitted wide protest against the dismissal of General MacArthur in 1951, and that of the Soviet Union, which "shrouded in secrecy" the dismissal of General Zhukov a few years later.[23] This concern is with the *general functioning* of the social system with regard to protest, and seeks to set a context for the behavior of *all* groups within that social system.[24]

It is neither practical nor useful to indulge in an elaborate critique of these approaches. A brief discussion of their weaknesses will help to clarify the thrust of the theory presented in this work.

First, the tremendous emphasis on the psychology of social movement membership is a simple extension of the assumptions of irrationality which permeate so much work in this field. Once a theorist assumes that the ideas that move social protest are "akin to magical beliefs"[25] and that the arguments that inform them are "of such an inferior kind that it is only by way of analogy that they can be described as reasoning,"[26] then it makes perfect sense to search everywhere for the sources of these peculiar psychic states. One logical place to look is in the parent social structure, and this explains the extensive literature in this area.

We have already dealt in some detail with the inadequacies of postulating irrational or arational motives in the discussion of protest groups, so we need not repeat that discussion here. Instead we can focus on the thrust of this work on membership psyche: the finding that different groups of people have different collective personalities. Social psychological social movement theorists posit "psychic states" as part of the social system—a more or less regular attribute of particular social roles. For example, the middle class is supposed to be optimistic and confident of its own power, while the lower class feels paranoid and impotent. This "regularity"[27] is explained as a *part* of the roles and culture of these groups, a social commodity that is the property of the collectivity and is transmitted whole to the individual as a part of his or her heritage. This ideational heritage is the soil in which social movements grow. Thus, the impulse to protest is a consequence of the simultaneous reactions of similar minds to similar conditions.

This is an enticing argument, but it is wrong. The psychic states that inform social protest are not part of the system so much as they are reactions to it. People are moved to action by *newly formed* convictions about the existence of a problem

[23] Smelser, *op. cit.,* p. 280.
[24] For examples of this sort of analysis see Smelser, *op. cit.,* pp. 280–287, 306–310; Lang and Lang *op. cit.,* pp. 16–19.
[25] Smelser, *op. cit.,* p. 8.
[26] Georges LeBon, *The Crowd* (London, 1952), p. 65.
[27] All such generalizations are probably useless. See Chapter 10 of this volume, "The Class Makeup of the Organization."

or how to alter a bad situation. The emotions that inform these actions are surprise, anger, and hopefulness, not deep-seated psychic states. The emotions involved are transitory and are the straightforward coordinates of a set of beliefs. They do not have an independent existence and they do not exercise an independent influence on the activities of the group. Therefore, the study of psychic states is pretty much irrelevant to understanding the behavior of protest groups.

By making this contrast explicit, we can forestall confusion in the later analysis. The discussion of protest group behavior and the detailed analysis of the Farmers' Alliance in this book is devoid of discussion of psychological processes. This is not because the members of protest groups are without psyches, and it is not because emotion and psychological processes play no role. It is because the role of the "non-rational" factors is derivative—they correlate with and reflect the logic of the situation and the beliefs that arise from it. We shall return to this issue in Chapter 10.

We can now turn our attention to the second aspect of social structure which is usually discussed in social movement literature: system malfunctions that generate social movements. This orientation has produced useful insights, but it is primitive, and it leads to analyses that inaccurately separate the protest organization from its parent structure. It also generates a pathological view of social protest.

Consider the origins of the Farmers' Alliance. Briefly stated, a "system malfunction" theory would look at the functioning of the tenancy system. It would discover that the tenancy system was creating poverty and economic insecurity. This misery triggered discontent and from this discontent arose the Alliance. But if we were to leave it at that, we would have hardly begun to understand the Alliance. The same excruciating oppression existed before and after the Alliance and it produced a great variety of responses besides protest activity. Why did the Alliance come into being when it did, and why did it take the form it did?

Unfortunately, theories of "system malfunction" do not usually look to the parent structure for the answer to this question. Instead, the timing and shape of protest are seen as a function of the psyches of the membership, and "one may assume that movements recruited from the same universe are broadly similar."[28] It does not matter what the source or purpose of protest is—people from similar demographic categories produce similar movements.

We have returned once again to the issue of individual and collective psyches, but only for a moment. "System malfunction" theories are bound up with the social psychological approach to social protest and they lead to a simpleminded analysis of the parent structure. If, on the other hand, a rationalist perspective is taken, it leads directly to a detailed analysis of the parent structure.

Our analysis of tenancy demonstrates that the 1880s and 1890s were a period of lienization, tenantization, and immiseration for yeomen and tenant farmers; competition, monopolization, and centralization among merchants and landlords. For those who suffered, the whole system was a monstrosity, but to those who prospered, the main problem was laborers who rebelled against a just system which

---

[28] Lang and Lang, *op. cit.*, p. 531.

rewarded the worthy. This central conflict and many peripheral ones were intrinsic to the system; no amount of patchwork would eliminate the centralization process, the day-to-day struggles between tenant and landlord, and the myriad competitions within the complicated structure.

There is a complexity to this system which is reproduced in the complexity of response of its victims. It produced thousands of different kinds of miseries, which produced thousands of different kinds of discontents, which produced thousands of different kinds of potential solutions. The Farmers' Alliance developed after the tenancy system had matured and hardened, after many thousands of other solutions had failed, and after hard work at communication had been done. Its form— from clubs built around supply centers to postharvest conventions—was determined by the workings of the system. And its activities—from local boycotts to statewide cooperatives—were directly linked to the structure of the system.

A "system malfunction" analysis fails to study the parent structure closely, and therefore it fails to trace the myriad ways in which the system determines the structure and functioning of the protest organizations it spawns. This failure then leads to another, because without such an analysis, it is impossible to understand why the protest group behaves in the unique manner it does. "System malfunction" analysts therefore search in the psyches of the members for the sources of the group's behavior, and all too frequently the explanations that emerge posit elaborate emotional pathologies.

We turn now to a discussion of the third emphasis in social movement literature. Analyses of "structural conduciveness" have yielded useful insights because they have sought the source of social movement behavior in the parent structures. However, the work in this area has generally had three major shortcomings.

First, it has often assumed that a given social structure was identically "conducive" to all protest organizations. For example, Smelser argues that a society which closes off peaceful reform invites violence.[29] But he pays no attention to the possibility that a society will resist certain reforms (and therefore invite violence), and allow others (and therefore preempt violence). The danger in this overly general analysis is apparent. If one assumes that tolerance for reform (or any other attribute) is a system trait, then after one protest group successfully initiates peaceful reform, any other group that engages in nonpeaceful action must be behaving irrationally. Unfortunately, this logic is applied over and over again in the social protest literature, without theorists even considering the possibility that the system treats different groups differently. As a consequence, much protest group behavior with origins in the behavior of the parent system is incorrectly attributed to pathological sources.

Second, such work fails to analyze the subsystems which are the proximate cause of the protest organization. For example, Smelser emphasizes the role of communication in the development of protest.[30] But he fails to see that the ability to

[29] Smelser, *op. cit.*, pp. 319–330.
[30] *Ibid.*

communicate can vary widely from structure to structure. As Marx noted long ago, one reason industrial workers are more organizable than farmers is that the modern factory brings a great many people with very similar grievances into near proximity. Communication and other traits of structural conduciveness, therefore, are "structure specific" and failure to note this can lead to important analytic errors.

Finally, structural conduciveness analysis has failed to take into account the ongoing and changing relationship between a protest group and its parent structure. The size, shape, demands, and tactics of the organization will vary over time and the response of the larger structure will vary also. Social structures are living, changing organisms. When a protest organization challenges them, they act to defend themselves in a variety of ways which evolve from and respond to the protest activities. The assumption that the parent structure has fixed modes of behavior leads to a limited understanding of protest behavior, because it analyzes only one-half of the situation. One needs to look back and forth from the protest group to the social structure to understand the behavior on either side.[31]

Structured Ignorance

The tenancy system generated immiseration and poverty. Millions of individuals experienced this process, and certainly the similarities of their lives were striking. But the focused vision of hindsight allows us to strip away the less central features of this situation which, at the time, obscured these similarities. One tenant fell into debt because his child required expensive medical care, another's crop was hit by blight. A third had risen out of debt twice before, so why not this third time? One yeoman farmer fell into debt because his dedication to work was undermined by a family tragedy; another made a series of stupid decisions in selling his crop. The specific experiences *were* different, and the similarities were not easily perceived at the time.

Any structure capable of generating a protest group will generate myriad different experiences. However much unity of causation exists among these experiences, this unity is concealed from the naked eye, and the discovery of that unity is therefore rendered problematical. And for those who discover that their plight is linked to that of other people, there remains the equally complicated task of separating the actual mechanisms of misery from many equally plausible, but false, candidates for the honor. With only the limited vision available from their own experience, this task may, in fact, be an impossible one.

---

[31] Oberschall, *op. cit.*, presents a theory of social movements which avoids most of the problems of previous efforts at explaining the behavior of social movements from a structural perspective. His book contains a great many important and challenging ideas, especially about the genesis of social movements (see pp. 118–145), based upon structural conduciveness arguments. However, Oberschall fails to incorporate into his model the dynamic character of the relationship between social protest and the parent structure. His discussion of the genesis of violence and radicalism lays too heavy a burden upon the original social conditions and not enough emphasis upon the outcome of attempts at social change, including the changing interaction between social structure and protest organizations.

This is the essence of structured ignorance. The structure of an ongoing social organization is masked from the individuals enmeshed in it. Each person sees only a small part of the system, and this limited view admits to many, many different interpretations. Only one of these interpretations is true, but all are plausible. The structure, because of its compartmentalized complexity, creates and maintains ignorance.

Nevertheless, it would seem that such structured ignorance is easily reduced by pooling different individuals' experiences, by careful study of the system, or by experimentation with different activities to see which one remedies the problems. But such strategies are not equally, or even minimally, available to everyone in a given structure.

In the contradiction between landlord and tenant, the landlord was dominant in everyday affairs. Therefore, if the landlord experienced frustration of his needs, he could experiment with many tactics that might increase his return. This experimentation was limited in numerous ways by the potential and actual resistence of the tenants, but this was minimal compared to the limits set on tenant experimentation by landlord dominance. Landlords were, therefore, in a much better position to try new ideas than were tenants. Furthermore, they were also in a much better position to study the system, since their dominant position allowed them to collect information. And landlords had the resources to expend in the research process, while individual tenants could afford neither the time nor the money needed for this. Finally, there were relatively few landlords compared to the huge number of tenants. Landlords could easily come together to compare experiences, while tenants had a difficult time achieving this unity.

Therefore, the situation that created and maintained landlord dominance also placed the landlords in an ideal position to reduce their own structured ignorance, whereas tenants and yeomen had few chances to do so. On a day-to-day basis, consequently, the amount of structured ignorance remained very high among the tenants, while it was substantially reduced among landlords.

This imbalance exists in most structures marked by the sort of contradictions that characterized tenancy. The elite, with its day-to-day dominance, can reduce structured ignorance whenever dysfunctions begin to occur. The process is by no means routinized, nor are solutions guaranteed, but the prerequisites of fruitful action are readily available. For the rank and file, however, just meeting these prerequisites is a major hurdle. Whether or not this obstacle is overcome is one of the crucial questions in redressing grievances.

One way to overcome the obstacle is for the rank and file to utilize the resources of the elite to reduce structured ignorance. By pooling the knowledge of landlord and tenant, by using landlord resources to investigate the problems, and by using landlord dominance to introduce new cultivation strategies, tenants and landlords could increase their understanding of the system enough to discover solution to their grievances. This method depends upon an assumption about the tenancy system: that there existed a solution that would help both landlords and tenants. Because the main changes that helped landlords hurt tenants, and vice versa, this "cross-class" unity could not succeed. Moreover, such efforts had a profound impact on the nature of the structured ignorance which existed in the system. Without any efforts at reducing structured ignorance, each individual in a system would have a unique picture of the system. But efforts to reduce ignorance are in continual operation, whether they are casual conversations among tenants or major cultivation strategies initiated by landlords. Since the nature of tenancy dictated that landlords were dominant, the ignorance reduction efforts were aimed primarily at landlord problems. However, the elite had a stake in the "cross-class" efforts and sought understanding of tenant problems just as long as the actions that flowed from this understanding did not challenge landlord interest. Ideas that might help tenants and hurt landlords were not pursued, but those that might help both were pursued, along with those that helped landlords and hurt tenants.

This skewed effort meant that, at any given moment, there was under active scrutiny a finite number of ideas about how the system worked. These ideas—and their accompanying actions—varied from time to time and place to place because they were tested and altered by practice. But they always had the same character: The theory suggested that the problems were a consequence of tenant abuses; that the problems emanated from an outside force; or that the problems were inevitable. Because of landlord hegemony, the current theories did not see the problems as flowing from landlord abuse.

A social system, therefore, does more than create structured ignorance. Because of the differential access to the tests that reduce structured ignorance, the theories that arise to explain the common thread of the collective experience all have a "pro-elite" character. These theories gain temporary or long-term acceptance as the "explanation" for people's grievances. At any time, there may be several different theories accepted by different individuals, or different substructures, depending upon subtle combinations of information dispersal and different conditions that lend plausibility to differing ideas. But the number of competing theories is small compared to the wide variety of individual experiences. The elite's search for solutions to its own problems homogenizes the thought of the rank and file. And the prevailing theories, no matter how contradictory they may be in every other respect, are agreed on one fundamental point: Rank-and file grievances cannot be redressed through an attack on the elite. Thus, they create a more powerful form of structured ignorance—the systematic denial of accurate propositions.

Thus, when there exist real antagonisms between the elite and the rank and file, the routine processes of ignorance reduction will act to divert attention away from these antagonisms. Only the creation of an ignorance-reducing device that does not depend upon the power and resources of the elite will uncover and focus attention on these important features of the structure. This is the role of a protest organization. To reduce structured ignorance, people must pool their individual experience, study the situation, and experiment with new actions. Protest organizations bring non-elite people together around a set of problems so that their diverse experiences can be compared. By achieving large membership, these organizations can generate the needed resources for study and action by taxing each member a modest amount. And by allowing for coordination of members' actions, they can generate the power necessary to force the system to experiment with innovations aimed at redressing grievances.

In a sense, then, protest organizations are primarily ignorance-reducing devices specially adapted to uncover elite—non-elite antagonisms. The measure of their usefulness is their success in this educational effort, and they die if they fail to provide this service. As we shall see, the effort is complicated by a great many factors, and much of what follows will in some fundamental way be concerned with understanding the forces that inhibit or aid in the reduction of structured ignorance.

10

The Determinants of Organized
Protest—Part 1

Every activity undertaken by a mass-based protest organization—regardless of how simple it is in appearance—is actually the result of the interplay of seven factors.

1. The class makeup of the organization.
2. The internal structure of the organization.
3. The nature of the active and potential opposition.
4. The nature of the active and potential support.
5. The structural position of the organization's membership in the structure to be challenged.
6. The prevailing analysis of the situation.
7. Previous actions and their outcomes.

This chapter and Chapter 11 will discuss the important aspects of these determinants and point out major interactions among them.

The Class Makeup of the Organization

There are two ways to approach the question of "class": Most sociologists analyze social class as the cauldron in which an individual's personality is formed. For example, researchers with this orientation have attempted to demonstrate that blue collar workers are authoritarian,[1] that small businessmen are politically intolerant,[2] and so on. These collective personalities are then seen as the deter-

[1] Seymour Martin Lipset, *Political Man* (Garden City, N.Y., 1960), pp. 87–126, especially pp. 100–116. For a comprehensive review of this literature, see Alan C. Kerckhoff, *Socialization and Social Class* (Englewood Cliffs, N.J., 1972).

[2] Martin J. Trow, "Small Businessmen, Political Tolerance, and Support for McCarthy," in *Protest, Reform and Revolt*, ed. Joseph R. Gusfield (New York, 1970), pp. 403–418.

minants of a wide range of behavior, including the organizations such types join and the causes they espouse.[3] Thus, according to S. M. Lipset, the authoritarian blue-collar worker is attracted to, and helps to create, dictatorial and dogmatic political parties.[4] According to C. Kerr and A. Seigel, violent unionism among miners reflects their violent personalities.[5] According to S. Perlman, union demands for closed shops and job security reflect a pervasive pessimism among manual workers.[6]

Implicit in these theories is the denial that organizational structure and activity is conditioned by necessity. Kerr and Seigel do not even entertain the notion that violence may be necessary for miners to win strikes; Lipset wholeheartedly denies (without evidence) that, under certain conditions, highly structured and disciplined organizations might be the most efficient (if not the only) route to major social change.

Once again we are face to face with theories that postulate irrational or arational behavior as the basis of social movements. Richard Hofstadter's analysis of Populism is a particularly relevant case in point.[7] Beginning with the unstated premise that the electoral process presents a straightforward method for redress of grievances, he sets out to discover the psychological patterns that produced Populist mass protest instead of party politics. He makes no effort to assess the idea that the system was faulty, that militant action and radical analysis were functional and accurate, or that they were plausibly based on the general information available at that time. Claims of monopoly control, far-reaching oppression, and general exploitation are not seen as drastic but reasonable explanations of a great agricultural depression. Instead they become the "proof" that farmers in the South and in the West were individually and collectively paranoid. Hofstadter's assertions and assumptions have been refuted directly,[8] but the underlying style of analysis continues to be commonplace in both sociological and historical treatments of mass movements.

The bankruptcy of such an approach can be seen in two ways. First, attempts to prove the existence of such collective personalities have met with notable unsuccess. Most works, like that of Kerr and Seigel, provide absolutely no evidence to support their assertions.[9] Those which do present evidence tend to undermine their own argument. Lipset's meager data seem to suggest that authoritarianism among blue-collar workers is at most marginally greater than it is among other groups,

[3] See, for example, Samuel Lubell, *The Future of American Politics* (New York, 1952); and V. O. Key, *Politics, Parties and Pressure Groups* (New York, 1958), pp. 269–279, for the application of this logic to voting behavior.

[4] Lipset, *op. cit.*

[5] Clark Kerr and Abraham Siegel, "The Interindustry Propensity to Strike," in *Industrial Conflict*, ed. William Kornhauser et al. (New York, 1954), pp. 196–197.

[6] Selig Perlman, *Theory of the Labor Movement* (New York, 1928), p. 6–7.

[7] Richard Hofstadter, *The Age of Reform* (New York, 1959).

[8] Norman Pollack, *Populist Response to Industrial America* (Cambridge, Mass., 1968); Norman Pollack, "Hofstadter on Populism: A Critique of the Age of Reform," *Journal of Southern History* 26 (November 1960), pp. 478–500.

[9] Kerr and Seigel, *op. cit.*

especially when other variables are controlled.[10] More careful work makes the irrelevance of social class to personality even clearer. Kerckhoff's compendium of the most reliable studies indicates that social class accounts for no more than 20% of the variance in fundamental personality traits, and this figure is itself highly inflated by uncontrolled confounding variables.[11] Second, and more important, there has been no systematic effort to show the mechanisms and methods by which the personality of an organization can be made to duplicate the personality of its membership. Certainly this is a fruitless task, since even cursory knowledge of protest organizations reveals inconsistent and constantly evolving behavior. From 1884 to 1889, the Farmers' Alliance initiated all of the following activities:

1. Cooperative buying and selling.
2. Boycotts of merchants, including militant picket lines.
3. Lobbying state legislatures.
4. Electoral politics.
5. The creation of an entire countereconomy.

Analyzed in personality terms, this list would indicate at the same time retreatism, acting out, and communalism; it displays both rebelliousness and acceptance, violence and pacifism. If this reflects the personality of the membership, then the tenancy system had created a horde of ambulatory schizophrenics.

It seems most reasonable to assume that social structures like the tenancy system, however powerful they may be, produce a wide range of different personality types. The organizations that derive from these structures attract an equally wide range of personalities, even if they tend to appeal to one type more than another. And the effect of the personalities of members is subtle enough and complicated enough to make the simplistic "class" analysis utilized by Hofstadter and others extremely suspect, if not wholly useless.

How, then, do the social origins of the membership affect the organization? To begin with, we recall that protest organizations are *derivative*. They are created for the express purpose of attacking and defeating another structure, and in that sense they derive from it. An individual joins the group in order to redress grievances against the larger structure. With a few important exceptions, the organization plays a secondary role in the life of its members. If Alliance activities caused the crops to be neglected, the Alliancemen quit the Alliance, not the farm. More important, if the landlord found himself the member of an Alliance club which moved to reduce his rents, he would not support the tenant action against himself. He would argue for a reorientation that would serve his interests (attacking railroads, for example) or else leave (or try to destroy) the club. His primary loyalty was to his role as "landlord," not to his role as "Allianceman."

---

[10] Kerr and Siegel, *op. cit.*, for example, Tables I, IV, V, pp. 1, 102, 118. For instance, by using Tables I and IV and making simple calculations, we discover that while middle class (upper white collar) men are less authoritarian than blue collar men, their female counterparts are more authoritarian.

[11] Kerckhoff, *op. cit.*, pp. 123–124. For example, the correlation between social class origin on occupational aspirations is .37 (accounting for 14% of variance on this trait).

When we speak, then, of the "class makeup" of the organization, we do not refer to a collective personality. We speak instead of the "role" the members play in another structure. And when we refer to their "class interest," we must look at the needs and difficulties attached to that outside role, not to the personality traits it supposedly creates.

To say that a group of people has the same "class interest" does not imply that the members have the same "opinion" on all, or even most, issues. Quite the contrary. Precisely because individuals in the same class have widely varying personalities— and widely varying experiences with the system—they will advocate different solutions to their common problems. In part, the purpose of a protest organization is to assess all these ideas and choose those that will work. Frequently this process involves mistakes, disagreements, and controversy. But if the members share a common class interest, then a particular program will "succeed" or "fail" for all members, no matter what their original opinion of it. Its usefulness can therefore be evaluated by each individual, who sees if it has improved his or her situation. After many failures, much controversy, and extensive experimentation, the com- mon "interest" is transformed into a common consciousness and a generally accepted program which potentially serves the entire membership.[12]

The development of a program to serve the articulated class interest of a group's membership depends upon recruitment from a single class. Often, as in the case of the Farmers' Alliance, this does not happen. When individuals from different classes join the same group, class "contradictions" are internalized and become a factor in group behavior. In some cases, there is an underlying common interest which transcends surface differences; this was the case for tenant and yeoman differences in the Alliance. In other cases, there is an underlying antagonism which undermines apparent commonality; this was the case for yeomen and landlords within the Alliance.

The attempted resolution of nonantagonistic contradictions, and the attempted compromise of antagonistic ones, is a central function of organizational structure. The tempting assumption that these efforts are generally successful is, however, unwarranted and is yet another example of the "superrationality" hypothesis. Structured ignorance may produce programs that serve only one subgroup, and leadership–membership cleavages may interact with class differences to produce the dominance of one group. The analysis of organizational policy in terms of the class interests of members is therefore complicated by the probable existence of structural blocks to the development and expression of membership needs.

---

[12] The Farmers' Alliance, like most other protest groups, derived from a broad economic system, and its "class makeup" can therefore be determined in Marxist fashion: by the way the membership fitted into the productive system. However, the analysis presented here also applies to much more limited structures. For example, in modern universities, protest groups (like Students for a Democratic Society) attempt to articulate the needs of students on a "class" basis: in antagonism to those of the administration and sometimes the faculty. It may be possible to see these as reflections of broader classes: students representing the interests of the common people against the administration, which represents the corporate elite. Whether or not this is true, the protest group is still derivative from the university structure and will relate to that structure in much the same way the Farmers' Alliance related to the cotton tenancy structure. Ralf Dahrendorf, *Class and Class Conflict in Industrial Society* (Palo Alto, Calif., 1959), pp. 201–205, applies the term "class" in this broader way.

Internal Structure and Functioning of the Organization

A protest organization develops an internal social structure of its own. This structure is both a reflection and a cause of the activities which the group undertakes. We cannot fruitfully discuss this entire interaction, so we shall focus on its central role in determining leadership–membership relations. These relations are the touchstone of organizational success.

Robert Michels was the first academically respected social theorist to emphasize the crucial role that leadership–membership relations play in the life of voluntary organizations.[13] His main contribution was a forceful and persuasive discussion of the conditions leading to the development of oligarchy in voluntary organizations. However, like many of the modern academic analysts of social movements, Michels neglected the connections between protest organizations and their parent structures.[14] By correcting this deficiency, we can fit Michels' analysis into a broader theoretical context.[15]

We have already noted that a protest organization is required to mediate the differences among its constituent subgroups. The formation of a Michelsian oilgarchy is a distinct threat to this process, particularly if the leaders are largely recruited from only one of the constituent groups. Such a development may produce policies useful to a single sector only—perhaps a small minority—of the membership.

We have already discussed the development of just such a cleavage within the Alliance: The process of early organization and expansion resulted in the recruitment of planters and other elite individuals to leadership positions. This cleavage, in combination with the migration of organizational initiative into the state structures, interfered with membership control.[16] In general, if the leadership–membership cleavage is also a class cleavage, a protest organization is in deep trouble. The mediation and information dispersal functions are frustrated, and the process of developing a "class" program is threatened.

---

[13] Robert Michels, *Political Parties* (New York, 1966; originally published in 1916). A great many Marxist activists had concerned themselves with this issue before then, notably V. I. Lenin, whose polemic *What Is to Be Done* argued that the success or failure of revolutionary movements depends upon the creation of a hitherto unknown organizational form, the democractic–centralist party. Many of the ideas developed by Michels can be found in the corners of Lenin's analysis; the debate within the socialist movement which was generated by Lenin's argument, and by his creation of the first such democratic–centralist group, undoubtedly forms a large part of the intellectual backdrop to Michels. Ostrogroiski (*Democracy and the Organization of Political Parties*, translated from the French by Frederick Clark, New York, 1902, 2v.) in some ways anticipated Michels, but his work has failed to match the impact of Michels' in academic circles.

[14] See Chapter 9 of this volume.

[15] Despite widespread acceptance, Michels's ideas have not been extensively developed or elaborated. The most impressive effort is the essay by Mayer Zald and Roberta Ash, "Social Movement Organizations, Growth, Decay and Change," *Social Forces* 44 (March 1966), pp. 327–340, which points to weaknesses in the Michelsian system while developing some of its strengths. Strangely, in her challenging analysis *Social Movements in America* (Chicago, 1972), Ash fails to stress the sort of internal, structural factors indicated by both her own work and the Marxist tradition she draws upon. Seymour M. Lipset, *Union Democracy* (Garden City, N.Y., 1962), explicitly sets himself the task of empirically extending Michelsian analysis and his is probably the most widely known application of the theory. At first widely hailed as a research breakthrough, it is now becoming less popular as its inadequacies become clearer.

[16] See Chapters 6 and 7 of this volume.

According to Michels, oligarchic leadership attempts to preserve both the protest group and its own role inside it. It has no "outside" interests. We have just seen one way in which the leadership can have an "outside" interest—if the leadership is recruited from a certain group with grievances distinct from those of the bulk of the membership. But even without a homogeneous class background, a Michelsian leadership clique can acquire such an outside "class" affiliation. Consider for a moment the position of an oligarchy in a protest group. On the one hand, its tenure of office can be threatened by rank-and-file discontent which arises if the organization fails to redress grievances. On the other hand, the leadership is threatened by the "parent" structure, which would like to eliminate the entire organization and thus frustrate its demands. The leadership's conservative interest is served if it can negotiate a compromise with the outside structure involving a deescalation of demands in exchange for an acceptance of continued existence. The leadership, instead of mediating the internal conflicts within the organization, becomes a "mediator" between the membership and the parent structure. Moreover, if the oligarchy consolidates its internal power, it has less to fear from the membership, while the outside threat remains. If an oligarchic leadership attains complete control, it can abandon membership-oriented demands entirely and bargain for concessions from the parent structure that will serve leadership *as distinguished from* membership. Inside the organization, the leadership must attempt to win the membership away from its original orientation, and thus it becomes an agent for the parent structure inside the protest organization.

In other words, in a highly oligarchized protest organization, the only threat to the oligarchy is a concerted attack by the parent structure. To preclude such an attack, the oligarchy, must prevent the protest group from challenging that structure. However, the raison d'être of the protest group is just such a challenge; in order to keep membership loyalty, the entrenched leadership must rally people to unthreatening activities. In oligarchies, therefore, leadership behavior becomes predictable: Leaders will act to divert protest activities from those areas which the target structure will most resist. The equation of forces creates a coalition between the target structure and the movement leadership. This process, operating in conjunction with Michelsian forces, is a predominant pattern in protest groups, and it is of particular, importance in understanding the Southern Farmers' Alliance.

The development of oligarchy is related to the question of whether leadership or membership does the organizing for the organization. For example, an election campaign can be carried on in two very different ways. It can depend upon the candidate's speeches to project the ideas of the campaign, or it can depend on the rank and file to speak to their friends and acquaintances, canvass their neighbors, and take other actions to convince people to vote. In the first strategy, the leader (the candidate) is carrying the burden of reaching outsiders—this is "leadership organizing." The second strategy involves "membership organizing."

Though every organization engages in a mixture of membership and leadership organizing, it is usually possible to evaluate which type is predominant. We can also discern important organizational structures and patterns associated with each mode of organizing. In the electoral example, dependence on membership organizing implies that the rank and file must be equipped to convince and persuade others to vote for the candidate, a task requiring considerable information and motivation. The organization must therefore develop an educational structure capable of communicating changes in the campaign and answers to various problems that may arise suddenly. In contrast, a campaign that depends on the candidate—or a few leaders—to communicate with potential voters does not need this kind of structure. The membership role may be negligible, or it may be restricted to the collection of funds or the supplying of auditoriums and audiences. These tasks are more routinized, and entirely different structures are needed to regiment and coordinate them. A further implication of this distinction relates to the ability of the organization to change its activities quickly. If the organization depends upon membership organizing, any policy change requires a simultaneous change in behavior by all the members, a circumstance which necessitates tremendous organizational discipline. If, on the other hand, it depends upon leadership organizing, a change in policy might not imply a change in membership activity at all, and therefore little organizational discipline would be required. Thus, successful reliance on membership organizing implies either a stable set of policies or a high degree of organizational discipline.

Membership organizing is incompatible with oligarchy in protest organizations. When members carry the basic responsibility for relating to the "outside," they must understand and support the policies they are organizing around. If a policy is promulgated which is not consonant with their interest, then membership will become less enthusiastic as they become more knowledgeable. They will not work as hard and the program will falter. Moreover, since oligarchy leads to the creation of a coalition between protest leadership and the established structure, the natural mode of oligarchic behavior is for leadership to carry on negotiations with the outside, while membership acts to support the compromise outcome. Hence, oligarchy leads to both the reduced reliability of members as organizers and the increased necessity for leadership initiative.

In this section, we have scrutinized three important processes:

1. The development of oligarchy in an organization may proceed along Michelsian lines, except that the policies developed have a pattern which connects the protest group to the outside structure. One frequent occurrence is the recruitment of leadership that is class homogeneous, and this, combined, with oligarchical tendencies, results in policies that systematically represent a small minority of the organization. Alternately, an oligarchic leadership with no homogeneous class affiliation will discover that the major threat to its preservation is the opposition— the parent structure. To eliminate this danger, the oligarchy uses its power within the organization to divert energies away from activities which the parent structure resists, and therefore becomes within the organization an agent for the opposition.

2. Protest organizations can relate to the outside either through their leadership or their membership. Membership organizing depends upon mass understanding

of the issues, and it correlates with elaborate internal educational structures. It also requires a relatively stable policy or else a high degree of membership discipline and commitment. Leadership organizing correlates with flexible policies and bureaucratic structures.

3. Organizations with predominantly membership organizing are strongly resistant to oligarchy. Oligarchic organizations tend to rely increasingly on leadership organizing.

The Nature of the Active and Potential Opposition

The ultimate test of mass protest is the successful exercise of power over the parent structure. This success is dependent upon the structural position of the membership in the larger system (to be discussed below) and upon the vulnerabilities of the groups mobilized to protect the system. In choosing movement activities, a protest group can attain a degree of control over who the opposition will be, to what degree it will be mobilized, and in what ways it will be vulnerable. For example, in the aborted Clebourne convention, the Farmers' Alliance attempted to ensure the success of statewide electoral activity by controlling these aspects of the struggle. The Clebourne demands attacked railroads and industrialists while courting landlords and merchants. It selected the electoral arena, where the railroads seemed vulnerable to the welding of Alliance votes into the electoral machinery of the planter-oriented wing of the Democratic party (see Chapter 1). Other programs would have resulted in different allies, different opponents, and different organizing strategies.

Attempts by protest organizations to choose the sides and the terms of battle produce counterefforts by the newly mobilized opposition. Just as the Alliance preferred the Texas government as the arena in its fight with the railroads, the railroads preferred to move the battle into a locale more advantageous to themselves. In fact, when railroad control boards were established in many states, the railroads went to the federal government to challenge the laws behind the boards. They choose a new arena of battle and a new alignment of forces.

This points to a key variable in conflict situations: the *rigidity* of the contending forces. We have already mentioned the connection between membership control of organizing and the inability of a protest group to change activities. Without a high degree of organizational discipline, this rigidity can preclude many otherwise reasonable undertakings. The same applies to the opposition forces, but since the opposition generally utilizes institutionalized power, it does not face the difficulties associated with mass mobilization. Instead, it is constrained by the logic of the structure itself. For example, when the Farmers' Alliance began organizing boycotts and cooperative buying, the target (opposition) was the local merchants. One of the numerous counterstrategies adopted by the merchants called for them temporarily to lower their prices, thus creating a tremendous inducement to farmers to break the boycott or abandon the cooperative. Once the boycott was defeated, prices could be returned to their original level. This strategy was usually thwarted by the rigidity of the distribution system. Many local merchants were themselves indebted wholesalers who would not extend the credit necessary to sell below cost. Thus, this strategy was precluded by the nature of the merchants' involvement in the larger system. Rigidity of this sort is characteristic of all social structures and represents a major handicap in responding to the onslaught of reform efforts.

A second key variable that determines the nature and effectiveness of the resistance to reform is the possibility for escalation—the introduction of unanticipated new adversaries into the struggle. For example, when Alliance boycotts and co-operatives were effective enough to drive merchants into bankruptcy (or create a serious threat to their business), the wholesale supplier lost the money he had lent to the retailer. Moreover, large cooperatives exerted pressure on wholesalers to reduce prices or face a loss of business.

Wholesalers were therefore quick to learn that successful Alliance action meant lower profits for them, and this brought them into previously limited Alliance—merchant struggle (see Chapter 13). They withheld goods from beginning Alliance cooperatives and thus prevented them from developing into alternatives to the already functioning merchants. In order to avoid reliance on wholesalers, Alliance co-ops needed enlarged resources to pay cash or establish credit with manufacturers. Thus, the very success of cooperatives brought new opposition into the conflict that ended in their defeat. This is the process of escalation, a potential factor in every reform situation.

A third factor in determining the ability of the opposition to respond is the *organizability* of the opposition group. In some cases, the opposition is already highly organized and this issue has reduced importance. However, in many cases, there are structural features in the situation which affect the ability of the opposition to organize. For example, when the Alliance began merchant boycotts it took advantage of the competition among merchants. Obviously, if all merchants within reach agreed not to sell to Alliance members (as sometimes happened), this "counter-boycott" would have defeated the tactic. However, the profit motive and the rigidity of the economic structure made it very difficult for this type of organization to occur, and merchants were therefore picked off one at a time.

On the other hand, the Clebourne demands attempted to avoid conflict with landlords partly because the landlord—merchants would be a formidable opposition in the electoral arena. Thus, organizability came into play in the selection of both tactics—in the one, the Alliance selected a tactic partly because it split merchants apart; in the other, a program was designed to avoid the opposition of a well-oiled landlord—merchant organization in the arena of battle.

Naturally, the question of organizability of the opposition is as complex as the question of organizability of the protest organization itself. However, one important difference should be noted: Usually a protest organization attempts to use non-institutional power to accomplish changes. This usually places the protest group in conflict with the state apparatus—if not directly, then potentially. In contrast, the opposition mostly utilizes institutional power, implying routinized channels of communication and a much more well-defined description of organizability. Therefore, while a protest group may be plagued with uncertainty about its own resources, the opposition's resources are most often much clearer and well defined.

Two major points have been made in this discussion:

1. The protest organization can, to a certain extent, control both the nature and scope of the opposition. By choosing among several different possible solutions to the membership's problems, the group can bring itself into conflict with one group and prevent conflict with others. At the same time, it can choose weapons that will bring it into conflict with all or only part of the opposition group and in an arena of its own choosing.

2. The opposition is affected in its response by its own position in the social structure. Three important dimensions of this limitation can be discovered. First, *rigidity* reflects the inability of the opposition to adopt certain countertactics because the structure of the whole system prevents such action. Second, *escalation* occurs when the results of the protest organization's activity brings new groups into opposition which were not originally involved. These new groups bring with them new weapons and different vulnerabilities. Third, the *organizability* of the opposition is a key element in determining how it will respond to any given strategy or action. This organizability is affected by many things and is similar to the problem of organization faced by the protest group, except that the institutional power which usually lies behind the opposition results in a more clear-cut and well-defined set of weapons and vulnerabilities.

The Nature of the Active and Potential Support

The nature of the active support has profound effects upon the policies or actions undertaken. We can begin with an enumeration of several obvious variables.

Demographic Variables

The size of an organization is clearly a critical factor in determining its behavior. For example, the number of members was an important determinant of the level of the system which the Alliance attacked and was a factor in the Alliance's entering electoral politics. The geographical spread of the membership is also important. For example, it was not until the Alliance had established itself in a large number of localities that it felt ready to enter statewide politics. Resources of the membership is yet another factor. The early reliance upon cooperatives required members who had at least a small amount to ready cash. When wholesalers boycotted these stores, the cash needs increased tremendously, and this lack of resources forced an abandonment of local action.

Another structural variable is the *physical arrangement* of the membership. The Alliance pattern of organizing around the county seats where farmers traded had advantages and disadvantages. Boycotts of merchants were easily arranged, since all Alliance members who patronized the same merchant would be likely to be in the same county. But unified action against a large landlord was difficult if his holdings were spread across county lines. Similarily, when electoral activity began, many clubs found themselves with membership spread over two or more legislative districts—and they had to reorganize into electoral units.

These fundamental features of membership demography all play roles in organizational behavior. The size, geography, resources, and arrangement of the support facilitate some activities and inhibit others.

Sources of Experience and Understanding

A complicated and crucial variable determining the direction of the organization is the *experience and understanding* of the membership. For example, a preponderance of new members in the group will result in a tendency to support policies that have been discredited by past experience. In other words, the common experience and history of an organization affects its behavior only to the extent that the membership has itself been a part of that experience and history.

Connected to the newness of the membership are the experiences that members bring with them into the organization. Particularly relevant is experience in other protest groups. For example, many Alliance members had been active in the Grange, a farmers' group that had swept the South in the late 1870s—and then collapsed after the failure of cooperatives and Greenback party politics. These experiences were transmitted to the Alliance by the individuals who were involved: The failures were deterrents to similar mistakes and the successes became guidelines for Alliance activities.

Another source of outside experience is the class position of the membership. The position of membership in the parent structure exposes individuals to experiences that condition their support for potential programs. Consider a Southern yeoman who worked hard at rising into the landlord class. Hard times did not necessarily remove this ambition; many yeomen sought reforms that would reopen the avenues into wealth. Others accepted their new status as tenants and sought reforms to ease the burden of all tenants, instead of reforms to make it easier for a few to rise out of that status. The two attitudes imply entirely different sets of demands: The first emphasizes the return of liened land and market reforms, while the second implies rent reduction and freedom from supervision.

If the Alliance membership had been prosperous in the past and saw clearly the possibility of rising out of yeoman status, they would be most enthusiastic about the first sort of reforms. If, on the other hand, the membership were largely poor yeomen or tenants who had never been prosperous, they would be more enthusiastic about tenant-oriented demands. Thus, the type of demands the membership would support were in part determined by the collective experience in the tenancy system. Many of the variations among state Alliances as to policies and actions can be understood in these terms.

In discussing the experience and understanding of membership, it is important to keep in mind that the attitudes of the membership are only one factor in determining policy. Perhaps in a perfectly democratic organization, there is a congruence between membership attitude and organizational policy. However, in almost all cases, the structural factors we have outlined were important in determining policy, whether or not the membership wanted it that way. Furthermore, the different experiences and understanding among the internal groupings of an organization make it impossible to speak of the membership as having uniform attitudes or understanding.

Organizational Discipline and Membership Attitudes toward Policy

Even in the most undemocratic organizations, membership understanding directly affects organizational discipline. Only a member who truly believes in the group's policies is likely to expend a great deal of energy on them. It is easier to stay home than stand on a picket line, attend a meeting, or canvass friends. There is no remedy for such "laziness," except the conviction that the organization's policies—and the member's part in them—will really result in beneficial changes.

Many theorists have challenged this logic of "self-interest." Mancur Olson argues that no amount of self-interest or possible benefit can be the prime force behind participation in a voluntary organization like the Alliance. Regardless of how much the individual farmer could gain, he would adopt a "let George do it" attitude since he could "enjoy any improvements brought about by others whether or not he has worked in support of his organization."[17] Therefore, argues Olson, "it is certain that a collective good will *not* be provided unless there is coercion or some outside inducements that will lead the members of the large group to act in their common interest."[18]

The flaw in Olson's argument is revealed by an example. An Alliance boycott against a merchant succeeded if enough individuals refused to buy from him until he lowered prices. All the merchant's customers benefited from the lowered prices, but those who did not boycott benefited more, since they did not suffer the discomfort of having to switch stores or submit to whatever counterattacks the merchant initiated. According to Olson, this makes it impossible to organize a boycott on economic interest alone—each individual would reason, "I personally am better off by letting the others do it," and hence no one would boycott. Without some other inducement, such as friendship ties or coercion, few people would participate in the boycott.

But the farmers were also aware of this contradiction, and many felt the sacrifices of organizing work were not as bad as the consequences of failure. Even if those who did not participate were best off, the benefits of successful struggle outweighed its discomforts for those who did boycott.

A protest organization draws its membership from those who are acutely aware of the contradiction that Olson finds so compelling, and this is why these groups

[17] Mancur Olson, *The Logic of Collective Action* (New York, 1971), p. 16.
[18] *Ibid.*

almost invariably adopt slogans conveying the notion that "unity is strength." The understanding that mutual benefits can be gained only by first making mutual sacrifices is the keystone of the organization. But this understanding is activated only when the individual believes firmly that the action will succeed. A boycott that fails brings only grief to the activist—all of the detriments and none of the benefits. Therefore, even those who are ready to make the "sacrifice" involved in united action will not participate unless they are convinced of its probable success. This generates tremendous pressure for membership participation and understanding of the decisions made and actions carried out by an organization. Only such an immediacy can generate enough membership enthusiasm to make the policies work. The implications of this relationship extend throughout the discussion of organizational decisionmaking.

First, we can see the need for effective communications inside a protest organization; otherwise the membership cannot possibly understand the implications of decisions made at the top and will have little enthusiasm for action on these decisions at the grass roots. This lack of enthusiasm will be tolerable only if there is little or no need for grass roots action. Thus, in the Farmers' Alliance, lobbying activity grained its leverage by the threat of electoral action. However, since the threat did not need to be immediately exercised, there was no compelling force for informing the membership of the various policies advanced by the lobbyists. Later, when elections came and the membership had to vote for one candidate and not another, this demanded a massive education campaign. Thus, actions adopted by an organization will be in part determined by the ability of the organization to communicate to its membership an understanding of these decisions.

Second, this whole process can be reversed. If there is no need for membership to participate in the actions of the organization, then there is no need for communication at all. If an organization adopts policies that do not depend on the participation of its supporters, there is no reason for the membership to understand these policies, and the whole process of communication between top and bottom will disintegrate. Later, if new policies require real support, the organizational equipment will have dissolved and there will be no way to mobilize the necessary masses for enforcing the new policy.

Third, it is not necessarily true that a policy must be really beneficial for the membership to *believe* that it will be beneficial. In the case of the Clebourne demands, anti-railroad legislation and several of the other demands would not have resulted in any real gains for tenant farmers. Yet many tenants enthusiastically supported these demands because they thought these policies would benefit them. This points to a crucial relationship between organizational structure and organizational discipline: The involvement of people in policies that do not actually benefit them contains the seeds of its own alteration. Once large numbers of tenants had become involved in the Farmers' Alliance and had sufficient experience with demands like those set forth at Clebourne, disillusionment began to take hold among those who discovered the inadequacy of those solutions. Such disillusionment creates two contradictory forces in the organization. On one side, disillusioned membership tends to be less certain about the organization's usefulness and drops out, while those who believe in the policies remain. On the other side, if disillusionment strikes many members at the same time—as it would if a demand were won and then effected no change for a great bulk of the supporters—these members might have the strength to push the group toward new, very different actions. The success of such a movement would, of course, depend upon many structural features of the organization and the amount of commitment and enthusiasm the members shared. Its adoption and success would be determined by all the factors we have been discussing in this chapter.

Potential Support

Much of what has just been said about the active membership of a protest organization applies equally well to potential membership. Clearly, such variables as size, scope, physical arrangement, and outside experience of possible recruits will have a large impact on the policies and actions of the organization. But there are further considerations in regard to potential support. First, the process of activating potential support is by itself a special policy which involves decisions and structures different from those in activating support which has already been recruited to the organization. Thus, we speak of "organizers" who try to reach people not already in the organization and bring them into it. The nature of the potential support has a great impact on recruitment style, as does the state of the organization in the area of the potential recruits. During the period of rapid expansion, 1887–1889, two very different methods of recruitment were needed. In areas of great Alliance strength, the membership could canvass their neighbors and friends on ongoing projects. However, were there was little or no Alliance organization, outside organizers with special skills and abilities were needed. These outsider organizers tailored their appeal to the types of individuals they found in the as yet unorganized areas. And, since they were often influential statewide leaders, the statewide policies were tailored to the type of recruit the organization found in undeveloped areas.

A second important and related consideration was whether the potential support for group activities was to be brought into the organization or would remain formally outside of it. Consider, for example, the Clebourne demands, which the Farmers' Alliance hoped would attract the support of all rural groups. These demands attempted to unify planters and tenants and yeomen under the banner of fighting finance and industrial capitalists. However, the Alliance's constitution specifically excluded landlords and merchants from membership in the organization because of the class antagonisms which the Alliance perceived between tenant—yeomen and landlord—merchants (see Chapters 6–7). Thus, they sought to organize planters but not bring them into the organization. This strategy required a new organizational vehicle (the Democratic party) and a different style of organizing (lobbying). This contrasted sharply with the method of recruiting tenants and yeomen, who were brought into the organization through mass meetings and face-to-face proselytizing.

We see here a crucial force at work. The analysis of the protest group—in this case, the perceived antagonism between landlords and Alliancemen—partly determines the nature and style of the recruitment process. A circumstance that requires coalition with an otherwise unfriendly group creates complicated organizational problems requiring special structural arrangements. Indeed, the failure of the Alliance to master these structural problems vis-à-vis landlords resulted in the internalization of the antagonism (Chapters 6–7).

A potential supporter need not become a formal member. The principal determinant here is the need for organizational discipline. Protest organizations have meetings at which policy is determined; then its members participate in various activities in furthering these policies. Many people participate in the actions without attending policymaking meetings, but if the actions require understanding and commitment, few non-members will support them. To the extent that people are brought into membership, they can be expected to develop and maintain the understanding of complex and/or rapidly changing policy; therefore, full membership is intimately connected to organizational discipline.

Several important points have been made in this discussion:

1. The size, scope, and physical arrangement of membership have a direct effect on policies. An organization is bound by membership attributes which facilitate certain policies and make others impossible.

2. The experience and understanding of the active membership and the potential support are crucial in the success of actions. This effect reverberates through many aspects of decisionmaking, especially its effect on organizational discipline. Membership enthusiasm and energy is contingent on belief in the effectiveness of policy. This belief is contingent upon the collective experience of the membership inside and outside the organization, the structure of communication, the degree of membership participation in organizing, and the recruitment process.

3. Potential membership can be mobilized only if the organization has special structures and activities to accomplish this. These structures themselves represent decisions of the organization.

4. Potential supporters can be activated in three different ways. They can be brought directly into membership; they can become nonaffiliated supporters; or through coalition they can be allied with. The latter strategy is necessary when class antagonisms with other groups that might support some of the same demands are too great to allow for membership. Nonaffiliation occurs when the degree of discipline necessary for support is not sufficient to require full participation.

11

The Determinants of Organized Protest—Part 2

The Structural Position of the Organization's Membership in the Structure to Be Challenged

We now focus upon a particular feature of the class position of the membership: the potential leverage a group of people can exercise over the social structure. To illustrate this idea, we refer again to the consumer boycotts organized by the Alliance. The theory behind these boycotts was that by withholding patronage, the customers of a given store could exert pressure on the store's policy—in this case, to reduce prices and to alter credit arrangements. The merchant was forced to change his policy by the threat of bankruptcy. Here we have an example of the Farmers' Alliance taking advantage of the structural position of yeomanry in the cotton tenancy system. To demonstrate that this was, in fact, a structural feature of the unencumbered yeomanry, we note that debt peons had no choice of suppliers. Without the ability to change merchants, they could not use the consumer boycott as a weapon. Their position did, however, offer a different, less easily executed, alternative. They could refuse to produce cotton. The landlord could throw them off the land (if he could find replacements), but in doing so, he lost the power that debt peonage bestowed on him. Thus, even debt peons, if organized, could exert pressure based on the fact that the landlord or merchant could utilize lien leverage only if he allowed them to remain on the land. If they refused to work the land, the landlord was bound to lose.

Thus, in talking of the position of the membership in the large system, we are looking at the basis of power which an organization hopes to develop. To understand the nature of this power and its potential, we must raise and discuss several issues about what constitutes effective leverage.

Power can be conceived of as the ability of one person or group of people to force another person or group of people to do something *against their will*. Underlying this coercion is the creation of a circumstance in which the other alternatives open

171

to the coerced party are less attractive than the one the powerholder wants chosen. The most blunt and obvious form of power is to credibly threaten a victim with death unless he or she chooses to do one's bidding. Some people will choose death; most will submit.

Social structures create power relationships. The coercion applied is not necessarily a threat of violence; more often it is the threat of depriving the individual of something which, by the fact of his or her role in the structure, he or she desires. A familiar example is the power of an employer over his employees. The employees work because they desire the pay. Whenever an employer gives an order, it carries the threat of job loss behind it—the job situation is one that exchanges obedience for payment. This same sort of power was exercised by the merchant over tenants. They could purchase from no one but him, so unless they were willing to obey various commands, such as which crops to plant, he could prevent them from eating. This threat was usually sufficient to make the choice certain, and therefore the merchant came to exercise routinized power over his tenants. They consistently did what he said rather than face the alternative of not getting supplies.

We see here the exercise of *structural power*, which is recognizable by the fact that the structure in question could not function without the consistent and routinized exercise of such power. It is not possible to imagine a company functioning in any recognizable way without the employer ordering his employees to do certain things, or for the tenancy system to be anything like what it was without the power of decision conveyed by lienholding. In fact, employees who do not value their job enough to follow orders soon quit or are fired, and tenants who refused to obey their lienholders soon found themselves without livelihood. The system is self-perpetuating in that the structure constantly purifies itself of those who do not fit into the power relations it requires.

We can therefore define structural power as the set of power relations that is required for any given structure to continue to function in its usual manner. Lurking beyond structural power, however, is another sort of power which is in some senses its exact opposite. Since a structure cannot function without the routinized exercise of structural power, any threat to structural power becomes a threat to that system itself. Thus, if employees suddenly began refusing to obey orders, the company in question could not function. Or if tenants simply disobeyed the merchant's order to grow cotton, the tenancy system would collapse. Such disobedience, however, depends on the ability of the bulk of employees or tenants to coordinate their action and to exercise discipline so that they can create a serious threat. Thus, if one or two workers refuse to obey orders, they can be fired and replaced. But if all stop work simultaneously, all the conditions of power are present. The workers can prevent the employer from continuing to function unless he submits to certain demands. If he values the functioning of the system, he must submit to the demands of the workers.

Thus, we see a subtle, but very important, relationship between structural power and those who are subject to it. On the one hand, these power relations define the functioning of any ongoing system; on the other hand, the ability to disrupt these relationships is exactly the sort of leverage which can be used to *alter* the functioning of the system. Thus, *any system contains within itself the possibility of a power strong enough to alter it.*

This relationship has been described earlier—it is what we called a *contradiction.* A structure or system creates two antagonistic groups (say, landlords and tenants) and each is necessary for the continued functioning of the system. One group (the merchant–landlords) exercises routinized power. The other group (the tenants) posseses the possibility of refusing to accept this authority, and therefore possesses the possibility of calling the existence of the system into question. This possibility constitutes a lever against the system—the lever which can force the system to change in order to preserve itself.

The subordinate group does not possess active power. It is subordinate precisely because its potential power is not activated by the normal functioning of the system. Its power becomes real only when it can form and maintain an *organization independent of the original structure*, which has a membership extensive enough and disciplined enough to call into question the continued functioning of the system.

We can illustrate this by returning to the example of workers or tenants facing an employer or a merchant–landlord. In both cases, the power of the subordinate group is contingent upon sufficient numbers withdrawing their cooperation in unison. If too few participate, the employer or merchant can replace them. If they are unable to coordinate their actions, they will not constitute a real threat. It is only when a vast number of tenants refuse to obey the merchant's orders simultaneously that the system—the production of cotton for his profit—is threatened. It is only when a large number of workers refuse to obey orders that the functioning of the factory or business enterprise is threatened. In both cases, the coordinated refusal is dependent upon the creation of workable independent protest groups. These groups cannot be dependent on, or embedded in, the original system, since that system is based on the exercise of routinized power by the dominant group. A threat to the continuing functioning of a system cannot be mounted by the system itself.

This principle—that the system cannot mount a threat against itself—entails many subtle applications in the functioning of a protest group. It is not always clear if a strategy involves such a situation, since the boundaries of the system are not always well defined. For example, wholesalers often refused to do business with successful cooperatives, for they had a financial stake in the retailers the coops threatened. Thus, the structural power of the system—the power of the wholesalers to refuse to sell—was used to defend the system. Furthermore, this reaction revealed that the tactic of cooperatives actually depended upon the structural power of the system itself: the routinized power of wholesalers to grant or withhold patronage. When the cooperatives demonstrated their ability to change the system, this dependence was revealed in the counterattack by the merchants.

We have now enunciated a crucial principle in understanding the development and role of protest organizations: An effective challenge to the internal power relations in a system can be mounted only when the subordinate group can organize itself outside that system. Before developing this principle further, we must first clarify the nature of the power which is exercised in these situations.

First, structural leverage is fundamentally superior to other types of power. Any group of people, if they were determined enough, could disrupt the functioning of any social structure or organization. For example, a group of bandits could force a merchant to give them his cash by threatening to burn down his store. This would constitute a real threat to the system of tenancy in the area, and the bandits might very well succeed in exercising power over the merchant. Analogously, the tenants, instead of refusing to work, could bring guns and obtain free merchandise by threatening to burn down the store. These actions constitute power, but the power is not derived from roles played within the system. Similarly, if tenants imposed their will on the landlord by keeping him awake with noisy demonstrations outside his home each night, they would also be utilizing power which does not depend on the role of the tenants in the cotton production system.

The last example reveals an important aspect of some attempts to exercise power: They can threaten individuals without regard to their role in the structure. Thus, the tenants could be frustrated if the merchant simply hired someone to run the store who could sleep through the noise, and then left town. The harassment would have been ineffective because it did not threaten the system's functioning. Similarly, the vulnerability of the merchant to a holdup can be remedied without fundamentally altering the tenancy system. Safety devices, armed guards, or fireproofed stores, for instance, could protect a storekeeper from this action. However, no change could be made in the tenancy system that would allow it to function without the labor of the tenants. Therefore, the only unanswerable power is that which develops from a refusal to play one's appointed role within the system.

Second, the use of this structural leverage is limited to the particular structure in which the group is embedded. A strike by one set of tenants would not influence the behavior of a merchant who did not do business with them. Similarly, tenants could not expect their strike against the merchant to exert pressure upon a factory owner who was polluting their water supply. The equation of "leverage" therefore involves the *source* of the problem to be solved. If the complaints of tenants cannot be remedied by the merchant, then exerting leverage on him will be ineffective in solving the problems.

However, it must be kept in mind that the "system" we speak of may be larger or smaller, depending upon the situation and the groups organized. Thus, we have pointed out that tenants were related to the particular merchants who held liens over them, and could organize to use leverage against these merchants. But, looked at from another perspective, the tenancy system included the wholesaler who supplied several merchants at once. Tenants could organize together and, by coordinating their actions on a broader basis, threaten the wholesale merchant with a refusal to patronize any of his retailers. This would exert effective leverage on the larger system.

Thus, the system under attack may vary, depending upon the extent of organization and the nature of the changes required. Systems and structures are embedded within each other, and different organizing strategies can be developed in order to effect different changes in policy by different groups of powerholders.

Third, any group of people is involved in several different structures simultaneously. Tenants in the South were not only involved in a cotton tenancy structure with landlords or merchants, they were also involved in county governmental structures, in state political systems, in any number of voluntary organizations, and in such structures as families or friendship networks. These structures coexisted and often intersected, so that the selection of which structure to operate in could become a serious problem in attempting to settle grievances.

If we return once again to the Clebourne demands, we can see the impact these notions of structural leverage had on the decisions made by the Texas Farmers' Alliance. The early boycott campaigns had attempted to develop the structural leverage of yeomen within the supply system associated with cotton farming. Utilizing the coordination made possible by the Alliance, yeomen had withdrawn their obedience to the price setting of merchants by buying elsewhere or forming cooperatives and had thereby attempted to activate their latent power. Unfortunately, the effectiveness of the organization resulted in pressure on wholesalers, who counterattacked by refusing to extend credit to the alternative stores set up by the Alliance. Sometimes the Alliance countered by reorganizing itself to exert effective leverage on the wholesalers. Other times, such as at Clebourne, it sought to move into a new arena—the political system. This strategy began with an analysis that found solutions in an attack on railroads and banks but recognized the absence of potential structural leverage over these institutions. Therefore, leverage was to be applied in the political system, which in turn would exert leverage on the railroad and monetary systems.

In order to exert leverage in the political system, the Alliance needed to activate its potential power as a bloc of votes. During the 1870s and early 1880s, political stability in the South rested upon a divided farmer vote. The development of a united bloc of farm votes shifting together could, presumably, disrupt the system by repeatedly removing incumbent officeholders until the desired changes were made. While in appearance this threat of electoral disruption seems analogous to boycotts strikes, it had a peculiar recursive quality. Without the guarantee of fair elections conducted without fraud, the Alliance threat was meaningless. Such a guarantee could be given by the government only, and therefore the Alliance strategy of exercising leverage over government depended upon the government itself.

This dependence seems at first to be irrelevant, since we do not ordinarily expect government officeholders to defend their incumbency (and therefore their policies) through fraud. However, such a defense has repeatedly been attempted, successfully so against the Populist party.[1] The defeat of the incumbent depends upon the ability of the defrauded voters to organize *outside* the electoral system, to mount a credible threat of wider disruption. Therefore, successful electoral activity depends

---

[1] See, for example, C. Vann Woodward, *Tom Watson, Agrarian Rebel* (Baton Rouge, 1939).

upon either the "goodwill" of those under attack or else upon the creation of an *outside* deterrent against fraud. It is not a self-contained strategy.

Thus, we arrive at a fourth dimension to the use of structural power. In a boycott, the Alliance did not utilize tools provided by the parent structure: The boycott was not a routinized part of the tenancy system. On the other hand, the use of the electoral process is a built-in part of the governmental system, and when the Alliance turned to this as its tool of leverage, it was using a tool which depended for its efficacy on governmental power. The first is noninstitutional power; the second is institutionalized power (Chapter 8).

This distinction reveals a certain circularity in the logic of electoral protest. Such protest is effective only insofar as it creates a genuine threat to the current office-holders' incumbency. Such a threat, however, large the bloc of votes, exists only when fair elections are assured. Fair elections can be guaranteed only if the current officeholders, who control the election process, are willing to allow them. Therefore, a real electoral threat to current policy is dependent upon the sufferance of the officials who created the discontent in the first place.

The apparent weakness of this logic is the possibility that political officeholders do not have control over elections: The legal network, enforced by courts and police, does not respond to the needs of elected officials. Put another way, the state legislature could be dominated by pro-merchant forces, but the electoral apparatus might be controlled by individuals with little stake in tenancy issues. In this situation, a pro-yeoman majority need not fear the use of fraud against electoral protest.

How often does such "divided control" exist within a social or political system? In appearance, it seems quite frequent, but it is actually both rare and unstable. If two parts of a system are controlled by "antagonistic" interests (as our Alliance example suggests), they are brought into conflict with each other. Because they are part of the same system, both sectors are capable of disrupting its functioning, and whichever side loses a particular battle will be tempted to disrupt the structure in order to retrieve its loss. Such disruption will take place only when the issue is important enough to merit it, but antagonistic situations create issues of this gravity. Such an effort to reverse a defeat leads to a struggle for power with each side determined to acquire control over the entire system. Disruption will appear and reappear until one side wins.

To see this, it is useful to recall the conflict between the landlord and the merchant. Each had power. The landlord controlled the land and this gave him leverage in the system. The merchant had supplies and credit and this gave him leverage. They were unable to coexist, since the antagonism between them forced them to struggle over control of the crop. Eventually one destroyed the other or reduced him to a subordinate, unchallenging position.

In the context of Alliance electoral action, the Alliance sought to wrest control of government, either from landlord interests or from representatives of railroads and banks, in order to advance the cause—farmer prosperity—at their expense. These conflicts were "antagonistic" (see Chapter 10, "The Class Make-up of the

Organization") and therefore the opposition could be expected to use fraud, corruption, and any other means to maintain control of the government apparatus. Since the Alliance began with no sector of the government under its control, it had no internal leverage: The opposition controlled all sectors and could be expected to utilize them in the counterattack. The use of voting blocs depended upon cooperation from the system which was not forthcoming. Therefore, voting, like cooperatives, was doomed to failure by its ultimate reliance on institutional power.

What is most important in this discussion is the fact that in a situation of conflict between two groups in one structure, one or the other group dominates all structural modes of power. Those structural levers which the subordinate group gains control of are guaranteed by some outside force or else they are ultimately captured by the dominant group and rendered useless. Effective protest relies on non-institutional power.

We have made several points in this discussion:

1. Every functioning system has a set of routinized power relations in effect on a day-to-day basis. This is structural power since the structure could not function without the existence and use of this power.
2. Those who are subject to this structural power possess a latent power deriving from the possibility of refusing to abide by the power exercised over them. Since the system depends on their obedience, it cannot function if the subordinates refuse to obey the commands given them.
3. This latent power can be exercised only if the subordinate group organizes itself. Only by united, common action can the ability to disrupt become activated, since any individual could be replaced with little harm to the system.
4. The organization of the subordinate group must be carried out independently of the structure itself. If this is not done, then the exercise of leverage *against* the structure will fail since the structure will use its power to frustrate the effectiveness of the action.
5. Power exercised by a group that depends on its place in the structure and its ability to withhold obedience to the structural power relations is non-institutional in form and exists independent of state power as well as structural power.

The Prevailing Analysis of the Situation

The Question of "Accuracy"

So far, our discussion has focused on the objective situation in which a group operates, but it is often hindsight alone which allows a full understanding of this reality. At the time an organization or protest group adopts a plan of action, the situation is filled with ambiguities. Many facts are unavailable, many ideas are unclearly formed, and there are competing explanations for even agreed upon facts. The prevailing analysis is highly inaccurate, and it may, in fact, mislead the organization into actions that do not have the slimmest hope of redressing the members' grievances.

The success of a protest organization depends upon a realistic assessment of its situation, and therefore the development and acceptance of an accurate analysis by the membership. Our concern in this section is to discuss the factors that condition this process. In doing so, we shall focus on whether or not the prevailing analysis is *correct*, whether it provides people with an accurate and usable portrait of their problems.

There is almost no discussion in the literature on social movements about this central problem. Herbert Blumer, in his widely cited essay, characterizes a usable analysis as "prestigious," "respectable," and "appealing." It does not need to be "accurate."[2] Smelser, in a 50-page discussion of "generalized beliefs," nowhere raises the question of accuracy. His treatise on collective behavior offers no discussion of the implications of masses of individuals acting upon false or near-false analyses of their circumstance.[3]

The reason for this neglect is made explicit by Turner and Killian. "Certainly," they assert, a protester "will impute a source" to his or her problems, but

> it does not greatly matter whether he identifies the nature and source correctly or not because his actions seldom succeed in eliminating the cause as he identifies it. Unless the imputed source can be successfully eliminated, when it would be possible to see whether the discontent subsides, it is normally impossible to know whether the source has been correctly identified or not. Hence the individual's conviction that he correctly understands his feelings is based on other considerations.[4]

This assertion is not defended—it is seen as self-evident. And behind it is the same "irrational" view of people that we have already discussed. According to Turner and Killian, protesters do not adopt an analysis because it fits best with the evidence at hand; they adopt one because it fits with their "conceptions about human motivation," because they find "social support" for this view, and because the actions that flow from it "are in themselves gratifying."[5]

Two examples will illustrate the application of this theory of protest behavior. James R. McGovern approaches the women's movement through an "in-depth" psychological analysis of the "model feminist." "This approach," he argues, reveals the movement

> as a relationship between the drives of leaders and its social achievements. It also demonstrates the real role of fantasy in sustaining what for most followers of a movement is merely its 'truth'.

---

[2] Herbert Blumer, "Social Movements," in *Studies in Social Movements* ed. Barry McLaughlin (New York, 1969), pp. 19–20.

[3] Neil Smelser, *Theory of Collective Behavior* (New York, 1962), especially pp. 79–130.

[4] Ralph H. Turner and Lewis M. Killian, *Collective Behavior*, 2d ed. (Englewood Cliffs, N.J., 1972), p. 249.

[5] *Ibid.*

But it underscores as well the important contributions of the neurotic personality to historical change and conversely illustrates how ideology and organization serve underlying needs and purposes of such personalities.[6]

Turner and Killian propose a similar, though not as declamatory, interpretation of the sources of discontent among poor people. "It is reasonable," they assert, "to suppose that people feel powerless because they have been exposed to this set of ideas under suitable circumstances rather than because their actual state of powerlessness has led them to feel powerless."[7]

Blumer, Smelser, Turner and Killian, and other social psychological theorists of protest groups assume that the accuracy of the analysis is *irrelevant*. Protesters have no way to know the truth of their ideas, and they are not led to them by any particular search for truth. Beliefs fill psychological needs and are "arational." As Smelser puts it: "Beliefs associated with collective behavior differ . . . from many of those which characterize everyday action."[8]

The lynchpin of this view is the notion that people have no way of knowing whether or not their analysis is correct—"it is normally impossible to know whether the source has been correctly identified or not." From this assertion the rest follows: If people have no way of checking the truth of their analysis, they must accept or reject it according to some "arational" criterion. Certainly this logic applies to a great many general beliefs which people have. But it has only a secondary importance in explaining the ideology of protest groups, because protesters *can* test the accuracy of their ideas. Indeed, the history of protest organizations can be viewed as a laboratory in which the truth of their understanding is constantly tested by the successes and failures of the movement.

The basic process is actually quite simple, though many conflicting forces enter to complicate it. We can begin by noting that the analysis that a protest group adopts is used as a tool, a guide to actions against the system. Its accuracy is tested by those actions. If they are successful, the analysis must in some important respects be accurate and it will probably remain unchanged. If the actions are unsuccessful, then there must be crucial flaws in the analysis, and it will probably be changed.

What are the objections to this "rationalist," "hypothesis testing" model? First, many sociologists argue that there is no way to measure "success" and therefore no way to test an analysis. Turner and Killian conclude, for example, that the "decision to describe a movement as successful or unsuccessful depends upon the perspective of the observer."[9] Any outcome will seem "successful" to some, "unsuccessful" to others.

But this argument ignores the very high degree of unanimity of "perspective" that protest group membership can and does obtain. The overwhelming majority

[6] James P. McGovern, "Anna Howard Shaw: New Approaches to Feminism," *Journal of Social History* 3 (Winter 1969–1970), p. 153, quoted in Linda Gordon *et al.*, "A Review of Sexism in American Historical Writing," *Women's Studies* 1 (1972), p. 145.
[7] Turner and Killian, *op. cit.*, p. 249.
[8] Smelser, *op. cit.*, p. 79.
[9] Turner and Killian, *op. cit.*, p. 256.

of farmers joined the Farmers' Alliance to change specific features of their daily existence. One of these day-to-day features was high supply prices, and the Alliance organized boycotts in an attempt to reduce them. It was not hard to assess these actions, because prices either dropped or they did not. If they succeeded, it was clear; if they failed, it was also clear. Because of the common perspective—the desire for lower prices—the Turner and Killian assertion that different perspectives would reach different conclusions does not apply. Certainly some individuals joint protest groups in order to advance themselves, others join out of a need for social life, camaraderie, and soon. But even most of these individuals are deeply committed to the predominant perspective—the desire to redress certain kinds of grievances.[10] Hence, most protest groups have a very well-defined perspective: They are successful if they alleviate the day-to-day problems that gave birth to the group. The analysis is evaluated according to its ability to guide the group to this kind of success.

A second objection to the rationalist model presented here is its simplicity. Any social structure, say the critics, is too complicated to be so simply manipulated. If a farmer joined the Alliance, and the next year he did very well, he should not assume that his Alliance activities caused his prosperity. It could have been good weather, economic fluctuations, bad crops in other parts of the world, or even luck. Two facets of this argument need discussion.

First, farmers, unionists, and members of other protest groups are not stupid. They can assess evidence and make judgments about causation. If a farmer participated in a boycott that failed to lower prices, he would not likely claim that this was the cause of his better year. If the price of cotton suddenly rose, few farmers—regardless of how committed they were to the Alliance—would deny that economic fluctuations were not a possible cause (unless they had clear evidence to the contrary).

Second, there are many situations in which causation is complicated or ambiguous. In these circumstances, most people do not revise their ideas much, but neither do they become more attached to them. Incorrect analyses will continue to be used unless actions or events arise to discredit them clearly. And since reality is complicated, partially accurate analyses may be used for long periods. But this certainly differs from Turner and Killian's view that rational evaluation has little to do with individual or organizational behavior. For example, the Clebourne convention was responding to the failure of local boycotts and cooperatives. Some individuals argued that these failures proved the bankruptcy of economic protest and the necessity of political action. Others argued that they showed only that the scope of economic action should be broadened to district, state, and national levels. The evidence could not resolve this dispute and the ambiguity created the basis

---

[10] Only a few individuals join organizations with a predominant commitment to their own ambitions, social needs, etc. While they are a relative handful, they can substantially alter the organization's behavior if they possess needed resources or attain influential positions within the organization. Much of the discussion in this theoretical chapter and the study of Alliance activity is devoted to understanding how and when these situations arise.

for the sharp conflict at Clebourne. But the evidence was clear on the main point: Boycotts and other uncoordinated local actions would not work. And the membership, no matter how congenial this orientation was to them psychologically, turned away from it. If the social psychological theorists were correct, the organization would have clung to local actions because these actions conformed to the members' "conceptions of human motivation," they found "social support" for them, and they were "in themselves gratifying."

A third objection to the rationalist model argues, that if it is possible for protest groups to act on incorrect analyses over and over again with apparent success, then it must be irrelevant whether the analysis is correct. To meet this objection, we must distinguish between general theories and specific tactics. Organizational membership can easily measure the success of many specific tactics: If the actions result in concrete beneficial changes, they are successful; if they do not, they are unsuccessful. Thus, protest groups change tactics frequently, adopting new ones and discarding old ones that have failed. The history of the Farmers' Alliance can be told in terms of the migration from one tactic to another.

On the other hand, theories are harder to test. Even if one tactic fails, this failure may be a misapplication of a theory instead of an invalidation of it. For this reason, overall orientations remain more stable. But this does not mean that they do not change. If the organization is repeatedly unsuccessful, people within the organization will begin to adopt new analyses which they think will produce more successfull actions.[11] Such new analyses are either borrowed from other groups or else developed within the organization. In either case, a "debate" arises which can result in organizational "test" of the competing theories: actions taken on the basis of one theory whose results are seen as the crucial evidence of its validity. When a new theory proves more useful, it will ordinarily be adopted to replace the old one. Of course, this theory may also be inaccurate. There is no guarantee that it will be a perfect analysis.

The Clebourne demands offer an instructive illustration of this process. The local cooperatives and boycotts of the Alliance had been successfully thwarted and their initial successes had begun to falter. Repeated failure called for a reassessment of the strategy. This reassessment involved questioning the basic assumptions about the tenancy system held by many Alliancemen up until then. For example, cooperative stores had failed partly because wholesalers refused to supply them. This forced many individuals to change their view of who the opposition included instead of seeing their enemy as mainly the retail merchants, they began to analyze their plight as a consequence of the structure of supply.

Out of this questioning emerged two competing theories. In one theory, the Alliance could best succeed by pushing the state government into regulating the supply system. This analysis lay behind the Clebourne demands. Afterward, this

---

[11] Social movement literature is almost devoid of any attention to this process. Turner and Killian, *op. cit.*, ch. 14, especially pp. 284–288, for example, devote many pages to discussing the development and alteration of movement ideology. But nowhere do they mention the possibility that such changes flow from "learning from mistakes."

policy was reversed and the Alliance embarked upon an organizing drive to widen its membership base. Behind this policy was an analysis that held that a broad enough membership base could exercise sufficient economic leverage to alter the system. Thus, the two new analyses each embraced the lesson from the previous failures, but they disagreed on other, untested, aspects of the system. The latter strategy was pursued with only partial success for 5 years before it was abandoned.

Thus, while the rational evaluation of tactics is straightforward and generally results in rapid change, the testing of broader, strategic orientations is slower and more problematical. But the process occurs, with all its complications. And the accuracy of the broad theory is central to the organization because tactical actions are guided by strategic views. The day-to-day success of the protest group is profoundly affected by the theoretical orientation.

We can now turn to a fourth objection to the "hypothesis testing" view of movement ideology. If people accept or reject analyses according to their accuracy in guiding action, why do so many protest groups survive with obviously mistaken and even self-contradictory ideologies. There are five major responses to this.

First, we have already discussed in Chapter 9 the origins of ideological disagreement. The varying experiences of different individuals and the operation of structured ignorance make many inaccurate hypotheses plausible. And the complexity of society always allows for incorrect interpretations of any set of events. The wide diversity of correct and incorrect ideas found among similarly situated people can be explained with little reference to psychological or pathological variables.

Second, inaccuracy is rapidly decreased by the activities of social movements. Before a protest group arises, individuals may have limited facts with which to assess their circumstances. But this ignorance is reduced because members learn from each other's experience and because the organization initiates and carries through actions aimed at changing the situation. The various theories are tested by these actions, and a homogenization occurs.

Third, movements with ineffective or mistaken ideologies do not usually survive. The biography of the overwhelming majority of protest groups is quite simple. They form over a particular issue and analysis. They act on this theory. They fail. They die. Because they did not have a correct analysis, they could not redress grievances and they therefore did not attract people. There are two frequent variants of this pattern. In one, the group has initial success and grows, but then it fails and dies. In this case, the analysis had some validity but not enough to answer the first counterattack. In the second variant, a handful of diehards maintains the group after it has lost all chance of effectiveness. In this case, perhaps the elaborate psychological analyses are in order, but the main feature is still that inaccurate analysis results in failure. Social movement theorists rarely study these ineffective groups, but they are important in understanding the social process of protest organizations. By and large, groups with analyses that do not have a probable ·chance to accomplish change die, remain tiny, or totally change their orientation. Only those with accurate analyses will grow and survive.

Fourth, the small minority of protest groups that do grow and prosper have accurate analyses of the crucial aspects of their situation. Consider labor unions:

The central theory which informs their activities is that management and labor are in contradiction to each other. Management will refuse pay raises, working-condition improvements, and fringe benefits unless the workers resort to force or threaten to use force. This view, which is now accepted by most students of unions, was a radical and blasphemous idea before unionization was successful. Long before social scientists endorsed this analysis, laborers in large numbers came to understand and act upon it. In doing so, they established its validity. Had strikes mainly failed, the union movement would have had to find another tactic or else disappear.

Sometimes, the rationality of movement ideology is not readily apparent. The Farmers' Alliance adopted an extremely negative view of the American economic system. Alliancemen were ridiculed and called crazy, reds, radicals, and so forth, and their ideas were scorned in the press.[12] But later analyses of the social system and the Alliance challenge to it have softened that view. Today, most accounts endorse Alliance contentions that the economic system exploited the farmer, that railroads abused their power, that monopolistic tendencies in banking and industry acted to increase the misery of the poor, and that this entire situation was worsened by corrupt politicians who gave aid and comfort to these abusers.[13]

If one reviews the history of large protest organizations and movements, one finds the pattern very similar. The analysis that they endorse is at first reviled and denied by the established experts. But later their ideas are found to have had validity, their analysis is at least partially endorsed; and the actions based on them are largely justified.[14]

Fifth, the parts of the analysis that remain inaccurate are mostly abstract. The activities of protest groups test and retest the theories that guide them. But some of the general assertions are difficult to assess. None of the actions—successes or failures—reflects on their accuracy because these features of the theory do not dictate specific actions. A group can proceed for many years without scrutinizing certain parts of its ideology (or without resolving ideological differences between two subgroups) because there is no action based on them. All too often, theorists of social protest focus upon the most abstract parts of movement theories, find faults, and conclude that the accuracy of the ideas was not an issue. Unused portions of an analysis have minor roles in the life of a protest group. Sometimes they are matters of some dispute; sometimes they are important only to a small segment of the group; and sometimes they are inactively endorsed by most of the membership. But as long as they do not dictate policy, they will have little force.

---

[12]For example, see "Crazes," *Nation* 53 (November 26, 1891), p. 403; Hon. John Davis, "Communism or Capitalism—The Real Issue Before the People," *Arena* 6 (September 1893), pp. 417–419; "The Real Issues," *Harper's Weekly* 34 (October 25, 1890), p. 822; Frank B. Tracy, "Rise and Doom of the Populist Party," *Forum* 16 (October 1893), pp. 240–251.

[13]C. Vann Woodward, *Origins of the New South, 1877–1913* (Baton Rouge, 1951). This is the most widely respected history of this period, and in broad terms it supports the basic views of the Farmers' Alliance.

[14]The student movement of the 1960s is just beginning to be reevaluated in this way. See Max Heirich, *The Spiral of Conflict, Berkeley, 1964* (New York, 1968), for a detailed analysis of the rationality of the students' ideas and actions in the free speech movement, the first major white student protest of the 1960s.

How the Analysis Affects Leadership and vice versa

Any organization contains competing ideas, and choosing among programs premised upon competing analyses is a frequently utilized procedure. It is therefore useful to frame our discussion of "prevailing analysis" in terms of the competition among two or more sets of analyses—only one of which can prevail at a given time. We should not, however, lose track of two important facts. The adoption of one "analysis" over another does not necessarily imply a permanent ascendancy, nor does it imply that the organization will follow that analysis without fail. As with all aspects of organizational behavior, the situation is fluid and changing and need not be wholly consistent either among internal elements or over time. For example, only 6 months after the Clebourne demands shifted the Alliance into politics, the Waco convention shifted it back to economic action.

Just as internal structure may prevent the adoption of a policy that is in the interests of a majority of the group, it may also prevent the adoption of a potentially popular analysis. The internal structure of the organization may contribute to "structurered ignorance": Constraints on the free flow of information may prevent the accurate assessment of experience and inhibit the collective evaluation of competing analyses. Most important in this regard is the central role played by leadership.

The operation of the early cooperatives required business expertise, and the local leadership, which was recruited on the basis of possessing this expertise, was embarrassed by the failure of these local enterprises. The statewide leadership was not bound in the same way to these policies, and it sought to initiate statewide actions that would tilt the center of gravity toward itself. When the controversy developed within the Alliance over the Clebourne demands, it is not surprising that the local leaders were lined up against statewide political action, while the statewide leadership generally supported it.

Here we see an interaction between analysis and structure. In the first instance, the analysis of how the merchants could be successfully attacked led to the formation of cooperatives. One of the implications of this structural development was the elevation of individuals with business experience to local leadership positions, while men with different abilities rose to statewide leadership positions. Later, upon the failure of the boycotts and cooperatives, these two different leadership groups offered different analyses of the problems—the local leaders tried to avoid an analysis that posed the economic programs as hopeless, while the statewide leadership argued for more political analyses which served its interest.

We have arrived at a cycle of causation: An accepted analysis prescribes the form or structure required to enact it; and thus the analysis determines the structure in part. The new structure then elevates certain people to positions of leadership, while preventing others from rising. This "unrepresentative" leadership then determines what new analyses will be presented to the organization.

Several important conclusions can be drawn from this. First, leadership groups are often the source of "new ideas." After a failure, individual members have great difficulty reaching people with new ideas. Leaders, on the other hand, are ideally situated to accomplish this. Thus, in many situations, leaders define the terms of debate and present analyses for approval or veto. If the leadership promotes only those analyses which defend its own interests, it may be very difficult for a more correct analysis to gain currency. We see here, then, the possibility of "structured ignorance" emanating from within the group itself. The process of "hypothesis testing" can be weakened because the leadership presents only those hypotheses which are acceptable to it. Even if the membership consistently rejects these analyses, better proposals may never be discussed.

Second, the existence of two competing leadership groups does not necessarily guarantee the promotion of the best strategy. There is a disarming logic—most forcefully presented by S. M. Lipset[15]—that when two leadership groups compete for membership support, they will each attempt to find and present the most beneficial policy for the membership. According to this view, this pattern is made inevitable by competition carried on in much the same way that two businesses often compete by lowering prices to a minimum level. But just as competitive pricing frequently breaks down in the economic realm, so does "competitive policy formation" break down in protest movements. Many potential activities would undermine the strength of *both* leadership groups, and therefore neither presses for these policies. For example, at no time in Alliance history did either state leadership or local leadership show any interest in creating a *centralized* national organization, however promising this might have been in terms of successful reform activity. Thus, even with competing leadership groups, there is no guarantee that all potentially successful ideas will be widely circulated and discussed. There may be more variety, but this variety may still be very limited and it may exclude the most relevant new ideas.

Third, a perfectly "democratic" organization can adopt and readopt useless programs, pursue failing activities, and embrace false theories without any mass irrationality or psychopathology present among the membership. The pursuit of a plausible, promising program can lead to the recruitment of leadership with interests that conflict with the needs of the rank and file. If this leadership group (or groups) is in a position to influence the dissemination of ideas within the organization, debates within the group will exclude those ideas uncongenial to the leadership. Without the entire range of alternatives, membership suffers from structural ignorance and may be repeatedly forced to choose among several bad programs. In this circumstance, the decision taken, however democratic the procedure is, will be less than satisfactory. Even if the newly adopted program fails and is soon discarded, this may not bring the group closer to a better program since the ensuing debate will still be restricted because of control over information dispersal exercised by the leadership group.

Thus, within a "democratic" decisionmaking procedure, certain solutions may

[15] S. M. Lipset, *Union Democracy* (Garden City, N.Y., 1962); see also Robert Dahl, *Preface to Democratic Theory* (Chicago, 1956); Arnold Rose, *The Power Structure* (New York, 1966).

never be considered, never be given a fair hearing, and therefore never be adopted, because a more or less cohesive leadership group has excluded promising proposals that threaten its position. The organization may cling tenaciously to a small number of failing or marginally successful activities, or it may wander among a great many different programs. In either case, it suffers from ossification and will lose in some degree its ability to learn and grow from experience.

Apparently democratic organizations are not necessarily democratic. The structural "solution" to democracy in which policies are created by competing elites and subjected to membership approval, proposed by Lipset and other pluralist political theorists, fails to take into account the restriction of debate we have discussed here.[16]

The connection between analysis and leadership is complicated and circular. Any analysis that is acted upon results in the creation of certain structures and, perhaps most important, certain leadership—membership relations. Since leadership often controls information flow, the next set of ideas will be filtered before it reaches a wide audience. If leadership is in some way unified around one orientation and/or against others, the terms of debate will be restricted and the organization itself will contribute to the creation and maintenance of structural ignorance. Faulty analysis will become more probable, and actions will become less successful. Especially in times of crisis—when the organization needs new programs to replace failing ones—this structured inefficiency can destroy the usefulness of a protest group.

How the Analysis Affects Recruitment Patterns and vice versa

The analysis an organization endorses has a substantial impact on recruitment. Many individuals judge a group by its appeal, and different people find different analyses "appealing." Differential appeal has to do with "psychological" variables, but mainly it relates to the different ways in which potential members have related to the "parent" structure.

A tenant, for example, related to the supply and selling systems almost exclusively through his or her merchant—landlord. He or she had little or no experience with marketing, selective buying, and transportation problems. His or her main concern centered around how to control, handle, or eliminate the merchant as a dominating influence. As a consequence, he or she was more easily organized to attack this visible enemy—the merchant or landlord—than the invisible enemy—the railroad. The yeoman, or former yeoman, on the other hand, had experiences with marketing and transport and perhaps with selective buying. Therefore, his or her vision of change included the possible reform of transport and merchandising systems.

This differential appeal exists above and beyond actual differences in "class

---

[16] Lipset, *op. cit.*

interest." While some of the yeoman demands against railroads would not have benefited tenants, others would have. Lack of experience with the marketing system made it difficult for tenants to see that these demands were in their interest. They needed ideas and materials that would explain how the proposed reforms would address their problems.

The prevailing analysis, then, in part determines who will join a movement. It also determines what kind of agitation and proselytizing must take place to educate those who do not immediately see the connection between the proposed program and their own problems.

A protest organization feels pressure to tailor its analysis to avoid the opposition of as many people as possible, and to include the support of as many people as possible. Even after a policy is set, the analysis of that policy can be altered to win the support of fresh groups. The analysis therefore undergoes progressive change as the organization discovers which arguments win support and which ones mobilize the opposition. Sometimes this results in the alteration or elimination of demands.

The structural location of the organization's membership has a profound effect on the analysis of the situation. Any protest organization searches for an understanding that harnesses the structural power its members can exercise. This requires that the organization pay careful attention to the past experiences of its members and other people in similar circumstances. It may also demand a kind of division of labor among varying subgroups—with each one exacting leverage when and where it can.

In some circumstances, groups find it impossible to develop potent leverage over the structure they wish to change. In these cases, the survival of the organization depends upon the development of new analyses which will lead to successful action. Most often the organization does indeed die, but in a few cases, it embarks upon a major transformation.

First, the organization can explicitly seek to organize a group with enough structural leverage to achieve its goals. Here an analysis of structural impotence leads to an attempt to change the class basis of the supporters. It can mean revamping several important but expendable parts of the previous analysis in order to appeal to this new group of supporters. An example of this was the decision of the Alliance to tailor its Clebourne demands to the needs of the large planters so that the Alliance could take advantage of the position the planters held in the political structure.

Second, the organization can embrace the structural powerlessness of its membership and attempt to develop power outside the structural relations of the system which is to be changed. The most dramatic and important indicator of this is the adoption of terror tactics which depend on the single-handed bravery of the individual terrorist. The basis of power behind these tactics (whether they be terror or something less dramatic) is the disruption of the structure "from without"— disruption without the use of structural leverage by those upon whom the system depends for its existence. It represents an analysis that "we cannot really exercise power" followed by a new analysis that the way to exercise power is to challenge the structure without organizing those within it.

Analysis and recruitment are ultimately connected by the strands of organizational success. The prevailing analysis creates recruitment patterns through its differential appeal among prospective supporters, and the entry of these supporters into protest activity is the prerequisite for successful application of the analysis. This recursive relationship is then complicated by the intervention of a wide range of other circumstances.

Our discussion of the role played by analysis and ideology is not a complete catalogue of the constant and complicated interchange between the guiding ideas of an organization and its activities. We have restricted ourselves to a review of several of the central themes in this interchange.

1. Protest groups use their analysis to guide action, and therefore the *accuracy* of the analysis used is a central factor in its effectiveness and its survival.

2. While the class position of membership is a major determinant of what initial analysis is adopted, programmatic activities create feedback which results in a fluid and constantly changing set of ideas. If some structural arrangement prevents this "organizational learning" from occurring, then the group must become less and less successful and die.

3. The analysis leads to actions and thus to particular organizational forms. Once these forms develop, they place leverage in the hands of leadership which has been recruited to advance certain programs. Thus, the leadership created by an analysis will have a major influence on the debate following the failure of the analysis. A cycle is set up, with analysis influencing the particular type of leadership, which in turn influences whatever changes occur in the analysis.

4. This analysis—leadership cycle is central to maintenance of organizational democracy. Either through the operation of internal structural processes or through external connections, the leadership may have some or many interests in contradiction with those of the membership. If the organizational structure allows for leadership domination of internal debate, then when new analyses are being considered to replace failures, the membership will not be systematically exposed to ideas that conflict with leadership needs. The existence of competing leadership groups may not lessen this since in many situations the competing groups both seek to exclude whole categories of analysis.

5. The potential support and opposition will put pressure on the analysis developed since analyses will be tailored to winning support or neutralizing potential opposition.

6. The structural position of the membership and of the potential membership will direct the analysis of the organization toward the development of its latent structural power. In addition, the lack of power or the ineffective use of potential structural power will result in an "analytic crisis" which will destroy the organization unless a new understanding develops of how to exercise power.

The Previous Actions and Their Outcomes

We have already discussed the impact of previous actions undertaken by an organization on both the structure and analysis of that organization. The undertaking of a certain action requires the construction of a certain type of organization. This organizational structure then puts limits on the ability of that organization to undertake various new projects—the structure is amenable to some projects but not to others. In much the same way, we can review the influence of previous actions on the potential and active support or opposition, on the structural role of the membership in the larger system, and upon the prevailing analysis. Much of this work has been done in the preceding sections and need not be reiterated here. This section is devoted to the two important principles of "organizational learning" and "membership demoralization." Both of these are integrally connected with the success or failure of organizational enterprises, and they play an important role in determining new actions.

The Farmers' Alliance recruited its farmer membership on the hope that united action would result in an improvement in the situation of yeomen and tenant farmers. By and large, protest groups contain individuals with this sort of straightforward purpose, and while there were myriad other motivating reasons—some consonant and some dissonant with this basic motive—it is possible and fruitful to ignore these here. In this section, therefore, we deal with the relationship of past actions to the basic goals of membership of the organization. It is this relationship which is important in understanding membership demoralization.

We have already emphasized that a key variable in the ability of an organization to carry out its agreed upon goals is organizational discipline: the ability to motivate membership to act and change its action in unison. Central to this discipline is rank-and-file understanding of the way the organization's program will produce the desired reforms.

The counterpart to discipline is "demoralization." Demoralization means that a member does not believe that the organization's action, or his or her own part in the organization's action, will have any real effect. People are unwilling to do the work necessary to sustain such action, and they are unwilling to coordinate their efforts with those of others to create disciplined organizational behavior. Members drop away and the organization cannot continue to function.

The question of demoralization is related to that of attracting membership. Recruitment is largely based on convincing those outside the organization that its programs will, in fact, help them. Thus, any organization is faced with two related but distinct problems. On the one hand, it looks out to a possible membership which must be convinced of the efficacy of the organization in winning the changes they wish. (Many, of course, must be convinced that changes are needed.) On the other hand, those already inside the organization must be constantly reinforced in their belief that the organization is succeeding.

The results of previous actions affect both the recruitment of new membership and the maintenance of discipline among old membership. The chief evidence for the efficacy of an organization is the result of the actions it takes. To the extent that these actions produce meaningful reforms, the organization validates its claim upon its membership's time and energy. Organizational discipline is therefore intimately related to the successful completion of various undertakings or projects. Similarly, potential new members are attracted by a proven ability to produce results. Recruitment is therefore also tied to organizational success.

It is easy to see the effect of success, but not so easy to see the effect of failure. Failure does not lead to demoralization unless the membership's faith in the organization's ability to succeed is shaken.

There often exist ambiguous situations in which it is hard to tell whether or not the organization has succeeded, and the membership can be led to believe in success where failure has actually resulted. For example, one of the Clebourne demands called for railroad control. Texas did form a Railroad Control Board, which had as its purpose the control of railroad rates. The board fell into the hands of the railroads themselves, however, and did not effectively control rates. However, when this bill was first passed, it appeared to be an important victory to those who wished to achieve lower rates and it stood as important evidence of the effectiveness of the Alliance. On the basis of this, many people joined the Alliance and worked within it.

However, the final test of all actions taken by an organization is whether they influence the lives of the members themselves. In the long run, unless the constituency sees a change in the original problems, it will begin to lose faith in the organization and fall away from it. Thus, the expedient of convincing individuals that success has been achieved works in the short run only—the long run will produce no perceptible changes and demoralization will follow.

Consider the implications of demoralization resulting from long-term failure. First, there is in voluntary organizations an inherent pressure toward a fundamental democracy. Unless the organization meets the basic needs that led its membership to join, the membership will leave and the organization will disintegrate. Voluntary organizations cannot survive unless they can maintain the interest and involvement of their membership, and this interest and involvement can be maintained in the long run only by the accomplishment of real changes which can be perceived by the membership and potential membership. A leadership unresponsive to the needs of its constituency is left without a constituency.

This process is magnified in protest organizations. Since protest organizations are always faced with an adversary who seeks to defeat the movement's demands, any failure of the organization is likely to be publicized by the structure under attack. Moreover, the derivative nature of protest groups means that the membership is in day-to-day contact with the opposition. The ability to fool the membership is moderated tremendously by the ability of the adversary to publicize any inaccuracies of analysis or reporting that might be present inside the organization.

Second, leadership groups are particularly threatened by the failure of any project. Unless failure can be avoided or covered over, it will result in the membership's becoming demoralized, and the strength of the organization will begin to dissipate. If the leadership is more committed to the continuation of the organization than to the membership, this commitment creates powerful pressure for avoidance of failure to take precedence over successful achievement of ends. Among the possible results are several of consequence in understanding the Farmer's Alliance:

1. Programs are adopted which have obscure or abstract results. Thus, the membership cannot easily perceive whether or not the action has been successful and must depend on the leadership to be their "eyes" and "ears."
2. Actions are taken which will find favor with the mass media—and often with the obvious adversary, so that the lack of success will not be immediately exposed by an adversary well equipped to inform the membership.
3. Programs are adopted which have a good chance of success, so that failure can be avoided. Whether or not these programs meet basic needs is less important than whether actions are successful.

All these possibilities only postpone the demoralization of the membership, since they all sacrifice long-range success in favor of short-run achievements. Therefore, none of them actually resolves the contradiction between the inability of an organization to meet basic needs and the necessity of its satisfying its membership in order to survive.

This brings us to the third implication of the threat of demoralization. If the leadership becomes fundamentally separated from its membership in terms of class interest, then it can begin pursuing goals which will not, in fact, aid the membership. If this occurs, then the leadership can expect long-run demoralization of its membership, though in the short run, it may be able to maintain considerable membership size and discipline. However, if the leadership adopts policies that depend upon the *threat* of membership action without having actually to realize that action, it can wield great influence without needing to mobilize the membership. Thus, lobbying in a state legislature may be effective because of the threat of votes, but those votes need not be mobilized. This kind of threat power can enable the leadership of an organization to utilize *past* membership discipline to achieve ends for which the organization could not motivate the membership to work. Naturally, this would depend on fooling an adversary into believing that the membership was sufficiently committed to the action so that they would act if necessary.

What this implies is that when an organization only poses the threat of mass action, there is no real test of whether the action is actually supported by the membership. Therefore, it is possible for a dead or dying organization to wield power, despite its inability actually to mobilize its membership.

There is one escape from the "failure—demoralization" pattern: if the membership retains its faith that the organization will ultimately prove successful. There is the old slogan—"learn from mistakes"—which has a special meaning when we speak of protest organizations. To the extent that an organization can turn an unsuccessful attempt at meeting its basic goals into a clearer strategy for accomplishing them later, we can say that the organization has "learned" from its mistakes. What is important here is to distinguish between some individuals or groups within an organization learning from previous action and the organization's actually changing its structural behavior in light of this. The former is an abstracted and useless learning in terms of convincing members that the organization can meet their needs, while the latter indicates that the organization as a whole has changed its behavior in light of previous failures.

We have spoken before of the constraints that organizational structure puts upon the adoption of various policies. Different actions require different structures. Sometimes, it is impossible for an organization to adopt a policy simply because it does not have the structure to enforce it. For example, in 1886, the Texas Alliance could not initiate a policy of pressuring the federal government because it did not have the necessary interstate structure.

When an organization has attempted to achieve its ends through one policy and has failed, then the keynote of real organizational "learning" is whether or not it dismantles the structures built to enhance and realize that policy. A failure must be accompanied by an analysis of why that failure took place, but it also requires a structural alteration to match the needs of the new policy.

It is at this node, when policies have failed and new ones are adopted, that the role of analysis is most direct and urgent. There is, in a sense, a structural interregnum during which the organization must rearrange itself and create a new structure conducive to the new policies and actions to be undertaken. The rearrangement must be made according to an understanding of what is needed—this understanding is what we call an analysis. To the extent that analyses are really important in organizations, they play their crucial role at these moments.

In order for an organization to learn from its experiences, it must change its functioning on the basis of them. A changed organization is one with a different structure—a structure tailored to the new policies, designed to realize the new goals that have been established.

12

The Life of Protest Organizations

Protest organizations survive or die according to how successfully they redress the grievances of their membership. Predicting their ultimate fate in therefore involves understanding how and why they succeed or fail. The preceding chapters have elaborated on a great many determinants of this; this chapter seeks to distill these lengthy discussions into a coherent set of analytic principles.

First, we address a central issue: Under what circumstances will protest activity succeed in altering the parent structure in a way that advances the interests of its membership? The necessary and sufficient conditions are these:

1. The changes demanded from the system must be beneficial to the protest group membership.
2. The group must adopt a tactic to disrupt or threaten to disrupt the normal functioning of the system. That is, the group must develop the latent structural power of its membership.
3. The group must organize a sufficient proportion of those with grievances to activate the mass character of their structural power.
4. The group must develop sufficient organizational discipline so that the membership can coordinate the changes of action necessary to exercise structural leverage.

Each of these conditions is created by other, preceding conditions. We shall therefore discuss them in turn. This discussion will summarize most of the important principles developed in Chapters 8–11. One central issue which spans all others will then be treated: the development of oligarchy. Finally, we shall briefly focus on the connection between the dynamics discussed here and the birth and death of protest organizations.

1. *Correct demands.* The development of correct demands depends upon successful reduction of structured ignorance. Our discussion of the conditions under which this takes place may be summarized in five propositions.

a. If the membership is "class homogeneous," then discovering demands that
    serve all members is relatively simple. If many different classes are involved,
    a common interest must be discovered. In some cases, no such common
    interest exists.
b. The parent social structure acts in the interest of the elite and therefore all
    ignorance-reducing efforts carried on by the parent structure mask the anta-
    gonisms between the rank and file and the elite.
c. Protest groups, because they arise with the purpose of attacking and changing
    the structure, embrace theories that perceive these elite—non-elite anta-
    gonisms. Protest organizations are the main method by which structured
    ignorance about these antagonistic aspects of the social system is reduced.
d. If there is substantial membership participation in, and information about,
    demands and activities, demands that fail to serve membership needs will be
    discarded. Therefore, in a nonoligarchic protest group, organizational learn-
    ing takes place. The "learning" process involves the following sequence:
    Inaccurate analysis leads to incorrect demands. Incorrect demands fail to
    redress grievances and this development triggers internal debate and analysis.
    Structured ignorance is reduced and new—more accurate—analyses are
    adopted. Over time, the organization's analysis becomes more and more
    accurate.
e. Leadership with a class or structural interest different from that of the
    membership is the main obstacle to organizational learning, if it has partial
    or total control of information dispersal. After a failure has been recognized,
    leadership from a single subgroup in the organization will push the debate
    into new analyses that serve its own subgroup. Internally developed struc-
    tural elites will act to preserve their own position by suppressing analyses
    that emphsize antagonism with the parent structure. In either case, non-
    responsive leadership perpetuates and contributes to structured ignorance by
    failing to disseminate ideas and analyses antagonistic to their interest.

2. *Correct tactics.* A protest organization will win a demand if it utilizes its
position within the system to disrupt or threaten to disrupt the system. The
determinants of correct tactics may be summarized in four propositions.

a. If the protest organization is "class homogeneous," it will have a restricted
    number of tactics available to it. If it has individuals from many different
    classes, its available tactics increase.
b. Tactics that disrupt one element of the system while leaving the remaining
    elements unthreatened can focus the attack, restrict the opposition, and aug-
    ment the chances of success.
c. Focused attacks will not work unless the element under attack has the re-
    sources to grant the demand.
d. Most frequently, focused attacks are defeated by "escalation." They depend
    upon the noninvolvement by other, unattached, elements in the system. In a
    tightly connected structure, attack on one element may affect other, more

powerful, elements. These elements may have resources capable of defeating the focused attack and will therefore overwhelm the protest group.

3. *Size and growth.* A protest organization will maintain old membership and attract new supporters to the degree that it seems capable of redressing membership grievances. In one sense, then, the growth process is circular—the group needs a large membership to succeed, and it needs success to grow. The unraveling of this cycle may be summarized in five propositions.

   a. Worsening conditions create multiple grievances, eliminate many previous plausible solutions, and force individuals actively to seek methods of redress.
   b. Individuals who actively try other solutions to their grievances but fail will search for new methods and therefore may join a protest group.
   c. People whose class position and particular history in the system allows them to see the immediate advantages of protest group programs will most readily join the group.
   d. A protest organization will attract membership from particular groups to the degree that it develops and broadcasts an analysis that connects the organizational program to those groups' needs.
   e. If an organization uses its initial resources to win smaller successes and to bring its program to appropriate groups, these activities will produce a larger membership and therefore the potential for larger successes.

4. *Organizational discipline.* Organizational discipline and membership demoralization are the extremes within which participation takes place. They describe the degree to which the rank and file of an organization is willing to change its activities in order to advance organizational goals. The factors that determine discipline and demoralization are identical to those which determine membership increase and decrease. Here we shall delineate the broad connections between the organizational discipline—membership demoralization dimension and organizational behavior.

   a. Membership will be more disciplined to the degree that it believes organizational activities will be successful in redressing grievances. Therefore, success increases discipline; organizational learning increases discipline; and failure increases demoralization.
   b. Membership understanding of organizational policies leads to discipline. Lack of understanding increases demoralization. Therefore, any structural feature that decreases membership information about, and understanding of, the protest group's activities will decrease discipline and increase demoralization. In particular, oligarchy will have this effect, as will multiclass membership without a well-developed analysis.
   c. If the membership is responsible for outside organizing, it must be well informed about policy, the prerequisite for discipline. Hence, membership organizing implies organizational discipline (though the reverse may not hold). Since oligarchy means that the organization does not reduce structured ignorance (1.d) and this produces demoralization (4.a), oligarchy and

membership responsibility for organizing are incompatible. When such a structural arrangement occurs, one or the other is eliminated.

5. *Oligarchy.* The development of oligarchy depends upon the leadership's possessing or developing different interests from most of the membership. This, in combination with other factors, produces elite control.

   a. Recruitment of leaders from a single subgroup in the organization creates a leadership with different interests from those of the membership.

   b. Michelsian processes tend to create separate interests within any stable, privileged leadership group.

   c. Different leadership interests plus leadership control of information dispersal will result in oligarchy. Even if membership does the organizing, the process of organizational learning will be frustrated and membership demoralization will set in, shifting organizing responsibility to leadership.

   d. Different leadership interests plus leadership responsibility for outside organizing will result in oligarchy. Even if membership retains open channels of communication, the leadership will recruit the new membership and execute programs in its own interest. The new information based on these activities will be under the control of the leadership.

   e. Inaccurate analysis may lead to oligarchy if it produces the conditions of oligarchy. Thus, a mistaken program can produce a leadership structure that defeats attempts at understanding the past failures.

   f. Oligarchic leadership—especially that developed in a Michelsian manner—becomes within the protest group more and more an agency of the parent structure. This process results in the muting and diverting of tendencies to perceive antagonisms with the structure, as well as an increasingly demoralized membership.

The Birth and Death of Protest

The analysis of protest organizations presented in this book focuses upon the behavior of an ongoing group. As such, it seems to omit two crucial subjects—the origins of the organization and the causes and processes of its disintegration. This neglect is due partly to the necessity to limit the scope of the analysis. However, it is also a reflection of the underlying perspective presented here, which attaches less importance to "birth" and "death" than it does to "process." A brief discussion of these endpoints in the life of an organization will not only outline the approach to understanding them but also provide an argument for the generalizability of the analysis.

To the degree that social structures generate grievances, they will generate activities that attempt to redress grievances. Most efforts at correction do not involve protest, and the vast bulk of grievances are redressed without any disruption of the system. However, systems like tenancy have deep structural forces which create and maintain widespread misery. Attempts by individuals to reduce this sort of problem mostly fail, and therefore a large number of people are constantly trying a wide variety of solutions. Organized protest will certainly be one of the solutions tried.

Whenever a social organization generates persistent grievances, it generates persistent protest as well. And, since all the current social systems have structures which generate grievances, protest groups are endemic. Therefore, the answer to the question "When will protest groups arise?" is very simple: all the time.

But this seems quite inaccurate, considering that some societies have suppressed all protest; others seem to go through periods of calm and periods of disruption; and only a few face constant strife.

However, the contradiction is more apparent than real, since we have not excluded from the category "protest organization" even the smallest, most transient group. When protest is a consistent feature of a social structure, protest groups arise constantly, but it does not guarantee that even a single one will become large enough or live long enough to affect the functioning of the parent structure.

In the most chaotic society, wracked by constant protest, there are myriad small groups with no impact, and only a few that successfully challenge the structure they aim to reform. And, in the most repressive and the most placid systems, the contradictions produce countless protest groups, but their fate is to arise and die without impact. The problem is not how protest groups arise, but why in some circumstances a few achieve enough strength to affect the parent structure, while in other circumstances none has any impact and all die prematurely.

This reformulation makes issues about the birth of protest more manageable. They fall under the rubric of conditions that cause protest groups to grow in size and strength, a topic that has received considerable attention in our previous analysis. Certainly, there are some unique features to the early organizing process, but basically it follows the same pattern as later organizational behavior.

For example, a particularly vexing irregularity is reflected in the fact that some protest groups seem to "borrow" the structure of some other institution and convert it into a protest organization when mass grievances arise. Naturally such a group will have a faster initial growth than one that painstakingly creates a new organization from scratch. But the reasons that preexisting structures spur initial growth can be broken down into constituent parts which can be found in the analysis presented here. For example, the use of a preexisting structure provides ready-made channels of communication with which to reduce structural ignorance. A preexisting structure may represent a uninamous previous analysis. Thus, the individuals involved may be convinced of the efficacy of the protest by the same events or arguments. By beginning with a large group of people, the organization may have enough membership to undertake actions a smaller group could not, and this initial success might attract enough new membership to guarantee future life.

Furthermore, even the question of when such preexisting structures will exist can be recast in the terms of the analysis presented here. If the system is highly integrated and all the existing structures are mutually dependent, protest against one will "escalate" to the others. This will eliminate the possibility of using preexisting structures. Such a dependence relationship certainly can be difficult to discern, and the focus of this work is not the particular problem of describing what sort of structures are highly integrated and which are not.

Nevertheless, the principles of "organizational birth" are not different from those of organizational growth. A group will become large enough to be noticed if it undertakes actions that successfully redress grievances of its membership base, and such success, for the smallest incipient group or the largest borrowed structure, depends upon the same general principles.

Almost all protest organizations die aborning, and their deaths are prototypical of the demise of all protest groups. Most groups form, undertake a failing activity, and dissolve. They die because they have failed to serve their membership and they have offered no credible evidence of organizational learning that promises future success. The actual process is simple: Failure leads to membership demoralization which deprives the group of all its resources. Without resources it cannot act, and therefore it dies.

Large groups behave in basically the same way. When activities fail to redress membership grievances, demoralization will result. If there is a backlog of success and a lively intraorganizational communications system, then organizational learning will limit demoralization enough to allow for further action. But if there are no successful activities which validate at least some aspects of the prevailing analysis, increasing numbers of members will fail to exhibit enough organizational discipline to sustain the group's activities. A large group becomes a small group and the small group dies.

Obviously this simplifies the process, but the principles remain intact in more complex situations. Though many labor unions have died in roughly the same way described in this section, certain ones seem now to remain, whether or not they maintain membership discipline. This phenomenon can be understood if we note that the sustenance of these permanent unions depends upon their connection to the parent structure. For example, union "recognition" implies that the corporation collects dues for the union leadership and confers many privileges upon its officers. The structure of the organization is accordingly altered by these relationships, and it is hard to determine whether the movement is indeed a "protest" organization in the sense we use the term here. This outcome is a logical extension of the dynamics of oligarchy, which we have discussed in our analysis.

We see, then, the symmetry in birth and death. Groups may build themselves slowly from scratch or they may begin by borrowing a preexisting structure. They may wither away and die or they may be transformed into a non-protest group. The processes that condition these births and deaths are largely analyzed here, but the detailed attention they require is beyond the scope of this research.

IV

THE PROCESS OF ALLIANCE PROTEST

13

Local Economic Action and the Process of Escalation

In fact you may go, one and all,
From sunny South to mountains tall,
And not one time will you see
One who'll sell you goods like me.

Soon we'll have our line complete,
And we defy any one to compete,
For there is a thousand or more
Bargains at the Alliance store,

Now we'll add just one word more,
The place to buy is at the Alliance store,
A new frame house built neat and well,
Just in front of the Guthrie Hotel.

[R. F. Moore, *Raleigh Progressive Farmer*, November 5, 1889]

In developing and pursuing programs, farmers' organizations faced the system of cotton cultivation in two directions at once. They could look at their plight in terms of the supply system, focusing on the high cost of purchasing the materials necessary to run their farms, or they could see it in terms of the marketing system, focusing on low prices for cotton and high costs attached to the selling process. Since tenantization tended to bring about a marriage of these two systems (most farmers bought their supplies and sold their product to the same merchant—landlord), the target was often the same regardless of which choice was made.

The two systems were attacked separately because the marketing system was approached without the merchant as the primary target. One reason was that the early membership, who had not fallen completely into tenancy, could directly benefit from reduction of marketing costs. A second reason was the looseness of the control that merchants and landlords exercised over the marketing process.

While frequently the lien system gave them the necessary leverage to force their debtors to sell to them, under certain conditions even heavily indebted yeomen and tenants were able to market their cotton elsewhere. Therefore, many tenants supported these actions in the hope that they would destroy the buying monopoly of the lienholder.

Nevertheless, there remained a great many tenants or yeomen who had to sell immediately to their lienholder and therefore had little to gain from such actions as the bulking of cotton or the running of independent warehousing. [1] The adoption of marketing projects therefore partly indicated the congeniality of the Alliance to the interests of the more prosperous farmers. Partly it indicated the presence of a particular analysis which argued that such actions would indirectly help the poorer farmers: If Alliance action raised cotton market prices, the merchant would pay more, even to debt peons. Though we have seen that this was hardly inevitable, the structured ignorance in the system made it apparently so, and only direct experience could clarify the situation.

Thus, if we consider the membership of the Alliance, we can distinguish three groups with three different orientations to marketing programs. The prosperous yeomen supported such activities because they would raise prices or lower marketing costs and therefore increase their return. Many tenants and yeomen who were tied to merchants hoped that marketing programs would free them from the purchasing monopoly. Poor tenants who had no hope of independent marketing looked for a general price increase or lower costs which would be passed on to them. Two groups of farmers hoped to benefit directly; the third hoped to benefit indirectly.

This example contains the key to understanding the development of political analysis in an organization. It was not simply a matter of rationalizing or motivating action, but an extension of the internal contradictions that required one or another group to accept programs that were not immediately beneficial to them. The analysis presented the vision of the less obvious, indirect benefits of that action.

Another feature of early activities was the contrast between two different tactical orientations: pressuring the system and developing counterinstitutions. In the former case, the farmers attempted to force changes through the use of boycotts or strikes. In the latter case, the Alliance attempted to replace some institution in the system with one of its own which would be operated more fairly.

The contrast between pressure tactics and counterinstitutions can best be made by proceeding to a discussion of local Alliance attacks upon the structure of supply in the tenant system. One important result of monopoly selling created by the crop lien system was that a farmer's complaints about high prices were directed at a single firm. Furthermore, each merchant had a whole group of farmers he supplied and therefore a whole group of complaints when prices were high. The concentration of business and the development of general stores—a necessity under the lien system—meant that the farmers were *organized by the system* into

---

[1] See Chapters 2–5 for a full discussion of these relationships.

Supply under the lien system

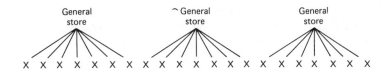

Supply under a noncredit system

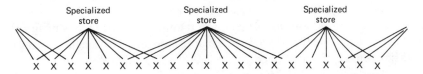

Figure 13.1   *The structural vulnerability of the retail merchant.*

groups. These groups, if coordinated, could exert great leverage against the merchant, since they represented his entire livelihood.

The importance of this structural feature of the system can be seen in comparing such an arrangement with one more typical of noncredit systems. (Figure 13.1 schematically makes this comparison.) A noncredit system encouraged the development of specialized stores, with each buyer purchasing from several different merchants. Price rises appeared as "inflation"—a general price rise. Successful action taken against any particular merchant would not greatly lessen the problem, and therefore such action was not as appealing. Moreover, a group of farmers who patronized one shop for their grain might not all have the same meat supplier. Therefore, there was no group readily available which had common complaints about a large enough group of common merchants to make common protest worthwhile. The unity inherent in the tenancy system did not exist.

The principal pressure tactic used by the Alliance against the supply system was the trade agreement. The Alliance appointed a trade committee which surveyed various merchants and signed an agreement with one of them, guaranteeing all the Alliance's business in exchange for lower prices. In order to assure enforcement, the Alliance sometimes even placed a man in the store to oversee sales and check the books.[2]

There was great incentive for a merchant to enter into one of these agreements. In the lien system—general store arrangement, the loss or gain of even one customer

[2] For descriptions of trade agreements see the following. Ralph A. Smith, "'Macuneism' or the Farmers of Texas in Business," *Journal of Southern History* 13 (May 1947), p. 221; Nelson A. Dunning, ed., *Farmers' Alliance History and Agricultural Digest* (Washington, D.C., 1891), pp. 356–357; Robert Lee Hunt, *A History of Farmers' Movements in the Southwest 1873–1925* (College Station, Tex. 1935), p. 37; *Raleigh Progressive Farmer,* July 16, 1889; *ibid.,* April 22, 1890; *Florida Dispatch,* March 14, 1889; William D. Sheldon, *Populism in the Old Dominion* (Princeton, 1935), p. 43; W. Scott Morgan, *History of the Wheel and Alliance and the Impending Revolution* (Fort Riley, Kans., 1891), p. 103.

mattered a great deal to a given merchant. The loss or gain of a substantial number—the membership of an entire Alliance—could mean ruin or boom. New
customers were tied to him for the entire crop year, and his business could be
doubled or tripled. A boycott, on the other hand, meant that a merchant's customers signed liens with someone else. He lost their business for the entire year,
since they would be forced to patronize their new lienholder exclusively.

The Alliance promise of business or threat of boycott was credible only if its
membership could really switch merchants. Heavily indebted yeomen or tenants
who still owed their lienholder money at the end of one year could not switch
the next year and therefore could not use this tactic. Trade agreements were therefore powerful weapons which could easily be wielded, but only by those farmers
prosperous enough to have a choice of merchants.

Cooperative stores, the main counterinstitutional attack upon the supply system,
had been tried many times before the Alliance arose. In fact, cooperatives had been
a major project of the Grange, which preceded the Alliance in many states. In
1888, there were still 226 surviving Grange cooperatives worth some $63,835
and doing $600,000 of business.[3]

The Alliance co-ops were typical of their day. They were formed by the Alliance
group, with members buying shares (if they could afford them) and electing the
managers and directors. Frequently, an experienced storeowner was hired, though
sometimes the manager was recruited from the membership.[4] The cooperative
had the goal of eliminating the retail merchant from the supply system altogether.
The cooperative acted as a retailer. It bought from the wholesalers and sold to the
farmers at prices just slightly above wholesale. The huge markups taken by the
local merchants were returned to the farmer. The potential savings were enormous,
but, like trade agreements, cooperatives could be initiated only by farmers who
had escaped permanent debt.[5]

One difference between co-ops and trade agreements involved the need for credit.
Co-ops rarely gave credit, since credit selling required large amounts of capital
with which to buy supplies until the crop came in and the farmers were solvent.
Needless to say, it was hard for a group of nearly insolvent farmers to finance a store
that would cover their own debts. It was one thing to threaten to change merchants
and another to have $5 to spare for a share in a cooperative. As one club member
wrote: "The trouble is that most of our farmers do not have the cash to buy their
supplies."[6]

A second difference was that cooperatives were a much better tactic where
general stores did not dominate. As our discussion indicates, trade agreements

---

[3] *Appleton's Annual Cyclopedia,* 1888, (New York, 1229), p. 243.

[4] A good description of Alliance cooperatives can be found in Morgan, *op. cit.*, pp. 162–184; see also *Raleigh Progressive Farmer,* April 23, 1889; *ibid.,* May 14, 21, 1889; *ibid.,* November 5, 1889; *ibid.,* January 7, 1890.

[5] Discussion of cooperatives appears in William W. Rogers, "The Farmers" Alliance in Alabama," *Alabama Review* 15 (January 1962), p. 12–14; *Memorial Record of Alabama* (Madison, 1893), 2, p. 897; Morgan, *op. cit.,* p. 113; Sheldon, *op. cit.,* p. 42; *Florida Dispatch,* November 11, 1887; *ibid.,* November 14, 1889; *National Economist,* June 14, 1890. Examples of trade agreements are described in *Florida Dispatch* , March 14, 1889; Sheldon, *op. cit.,* p. 43; Morgan, *op. cit.,* p. 103.

[6] *Raleigh Progressive Farmer,* February 12, 1889.

meant little if the merchant signing them could meet only a small part of the farmers' needs. On the other hand, a cooperative could act as a general store and therefore bypass several other stores at once. Cooperatives were therefore more attractive in the most prosperous areas, because it was only in those areas that the lien system had not driven the specialty store out of business.

Thus, the favor with which the earlier Grange movement had viewed co-operatives is understandable. In those days, there were more solvent farmers. The spread of the tenancy system and the increasing indebtedness of the yeomen meant that fewer and fewer farmers were prosperous enough to initiate the co-ops, while many more areas had converted to the general store system of marketing. As the years passed and the Alliance replaced the Grange, the trade agreement grew more popular, while the resources for the cooperatives were diminished.

The third important difference between the two tactics had to do with perman-ence. A co-op could provide good service year after year, but a trade agreement had to be constantly enforced and reenforced. Each year the merchant sought to extricate himself from the agreement and each month he wanted to raise his prices. Unless the Alliance maintained a credible threat all the time, the agree-ment could be violated. Clearly, the cooperative was a preferable alternative, since it resulted in minimal prices without constant Alliance activity. However, it was more difficult to organize.

These differences are illustrative of the contrasts between pressure tactics and counterinstitutions. The former are applicable when a group has few resources to invest in the solution—the plight of the poorer members of any group. The counter-institution has the advantage of being a solution which, if successful, does not require constant mobilization and protest activity.

The two tactics, cooperatives and trade agreements, spread in the South during the early days of the Alliance, but the fragmentary evidence does not allow us to assess definitively which tactic was used in which areas. The evidence does, how-ever, give us an idea of what became of these programs. It is their fate which con-cerns us here, because the results of these efforts help us understand the process of organizational change.

Several problems limited the usefulness of trade agreements. Merchants in a vicinity could enter into an arrangement by which none of them would sign a trade agreement with the Alliance. One observer described the situation this way:

> The merchants . . . believed themselves innocent of any wrong-doing, and took offense in many instances at the movement to make them the 'goats' of the Alliance schemes. In some towns all the merchants declined to bid for the Alliance business. This natural-ly added fuel to the flame of emotionalism and the Alliance found it easy to persuade its members that the merchants were combining to defeat the Alliance.[7]

Merchants also tried to undermine trade agreements. Several methods were available. By threatening to withhold credit or by exacting extra interest for credit,

[7] Hunt, *op. cit.*, p. 31.

the merchants retrieved the money lost from the agreement. Or, after eroding organizational discipline, merchants could simply refuse to abide by the agreement and return to the old pricing. In Chatham County, North Carolina, a successful trade agreement in 1888 led to an agreement among all merchants in the county to refuse credit to any Alliance member. The locals, without a strong state organization to back them, were forced into an abortive cooperative store which also failed.[8]

Although these tactics were often successful, their effectiveness depended in part on the inadequacies of the Alliance. Careful and thorough organization and a well-informed membership could prevent the erosion of agreements. A well-disciplined organization could outlast the unity of the highly competitive merchants, any one of whom could make a great deal of money by breaking unity and signing a lucrative trade agreement with a large Alliance. One group of merchants attempted to frustrate a trade agreement with a plow store by selling competing plows at lower prices. An Alliance boycott of all participating merchants was the successful response.[9]

When merchants were really dominated by the selective buying power of the Alliance, pressure began to be felt by the rest of the supply system. The repeated application of threatened boycotts could drive prices so low that they began to cut into the margin of the wholesaler. Furthermore, many retailers were in debt to wholesalers, so the wholesalers had a stake in retail profits. A bankrupt or unprofitable retail store might deprive the wholesaler of payment on loans or repayment for goods delivered.

The success of trade agreements automatically triggered a new situation— the activation of the wholesale merchants, who lost money if retailers lost money.[10] In most cases, wholesalers refused to give credit to merchants who signed Alliance trade agreements. This "triggering" of a new situation occurred with the successful application of cooperation as well. We shall discuss this phenomenon more extensively after we look at the problem that cooperatives encountered.

Cooperatives were even more powerful than trade agreements in competing with merchants. If the Alliance handled its accounts well, made solid arrangements for financing, and established reasonable ties with wholesalers, local merchants had little leverage over the operation. One workable strategy was to undersell the co-op, drive it out of business, and then return prices to their previous level. Such strategies were successfully initiated, but they depended upon the ignorance of the Alliance supporters:

> For example, if a mercantile house is in the habit of selling a certain line of tobacco at 50 cents . . . and we establish a co-operative store reducing the price to 40 cents, all the consumers of that tobacco are 10 cents better off [because the merchant] comes

[8] *Raleigh Progressive Farmer*, February 12, 1889. For other examples see Hunt, *op. cit.*, p. 31; Smith, *op. cit.*, p. 223.
[9] *Raleigh Progressive Farmer*, February 19, 1889.
[10] This assertion would be more properly expressed if we noted that wholesalers stood to lose if *established* retailers lost money. Certainly, a new retail merchant would not be a good credit risk and therefore would have to provide his own money. The established stores, however, found credit available and were often in long-term debt. See Chapters 3–4.

down to 40 cents. They are not buying relatively cheaper from our own co-operative store than they could from the merchant. Many who could not look deeper than the surface and have forgotten that it sold at 50 cents prior to the inauguration of the co-operative store claim that the enterprise is of no benefit because outsiders are selling equally as cheap, or say perhaps 5 cents cheaper and thus those who should be our friends are often found to be its enemy. . . .[11]

When the farmers were knowledgeable, such merchant counterattacks made things worse for the merchants. In Gaston County, North Carolina, local merchants who undersold the Alliance were happily patronized by Alliancemen who promptly rebated 5% of the purchase price to the Alliance co-op. The farmers saved money, the co-op was subsidized, and the merchants footed the bill.[12] Another North Carolina county co-op at first restricted itself to a few items. It was disrupted only slightly by the efforts of local merchants to undersell its products, but the county Alliance, incensed at the attack, declared all-out war on the merchants and expanded their cooperative. They vowed a fight to the death, with the need for credit the only block to Alliance victory:

Now, sir, as our Alliance cause progresses, two things I observe; first, that there is an incalculable amount of good that we can accomplish, and, second, that nothing short of conflict will accomplish it. United effort, skillful management; in connection with that degree of pluck and energy which has long since characterized the Southern patriot, will prove equal to almost any emergency. That the merchant should say to us that we are not to buy direct from manufacturers, but that the goods must pass through their hands at a profit, in which the buyer has no voice, is an insult of the most damnable character; gird on your armor, brethren; our foe is formidable, and our struggle will be severe; but the glory of the victor is measured thereby. Those whom we have so long fed and fattened will die hard. Strive to do all the business through your Agent possible; ever keep your eyes on the cash system as our surest anchor; curtail your business with a view to that end. There is no use to talk of absolute independence with no money in our pockets, and we may as well give the merchants credit for knowing it.[13]

A well-organized Alliance cooperative movement with good membership discipline could defeat the merchants in a straight economic confrontation. In many cases, the merchants resisted at first but ultimately capitulated to trade agreements as the lesser evil.[14] In other places, they attempted noneconomic counterattacks. An Alliance co-op was burned to the ground in Graham, Georgia, and the merchants in Henderson County, North Carolina, offered a large reward to stop the Alliance.[15] But these tactics were hardly a consistent solution.

[11] *Southern Mercury,* December 11, 1887; *Raleigh Progressive Farmer,* December 15, 1887.
[12] *Raleigh Progressive Farmer,* April 2, 1889.
[13] *Raleigh Progressive Farmer,* February 26, 1889.
[14] *Raleigh Progressive Farmer,* February 19, 1889; *ibid.,* April 30, 1889; *ibid.,* May 14, 1889; *ibid.,* June 25, 1889.
[15] *Raleigh Progressive Farmer,* May 13, 1890; *ibid.,* December 18, 1888.

The real threats to the local supply actions were located inside the Alliance itself and above the merchants. By 1889, one Alliance leader had learned an important but simple lesson about co-ops: "they create merchants."[16] And indeed this was one of the principal results of efforts at cooperation. Because it was tempting for the management of these firms to copy the successful methods of the other merchants, many times the cooperatives developed into ordinary merchant stores with stockholders making the profits the merchant would have made. This tendency was, of course, reinforced by the whole structure of supply, which placed the merchant at the end of a chain of coercive conditions. His profit margin might not be very large, especially before he became established, and the high prices he charged were frequently necessary to finance his own debt to banks and wholesalers. Thus, the new co-op store might rapidly turn into just another retail merchant.

A co-op that did not create a merchant might very well create a bankruptcy. The financial inadequacies of Alliancemen-turned-businessmen were multiplied by the low profit orientations, which required unusual business acumen. Men with such skills generally wanted to work for themselves and not for the Alliance. This accounts for the large number of complaints about financial irresponsibility among Alliance co-op managers.[17] It also puts into perspective the frequency with which bankruptcies occurred among these stores.

One type of bankruptcy is of special interest to us here. In some cases, the Alliance store was more or less driven out of business because of discriminatory practices directed against it by the rest of the supply structure. Alliance cooperatives often found it difficult to get bank loans in situations where ordinary retail merchants would have had little trouble.[18] They also found more restrictive credit policies among wholesale merchants; sometimes the wholesalers simply refused to sell at any price.[19]

The problems of cooperatives were often dramatic and public. This had the added effect of publicly discrediting Alliance enterprises and thus making it difficult for the Alliance to recover. The closure of an Alliance store in Tuskaloosa, Alabama, was deemed worthy of coverage in the major Mobile paper:

> *The doors of the Tuskaloosa Alliance and Mercantile Company were closed today by the sheriff. Attachments amounting to $2,800 were served in favor of the Birmingham Dry Goods Company, of Birmingham, and J. H. Fitts & Co., of Tuskaloosa. The liabilities are about $7,000, assets $5,000.*[20]

These kinds of actions were the result of the same process we outlined for trade agreements. A successful cooperative store sold goods more cheaply. The

---

[16] *National Economist*, August 24, 1889.

[17] See, for example, report by President H. C. Martin of the Florida Alliance, January 3, 1889, in *Florida Dispatch*, February 14, 1889.

[18] Morgan, *op. cit.*, pp. 116–119; Smith, *op. cit.*, pp. 227–228.

[19] *National Economist*, July 5, 1890.

[20] *Mobile Daily Register*, May 17, 1892.

lower prices enabled it to sell to more and more farmers, as the news of cheap supplies traveled. This siphoned off customers from the other retailers, reduced their profits, and threatened their ability to redeem debts from banks and whole-salers. This was enough to turn these institutions against the Alliance stores.

This is *escalation* by the established structure. When Alliance attacks against a lower level in the system were transmitted to a higher level, that part of the struc-ture took action to protect the status quo. The process was bluntly described by an official Alliance historian:

> The merchants fought it [the Alliance co-op] because it was interfering with their business. The commission men opposed it because it was an encroachment upon their established trade; and the manufacturers boycotted it because it was premeditated war upon high prices and enormous profits.[21]

So far, we have looked at two sets of opening moves in an elaborate chess game. The Alliance began by initiating trade agreements or cooperatives, and the effect of these—when successful—was to create tension in the structure of supply and an escalation of the conflict to a higher level. To clarify this, it may be useful to describe again the key elements of the escalation process.

Any continuing structure acts in a routine manner in accord with certain pre-dictable principles. The day-to-day operation of any functioning system can be described according to these principles. The Alliance attempted to turn these prin-ciples to their advantage. For example, the application of trade agreements depended upon the operation of the profit motive and competition among merchants, which usually forced at least one merchant to capitulate. The operation of cooperatives depended upon the willingness of wholesalers to supply any store as well as the availability of credit to any enterprise that could make repayment.

However, the laws governing the operation of a system are not immutable. They can change and they do, given certain kinds of stimuli. A system has elaborate de-fense mechanisms which set off alarms when elements of it are threatened, calling forth new possibilities that are not routine and do not abide by the principles of its operation. One such response is exemplified by the merchants' of a community uniting and refusing to sign any agreements. This action was not routine; it did not follow the principles of competition and individual profit. Instead it violated these principles in pursuit of another one—collective action for mutual benefit.

This behavior can be characterized as a "reaction" to the stimulus created by the Alliance. We should note that such reactions are not always necessary to defeat an attack. In the example of trade agreements, the normal profit motive led store-keepers to try to undermine the agreements, and frequently they were successful. In the case of cooperatives, the normal operation of the system worked to deprive

---

[21] Morgan, *op. cit.*, p. 119. It would not be right to assert that opposition to the Alliance was restricted to such civilized actions. Other counterattacks included everything from "spreading rumors" (Smith, *op. cit.*, p. 228) to burning down stores (*Union Springs [Ala.] Herald*, November 11, 1891).

the Alliance cooperatives of good management and of easy credit. By themselves these everyday factors defeated many attempted cooperatives. When this occurred, no alarms were sounded within the system and no formal reaction took place.

Escalation is a particular form of reaction. In the case of escalation, the elements in the structure which do not follow routine principles are above the level that the Alliance (or any other group) attacks. Thus, while the trade agreements and cooperatives attacked retailers, the reaction came from wholesalers and banks.

The significance of escalation is that it creates a structural "mismatch." In our example, the Alliance created an organization capable of altering the retail sales subsystem and defeating the reactions of the retailers. However, it found itself confronting the wholesalers, who should have been unwitting allies. The Alliance structure was not prepared for this new adversary; it was not constructed to operate at this new level. Hence the mismatch.

For example, the farmers of Franklin County, North Carolina, attempted to buy plows and other iron implements directly from the Stonewall Company. Stonewall, mindful of its interdependence with local merchants, quoted the Alliance co-op prices far higher than it was charging retail merchants for the same merchandise. In an attempt to defeat this escalation, the county organization vowed not to purchase Stonewall equipment, but such a boycott lacked the statewide scope needed to exercise real leverage over the company.[22]

This sort of escalation destroyed all the local supply schemes which had avoided bankruptcy and other internal devastations. The early history of the Southern Alliance is one of discovering the myriad ways in which escalation could take place. Locals in the Southeast discovered in early 1889 that all the wholesalers in Norfolk, Virginia, had agreed to boycott Alliance co-ops.[23] Manufacturers all over the country boycotted the Alliance: Mississippi locals could not get wholesale farm implements, clubs in North Carolina were denied wholesale prices on shoes, and Texas farmers could not buy flour directly from the mill.[24] Alabama and South Carolina banks foreclosed on Alliance mortgages. Virginia railroads refused to give discount shipment rates available to other large customers.[25]

Locals tried many things to defeat these escalations, but a small group of farmers in one county could rarely exercise leverage over big city wholesalers, railroads, banks, and manufacturers. In rare cases, consumer boycotts worked; sometimes the locals successfully induced some wholesalers to break boycotts, and a few manufacturing enterprises were established to produce the items of escalating firms. But these were the exceptions.[26]

[22] *Raleigh Progressive Farmer*, March 5, 1889. The boycott did get some out-of-county support. See *Raleigh Progressive Farmer*, April 2, 1889.

[23] *Raleigh Progressive Farmer*, May 28, 1889.

[24] *Raleigh Progressive Farmer*, February 26, 1889; *ibid.*, October 23, 1889; *ibid.*, February 19, 1889; see also *ibid.*, March 5, 1889; *ibid.*, July 9, 1889; *ibid.*, September 24, 1889.

[25] *Raleigh Progressive Farmer*, July 30, 1889; *ibid.*, January 14, 1890; *ibid.*, March 11, 1890; see also *Oxford* (Ga.) *Day*, August 1890.

[26] For examples of many attempts and a few successes see *Raleigh Progressive Farmer*, February 19, 26, 1889; *ibid.*, March 5, 1889; *ibid.*, May 28, 1889; *ibid.*, September 24, 1889; *ibid.*, January 14, 1890; *ibid.*, February 4, 1890; *ibid.*, June 10, 1890; *ibid.*, September 2, 1890. *Oxford* (Ga.) *Day*, August 1890; *Southern Alliance Farmer* (Quitman, Ga), September 1890.

The Alliance response to defeat often involved giving up the frustrated action and adopting a new program. Such a shift tried to sidestep the obstacle that had defeated the co-op or trade agreement. For example, if a co-op were defeated through escalation, the group might try to pressure local merchants through trade agreements, since it was not necessarily clear that a similar escalation would take place against these. In any case, it was by no means obvious that bulk sales would be defeated by escalation whatever the fate of co-operatives had been.

Thus, the tactic of the shift—as distinguished from the counterattack—tried to sidestep, rather than defeat, the newly uncovered adversary. It had the advantage of not requiring a broader organization; it seemed possible for such a sidestepping to be accomplished at the same level as the previous failure. This led to the attack on the marketing system.

One strategy was "cotton bulking." If the farmers in any given area cooperated, they could either sell together at a distant market or else provide enough cotton to attract buyers to their town. Either way, this cut out the buyers' agent (including the retail merchant)—thus saving the commissions paid to these middlemen. It gave the Alliance members real bargaining powers vis-à-vis the buyers, who were willing to pay extra for guaranteed quality cotton in large quantities which could be shipped directly to factories. Cotton bulking plans took two forms. In one procedure, the local Alliance built or bought a warehouse and held all the members' cotton until a fair price was offered.[27] The other procedure involved a preharvest agreement by farmers to sell en masse. A representative was then sent to a major market town to negotiate the bulk sale. This procedure offered a guaranteed sale before the cotton came in and did not put financial pressure upon the farmer at harvesttime.[28]

Various Alliance estimates indicate that these systems augmented income as much as 25%.[29] Price increases of 2¢ per pound were not unknown, though actual profits were lessened by expenses.[30] Perhaps typical was a Spalding County, Georgia, warehouse which returned $4000 to Alliancemen, an income increase of about 15% per farmer.[31]

These two strategies correspond to the two major tactics against the supply system. The warehouse system depended upon the collection of funds beforehand and upon the ability of the farmers to hold their crops. It had the advantage of holding out the promise of a permanent solution, since the warehouse, once set up, would continue "automatically." It was, in short, a counterinstitution. The mass

[27] For descriptions of such warehouses see Morgan, *op. cit.*, p. 113; *National Economist*, March 8, 1890; *ibid.*, May 3, 1890; *Memorial Record of Alabama, op. cit.*, vol. 2, p. 879; Smith, *op. cit.*, p. 224; *Florida Dispatch*, July 11, 1889; *ibid.*, September 26, 1889; *Raleigh Progressive Farmer*, February 19, 26, 1889; *ibid.*, March 5, 1889; *ibid.*, July 9, 1889; *ibid.*, November 5, 1889.

[28] Descriptions of this strategy can be found in Smith, *op. cit.*, p. 225; *Florida Dispatch*, August 8, 1889; Billy M. Jones, *The Search for Maturity* (Austin, 1965), p. 130; Morgan, *op. cit.*, pp. 194—196; Dunning, *op. cit.*, p. 357; *Raleigh News and Observer*, December 28, 1888; *Raleigh Progressive Farmer*, January 7, 1890.

[29] Smith, *op. cit.*, p. 224; Morgan, *op. cit.*, p. 196.

[30] *Florida Dispatch*, October 17, 1889; *ibid.*, November 7, 1889; *National Economist*, May 3, 1890; *Raleigh Progressive Farmer*, April 4, 1889.

[31] *Raleigh Progressive Farmer*, March 5, 1889.

selling plan was a pressure tactic which did not require many resources and depended only upon the ability of the members to choose their buyer. It applied pressure to the sales system and made competition work for the farmer. It had the disadvantage that the whole process had to be repeated' each year.[32]

There were many ways these programs could fail without any system reaction at all. The normal workings of the marketing system made if difficult for the small farmer to sell to anyone but his lienholder. The difficulties of transporting cotton and the routinized nature of buyer—agent connections made it hard for bulking plans to succeed. Even several years of successful bulk selling did not guarantee success the next year. The time and expertise needed to accomplish these programs were scarce in the organization. For all these reasons, the bulk selling plan could fail.

But if they succeeded, or started to succeed, they were met by reactions from the system of marketing. These reactions came initially from the local buyers themselves. In the same manner as the merchants—many were merchants—they could and did band together to refuse to buy any cotton en masse or at increased prices. The tobacco warehouses in Danville, Virginia, did exactly this. When the Alliance approached them with a bulk selling proposition, the warehousemen formed a miniature trust which enforced sanctions against any business that gave the Alliance better prices. The local Alliances were forced to deal with distant markets, and their efforts were unsuccessful.[33]

Unfortunately for the buyers, it was usually possible for a well-organized Alliance to defeat such a counterattack. When the Granville County, North Carolina, buyers refused to reduce sales charges from 5% to $2\frac{1}{2}$% in return for bulked Alliance tobacco, the county organization established its own warehouse. In 3 months, this warehouse became the largest one in Oxford, North Carolina, a tobacco market for 12 counties in 3 states. Because of its low service charge, the farmer could save as much as 20% of his crop value, so that the Alliance warehouse attracted many non-Alliance tobacco growers.[34] In general, local buyers had difficulty resisting the pressure of a united and well-organized county Alliance.[35]

Escalation against cotton and tobacco bulking took two forms. First, the entire cotton marketing system was hooked into the welfare of the local buyers. Railroads, for example, had long-term transport agreements with many of their customers. If these customers went out of business, the railroads lost money. The new Alliance business was not new to them. Similarly, the manufacturers depended upon a steady source of supply from large cotton factors. Direct purchase from Alliancemen might mean lower prices at harvesttime, but it also meant no cotton at other times.

---

[32] Each of these strategies had aspects of the other. Through the warehouse plan an Alliance hoped to negotiate directly with the buyers and thereby bypass the agents. This negotiation could be seen as a form of pressure, but it did not always involve a united group of farmers in the bargaining. Thus, it was possible for a warehouse also to serve as a mass selling plan. On the other hand, the mass selling plan bypassed the local merchant to reach the higher prices.

[33] *Raleigh Progressive Farmer*, February 12, 1889.

[34] *Raleigh Progressive Farmer*, February 12, 1889.

[35] For further examples see Dunning, *op. cit.*, p. 357.

Thus, successful cotton bulking plans put pressure on more than the buyers. It threatened railroads and manufacturers and moved them to aid the buyers in defeating the Alliance. This escalation, like that associated with cooperatives and trade agreements, caught the farmers organizationally defenseless. There was little the Alliance could immediately do if the railroads refused to accept or charged extremely high rates for bulked cotton for through shipment.[36] Nor could they easily respond if the city buyers or manufacturers refused to buy, even at a lower price than they were paying to others.[37]

Bulk selling also produced another direction of escalation—the use of local government to defeat Alliance action. Bulk selling programs often found themselves defeated by new laws. Alliance warehouses were forced to pay exorbitant taxes to erect new structures, their customers had to pay extensive tolls for hauling cotton through town, and new zoning regulations made land prices too high.[38] This political retaliation differed in many ways from the economic escalation we have already discussed. But it was an escalation, since it was a nonroutine reaction of the system which brought into the power struggle an element the Alliance had not directly attacked. The difference lies in that the reaction came from a different system entirely. In another context, we shall discuss the conditions and results of this form of escalation.

Various sorts of escalation frustrated the entire local thrust of the Alliance, and it made the whole organizational structure obsolete. Despite Alliance attempts to switch from one locally oriented economic action to another, the process of escalation could always frustrate the local actions. Even if short-term victories were achieved, long-run failure was inevitable.

A great many Alliance activities did, in fact, succeed for a time. These successes saved local farmers many thousands of dollars. A co-op store in Chatham County, North Carolina, reduced prices in the area as much as 40%.[39] A warehouse in Henderson, North Carolina, created the highest tobacco prices in a decade.[40] A cooperative ginning enterprise in Grayson County, Texas, saved $1680 in 2 years.[41] Cooperative fertilizer purchasing saved farmers hundreds of thousands of dollars.[42] In 1888, the combined effects of several enterprises saved the Union County, North Carolina, Alliancemen $20,000, cut land mortgages in Durham County in half, and netted a 90% reduction in crop liens in Sandy Creek.[43] Indeed, the Alliance discovered that *successful* cooperation was the *cause* of escalation—The more successful the Alliance action, the more ferocious the counterattack:

[36] Dunning, *op. cit.*, pp. 226–227; *Raleigh Progressive Farmer*, March 11, 1890.

[37] Smith, *op. cit.*, p. 224; *Raleigh News and Observer*, October 19, 1889; *Raleigh Progressive Farmer*, July 17, 1888.

[38] *Raleigh News and Observer*, October 19, 1889; Smith, *op. cit.*, p. 221.

[39] *Raleigh Progressive Farmer*, February 5, 1889; *ibid.*, March 12, 1889.

[40] *Raleigh Progressive Farmer*, August 13, 1889.

[41] *Southern Mercury*, March 17, 1890.

[42] *Raleigh Progressive Farmer*, February 28, 1888; *ibid.*, June 5, 19, 1888; *ibid.*, May 14, 1889; *ibid.*, June 4, 1889.

[43] *Raleigh Progressive Farmer*, March 12, 1889; *ibid.*, June 26, 1888; *ibid.*, July 10, 1888; *ibid.*, April 21, 1889; *ibid.*, June 4, 1889; *ibid.*, November 5, 1889; *ibid.*, December 17, 1889; *ibid.*, January 7, 1890; *ibid.*, March 4, 1890; *ibid.*, June 10, 1890; *Greenville* (Ga.) *Free Press*, April 23, 1889.

> *Not until a co-operative enterprise shows signs of unmistakeable victory does the opposition crystalize and unite their whole force to drive it out of existence.*[44]

The appropriate response for the Alliance was an analogous escalation of its own. If the wholesale merchants sided with the retailers, then the Alliance could pressure the wholesalers or bypass them with a counterinstitution. If the railroads, manufacturers, or city buyers were acting to frustrate bulk selling, pressure could be brought to bear upon them.

The counter-attacks reflected this logic. In North Carolina, a statewide cotton bulking program was initiated. All Alliance cotton was brought to regional warehouses, where it was stored for 25¢ per bale. The Alliance gave farmers advances on their sales to help them escape the creditors who might otherwise force early selling. This bulked cotton was then withheld from the market either until the sales structure responded or until the supply of cotton dried up and the manufacturers were forced to buy from the Alliance.[45]

The national Alliance tried to organize a national bulking plan that would eliminate everyone in the sales system except the manufacturer. The idea was to get each farmer to specify the amount of cotton he would harvest, the grade, and the time of harvest. The national office would contact all the manufacturers and guarantee them the grade of cotton in the quantity they wanted at the time they wanted.[46] To enforce this program, attempts were made to have all growers withhold their cotton until sales agreements were made.[47]

These two programs were logical extensions of warehousing, on the one hand, and mass selling, on the other. Similar extensions were available in the supply system. When fertilizer manufacturers stopped selling directly to the Alliance, North Carolina county clubs responded with the battle cry "no Alliance man ought to patronize any company that will not sell to them through an Alliance agent" and organized a boycott of all "manipulated guano." To bypass counterattacking wholesalers, 22 state business departments tried to organize a national cooperative.[48]

Counterattacks also took less direct forms. Many state and regional groups attempted to bypass cotton buyers entirely by building Alliance cotton factories, thus creating their own market for cotton.[49] The sales system was attacked by state Alliances which organized everything from fertilizer to shoe factories in an attempt to lower supply costs.[50]

There is much to be said concerning these escalations by the Alliance, and we

[44] C. W. Macune, writing in *Southern Mercury*, December 1887, reprinted in *Raleigh Progressive Farmer*, December 15, 1887.

[45] *Raleigh News and Observer*, September 15, 1889.

[46] *Raleigh News and Observer*, December 28, 1888; *National Economist*, March 14, 1889.

[47] *National Economist*, September 7, 1889; *Florida Dispatch*, September 19, 1889.

[48] *Raleigh Progressive Farmer*, March 5, 1889; *ibid.*, November 20, 1888; *ibid.*, January 1, 22, 29, 1889; *ibid.*, February 5, 12, 19, 1889.

[49] *Florida Dispatch*, April 4, 1889; *National Economist*, April 8, 1889; Smith, *op. cit.*, pp. 224—225; Rogers, *op. cit.*, pp. 13—14.

[50] *Florida Dispatch*, February 28, 1889; *ibid.*, October 17, 1889; *National Economist*, September 21, 1889; *ibid.*, November 16, 1889; *ibid.*, April 19, 1890; Rogers, *op. cit.*, pp. 13—14; Sheldon, *op. cit.*, p. 44; *Raleigh Progressive Farmer*, February 12, 1889.

shall shortly turn to a detailed discussion of them. This discussion will focus on the Alliance Exchanges, the most prevalent, elaborate, and detailed response of the Alliance to the establishment's escalation.

Before proceeding to that discussion, however, we should summarize the experience of the Alliance with local economic actions, perhaps most succinctly summarized by an Alliance leader:

> In their efforts to perfect a trade system for their mutual good, through corresponding with manufacturers, they were always a referred by them to their agents. In their communications to wholesale men, for trade, they were continually referred by them to the retail merchant. In the disposition of their cotton, in trying to reach the manufacturer, they were met by the "bulls" and "bears" in the cotton market. Hence the Alliance [established] cotton yards of their own, for the purpose of bulking their cotton and selling, if possible, directly to the factories. This was done to some extent, but was violently opposed by the cotton buyers and speculators. In some towns, it is said that farmers could not purchase land to be used for such purposes, so strong was the prejudice of the merchants against the Alliance.[51]

As this passage describes, the problem the Alliance faced was escalation of the struggle to a level where the system was invulnerable. The ultimate sanction applicable to the Alliance was this escalation, and it worked.

We have been developing in this chapter a picture of Alliance protest as a game of chess. Basing its calculations on the routine operation of the system, the Alliance made a move which, if the system continued to function smoothly, would work to the advantage of the farmers. When the Alliance successfully executed its action, it did gain the advantage temporarily. However, the nature of the system was such that Alliance success weakened and threatened more than the level of the system initially attacked. When other parts of the system felt the pressure, they reorganized themselves and performed nonroutine actions to prevent Alliance success. These were the responding moves in the chess game—new moves which caught the Alliance organizationally offguard by creating a mismatch between the Alliance, which was organized to attack one level of the system, and the structure, which counterattacked on another level. The frustration experienced by the Alliance, and the vision of counterattack, were aptly expressed by one North Carolina farmer:

> What can a single Alliance do? Are we not wasting our energies in resolves, and as someone has said, making a guerrilla fight, instead of bringing into the conflict the force of our organization. . . . Would it not be a good plan to send to county and subordinate Alliances those questions of vital import to be discussed and voted on and the result of each reported back through the same channels. When a measure is adopted let it be known, as a rule, to be observed by the entire order. . . .
>
> The point I wish to make is that we should bring the whole force of our order to bear whenever we undertake to remedy anything beyond our individual and local spheres. . . ."[52]

---

[51] Quoted in Dunning, op. cit., p. 39.

[52] Raleigh Progressive Farmer, March 5, 1889.

14

The Alliance Exchange: The Ultimate Counterinstitution

By the aid of Jehovah's omnipotent hand,
 Our banner shall wave over Columbia's bright land;
And the blue-tinted valuts of the star-spangled dome,
 O'ershadow the farmers' happy, sweet, happy home.

Then we'll shout the glad tidings across the deep sea,
 That American farmers are happy and free,
To the breezes of Heaven our banners unfurl,
 And the Farmers' Alliance is leading the world.

[Rowan County (North Carolina) Club 829, *Raleigh Progressive Farmer*, December 10, 1889]

The Farmers' Alliance Exchanges were the most ambitious counterinstitutions ever undertaken by an American protest movement. In one swoop, they promised to revolutionize and civilize the cotton and tobacco cultivation systems, replace one-crop tenancy, and establish a nonhierarchical collective farming community. The Exchanges sought to eliminate merchants, wholesalers, and factors from the cotton culture; and they promised to reduce the power of the crop lien, the railroads, and the banking system to manageable proportions.

The plan was massively simpleminded, but subtly ingenious. All Alliance members assessed their supply needs at the beginning of the growing season. These needs were converted into lists by the local clubs and sent, along with crop liens, mortgages, and cash, to the state business agent. The accumulated securities offered by the entire statewide membership provided collateral for yearlong credit from banks and manufacturers. This credit, combined with a cash pool created out of stock sales and money payments, financed the purchase—directly from the manufacturers, the mills, and the importers—of practically all the supplies needed by the individual farmer.

217

In the fall, samples of picked crops were sent to the Exchange while the product was bulked at local Alliance warehouses. The Alliance Exchange, by combining the small amounts from widely separated farmers into huge lots, sold the cotton and/or tobacco directly to the exporter or manufacturer.

The elegance of the plan was that it would replace much of both the supply and marketing systems of cotton tenancy, while returning huge savings to the local farmer:

1. Instead of dependence upon the exorbitant crop lien, farmers, by bulking their notes, would be borrowing at bank rates.
2. The local merchant—landlord, who had essentially controlled cotton cultivation and appropriated the farmer's labor, would be eliminated as a factor in supplying farmers.
3. The entire marketing system would be short-circuited, with the elaborate structure of merchant—landlord—cotton exchange interdependence replaced with straightforward producer—manufacturer commerce.
4. Bottlenecks created by railroads, wholesalers, landlord-controlled local banks, and other peripheral, but powerful, elements in the tenancy system would be broken by the immense structural leverage generated by the economies of scale the Exchange produced.

And it worked. Even in the relatively modest forms ultimately achieved, the Exchanges devastated the economic status quo. In Texas, the Exchange reduced the farmers' supply bill by 40%, produced a general 20% price deflation, and saved farmers more than $6 million.[1] In some areas of North Carolina, it reduced prices as much as 60%, undermined the crop lien system, and had continued economic impact for 10 years after its demise.[2] The Louisiana Exchange claimed credit for $450,000 supply savings in 1889 despite significant setbacks.[3] With only a tiny capital fund, the Tennessee Exchange generated up to $25,000 per month in business at wholesale prices.[4] The Georgia Exchange saved farmers $200,000 in fertilizer bills in 1890, and the South Carolina operation reported a comparable savings.[5]

These successes are apparent in this extract from *Dunn's Weekly*:

> *In some Southern states trade is seriously affected for the time by the operations of the Farmers' Alliances, which enlist farmers in co-operative trading and absorb money which might otherwise go to settle indebtedness with merchants. The results in some localities almost paralyze trade.*[6]

[1] C. W. Macune, "The Farmers' Alliance" (typescript on file at University of Texas, 1920), p. 35; *Progressive Raleigh Farmer*, January 19, 1889.
[2] *Report of the Industrial Commission on Agriculture and Agricultural Labor* 57th Cong., 1st sess., 1901, H.R. 179, pp. 435—436.
[3] *Raleigh Progressive Farmer*, October 22, 1889; *ibid.*, April 23, 1889.
[4] *Raleigh Progressive Farmer*, April 23, 1889.
[5] *Buchanan* (Ga.) *Messenger*, April 1, 1890; *ibid.*, May 6, 1890.
[6] *Dunn's Weekly*, December 21, 1889.

But it also failed. No Exchange had two successful years and none of them lasted past 1892. And, like the local Alliance actions, the process of escalation made their success the cause of their destruction.

To understand the outcome of Exchange programs, we must begin with their structural origins in the failure of local economic action. These failures led to extensive demoralization and disillusionment which threatened the disintegration of the Alliance:

> Try and impress upon your neighbor the advantages of the Alliance, put your shoulder to the wheel and keep it steadily moving, otherwise this great and noble cause will pass into dire obliviousness.[7]

The threat of oblivion was real. Wherever local action failed, demoralization set in. In North Carolina, the bad time hit in late 1889. During that period, many locals reported membership dropouts and apathy.[8] One club with 138 members had less than half in good standing.[9] Another club expelled 40% of its membership because they refused to help in any activities.[10]

The organization would disintegrate without a new program which held the promise of success. And to validate that promise, a new analysis was needed to demonstrate why this would work where the others had not. People could be motivated by the vision of success, and the presentation and promotion of this vision were especially important at the moment of failure:

> The Atlantic Alliance after a long and dreary season—poverty striken, ill spoken of and many other drawbacks—we still try in our weakness to bear up the Alliance banner and rally the members. Last Saturday was our meeting at which we tried to discuss the propriety of raising the State Agency [Exchange] Fund, as we do believe this to be the vital cord to the relief of our depressed condition, financially.[11]

However, in order for such a vision to arise and a new program to be formulated, more was required than a simple failure. The local programs tended to fail at different times. While one local group tried to figure out a new strategy, the others were hard at work on another local action. This lack of coordination made it difficult for groups to unite in a common new strategy. It created tremendous organizational impetus for new ideas to be tailored for the country, the focus of the early actions. Even if a county had developed a successful statewide program, it would have great difficulty in interesting other counties in it while they were busily engaged in building a cooperative or a warehouse.

---

[7] *Raleigh Progressive Farmer*, April 9, 1889.

[8] *Raleigh Progressive Farmer*, July–December 1889; All, for example, *ibid.*, August 6, 1889; *ibid.*, September 3, 1889; *ibid.*, November 19, 1889; *ibid.*, December 24, 1889.

[9] *Raleigh Progressive Farmer*, October 1, 1889.

[10] *Raleigh Progressive Farmer*, July 16, 1889.

[11] *Raleigh Progressive Farmer*, February 9, 1889.

Thus, continued failure at the local level could result in a shifting about among various locally oriented programs, along with an attrition process as local groups became convinced that no local action could work.

To escape this morass, the Alliance had to act at the state level to move the entire organization, and this is what occurred at the Waco convention of the Texas Alliance. The result was the adoption of the Alliance Exchange as the central program of the organization. That convention is worth reviewing here to see the relationship between these conditions and previous Alliance activity.

To begin, the partial success of the local programs had measurably increased the size of the Alliance and therefore given it the strength necessary to undertake a statewide project. The unsuccessful local actions had been essential to the establishment of a viable statewide group, though a delicate balance existed. If the group had not responded to local failure, the new membership would have slipped away, and the organization would have disintegrated. In part, this is what had happened in 1882.

The enlarged organization had set into motion other forces that equipped the state organization to play a central role. In 1884 and 1885, a number of developments (discussed in Chapters 6–7) had strengthened the state Alliances vis-à-vis the local clubs, and a large number of new recruits had been brought into the organization on the basis of the hope for statewide action. Furthermore, defeats suffered by the local groups had resulted in a need for the state organization to provide new orientations even when they were locally oriented.

Much of the shifting about from one program to another took place because one county group did not know that the tactic they were adopting had already failed in another county. The development of Alliance newspapers, which allowed for communication among locals, advertised the pitfalls of these activities even in areas that had not yet explored all the immediate possibilities. As time went on, the whole organization began to react to failures and to adopt similar amelioratives simultaneously—like new accounting systems. This in turn meant that the local actions were more likely to fail simultaneously.

The same forces that moved the organization to seek statewide economic organization impelled it to explore political action, especially in 1886, an election year. The conflict over political or economic orientations crystallized at the Cleburne convention, where the first political program was adopted. Powerful forces were pressing for political action, and the frustration of local ventures made this idea very appealing to the rank and file. Those forces inside the Alliance which opposed entering politics were pushed, even forced, by circumstances to propose an economic program that could replace the local focus. They responded by proposing the Exchange.

This chronology indicates the conditions under which a protest organization would escalate in the face of escalation. First, there needed to be a growing frustration with local actions. Second, the organization needed to have an organizational basis upon which to build the bigger program. Third, there had to be groups within the organization that could propose and press for the broader program.

We also get another glimpse of the way analysis and ideology are developed. In this case, an organizational crisis led to a conflict between political and economic orientations. To buttress the two sides' arguments, analyses were developed to give the vision of what would occur if each one were selected. Crisis led to conflict which led to analysis.

The Exchange was a dramatic and inspiring program. It fit with the collective experience of the organization and seemed within the Alliance's resources.[12] It aspired to be the sole economic institution with which the individual farmer would do business. He or she bought supplies from the Exchange and sold the crop through it. If the Exchange operated correctly, the local merchant would be driven out of business because his customers would buy only the most insignificant items from him.

Each sub-Alliance would meet and fill out collective order forms for its members. Through this procedure, the state organization would have orders for many thousands of each item needed. Because of the quantities it ordered, the Exchange could deal directly with the manufacturers of most items and could demand a tremendous discount because it was a bulk purchaser and ordered all items to be delivered to one place at one time. The filled orders would be sent by the Exchange to county groups for distribution to the clubs.

The Exchange would sell to the farmers at the price it cost the Exchange, after expenses were met. The procedure cut out both wholesalers and retailers. It lessened the cost of shipment and delivery, and it drastically reduced the costs of overhead and advertising, which otherwise were paid for by the customer in the form of raised prices.

At harvesttime, the subordinate Alliances would canvass all participating farmers and assess their prospective crop. With this information, the Alliance would have selling control over a vast amount of cotton and would have detailed knowledge of its quality and the time it would be available. On this basis, preliminary contact would be made with manufacturers. When the cotton was picked, there probably would be a buyer waiting for it. If not, then the farmers would send a sample (or possibly the crop) to the central Exchange. With the cotton on hand and with access to the most important buyers (who would be attracted by the virtual monopoly the Alliance had on cotton) the Exchange could sell rapidly.

Because of sales directly to the manufacturer and because the sales were in bulk, the Alliance could save much money for the farmers. The commissions paid to the purchasing agents (especially local merchants) would be eliminated. Bypassing the city buyers and factors, would eliminate another set of commissions. The bulk sales meant that shipment could be made from farm to factory on a through bill of lading, thus eliminating the extra costs of shipping first to a market city and then

[12] This description is taken from Nelson A. Dunning, ed., *Farmers' Alliance History and Agricultural Digest* (Washington, D.C., 1891), pp. 358–367; W. Scott Morgan, *History of the Wheel and Alliance and the Impending Revolution* (Fort Scott, Kans., 1889), pp. 184–189; Robert Lee Hunt, *A History of Farmers' Movements in the Southwest, 1873–1925* (College Station, Tex., 1935), p. 37; Ralph A. Smith, "'Macuneism,' or the Farmers of Texas in Business," *Journal of Southern History* 13 (May 1947), pp. 230–240.

again, as well as taking advantage of the low long-distance railroad rates. The idea held the promise of earning the farmer as much as 3¢ per pound of cotton grown, a 40% increase in income.

Most Exchanges dealt collectively with the subordinate Alliance and not with the individual: Large orders and sales were necessary for effective use of the Exchange. Further motivating this collective action was the credit system. The Exchanges were forced to give credit to their customers, since most farmers could not otherwise buy supplies. To ensure credit, the locals signed a joint note with the Exchange, each one guaranteeing the others' credit and thereby strongly increasing the likelihood of repayment. Such a note would be much more easily converted to bank loans.

Since the Exchange was largely a credit business before the harvest, it would need credit itself to finance its various purchases.[13] The Exchange would obtain credit either from the manufacturers on the basis of its good name or by using the farmers' notes as collateral against bank loans, in the same way retail merchants did.[14]

A liquid Exchange could also serve its membership in other ways. Members could get money loans from the organization. It could become a bank for the members, so that it might someday be self-financing. Members who could not afford to hold a crop could sell it to the Exchange or obtain credit on purchases from the Exchange. There were other advantages to the Exchange. Even those who did not participate would benefit. In order to compete with the Exchange, local retailers had to lower prices and local cotton buyers had to raise their bids. Furthermore, the Exchange was able to inform local farmers who were not selling through the Alliance that cotton prices had risen, so they would not be cheated by buyers.

The Exchange was to be self-sustaining, but in order to begin operations, it needed a large sum to finance its initial purchases, to buy warehouses and stores, and to help establish a credit rating. This money was to be obtained through collections either from members or subordinate Alliances. The financing tied in with the structure of the Exchange operation, since donations could be made a prerequisite for participation in the decisionmaking apparatus.

Typically, the Exchange would sell stock to subordinate Alliances. Only member-subs could use the Exchange, so the purchase of stock for, let us say, $100, was like a membership fee. Member-subs then appointed a business agent to oversee their relations with the Exchange. A county business agent coordinated purchasing for the various subs in his area and oversaw deliveries. If there was an Exchange store located in the county, then a manager and governing board were needed. Depending upon the state, the control of the local store could fall under the jurisdiction of the state, or under the authority of the county Alliance, or under the jurisdiction of a newly formed group of stockholders in the Exchange.

[13] Hunt, *op. cit.*, p. 38.

[14] A typical exchange constitution can be found in "Proceedings of the North Carolina State Farmers' Alliance, 1888" (Raleigh, N. C., August 14, 1888), reprinted in *Raleigh Progressive Farmer*, August 21, 1888. Bylaws of the Texas Exchange can be found in *Raleigh Progressive Farmer*, July 17, 1888.

Operated maximally, the Exchange would buy from the manufacturer and eliminate both wholesale and retail merchants from the supply system. It would sell directly to the cotton factory and leave the agents, the factors, and most of the shippers out of the sales process. The whole economic system of cotton growing would be replaced. The only survivor would be bank financing, which would soon be eliminated. There were even plans for the Alliance to construct factories to manufacture its own supplies and cotton mills to process the farmers' cotton.[15]

We have previously discussed the distinction between counterinstitutions and pressure tactics. The former attempt to bypass some element of the system and replace it with a new structures. To explain why the Exchange arose and, in particular, why the Alliance did not adopt a pressure tactic, we need look further at this distinction.

One advantage of the Exchange was that it could directly compete with merchants and cotton buyers. The Alliance members got immediate results since they got products for less. In fact, the farmers did not need to change any principle of their own economic behavior. They simply bought from the cheapest merchant— who happened to be the Exchange. This meant that the Exchange could initiate operations and increase its clientele simply by offering better terms then did other merchants. No real proselytizing needed to be done, and no analysis of Southern agriculture had to be forwarded to newcomers. The Exchange was simply a superior form of merchandising and selling. No real change in the understanding or behavior of the farmers was needed for the Exchange to succeed.

A pressure tactic, on the other hand, always depended upon nonroutine action by the membership. For example, trade agreements depended upon the threat that Alliancemen would boycott a store even if such a boycott were not immediately profitable to the farmers. Furthermore, the membership needed to act in keeping with the development of the boycott—granting or withholding patronage, depending upon the state of the struggle between the Alliance and the merchant. This activity often involved much short-term hardship for the boycotters.

What we are describing here is the need for organizational discipline, the ability of the organization to get its members to change their behavior for the benefit of the whole group: Pressure tactics depend upon a certain amount of organizational discipline which counterinstitutions do not require—at least in theory. The beauty of the counterinstitution is that it requires no alteration of normal behavior; therefore, it could appeal to a large number of people who did not subscribe to Alliance principles at all.

There is a second, related contrast between the Exchange and pressure tactics. The Exchange related to the outside structure strictly through its leadership. Whereas a pressure tactic required the visible and coordinated effort of the membership, the Exchange required that the officers contact the manufacturers, the banks, and the other structures to facilitate the activity. The membership did not need to act upon or influence the structure.

---

[15] Smith, *op. cit.*, 229; C. W. Macune, *op. cit.*, p. 16; *Florida Dispatch* (Tallahassee), April 4, 1889.

In North Carolina, the Exchange raised $50,000 in capital, and this required considerable discipline, since locals had to send much needed cash to the organization, with no immediate return.[16] Once sufficient money was collected, little further commitment was required of the membership. The state agent traveled to New York, made contact with manufacturers and large wholesalers, set up purchasing facilities and distribution methods, and announced he was in business.[17] The Exchange functioned much like a very large and very cheap mercantile house: It advertised prices in the paper, sent sales agents to local areas, and competed for farmers' business. The locals had no organizing role beyond collecting orders, and individual participation did not depend upon any principle beyond buying at the cheapest store.[18] The Exchange advertisements even sounded like those of other merchants.[19]

Here we see the importance of the "inside—outside" distinction for protest organizations. Counterinstitutions depend upon leadership for their institutional connections to the established structure; pressure tactics depend upon the membership to relate to the outside. Pressure tactics therefore require a larger degree of organizational discipline through counterinstitutions.

We can, then, review the early development of the Alliance and see how it fit together with the choice of the Exchange as the principal statewide program. The initiative of the organization at first came from local groups. This was largely a result of the inability of the organization to generate action at any other level, but it also reflected various aspects of the system the Alliance challenged. As the group developed these actions, several things happened. The enlarged groups generated a state leadership which had an interest in pursuing and developing policies that would move the locus of action to the state level. This state organization did not, however, have direct contact with, or loyalty from, the bulk of its membership, which had been recruited upon the basis of local action. Nevertheless, its strength grew, and as local actions were tried and failed, it played more and more of a coordination and communication role among the locals. As escalations frustrated local action, discontent and failure at the local level became more and more focused and therefore created a crisis situation that called for the development of a statewide program. The nature of this statewide program was in part determined by the unwillingness of the organization to enter partisan politics; it also was determined by the fact that an analysis arose which presented the Exchange as a possible solution to the problems facing farmers. This sort of idea—a counterinstitution—was compatible with the circumstances of the state leadership, which could not at first gain the real organizational loyalty and discipline necessary for pressure tactics. Though it had the capability to dominate the organization through its

[16] *Raleigh Progressive Farmer.*, June 12, 1888–November 11, 1889; (see) especially *ibid.*, June 19, 1888; *ibid.*, July 10, 24, 1888; *ibid.*, October 9, 30, 1888; *ibid.*, November 27, 1888; *ibid.*, April 2, 1889; *ibid.*, July 2, 1889; *ibid.*, August 20, 1889; "Proceedings of the North Carolina State Farmers' Alliance, 1888," *op. cit.*

[17] *Raleigh Progressive Farmer*, November 12, 19, 1889; *ibid.*, December 17, 1889.

[18] *Raleigh Progressive Farmer*, November 12, 26, 1889; *ibid.*, December 24, 1889.

[19] "I am now prepared to supply groceries in whole packages *only* at lowest prices. . . ." *Raleigh Progressive Farmer*, November 12, 1889; see also *ibid.*, December 17, 1889.

management of newspapers and its control of monetary resources, it did not have the necessary systematic contact with the membership, the confidence of the membership, or the understanding of the membership. All of these were needed for the successful mass action that pressure tactics were likely to require. Therefore, the counterinstitution, which hoped to motivate support through direct benefit in routine economic terms, was compatible with the organizational situation of the Alliance.

To understand the operation of the Exchange, and its effect upon the Alliance, we can usefully look at the development of two Exchanges. The Texas Exchange was the pioneering effort and faced many difficulties that others avoided. The Florida Exchange, a strong later effort, exemplifies the role played by the Exchange in building the Alliance.

The idea of the Exchange was first expressed at the Waco convention of the Texas Farmers' Alliance in February 1887; the Exchange opened in September of that year. Between these dates, a whole organization was designed and constructed.[20] The rudimentary structures of the Exchange were already available because many counties, as a result of trade agreements and other efforts, had business managers who could be transformed into Exchange representatives.[21] By spring, C. W. Macune, the newly elected state Alliance president, had called all business managers together. From that point on, organizing proceeded rapidly. Once a communications network was established, orders were collected and money raised to provide the initial capital.

This money collection was a deviation from the conception of the Exchange as a routine economic structure. To get it started required a certain degree of organizational discipline among the members. The original plan called for each of the approximately 150,000 Alliance members to donate $2 to the financing of the enterprise.[22] These donations were to come in two installments per year, until the organization was self-sustaining. Over time, the Exchange hoped to collect $500,000. Actually, this amount was never reached. As Table 14.1 shows, the Exchange began operation with almost no dues collected, and it entered the second year with only about one-tenth of its expected total. Over the entire history of the Texas Exchange, less than $100,000 was collected in membership dues.

The Alliance Exchange opened in Semptember 1887, too late for it to supply the farmers but just in time to aid in the sale of cotton. Despite the haste of organization, it made contacts with Northern cotton mills, secured lower transport rates through direct shipments, established cheap Alliance warehouses (25¢ per bale), and obtained loans by using stockpiled cotton as collateral. By early 1888, Alliancemen had pocketed perhaps $1 million because of higher prices and lower costs realized through the Exchange. In areas where merchants and factors had to raise prices to compete with the Exchange, profits were probably greater.[23]

---

[20] Smith, op. cit., p. 229.

[21] Smith, op. cit., p. 225.

[22] Clarence N. Ousley, "A Lesson in Co-operation," Popular Science Monthly 36 (April 1890), p. 821.

[23] Southern Mercury, September, 1887; Waco Star and Crescent, July 1887; ibid., Raleigh Progressive Farmer, July 7, 1887; ibid., September 29, 1887; ibid., January 19, 1888; Macune, op. cit., pp. 20–23.

TABLE 14.1
Membership Dues Contributed to the
Texas Alliance

Date	Total dollar amount contributed[a]
November 1887	1,800
January 1888	5,200
March 1888	17,000
April 1888	20,000
June 1888	30,000
July 1888	56,000
September 1888	58,000
December 1888	62,000
August 1889	67,000
December 1889	79,000

[a]Different dates have figures from different sources. Therefore, seeming discontinuities, like those for June, July, and September 1888, may be the result of conflicting sources.

Sources: Nelson A. Dunning, ed., *Farmers' Alliance History and Agricultural Digest* (Washington, D.C., 1891), p. 85; Robert Lee Hunt, *A History of Farmers' Movements in the Southwest, 1873–1925* (College Station, Tex. 1935), p. 38; W. Scott Morgan, *History of the Wheel and Alliance and the Impending Revolution* (Fort Scott, Kans., 1889), p. 338; Clarence N. Ousley, "A Lesson in Cooperation," *Popular Science Monthly* 36 (April 1890), p. 824; Ralph A. Smith, "'Macuneism,' or the Farmers of Texas in Business," *Journal of Southern History* 13 (May 1947), p. 235.

While this was an encouraging beginning, it nowhere approached its potential, given the approximately $50 million worth of cotton raised by Alliancemen that year. Besides the lack of time, the Exchange encountered one of the constraints of tenancy: Many farmers who were under lien could not sell to the Exchange because they were forced to sell to the lienholders. To remove this constraint, the Alliance directors voted in November 1887 to offer crop liens the following year.[24] This would involve finding a considerable credit source and the development of a credit collecting system.

The Texas Exchange developed the system of collective credit which was to be adopted in many other states. The Exchange took notes upon the entire cotton crop of the sub-Alliances. It charged no interest for these notes and made them due November 15, fully 45 days later than the notes given by other lienholders. The Exchange took orders from the whole sub-Alliance with the notes as collateral. These notes were then offered as collateral for bank loans with which to finance the purchase of supplies. As the crop came in, the notes could be redeemed from the banks.[25]

[24] Ousley, *op. cit.*, p. 823.

Once it became apparent that the Exchange would be a large, if not dominant, merchant, businessmen could see the advantage of having the institution locate in their towns. One newspaper estimated that local banks would net $100,000 per year from interest on Alliance notes.[26]

Dallas was chosen over Fort Worth and Waco because it offered a wide assortment of inducements. Included was a guarantee of $10,000 in cash, payment of rent until a building was completed in May 1888, a $16,000 corner lot, 50 acres of water worth $5000 and discounts on construction costs. In addition, the Alliance was promised $5000 cash, 50 additional acres, and 2 acres in the fairgrounds if it decided to build a large factory.[27]

Operating from its Dallas headquarters, with a new branch in Belden, the 1888 Texas Exchange seriously disrupted the routine of cotton supply. Beginning the year with less than $20,000 in cash, it managed to do a huge business backed by over $1 million on joint notes.[28]

> Purchases were made on a large scale to meet the demands for supplies. One order was placed with the manufacturer for one thousand wagons to be shipped to various points. These wagons were duly made and delivered and paid in full. Tobacco was purchased in carload lots; five hundred barrels of molasses was [sic] purchased at one time, and other things in proportion.[29]

The Exchange charged only cost plus 10%, yet netted $62,000 profit in 1888.[30] Moreover, with prices frequently less than half those of local merchants, it created a general deflation:

> There were so many farmers in the Exchange and their trade constituted such a large percentage of the gross volume of trade in the community in which they lived, that the fact was irresistible that all merchants found themselves trying to meet Alliance prices.[31]

The decline in prices varied from place to place, depending upon Alliance strength. In well-organized areas, it frequently reached 40%, and throughout the Cotton Belt, the average was about 20%.[32] For the year 1888, this meant approximately $10 million in savings for Texas farmers. Farmers who dealt exclusively with the Exchange could cut costs in half and increase returns by one-quarter; as a result, over 80% of the farms were profitable.[33]

[25] Dunning, *op. cit.*, pp. 85, 360–362; Hunt, *op. cit.*, p. 36; Ousley, *op. cit.*, p. 821; Macune, *op. cit.*, p. 30.

[26] *Waco Star and Crescent*, quoted in *Raleigh Progressive Farmer*, July 7, 1887.

[27] *Rockdale (Tex.) Messenger*, September 6, 1887; *Raleigh Progressive Farmer*, September 15, 1887; *ibid.*, January 15, 1889; Macune, *op. cit.*, p. 16; Hunt, *op. cit.*, p. 36; Smith, *op. cit.*, p. 229.

[28] *Raleigh Progressive Farmer*, January 15, 1889; Ousley, *op. cit.*, p. 824; Dunning, *op. cit.*, p. 85.

[29] Macune, *op. cit.*, p. 25.

[30] *Raleigh Progressive Farmer*, January 15, 1889.

[31] Macune, *op. cit.*, p. 29.

[32] Macune, *op. cit.*, p. 35; *Raleigh Progressive Farmer*, January 15, 1889.

[33] See Chapter 5 of this volume.

Despite this dazzling success in 1888, the Exchange did not last even until 1890.[34] The cotton sales program declined drastically in fall 1888, and in May 1889, all new income was devoted to debt payment instead of supply purchase. By October of that year, the Alliance no longer controlled the Exchange, and in December, the building was sold at auction.

This turnabout actually began in early 1888. After collecting nearly $1 million in joint notes, the Exchange had immediately begun supply purchasing from wholesalers all over the country. It took no more than a few months before the Dallas merchants—retail and wholesale—realized that the Exchange, by going to the manufacturers, was reducing their business. As the pressure from Exchange sales began to be felt, the merchants became even more alarmed, and a formal meeting was held in April to plot a counterstrategy. Local banks were represented at the meeting, since they had heavily invested in local mercantile efforts.

After the April meeting, the local banks declared that the Exchange was a charitable institution, not liable to suit, and therefore ineligible for loans. This decision was widely publicized and it brought forth protest from all over Texas, a large demonstration of incensed Alliancemen in Dallas, and a statewide Alliance boycott of Dallas merchants. The resolution passed by the Kosse district Alliance expresses the anger of this response:

> *Whereas by honest intentions upon our part we have made this effort [the Exchange] for relief from the consuming group of insatiable greed, but*
> *Whereas, the merchants and bankers have made a combined effort to destroy our credit, blight our prospects and ruin our honest and legitimate struggle for relief, and*
> *Whereas by so doing they put on the escutcheon of ruler and assume the role of master whose power and authority must not be questioned or gainsaid, and branded the farmers as slaves and unworthy of rights or privileges, save to do the bidding of their Master at his beck and call....*[35]

After such an immediate and militant uproar, the banks backed down. But despite the Exchange's formal eligibility for bank loans, no bank in Dallas, Houston, Galveston, or New Orleans would loan the Exchange money. This would have ordinarily prevented any substantial Exchange business, but out-of-town manufacturers and wholesalers had already sent huge amounts of merchandise on credit, assuming that Exchange notes would be routinely funded. These creditors met with the Exchange director in early May and agreed to carry the debts until harvest, provided the Alliance collected a large sum of money from its membership as collateral for the debt: $58,000 was collected, about 10% of the May debt, and this carried the organization until fall. When harvesttime came, the Exchange paid all

---

[34] This account of the demise of the Texas Exchange is taken from the following sources. Macune, *op. cit.*, pp. 24—35; *National Economist*, September 6, 1890; *Raleigh Progressive Farmer*, May 15, 1888; *ibid.*, July 17, 1888; *ibid.*, November 7, 1888; *ibid.*, January 15, 1889; *ibid.*, September 16, 1890; *Southern Mercury*, May 8, 1888; *ibid.*, October 1888; *Florida Dispatch*, May 23, 1889; Ousley, *op. cit.*, pp. 827—828.

[35] Reprinted in *Raleigh Progressive Farmer*, July 17, 1888.

its debts, showed a profit of $68,000, and clearly demonstrated its reliability as a borrower.

Nevertheless, the Exchange was doomed. Because it had no credit source, the cotton sales program had to be abandoned in the fall. That winter, the Exchange abandoned credit purchases because it could no longer obtain credit from the manufacturers. Even though they had all been paid the previous year, they were neither able nor willing to extend yearlong credit in the absence of bank backing. Without any credit, the Exchange could make only cash purchases. In 1889, it did almost no business.

In the flush of the 1888 success, the Alliance invested $45,000 in a permanent Dallas site. When the crisis caused by withdrawal of credit took hold that winter, this bill could not be paid, and it was this debt which precipitated the bankruptcy of the Exchange.

The ultimate counterinstitution was defeated by the ultimate escalation. Because of its resounding success in 1888, the Exchange undermined the prosperity of the mercantile class in Texas, and mercantile depression brought the entire business structure into the struggle. This united business community sought out and discovered an effective counterattack—withdrawal of credit. As soon as loans were denied, the Exchange was doomed. The logic of this was expressed by C. W. Macune even before the defeat:

> *As our Exchange develops new and conclusive evidence of success, the various forms of opposition and antagonism become more active and bitter, and show a tendency toward coalition or combination of all those forces that oppose the Alliance common course to destroy the organization.*[36]

The Exchange was a counterinstitution designed to replace substantial parts of the cotton supply and sales system. It failed because it depended upon the credit system to back its notes, and when the banks and manufacturers refused credit, it had no alternative.

This escalation might have been met with counterescalation. One such counterescalation involved pressuring banks into loaning the Exchange money. Partly, this was the tactic used to reverse the Dallas declaration that the Exchange was a "charitable institution," and an extended boycott of Dallas merchants might well have forced the local banks to accept the Exchange's notes. Such an action required a protracted struggle and a determined membership willing to make serious sacrifices, including temporarily higher prices, long waits for merchandise, and the extreme inconvenience of sending long distances to obtain merchandise. In short, it required organizational discipline. A second counterescalation would extend the Exchange to replace the credit system. By means of the Exchange, the Alliance had counterattacked escalating wholesalers who had destroyed the co-

---

[36] How the Merchants and Bankers of Dallas Have 'Bounced' the State Alliance and How They Got 'Bounced,'" *Southern Mercury*, May 7, 1888; reprinted in *Raleigh Progressive Farmer*, May 15, 1888.

ops. This policy could have been extended. The credit system had refused to do business with the Alliances so it, too, would be replaced. If manufacturers then joined the fight, they, too, would be replaced with Alliance factories.[37]

But such a plan required a large reserve of cash with which to make purchases. The Exchange needed to become a bank in which prosperous yeomen would deposit the money needed to finance the mass credit purchases of the less prosperous. At harvesttime, the money would be returned.

In essence, the Exchange fund was such a bank and its fate reveals the crucial problem the Alliance faced. By late 1888, the Exchange had $130,000 in its fund. Alliancemen had contributed $62,000 in stock purchases, and $68,000 was profit from the first year's enterprise.[38] This fund, augmented by new stock purchases, could have provided the basis for a restricted operation which would be expanded as each year's profits were reinvested. However, many members demanded the return of their contributions. This development reflected the pessimism generated by the attacks. The April declaration that the Exchange was not financially responsible had been withdrawn, but major Texas papers continued to publicize it. The newspapers also spread rumors of Exchange insolvency, and at least one report circulated statewide that the director had absconded with the funds. At the same time, merchants all over the state used their many thousands of salesmen to undermine confidence in the Exchange.[39]

The Alliance membership, instead of contributing to the Exchange fund, withdrew their support and made it impossible for the Alliance to counterattack bank escalation. They became demoralized as a result of the persistent (though unfounded) rumors about the insolvency of the Exchange. With demoralization came the decline in organizational discipline.

During this decline, there emerged the threat of legal prosecution against the leaders of the Texas Exchange. In order to forestall this move, and to reestablish the credibility of the leaders, the national Alliance in 1890 hired an outside auditor whose report blamed the failure of the Exchange on its "financial inadequacies"— an endorsement of the banks' refusal to grant credit—and upheld the honesty of the officers. Thus, the final judgment protected the leaders from prosecution while it declared the entire enterprise ill-conceived and doomed to failure.[40]

Ironically, the Exchange succumbed to the credit boycott because of its own greatest strength. Its great advantage was that it could appeal to Alliancemen and other farmers just like any other merchant. Its prices were much lower and that alone was enough to guarantee a large business. No special commitment was necessary, and therefore the relatively weak state organization could sustain it. However, when the banks attacked, and when newspaper stories questioned the Exchange's economic viability, the farmers treated the Exchange just like any other merchant: They began to shop elsewhere. Without deeper membership understanding of the

---

[37] Ibid.
[38] Ibid.
[39] Macune, op. cit., pp. 30–31; National Economist, September 6, 1890.
[40] Raleigh Progressive Farmer, September 16, 1890.

role played by the Exchange, of its larger potential, and of the mechanisms that created the attack on it, it could not defend itself.

In other words, organizational discipline was lacking because the membership had not been organized around the *analysis* that generated the Alliance. This lack of understanding was itself one reason the Exchange had been so appealing. And this same lack of discipline made mass boycotts impossible. The Texas Alliance had trapped itself in a vicious circle.

To analyze this dilemma further, we can scrutinize the history of the Florida Exchange. The idea of an Exchange was raised at the first Florida Alliance meeting in October 1887, but the organization was not at that time strong enough to sustain an Exchange. While the Exchange did begin operation in the summer of 1888, it was only of help in cotton and fruit marketing.[41] It did not operate on a broad basis until 1889.

As a result, the Florida Alliance could look carefully at the Texas experience and adjust its operations accordingly. In fact, the trials of the Texas Exchange caused an extensive debate about the efficacy of the Alliance itself.[42] The operation of the Florida Exchange reflected this debate and scrutiny. The chief target was the credit system. Plans were made to circumvent the banks through the deposit of farmers' savings with the Alliance. Also, liens would be given only to individuals who were good risks, thereby reducing the chances of default. The Alliance would develop factories to avoid dependence upon uncooperative manufacturers.[43] To boost commitment, the entire structure of the Alliance was to be used for the Exchange. (The original Texas Exchange had created a structure of business managers who worked separately from the Alliance structure.) In Florida, part of the Alliance dues went to the Exchange and the Alliance locals were the local body of the Exchange.[44] An extensive system of local outlets was planned and developed.[45]

These structural features would all have been hopeless unless the Exchange could reach the membership and motivate its support. To accomplish this, the Exchange found itself in the grass roots organizing business. Advertising circulars were printed which explained the Alliance and the Exchange and exhorted people to join.[46] A system of lecturers and circulars was begun in an attempt to contact and encourage all interested farmers inside and outside the Alliance.[47] The principal resources of the Alliance organizers were given over to talking to new and old members about the advantages of the Exchange,[48] and the result was

[41] *Florida Dispatch,* January 28, 1889; James O. Knauss, "The Farmers' Alliance in Florida," *South Atlantic Quarterly* 25 (July 1926), p. 305.

[42] See Knauss, *op. cit.,* pp. 305–307; *Florida Dispatch,* February 14, 1887; *ibid.,* February 21, 1887; *ibid.,* July 11, 1889.

[43] *Florida Dispatch,* January 28, 1889; *ibid.,* March 7, 1889; *ibid.,* April 4, 1889; *ibid.,* July 11, 1889.

[44] *Florida Dispatch,* March 7, 1889; various issues August–November 1889.

[45] Branch stores were established in at least 12 counties. *Florida Dispatch,* January 28, 1889; *ibid.,* May 9, 1889; *ibid.,* July 4, 11, 1889; *ibid.,* August 22, 1889; *ibid.,* September 5, 1889; *ibid.,* November 7, 21, 1889.

[46] *Florida Dispatch,* January 28, 1889.

[47] *National Economist,* April 8, 1889; *Florida Dispatch,* July 11, 1889.

[48] *Florida Dispatch,* September 12, 1889; *ibid.,* October 31, 1889.

considerable rank-and-file support.[49] A final innovation was an attempt to circumvent selling problems by establishing a New York office of the Exchange so that
the Alliance could reach the cotton manufacturers in exactly the same place the
other sellers did.

Despite these extensive efforts, the Florida Exchange showed a $15,000 deficit
in early 1891 and was totally bankrupt before 1892.[50] In this respect, it was typical:
None of the 13 Alliance Exchanges functioned successfully after 1890, though
several survived into 1892.[51] They all met with a fate similar to that of the Texas
and Florida Exchanges.[52] These failures had a profound effect upon later Alliance
policies, and therefore they merit particular attention.

One type of difficulty the Exchanges experienced was "internal." The most
frequent form of internal problem was membership apathy. This problem was
summarized in a letter to the Florida Exchange which stated: "It is hard to convince
them [Alliance members] that the Exchange is their institution, but consider it
as any other mercantile or commission house."[53] Another was inefficient operation
which resulted in high prices or financial difficulty or both.[54] A third was internal
friction which arose over the usefulness or efficacy of Exchange operations.[55]
Alliance newspapers and leaders opposed the idea or the reality of the Exchange.
They raised many objections to the idea and made public the problems we have
listed.[56]

None of these internal problems should have been deadly. There was no reason,
for example, that internal disputes over the idea should have weakened the

---

[49] *Florida Dispatch,* April 4, 1889; *ibid.,* July 11, 1889; *ibid.,* August 18, 1889; *ibid.,* October 21, 1889; *ibid.,* November 21, 1889.

[50] Knauss, *op. cit.,* p. 306; *Florida Dispatch,* January 28, 1889.

[51] The Thirteen Exchanges were: Alabama, Arkansas, Florida, Georgia, Kentucky, Louisiana, Maryland, Mississippi, North Carolina, South Carolina, Tennessee, and Texas.

[52] Below is a list of sources on various exchanges.

Alabama: Thomas M. Owen, *History of Alabama and Dictionary of Alabama Biography* (Chicago, 1921), vol. I, p. 564; *Appleton's Annual Encyclopedia* (Washington, D.C. 1890), p. 9; William A. Rogers, "The Farmers' Alliance in Alabama," *Alabama Review* 15 (January 1962), pp. 14–15; *Raleigh Progressive Farmer,* February 12, 1889; *ibid.,* March 12, 1889.

Arkansas: *National Economist,* March 14, 1889; Morgan, *op. cit.,* pp. 184–185.

Georgia: Alex M. Arnett, *The Populist Movement in Georgia,* Columbia University Studies in History, Economics and Public Law, vol. 104 (New York, 1922), p. 79; *Florida Dispatch,* October 10, 1889; Dunning, *op. cit.,* pp. 367–368; *National Economist,* March 14, 1889; *Raleigh Progressive Farmer,* July 10, 1888; *ibid.,* February 26, 1889; *ibid.,* January 14, 1890; *ibid.,* February 4, 1890.

Louisiana: *National Economist,* September 5, 1888; *Raleigh Progressive Farmer,* April 23, 1889; *ibid.,* October 22, 1889.

Maryland: *National Economist,* February 15, 1890.

Mississippi: *National Economist,* March 14, 1889; *Raleigh Progressive Farmer,* March 5, 1889.

North Carolina: F. G. Blood, ed., *Handbook and History of the National Farmers' Alliance and Industrial Union* (Washington, 1893), p. 52; *Raleigh News and Observer,* August 18, 1889; *ibid.,* January 25, 1888; Stuart Noblen, *Leonidas LaFayette Polk: Agrarian Crusader* (Chapel Hill, 1949), p. 208.

South Carolina: Blood, *op. cit.,* p. 57; *Raleigh Progressive Farmer,* May 6, 1890; *ibid.,* June 10, 1890.

[53] *Florida Dispatch,* July 4, 1889.

[54] See, for example, *Florida Dispatch,* January 16, 1890; Ousley, *op. cit.,* p. 827.

[55] Ousley, *op. cit.,* p. 827; Morgan, *op. cit.,* p. 339; *Florida Dispatch,* January 16, 1889; *ibid.,* March 14, 1889.

[56] The Georgia Alliance president resigned when he could not defeat the establishment of the Exchange. *Raleigh Progressive Farmer,* February 25, 1889.

Exchanges. Many times, such internal conflict strengthens a program by clarifying and correcting its weaknesses while advertising its strengths. Poor management could be corrected. And the lack of membership enthusiasm should not have substantially affected the operation, for if people treated it "like any other mercantile or commission house," the good Exchange could undersell and get all the business.

Clearly, something more fundamental underlay these internal problems. We have already seen a glimpse of what this was, in our discussion of the Texas Alliance. The Exchange simply could not outcompete other merchants, because it could not obtain credit like other merchants: Bank and manufacturer escalation prevented it from doing so. Therefore, the Alliance membership needed to make monetary and other commitments to the Exchange. Furthermore, given the slanderous attacks against the Exchange, members needed a great deal of commitment and confidence to purchase from, and donate to, the operation. Tremendous economic benefits would come about only after large cash reserves had been accumulated and perhaps factories built. Certainly no one was going to do such things for an ordinary mercantile house, and therefore Exchange success did depend upon commitment and loyalty from the Allianceman.

In Florida, the Exchange attempted to reach the membership with literature and organizers who pointed out the daily advantage of the Exchange and its long-range promise. Such organizing attempted to bolster the commitment of the members so that they would aid in the Exchange's battle for survival. The effect of these efforts cannot be accurately measured, but the failure of the Exchange shows that it was not successful.

The internal problems were, then, integrally bound up with the external problems. In a manner of speaking, the two could not be separated, since the one implied and created the other. The external problems that beset the Exchange began with the banks. Credit refusals and high interest were the central difficulties. But Exchanges also faced concerted action by local merchants, as well as manufacturers' boycotts against Exchange purchases or cotton sales.[57] By and large, these represented escalations against the Exchange and can be subjected to the same type of analysis that we made of the responses to the trade agreements, cooperatives, and bulking plans. But in this case, the counterattack open to the Alliance was not the same. No strategy short of an entire countereconomy would suffice, and the vague efforts to organize this were not successful.[58] The strategy of counterinstitutions had been followed to its logical end.

It might be expected that the Alliance would emerge considerably weakened from a failure like the Exchanges, but this was only partly the case. Disintegration or demoralization takes place when an old program is not replaced with a new one that could plausibly resolve the old problem. The Exchanges had had the curious

[57] For example, Morgan, *op. cit.*, p. 339; *Florida Dispatch*, August 8, 1889; Ousley, *op. cit.*, p. 825; *Dunning, op. cit.*, pp. 362–363; Smith, *op. cit.*, p. 234; *National Economist*, September 6, 1890.

[58] *National Economist*, July 15, 1889; *ibid.*, August 3, 1889; Dunning, *op. cit.*, p. 72; *Florida Dispatch*, November 7, 1887; Samuel Proctor, "The National Farmers' Alliance Convention of 1890 and its 'Ocala Demands,'" *Florida Historical Quarterly* 28 (January 1950), p. 177; Macune, *op. cit.*, pp. 32–33.

effect of eliminating their own proximate cause. A key reason that pressure tactics had been discarded in favor of the Exchange was that the structure of the organization had made such mobilization hard to accomplish. In the course of the Alliance's developing the Exchange, a massive effort had been made to reach the rank and file; this effort brought the state structure into direct contact with the membership. This direct contact made it possible for the state to undertake the mass mobilization required for large-scale pressure tactics. Moreover, the initial successes had created a flood of new membership with which to undertake massive statewide action. Thus, the failure of the Exchanges had created the conditions for their own successor—statewide and national pressure tactics.

15

The Great Jute Boycott

Rally together, you sons of toil,
  Falter not in our righteous cause,
As we love our home, our native soil,
  Band together for better laws;
Then strike out against this greedy trust,
  Gallant freemen, with all your might,
A blow to bring it down to the dust,
  Burying it forever from our sight.

[Robert J. Cour, Oxford, North Carolina,
Raleigh Progressive Farmer, January 14, 1890]

Jute bagging was an essential part of the marketing of cotton. Cotton came out of the gin as a loose, bulky product and was compressed into bales of 400–500 pounds for ease of shipment. These bales were held together by 6 boards on the edges and about 6 yards of wrapping made of jute (which looks like burlap). The whole bundle was then sold as a unit. Jute was grown in India and shipped to the United States, where it was made into wrapping cloth (called "bagging"). For each bale of cotton, the farmer spent about 50¢ for jute bagging.

When a bale was sold, it was weighed along with the bagging. To ascertain the weight of the cotton alone, 6% was reduced from the total. This reduction, called a *tare*, had been adopted just after the Civil War and reflected the 400-pound bales then in use. With 6 ties weighing 2 pounds each and 6 yards of bagging, the weight of the wrapping was about 24 pounds, or 6% of 400. If the bale were a little heavier, a little more bagging would be used and this would be paid for by a slightly larger deduction.

By 1890, the jute cloth weighed about 1¾ pounds per yard, and the boards weighed 1¾ pounds each. The bales averaged about 480 pounds.[1] Even with the extra cloth for the larger bales, the weight of the wrapping was never over 24 pounds (and usually closer to 20) but the tare was close to 30 pounds. This disparity cost the farmer about 50¢ on each bale, more than 1% of his or her selling price.

[1] *National Economist* (Washington, D.C.), October 5, 1889.

On August 1, 1888, the price of jute bagging rose from 7¢ to 11¾¢ per yard. Such a price rise was extraordinary, and the U.S. government immediately initiated an investigation. This investigation revealed what everyone already knew—that eight companies with two-thirds of the jute market had agreed upon the rise. A trust had been formed.[2]

Such an action was not illegal. In fact, it was looked upon by many as perfectly legitimate. Just before the furor over the jute price rise, a member of the plaid trust explained why these price fixing agreements arose:

> It is the play of Hamlet with Hamlet left out. There is no trust about it. It is merely an agreement between most of the mills making plaid goods not to pile up any more goods in their warehouses, and not to sell what they have on hand at ruinous prices.[3]

The effect of this price rise was small but not insignificant: about 25¢ per bale, or less than 1% of the purchase price. Nevertheless, a farmer with 50 acres might lose as much as $10 per year because of this price rise. Furthermore, a successful price rise might encourage another one. Prices of 25¢ per yard for jute did not seem out of the question. This meant a loss of about $1 per bale, a substantial amount.

This jute price rise was also significant in another way. It was the sort of rise that reached almost all farmers directly. Many of the most indebted tenants were still involved in the ginning and compressing of their cotton. Those who were not involved in ginning were charged for it and knew the costs involved. There had been much grumbling about the lightened bagging and ties, and farmers quickly noted any price increase in jute. A 68% rise in price was met with immediate discontent and disapproval.

If there had been no Alliance, such a price rise might not have produced any significant protest. The time and effort it takes to bring people together to protest meetings, to link up with other protesters, and to coordinate action would have overwhelmed the discontent, especially since it was generated by a loss of less than 1%. However, there was an Alliance, and this incident occurred when the Alliance was uniquely equipped to channel and organize just the sort of protest that would be effective against the jute trust.

The immediate reaction came at the local level. In routine meetings of subordinate and county Alliances, members called for action to combat the trust.[4] The issue was a popular one, and many moderate groups, including the Louisiana State Agricultural Society and the Interstate Farmers' Convention, joined the protest. Even conservative journals, such as the *Raleigh News and Observer*, editorialized against the trust.[5]

[2] *Raleigh News and Observer*, August 2, 1888; *ibid.*, September 1, 1888; Ralph A. Smith, "'Macuneism, or the Farmers of Texas in Business," *Journal of Southern History* 13 (May 1947), p. 236.

[3] *Raleigh News and and Observer*, June 30, 1888.

[4] Lucia E. Daniel, "The Louisiana People's Party," *Louisiana Historical Quarterly* 26 (October 1943), pp. 1064—1065; Smith, *op. cit.*, p. 236; W. Scott Morgan, *History of the Wheel and Alliance and the Impending Revolution* (Fort Scott, Kans., 1889), p. 104; *Raleigh News and Observer*, September 15, 1888; *Raleigh Progressive Farmer*, August 7, 14, 28, 1888.

[5] *Raleigh News and Observer*, September 16, 1888.

The state Alliances also took up the battle. As the state organizations met during the autumn of 1888, they considered a variety of actions. The Louisiana State Farmers' Union (the Alliance group in that state) called for a national boycott until the price came down, along with the establishment of a plant to manufacture cotton bagging to replace jute.[6] The Georgia state Alliance tried to arrange a boycott of jute by making an agreement with a company to buy cotton bagging.[7]

By September, there was general agreement favoring a national boycott of jute bagging, and a planning meeting was held in Washington, D.C.[8] The very existence of such a meeting was so ominous that the price of jute dropped immediately in some markets. Soon afterward, the boycott began to take hold all over the South.[9] Farmers bought second-hand jute bagging, cotton bagging, pine straw bagging, and any other wrap they could find. So great was the spirit that local farmers initiated boycotts against fertilizer in jute bags, jute twine, merchants who asked for jute-wrapped cotton, and newspapers that opposed the boycott.[10] In Raleigh, North Carolina,

> some of the dealers here who keep jute bagging have put it out of sight. The farmers cannot bear the sight of it and actually refuse to trade where it is kept.[11]

In Texas, the Alliance Exchange, which was as financially healthy as any Exchange ever was, used its economic clout to break the price. The Exchange bought a 50% interest in a cotton compress that was in financial difficulty, with the proviso that the owner sell the Exchange 10 carloads of jute bagging for 7.5¢ per yard. The Exchange then offered these 10 carloads for sale. This brought down the price to 7.5¢ on almost all the jute sold in the state.[12]

Taken by surprise, the trust had been beaten. The rapid Alliance action drove the price below pretrust levels and the jute manufacturers failed to show a profit in 1888.[13] All over the South, the Alliance clubs celebrated their victory.

> Whereas we have been successful in breaking down the bagging trust; therefore, we think it would be wise should the President of the State Alliance call a meeting of the State Alliance to confer in reference to other trusts.[14]

But this was only the opening round. Unless the Alliance planned ahead, cotton farmers could expect to pay 12¢ or more per yard for jute in 1889. Therefore, at the

---

[6] Daniel, *op. cit.*

[7] Morgan, *op. cit.*, p. 336.

[8] *Raleigh Progressive Farmer*, August 28, 1888; *ibid.*, September 4, 11, 18, 1888.

[9] *Raleigh Progressive Farmer*, September 18, 1888; *ibid.*, October 2, 9, 23, 1888; *ibid.*, December 25, 1889.

[10] *Raleigh Progressive Farmer*, September 4, 11, 18, 1888; *ibid.*, October 2, 9, 16, 23, 30, 1888; *ibid.*, November 6, 13, 20, 27, 1888.

[11] *Wilmington* (N.C.) *Messenger*, September 1888, quoted in *Raleigh Progressive Farmer*, September 25, 1888.

[12] Smith, *op. cit.*, pp. 236–237; C. W. Macune, "The Farmers' Alliance" (1920), pp. 26–28.

[13] *Raleigh Progressive Farmer*, July 7, 1889.

[14] *Raleigh Progressive Farmer*, January 8, 1889.

December 1888 national convention, a special jute committee worked on the strategy for successful further action.[15] It suggested a boycott if a substitute for the jute could be found. Two such substitutes seemed to be possible: pine straw bagging and cotton bagging. Actual production had not been worked out for either, and even if one of them became available, three problems still remained.

First, cotton buyers could refuse to accept bales wrapped in the substitute, so a successful boycott would need the cooperation of the cotton exchanges, which oversaw the sales of the crop. (These exchanges had nothing to do with Alliance Exchanges. They were the equivalent of the New York Stock Exchange; that is, they were where cotton was sold.) Second, both pine straw and cotton bagging would weigh considerably less than the jute bagging. The cotton wrapping weighed about 16 pounds instead of the established rate of about 29 pounds (6% of 480) and the actual rate of about 21 pounds. The current system cheated the farmer of about 10 pounds of cotton per bale, and a change would involve an additional loss of 4 pounds. The final problem was the availability of cotton or pine bagging and the price of production. Neither of these problems had been solved, and a permanent jute committee was established to keep track of the situation.

So far, nothing had been done. The national Alliance, busy with organizational and other problems, was unequipped to lead a jute boycott. It had just been formed, and it had none of the organizational equipment to carry the initiative. However, the state organizations were strong and did have the structural equipment.

The Georgia convention, held in April, was a particularly successful one. A boycott was voted, and the Alliance decided to use cotton bagging. The purchasing would begin in the spring of 1889 because manufacturers would not produce cotton bagging without a guaranteed market.[16] Two million yards of cotton bagging were ordered, and pressure was applied to force merchants to accept cotton wrapping with a 4% tare adjustment.[17]

The leaders of 11 state Alliances met in Birmingham in late April and returned to their state groups with the program for a full-scale boycott of jute.[18] Moreover, it was decided to use cotton bagging on a permanent basis. Calculations indicated that this practice would ultimately save cotton farmers $14 million even if jute were sold at its pretrust price of 7¢, while cotton bagging sold for 12¢.[19] So confident was

[15] "Proceedings of the National Farmers' Alliance and Industrial Union of America, Meridian, Mississippi, December 5, 1888," reprinted in *Raleigh Progressive Farmer*, December 25, 1888; *ibid.*, January 8, 1889; *National Economist*, March 14, 1889.

[16] *National Economist*, April 13, 20, 26, 1889; *Raleigh Progressive Farmer*, April 16, 1889.

[17] *Raleigh Progressive Farmer*, May 7, 1889; *National Economist*, April 13, 20, 26, 1889.

[18] "Proceedings of the Birmingham Conference, Farmers' Alliance and Agricultural Wheel, May 15–16," reprinted in *Raleigh Progressive Farmer*, May 28, 1889; see also *National Economist*, April 26, 1889; Morgan, *op. cit.*, p. 343. The meeting was actually held in late April, despite the dates listed on the proceedings.

[19] "Proceedings of the Birmingham Conference"; *Appleton's Annual Cyclopedia, 1889* (New York, 1890), p. 9; Morgan, *op. cit.*, p. 345; *National Economist*, May 1, 1889. This was not really a paradox. Cotton bagging could be processed with the cotton itself, meaning that it was possible (in the long run) that the farmer would be paid for his 6 pounds of cotton wrapping at the market rate. This would save the farmer around half the price of the bagging. Also, the use of cotton bagging would increase the market for cotton. Thus, the cost of a yard of cotton bagging would actually be nothing since the farmer would get half the price back from increased cotton sales and the other half back from the buyer who paid for the cotton bagging as processible cotton.

the convention that it refused an offer of 2 million yards of jute at pretrust prices.[20]

The plan of action was straightforward but difficult. Every county Alliance would be urged to meet in order to endorse the boycott. State organizations would send lecturers and organizers to help in this effort. At these county meetings, and at subordinate meetings which followed, members would be organized to make the boycott effective at the local level. All members would refuse to wrap their cotton in jute and would urge their neighbors to do the same. They would refuse to sell to any buyer who did not allow 8 extra pounds to adjust the tare. Members could order their cotton bagging through the state organizations. Members who broke the boycott were to be expelled from the organization.[21]

This strategy would pressure the buyers and cotton exchanges to accept cotton bagging and it would force an adjustment in the tare. It also guaranteed a market for the manufacturers of cotton bagging. The only problem was to carry out the boycott at the local level.

The process by which the great jute boycott developed reveals much about the functioning of the Alliance and much about the particular structure of the Alliance at that time. A successful boycott required that the local Alliances be the locus of action; the membership needed to take the initiative in making the strategy work. Unlike the Exchange, which had members relating to the Exchange and the Exchange making contact with manufacturers and others, the boycott called for the membership to buy their cotton bagging specially, to pressure merchants and buyers into accepting it, and to urge their friends to do the same. The upper organization could arrange to supply cotton bagging, but it could only encourage its membership to observe the boycott.

The national organization had almost no direct contact with the membership. It could not initiate a program and expect to move the membership afterward. Significantly, the boycott had been proposed at a special Georgia convention, which brought the local leadership to a statewide meeting. This was emblematic of the organizational situation. The national body was too weak to call the boycott. The state organ of Georgia could do so, but it recognized that success depended upon local groups. The special convention brought the proposals directly before the local leadership and gained their support. This reflected the locus of power for this action. The statewide leadership was not preeminent—it was not the principal opinion-maker for the membership. The local leadership was still strong and could make or break the boycott.

On the other hand, the locals were incapable of calling the boycott, since it had to be at least statewide, if not national, in scope. Therefore, local agitation had served the purpose of calling the problem to the attention of the states, but it could not by itself organize the boycott. The initiative needed to be taken by the states.

[20] "Proceedings of the Birmingham Conference."

[21] "Proceedings of the Birmingham Conference"; *Jacksonville Florida Dispatch*, June 20, 1889; *National Economist*, May 1, 8, 1889; *Raleigh Progressive Farmer*, May 21, 1889.

[22] *National Economist*, May 1, 1889; *ibid.*, August 3, 1889; *ibid.*, September 28, 1889; *ibid.*, November 23, 1889; *Raleigh News and Observer*, September 1, 1889; William W. Rogers, "The Farmers' Alliance in Alabama," *Alabama Review* 15 (January 1962), p. 16; Morgan, *op. cit.*, p. 335.

Thus, the jute boycott was a cooperative effort between the state organizations and the locals. Since the national Alliance was too weak to handle it, the boycott was run by a confederation of state Alliance leaders.

If the state structure had been stronger, if it had developed enough direct contact with the membership, it might not have needed to call conventions to organize support. It would have been equipped with organizers and lecturers, newspapers and finances so that it could reach individual members without the mediation and support of the local leadership. Had this been the case, however, the boycott might not have been called. At the time of the boycott, the Alliance Exchanges were at the peak of their activity, and the resources of the state organizations were deeply committed to making the Exchanges successful. This implied much more than a mere choosing of where to place resources. The two programs required different actions by the members and different functioning at the local level. The boycott needed a membership that was willing to take the short-run loss on cotton bagging for the long-run gain. The members needed to meet often, to negotiate with local merchants, and to organize their neighbors. Public support had to be built to keep the local population abreast of negotiations and progress so that sympathy and further support could be developed. The Exchange did not require frequent meetings, but it did require that the local representatives see the members frequently. Members needed to be persuaded to patronize the Exchange, but they did not need to make political and tactical decisions of their own. The Exchange decreased or eliminated the contact between the members and the established structure, while the boycott brought the members into greater and more involved contact.

Thus, the two programs, though not antagonistic, were in conflict. If the state organization had been very strong vis-à-vis the locals, it might have made a decision to forgo the boycott in favor of the long-range Exchange plans. But the state Alliances depended upon the locals for the success of the Exchange and had to respond to local needs. The jute trust was an appropriate target for this purpose.

Several actions aimed to bring the two programs into consonance. The most important was the idea of permanent conversion to cotton bagging, which would have made the bagging supply system a firm buttress for the Exchanges. Several Exchanges made special deals to supply cotton bagging—a commitment they could make only if they were sure of the boycott. Others built and financed factories to make the substitute product.[22] This permanent change to cotton held forth the promise of building the Exchange and strengthening the permanent organization.

After May 1889, the jute boycott divided into two parts: the development of support at the local level, and negotiation and bargaining at higher levels. During the summer months, agitation at the local level built for a strong boycott that fall. Orders were taken for cotton bagging, and various groups vocally supported the boycott.[23] Some local Alliances even built storage bins to hold unbaled cotton,

[23] A chronology of Florida actions can be found in the *Florida Dispatch*, various issues during July—August 1889. For some overall figures on local actions see *Jacksonville Florida Dispatch*, October 17, 1889. North Carolina actions can be found in *Raleigh Progressive Farmer*; Texas actions in *Southern Mercury*; and Arkansas actions in *Alliance Tocsin*, July—August, 1889.

thereby demonstrating their determination to hold the crop rather than wrap it in jute.[24]

These actions—public evidence of the credibility of Alliance threats—began to shake the cotton exchanges and the jute trust. As early as September 1888, reports circulated that the Liverpool cotton exchange, the preeminent market in the world, would accept cotton bagging, probably without a rise in the insurance rates.[25] Then, in early 1889, the New York cotton exchange endorsed cotton bagging and agreed to reduce the tare on cotton by 8 pounds.[26] A more important endorsement came several days later when the New Orleans exchange announced that it would also accept cotton bagging—on the same terms the New York exchange had set.[27] This was an acceptance of all the Alliance demands.

The New Orleans Plan, as it became known, spread to other cotton exchanges in the South; the plan was aided by a preliminary endorsement from Liverpool.[28] At the urging of the New Orleans exchange, several Southern exchanges met to develop a uniform policy. The results of this meeting would make or break the boycott, or so it seemed. It was here that the boycott looked best—a tare of 16 pounds for cotton compared to 24 pounds for jute was set.[29]

However, as several weeks went by, few of the exchanges actually followed this policy. Many refused to accept cotton bagging and those that did were not granting the 16-pound tare.[30] The situation at the important Galveston exchange, which at first endorsed the plan, revealed part of the problem: "A jute-factory in Galveston, the stock of which is owned by local merchants, has mustered sufficient backing to influence that exchange. . . ."[31] In Charleston, the same resistance emerged: Economic ties between jute factories and the local cotton merchants resulted in the refusal to accept any substitute bagging.[32]

These developments could have been overcome by routing cotton bales to the co-operating exchanges, an operation which the Alliance structure made possible. However, that summer, the Liverpool exchange announced that it would not adjust the tare.[33] Without this adjustment, farmers would lose about 50¢ per bale, a substantial part of their profits. The reasons for this resistance were not hard to find. First, jute was produced by British colonists in India, shipped in British vessels, and sold by British merchants—all having links to the Liverpool cotton exchange. Second, if cotton were used to cover the bales, this would absorb a considerable amount of American cotton which ordinarily was shipped to Britain. This decline

[24] *Raleigh Progressive Farmer*, August 13, 1889.

[25] *Raleigh News and Observer*, September 27, 1888.

[26] *National Economist*, May 8, 1889.

[27] *Ibid.*; *Raleigh Progressive Farmer*, September 17, 24, 1889.

[28] *Jacksonville Florida Dispatch*, August 22, 1889; *Raleigh Progressive Farmer*, September 17, 24, 1889; *National Economist*, August 24, 31, 1889.

[29] *National Economist*, September 21, 1889; *Raleigh Progressive Farmer*, September 17, 24, 1889.

[30] *Jacksonville Florida Dispatch*, October 17, 1889; *National Economist*, October 12, 1889; *ibid.*, November 16, 1889; *Raleigh News and Observer*, October 3, 1889; *Raleigh Progressive Farmer*, September 24, 1889; *ibid.*, October 1, 1889.

[31] *National Economist*, August 24, 1889.

[32] *Raleigh Progressive Farmer*, September 28, 1889; *ibid.*, October 1, 1889.

[33] *Jacksonville Florida Dispatch*, August 22, 1889; *ibid.*, September 5, 1889; *Raleigh Progressive Farmer*, August 13, 1889.

in supply would raise prices, thus increasing farmer income and decreasing London's factory profits; the manufacturers were also tied to the Liverpool merchants.[34]

Ironically, the Liverpool exchange had been accepting cotton bagging from Egypt for years. However, this was an entirely different matter, since the Egyptian cotton was British controlled from field to factory and therefore did not affect the financial interests of London merchants.[35]

Once again the Alliance found itself attacked from above. It had successfully organized against the jute trust only to find itself fighting the Liverpool exchange. And because Liverpool resisted, so did the American exchanges. The largest part of the cotton grown in the United States made its way to England through Liverpool, so American merchants who honored the New Orleans Plan would have had, to absorb a 50¢ per-bale loss on a high proportion of their commerce. A united front by American exchanges might have forced a reversal, but the exchanges had little incentive to develop this united front by themselves. Only consistent and powerful farmer pressure could move them.

The national cotton committee, representing each state Alliance, met in October to seek alternatives to their frustrated strategy of organizing and negotiating with cotton merchants. The committee called upon the membership of the Alliance to refuse to use anything except cotton bagging. All the local groups would call for their members to wrap their crop in cotton. If the merchant or buyer refused to buy, then the cotton would be taken elsewhere. If a buyer refused to give the weight adjustment, then the farmer would demand an extra $\frac{1}{2}$¢ per pound for his or her cotton.[36] Members had to be committed to this policy, since it was their determination alone that could bring the Liverpool exchange into line.

The Alliance national convention met in December under a cloud of gloom. There had been no adequate arrangement made with the exchanges, and many farmers had lost 50¢ or more on each bale because they had used cotton bagging. Many exchanges had refused to cooperate and had not been hurt financially. Exchanges that had cooperated with the boycotters had often lost money on the resale because the next buyer would not honor the New Orleans Plan. The Alliance could look forward to increased resistance the following year.

The manufacturing situation was also dim. Despite tremendous Alliance commitments, many farmers had been unable to obtain cotton bagging with which to wrap their crop.[37] The manufacturers were again demanding advance orders before committing themselves to producing cotton bagging.[38]

Nevertheless, the national convention was reluctant to give up the effort. The Alliance had invested a great deal of its organizational energy in a permanent change to cotton: Many Alliance factories were producing or attempting to produce

[34] *Atlanta Constitution*, August 7, 1889; Associated Press dispatch, August 24, 1889, printed in *Raleigh Progressive Farmer*, September 4, 1889.

[35] *Atlanta Constitution*, August 7, 1889.

[36] *Jacksonville Florida Dispatch*, October 10, 1889; *Raleigh News and Observer*, October 3, 1889.

[37] *Jacksonville Florida Dispatch*, December 5, 1889; *Raleigh Progressive Farmer*, October 15, 1889; *Alliance Tocsin*, November 1889.

[38] *National Economist*, February 22, 1890.

cotton bagging; and the Alliance Exchanges had been in part built around their ability to obtain cotton bagging. A return to jute would renew the threat of permanent high prices: The jute trust had incorporated itself as the American Manufacturing Company[39] and return to high prices was certain as soon as the threat of cotton bagging was weakened.

The national convention did not have the strength to act decisively; it first referred the problem to a committee and finally passed a resolution supporting cotton bagging. The matter was then referred to the states for action, since the national Alliance could not muster the strength to coordinate the effort.[40]

After some agitation by the states, another meeting of all the Southern cotton exchanges was called in March. The Alliance hoped to commit the exchanges to the cotton tare reduction. However, this meeting was totally unsuccessful; not a single cotton exchange sent a representative.[41] A national meeting of state Alliance representatives then denounced the cotton exchanges and reaffirmed the boycott, but the boycott never materialized.[42] The national convention in December 1890 denounced the exchanges for their lack of cooperation—and gave up the struggle.[43]

This failure of the Alliance program should be counterposed against the success of the boycott itself. The arguments the Alliance put forward for switching to cotton threatened the jute trust and established Alliance credibility. During the Birmingham convention in late April 1889, the trust negotiated with the Alliance, offering to lower the price of jute from 12½¢ per yard to 8⅜¢.[44] When the Alliance refused to call off the boycott, however, the offer was withdrawn.

The beginning of the summer saw the lines tightly drawn. While the trust had considerable power,[45] the farmers had the capacity to mount an effective boycott. All over the South, cotton farmers refused to wrap in jute. Early in the fall, when merchants withheld substitute bagging, cotton remained unsold and the price of cotton began to climb.[46] This terrified the cotton buyers and forced suppliers to produce acceptable wraps. In some places, jute wrapping had no market at all. Athens, Georgia, a major cotton depot, processed not one bale of jute-wrapped cotton in September, and other markets reported the same situation.[47] Secondary boycotts were initiated against merchants who sold jute, buyers who handled jute, and newspapers who supported jute.[48]

The farmers were not unhurt by their actions. Many were forced to absorb the 50¢ loss imposed by Liverpool, though others were able to pressure merchants into absorbing it. Some could not get cotton bagging and had their cotton confisc-

[39] Jacksonville Florida Dispatch, October 17, 1889.

[40] National Economist, December 24, 1889; Raleigh Progressive Farmer, December 17, 1889.

[41] National Economist, September 3, 1890; Atlanta Constitution, March 20, 1890.

[42] Atlanta Constitution, March 20, 1890.

[43] National Economist, December 20, 1890.

[44] Jacksonville Florida Dispatch, May 2, 1889; "Proceedings of the Birmingham Conference."

[45] Jacksonville Florida Dispatch, December 5, 1889; National Economist, August 10, 24, 1889; ibid., October 5, 1889.

[46] Associated Press, dispatch, August 24, 1889, printed in Raleigh Progressive Farmer, September 4, 1889.

[47] Raleigh Progressive Farmer, October 1, 1889; ibid., September 17, 1889; ibid., November 5, 1889.

[48] Raleigh Progressive Farmer, September 10, 17, 24, 1889; ibid., October 1, 8, 15, 1889; ibid., November 5, 12, 19, 26, 1889.

ated by lienholders. Still others were forced to rewrap their cotton at considerable expense.[49]

These developments may have hurt the farmers, but the trust, too, felt considerable pressure. Two weeks after the May meeting, jute was being offered to ginners and merchants for less than 8¢ per pound.[50] During the summer, the price dropped to a low of 6¢, 20% below the pretrust price.[51] Throughout the fall, the price remained low and the jute factories could not sell all their product. Desperate merchants, stuck with unsalable jute bagging, even tried dying it to make it appear to be a substitute.[52] When accounts were taken in December, the jute trust had lost money for a second year. It offered to sell at 7¢ in 1890 if the boycott were ended. And even though no formal agreement was reached, the 7¢ price obtained throughout the following year.[53] The Alliance had won its demand for cheaper jute bagging.

Prior to the jute boycott, Alliance successes had been reversed by escalation because the group lacked the understanding and organization to respond effectively. When the Liverpool exchange attacked the jute boycott, the Alliance could still win by relying upon membership enthusiasm and commitment to create extensive pressure against the entire marketing system. This leverage derived at once from the sophisticated membership, whose local boycotts ultimately reached the trust itself, and national organization, which had been painfully constructed from the wreckage of local and statewide programs.

And yet, just as the Alliance reached this maturity, the structural logic of oligarchization managed to grab defeat from the jaws of victory. The success had relied upon the organized action of local clubs, and the only guardian of this success would be the threat of a repeated boycott in 1890, 1891, and every subsequent year. The jute trust would raise prices just as soon as the credible threat of a boycott vanished. The Alliance could pursue the jute project only by continuing to rely upon membership action and initiative.

But this reliance was in direct contradiction to the rapidly crystalizing interest of the Alliance leadership. At the same time that the jute boycott had unveiled the strength of mass protest, it had also completed the organizational development of the Alliance, centralized the communications apparatus, and provided a national forum for the Alliance leadership. Men who had toiled anonymously to build the organization suddenly found themselves the subjects of interviews, the targets of reports, the featured speakers at assemblies. They became prominent citizens with an audience stretching far beyond the Alliance; and they eagerly courted this new constituency.

But the desire to reach outward was at odds with the sustenance and strengthening of membership commitment required by the continued boycott of jute. The jute

[49] *Raleigh Progressive Farmer*, October 15, 1889; *Alliance Tocsin*, November 1889; *Jacksonville Florida Dispatch*, December 5, 1889; *National Economist*, February 22, 1890.

[50] *Jacksonville Florida Dispatch*, August 22, 1889.

[51] *Raleigh Progressive Farmer*, August 27, 1889; *ibid.*, September 17, 1889.

[52] *Raleigh Progressive Farmer*, October 1, 1889.

[53] Rogers, *op. cit.*, p. 17; *Raleigh Progressive Farmer*, August 26, 1890.

boycott leadership had to devote its energies to the development and promulgation of the information and resources necessary for intelligent membership action. A cosmopolitan leadership would devote its energies to "outreach" agitation before non-Alliance audiences as well as negotiations with other elites.

This was not simply a conflict over how the leadership would spend its time. The continuation of the jute boycott would mean an increasing isolation for Alliance leadership. Liverpool had equivocated in 1888 but had resisted the boycott in 1889; the Southern cotton exchanges that had equivocated in 1889 might be firmly in the pro-jute camp in 1890. Many newspapers that had remained neutral in 1888 had attacked the boycott in 1889. How many more newspapers would do so in 1890? Even the U.S. government, neutral in 1888, had cut the jute tariff in 1889.[54] Would the government be even more anti-boycott in 1890?

The panorama of opportunity which stretched before the Alliance leadership depended in part on its ability to maintain good relations with other structures. If it fought the cotton exchanges, it would eliminate the promise of fruitful negotiations with major mercantile interests. If it alienated the newspapers, it would reduce its national exposure. If it antagonized the government, it would disconnect its political wires. And there was always the possibility that the jute boycott would lead to assaults on the integrity of Alliance leadership, as had happened during the Texas Exchange struggle.

Thus, the pursuit of the boycott was fraught with danger for the leadership, even while it held the promise of glorious success. This contradiction was made even sharper by the elite origins of the leaders. Their prosperity, their education, and their history of officeholding gave them ambitions which extended beyond economic improvement. Contacts made with large-scale merchants, with big city newspapers, and government officials were enough to kindle such ambition where none existed before. During 1889, the actions of Alliance leaders reflected this conflict. They sought out and pursued a strategy that would guarantee their leadership role while advancing the boycott at the same time. Their courtship of the Southern cotton exchanges reflected this concern, and their failure to win over these institutions was a major frustration. More broadly, the attempt to substitute cotton for jute bagging reflected the desire to avoid a constant struggle, to create a status quo that would defeat the jute trust, without constant membership mobilization and commitment.

Moreover, the tone of the 1889 convention reflected the reaction of Alliance leadership to the struggle that year. Instead of declaring a victory, they acknowledged defeat. When their 1890 attempts to organize the cotton exchanges failed, they did not pursue the boycott at the grass roots. Instead, they gave up. It was more important to guarantee leadership freedom than to guarantee cheap jute, and the boycott was abandoned.

The Alliance began the year 1890 in a good position to attack many elements in

[54] *Raleigh News and Observer*, December 5, 1889; *National Economist*, January 1, 1890; *Raleigh Progressive Farmer*, October 2, 1888; *ibid.*, October 15, 1889.

the system of cotton supply and sales. For the first time since the tenant farming system had begun to develop, farmers were in a position to mold and reshape its structure. But this restructuring never occurred because the actions necessary to accomplish it were fraught with dangers that threatened the personal and class aspirations of Alliance leadership. This group advocated programs that were not dangerous and, in this pursuit, they led the Alliance away from the possibility of successful reform.

16

The Farmers' Alliance in and around Richmond County, North Carolina

We have bound ourselves with ties of friendship,
    And around our banners we cry;
We are marching forward to victory.
    Yes, we are bound to win or die.

Chorus
As we march to victory
    We will wave our banners high,
And our song will ever be:
    We are bound to win or die.

We bid defiance to monopoly,
    We're bound our class to represent;
Let the enemy call us fools,
    As for that we don't care a cent.

We will never fail to do our duty,
    And we'll always be on the track;
We'll attend our Alliance meetings regular,
    And never, never, turn back.
[Charles B. Davis, *Raleigh Progressive Farmer*, August 26, 1890]

Richmond County, North Carolina, is located on the South Carolina border in the middle of the state. The Richmond region (including Union, Anson, Stanly, Montgomery, Moore, and Robeson counties) is at the southwestern end of the North Carolina Cotton Belt, which is a thick band through the middle of the state. In 1890, these counties were mostly yeoman, mostly white, and mostly depressed. Richmond was different in some respects: It was barely 50% yeoman and only 46% white.[1] But it was just as depressed as neighboring countries. In North Carolina, the crop lien was

[1] All figures unless otherwise noted are taken from *Eleventh Census* (1890), vol. 5 pp. 168–171, 395; U.S. Bureau of Census, *Negro Population, 1790–1915* (U.S. Govt. Printing Office, Washington, D.C., 1918), pp. 784–785.

automatic: As soon as supplies were taken on credit, the crop was mortgaged.[2] And, as happened in other regions, Richmond cotton would net perhaps five times as much credit as other crops.[3] By 1892, well over three-quarters of the farmers owed money, with close to one-half reduced to tenancy through hopeless debt.[4] In 1887, when Alliance organizers arrived, the Richmond County area was searching desperately for a solution:

> *We have seen more farmers this year with a disposition to learn something. Many of them are at their row's end. They have planted cotton and given mortgages until they have almost reduced themselves to the servitude of so many galley slaves. We do not believe we would be in error in saying that three-fourths of the real estate in Moore county is under mortgages. So great is the indebtedness that one of our merchants remarked that he hadn't looked in the face of a man for a month who did not owe him something. (Of course he meant the persons who dealt with him.) There is no healthy growth among a people in such a condition. Call a halt all along the lines, farmers, organize clubs, invite new ideas, seek reforms, create interest in your work.[5]*

North Carolina and Richmond County farmers, like farmers in many other areas, did not wait for the Alliance to arrive. Independent organizing efforts had already begun, and they reflected the same tendencies and tensions exhibited in the Alliance throughout the South.

The farmer's clubs of North Carolina were begun by L. L. Polk through his newspaper, the *Raleigh Progressive Farmer*.[6] After calling for such groups in his first issue February 10, 1886, Polk personally organized the first club, in Winston County, on April 10.[7] "Week after week during the following year the *Progressive Farmer* happily announced the birth and noted the progress of other clubs in various parts of the state."[8] As Polk's group became known, it uncovered already functioning clubs in other parts of the state, and these groups affiliated with the farmers' clubs and the *Raleigh Progressive Farmer*. Many of these already functioning groups, like the Farmers' Circle of Trinity, were basically identical to the clubs Polk was forming.[9] But others, like the Mountain Creek Farmers' Club of Richmond County, were dramatically different.[10]

First, and most important, most farmers' clubs were organized and led by rich

[2] *Agriculture Report*, p. 419. (A full citation of this work appears in note 3, Chapter 1 of this volume.)

[3] *Agriculture Report*, p. 436.

[4] *George Report*, pt. 1, pp. 475–480. (A full citation of this work appears in note 3, Chapter 1 of this volume.)

[5] *Moore County (N.C.) Central Express*, February 1887, reprinted in *Raleigh Progressive Farmer*, February 9, 1887; see also *Raleigh Progressive Farmer*, March 16, 1887.

[6] For discussions of this organization see text above; see also Stuart Noblen, *Leonidas Lafayette Polk, Agrarian Crusader* (Chapel Hill, 1949), pp. 147–160. A short and very inaccurate account appears in John D. Hicks, "The Farmers' Alliance in North Carolina," *North Carolina Historical Review* 2 (April 1925), pp. 169–170.

[7] Noblen, *op. cit.*, p. 158.

[8] Noblen, *op. cit.*, p. 158.

[9] *Raleigh Progressive Farmer*, April 28, 1886; *ibid.*, July 28, 1886; *ibid.*, January 5, 1887.

[10] The first mention of the Mountain Creek Club is in *Raleigh Progressive Farmer*, June 23, 1886. The differences began to emerge in the issue of July 7, 1886, when the history of the club was reported. Other counties also produced independent action. For examples, see *Raleigh Progressive Farmer*, July 21, 1886.

and prominent planters, while the Mountain Creek club was made up of poor yeo-men. While many farmers' clubs boasted that their membership was wholly or pre-dominantly prosperous, college educated, or professionally trained,[11] the Mountain Creek club designated itself as "poor."[12] Nearby Moore County sent 13 delegates to the state organizing convention, among them 5 prominent farmers who were elected officers. Mountain Creek, the largest and most successful club in the state, could afford to send only one delegate, and he was in no way prominent in the proceedings. No Mountain Creek representative appeared on the state executive committee.[13] The state organization elected a large planter and sugar mill operator as its president and boasted of his success in labor management.[14] The Mountain Creek club appointed a dirt farmer as business manager and listed dedication as his qualifying virtue.[15]

From these class differences flowed a great many others. The elite clubs devoted themselves to two main activities: education and expansion. The Trinity circle, designated by Polk as "among the foremost in the whole South,"[16] undertook not a single collective activity. Its meetings, devoted to discussions of "Grasses and Hay," "Clean Fields and Seeding," "Manure," and other educational topics, were led by trained experts or farmers with a history of success in the area.[17] The more energetic members gave speeches or wrote articles urging other farmers to form similar groups.[18] The Mountain Creek club had few meetings and fewer educational discussions because "we are not a talking club by any means; only a plain, plodding, persevering set of people. . . ."[19] And it did not attempt to organize any other groups at all—the members did not even know the organizational or economic status of the surrounding communities.[20]

Instead of education and expansion, Mountain Creek, and a few other yeoman-based clubs, devoted itself to collective action. These included crop and livestock competitions, community picnics, and various forms of mutual aid. But the central and focal activity was cooperative buying, the hallmark of all the groups that formed the Alliance.[21]

---

[11] *Raleigh Progressive Farmer*, March 24, 1886; *ibid.*, July 21, 28, 1886; *ibid.*, September 28, 1886; *ibid.*, December 1, 1886. The *Wilmington Star* said in May 1886; "The best farmers and wisest men in each county must compose the council [leadership]"; and the *Greensboro Patriot* pointedly called for the "leading farmers" to initiate the organizing (June 1886).

[12] *Raleigh Progressive Farmer*, May 5, 1887.

[13] "Proceedings of the Farmers' Mass Convention, January 26, 1887, Raleigh, N.C.," reprinted in *Raleigh Progressive Farmer*, February 9, 1887 (hereafter cited as "Proceedings"): see also *Raleigh Progressive Farmer*, March 2, 1887; *ibid.*, May 19, 1887.

[14] "Proceedings"; *Raleigh Progressive Farmer*, January 5, 1887; *ibid.*, February 2, 1887; *Raleigh News and Observer*, February 22, 1888.

[15] *Raleigh Progressive Farmer*, September 8, 1886.

[16] *Raleigh Progressive Farmer*, March 23, 1887.

[17] *Raleigh Progressive Farmer*, April 28, 1886; *ibid.*, May 12, 26, 1886; *ibid.*, June 9, 23, 1886; *ibid.*, July 7, 21, 1886.

[18] *Raleigh Progressive Farmer*, March 23, 1887.

[19] *Progressive Farmer*, May 5, 1887.

[20] *Ibid.*

[21] *Raleigh Progressive Farmer*, July 7, 1886; *ibid.*, September 8, 1886; *ibid.*, October 20, 1886; *ibid.*, January 19, 26, 1887; *ibid.*, March 5, 1887.

Thus, in North Carolina, even before the Alliance arrived, the conditions for internal conflict had begun to develop. Elite clubs stressed education which their membership could acquire and apply, while expanding their base to create the political support necessary to affect statewide policy. At its founding meeting, the North Carolina State Farmers' Association attempted to exert political power at the state government level. The group demanded a state agricultural college, a state agriculture department, and numerous other reforms aimed at facilitating the modernization and flexibility of large agricultural enterprises.[22] To give itself leverage, it embarked upon a broad mobilization around these issues, including membership drives and extensive articles in the *Raleigh Progressive Farmer* and other sympathetic newspapers.[23]

The yeoman clubs were interested in these activities, but they had little hope of benefiting from them. Yeoman farmers could not send their children to college; they could not afford expensive new tools and fertilizers; and they could not experiment with new crops unless they first escaped the system of lien and debt. Therefore, few yeomen joined the state group, and clubs like Mountain Creek marched off in their own direction, participating only marginally in the collective enterprises. Their own energies were devoted to the same local activities which the early Alliance generated throughout the South.

Co-op Buying in Mountain Creek

In January 1886, even before Polk began publishing the *Raleigh Progressive Farmer*, the six charter members of the Mountain Creek Farmers' Club began discussing their actual problems.[24] Unlike the farmers' clubs organized by Polk, the Mountain Creek club quickly exhausted discussion topics and exhortations about crop diversification; early in the spring, it established a cooperative buying plan almost identical to that established by local Alliances in towns all over the South:

> We all felt it was impossible for farmers to buy on time at prices varying from 40 to 70 percent over the wholesale price and pay in cotton at 8 to $8\frac{3}{4}$ cents per lb., and not be vastly worse off at the end of the year than at the beginning. This club, therefore, appointed James A. Ingram its agent, through whom everything is bought.[25]

Twenty members participated in this enterprise, and those without cash gave mortgages on their land. Obviously this excluded the most needy (and therefore most Blacks) from the organization, as did most early Alliances. The mortgages

---

[22] "Proceedings"; Noblen, *op. cit.*

[23] Noblen, *op. cit.*; *Raleigh News and Observer*, January 28, 1887; *Raleigh Progressive Farmer*, February 17, 1887; Hichs, *op. cit.*, pp. 169–170.

[24] Unfootnoted material for this discussion derives from long articles written by club Secretary Joseph Galloway and reprinted in *Raleigh Progressive Farmer*, July 7, 1886; *ibid.*, September 8, 1886; *ibid.*, October 20, 1886; *ibid.*, January 19, 1887; *ibid.*, May 5, 1887; see also *Raleigh Progressive Farmer*, January 26, 1887.

[25] *Raleigh Progressive Farmer*, July 7, 1886.

were borrowed against at the bank, and purchases were made from wholesalers, with "every member paying exact cost price, with interest, and any necessary expense."[26]

The plan worked extraordinarily well, with the average participant purchasing approximately $125 worth of goods for $75—a 40% reduction in cost on goods bought through the co-op. Furthermore:

> In spite of the short crops, the Club members are paying up, and no doubt will pay for what they have bought through the Club. But had they been compelled to pay time prices, most of them could not have paid out.[27]

This success brought many new members into the organization. By July, membership and increased to 50, where it remained until the August 19, 1886, picnic. After this event, and the extensive publicity given the group in the *Raleigh Progressive Farmer*, the Mountain Creek club expanded dramatically. The very next meeting had 19 new members and, by January 1, 1887, the membership was 112—this was just about twice the size of any other farmers' club in the state.[28]

Successful cooperation had generated this expansion. This is made clear by the concern and attention given to developing the program for the following year. Every member was assessed $1 to pay for erection of a store and meetinghouse. Modifications were made in the purchasing plan, including a proviso that the whole club would be collectively responsible for the default of any member. Provisions were made so that excess food from one member could be sold to another, thus extending the scope of the cooperative considerably. And protective secrecy began to appear in the form of a rule that any member revealing to an outsider prices paid for goods would be expelled.

With the flush of success, the Mountain Creek Farmers' Club looked ahead to a profitable year of cooperative buying and a return to prosperity. In the meantime, the Alliance had made its appearance.

The Alliance Enters North Carolina

Farmers' groups "spread like wildfire"[29] in the 1880s, but some wildfires spread faster than others. In North Carolina, a year had passed since L. L. Polk and the *Raleigh Progressive Farmer*—joined by at least 15 other newspapers—had begun urging the formation of farmers' clubs. Polk and others, like D. R. Reid of the Farmers' Circle of Trinity in Randolph County, had devoted themselves to traveling around the state in support of the organization.[30] Their efforts had borne fruit; at the

---

[26] *Ibid.*

[27] *Raleigh Progressive Farmer*, October 20, 1886.

[28] See *Raleigh Progressive Farmer*, March 16, 30, 1887; *ibid.*, April 14, 1887, for comparative figures.

[29] *Raleigh Progressive Farmer*, July 7, 1887.

[30] *Raleigh Progressive Farmer*, April 4, 1886; *ibid.*, May 26, 1886; *ibid.*, August 15, 1886; *ibid.*, September 1, 1886; *ibid.*, October 2, 1886; *ibid.*, November 3, 1886; *ibid.*, December 1, 1886; *ibid.*, May 19, 26, 1887; *ibid.*, June 9, 1887.

January 1887 state convention, 38 counties were represented.[31] Nevertheless, this progress was slow compared to the pace the Alliance set in early 1887.

After the Waco, Texas, meeting in January, the newly created national Alliance sent two organizers to North Carolina.[32] On May 12, 1887, J. B. Barry arrived in Raleigh and began his organizing with a call addressed to the Wake County Farmers' Institute.[33] One month later, the Wake County Alliance, with 12 clubs already functioning, was formed.[34] Wrote Barry, "I met the farmers in public meetings 27 times and 27 times they organized. . . . The farmers seem like unto ripe fruit—you can gather them by a gentle shake of the bush."[35] It had taken the farmers' club movement fully 6 months to generate its first county organization, with only 10 clubs organized.[36] In 6 months, the Alliance had at least 10 counties organized. Before it was a year old, it had absorbed the entire farmers' club movement.[37] Fifteen months after the first organizing began in Wake County, the North Carolina Farmers' Alliance reported 1018 local Alliances, 53 county organizations, and approximately 40,000 members.[38]

What was true for the state in general was even more true for the Richmond region. Because it was part of the Cotton Belt, this section had been a center of farmer club strength, with enough membership to support county organizations in 3 of the 7 counties.[39] Anson County, just west of Richmond, had 15 clubs, the second highest count in the state.[40] Six of the 7 counties had been represented at the state convention, with Anson sending 32 delegates, or 10% of the entire convention.[41]

But such success was small compared to the work of M. T. Sealey when he arrived from Texas in April 1887. He began his work in Robeson and Richmond Counties—neither extensively organized into clubs—and, by late June, had organized 25 clubs and formed them into county groups. In 3 months, the Alliance had as many clubs in these 2 counties as the farmers' clubs had managed in a whole year in 7 counties.[42] When Sealy turned his attention to the other counties, things moved just as quickly. In just 2 weeks, he organized 10 clubs and a county organization in Moore County.[43] In October, the Richmond region dominated the first state con-

[31] *Raleigh Progressive Farmer*, February 9, 1887; 36 counties sent delegates to the interstate farmers' convention in August. *Ibid.*, June 26, 1887.

[32] W. Scott Morgan, *History of the Wheel and Alliance and the Impending Revolution* (Fort Scott, Kans., 1889), p. 187.

[33] *Raleigh Progressive Farmer*, May 19, 1887.

[34] *Raleigh Progressive Farmer*, June 19, 1887.

[35] William L. Garvin and S. O. Dows, *History of the National Farmers' Alliance and Co-operative Union of America* (Jacksboro, Tex., 1887), pp. 49–50, quoted in Noblen, *op. cit.*, p. 205. For a similar statement see *Raleigh Progressive Farmer*, September 8, 1887.

[36] *Raleigh Progressive Farmer*, June 19, 1886, *ibid.*, August 11, 1886.

[37] Noblen, *op. cit.*, p. 205.

[38] Noblen, *op. cit.*, p. 205; Hicks, *op. cit.*, p. 170; *National Economist*, May 25, 1889; *ibid.*, August 24, 1889; *Raleigh News and Observer*, August 15, 16, 1888.

[39] *Raleigh Progressive Farmer*, September 28, 1886; *ibid.*, December 1, 1886; *ibid.*, March 3, 1887.

[40] *Raleigh Progressive Farmer*, June 2, 1887.

[41] "Proceedings."

[42] *Raleigh Progressive Farmer*, July 7, 1887.

[43] *Raleigh Progressive Farmer*, August 18, 1887; September 8, 22, 1887.

vention. It was held in Rockingham, county seat of Richmond; 3 of the 7 participating counties were from the immediate area; and over half the delegates came from nearby clubs.[44]

This Alliance strength in the Richmond region was not a result of previous work done by the farmers' clubs. Early success by Sealy came in exactly those regions untouched by the clubs. Anson County, the club stronghold, was not among the first to embrace the Alliance.[45] The evidence suggests that there may have been considerable explicit antagonism toward the Alliance and that headway was made only when the club leadership joined en masse.[46]

The Richmond organizing was not the work of a single, brilliant organizer. Sealy left the region in fall 1887, and a group of local organizers continued to expand the Alliance at breakneck speed. One individual must have set a record by organizing 12 subs in 8 days. By the summer of 1888, approximately 16 months after the first Alliance was organized at Ashpole in Robeson County, the Richmond region had 169 subs, an average of 24 clubs per county. This small cluster of seven counties accounted for nearly 20% of the state Alliance membership, and probably had more members than the entire statewide farmers' clubs at the pinnacle of their strength.[47]

The Alliance grew so fast because it combined the program and orientation of the Mountain Creek Farmers' Club with the statewide organizing perspective of Polk's North Carolina Farmers' Association. The clubs denied any intent to hurt merchants, and they undertook no project that could have done so.[48] The Alliance also denied any intention to "injure the business of certain other classes," but it added ominously, "unless others should conclude it is their right to boss our business."[49] And this, said the Alliance, was exactly what was happening:

> Trusts, pools and corners mean war upon the best interests of the people. . . [and] if we don't abolish them they will abolish us.[50]

In order to defeat this attack, the Alliance organizers told prospective members, organization was needed:

> The agriculturists of America, if united, are a power, and can, if they stand firm, successfully combat giant monopoly or any other power that seeks to oppress us. It may take a long and bitter fight to curb the wild, speculating craze and avaricious greed for gain that threatens to enslave the great mass of our people, but it is worth fighting for. The Wheel and Alliance and Grange are an organized effort in this direction.[51]

[44] *Raleigh Progressive Farmer*, October 13, 1887.
[45] *Raleigh Progressive Farmer*, January 12, 1888.
[46] *Raleigh Progressive Farmer*, January 19, 1887; *ibid.*, February 16, 1888.
[47] "Proceedings of the North Carolina Farmers' Alliance, Raleigh, N.C., August 14–16, 1888," reprinted in *Raleigh Progressive Farmer*, August 21, 1888; see also *Raleigh Progressive Farmer*, February 9, 1887; *ibid.*, April 20, 1887; *ibid.*, December 15, 1887; *ibid.*, January 5, 12, 26, 1888; *ibid.*, February 16, 28, 1888; *ibid.*, March 20, 1888.
[48] *Raleigh Progressive Farmer*, February 26, 1886.
[49] *Southern Mercury*, September 1887, quoted in *Raleigh Progressive Farmer*, September 8, 1887.
[50] *Nashville Weekly Toiler*, April 25, 1888.
[51] *Nashville Weekly Toiler*, April 25, 1888; see also *Raleigh Progressive Farmer*, April 21, 1887; *ibid.*, October 6, 1887; *ibid.*, Mary 1, 1888.

And this organization would create an economic unity among farmers capable of reforming and disciplining the entire economic system. The *Sanford Express*, an Alliance newspaper, gave both the strategy and tactics. The Alliance, it said, "seeks to adopt a cash system of trade that will do away with the mortgage system." Then it described exactly how to do this:

> ... *Cotton yards are being established where the farmer can deposit his product and on his certificate of deposit it is so arranged with the bank that he is allowed to draw three fourths of its value in cash. This arrangement enables him to hold his cotton and other products and not be obliged to sell at a sacrifice as many were compelled to do last fall. By concert of action then the price can be raised to something like the cost of production. The merchant calculates the cost of his wares before he sells, why not the farmer do the same? Just as long as the manufacturer is allowed to price the farmer's goods the same as his own, just so long will the farmer suffer at the hands of the manufacturer, because the farmer is consumer as well as purchaser.*
>
> *Already have offers been made from fertilizing companies to furnish fertilizer to the Alliance at reduced rates and the movers confidently expect a still greater reduction. Boards of trade are being established in every county organized, who are negotiating with manufacturers and wholesale houses for supplies necessary for the agriculturalist. We do not see therefore why the farmers shall not be greatly benefited by this move in the right direction. It is a stubborn and lamentable fact that our farmers as a class are becoming poorer and poorer every year and it seemed that there was no chance only for many of them to become veritable serfs as is the case with the laboring class of Ireland today; but we thank God there yet is hope, there is yet a "balm in Gilead." We urge the farmers then everywhere.to unite themselves in this grand scheme for their redemption. If you have no Alliances near you where you can join them call on one of our organizers and start one at once.*[52]

This strategy was recited to farmers' meetings, large and small. It was accompanied by glowing reports of dramatic successes all over the South and especially in Texas.[53] J. M. Barry, one of the Texas organizers, declared after only 4 months in the state: "In twelve months the farmers, mechanics, etc. will have as complete control of North Carolina as they have in Texas and will run their State to their own notion."[54]

The membership attracted by this appeal was not necessarily the elite agriculturalists. While reports from local chapters contained many references to rich and prominent farmers "coming to the front" and "lending with zeal and enthusiasm,"[55] there were increasing mentions of poor farmers, indebtedness, and oppression, as well as snide remarks about "would be aristocrats."[56] The Dyson Creek Alliance in

---

[52] Quoted in *Raleigh Progressive Farmer*, March 20, 1888.

[53] *Raleigh Progressive Farmer*, April 21, 1887; *ibid.*, May 5, 12, 1887.

[54] Printed in *Raleigh Progressive Farmer*, August 18, 1887.

[55] *Raleigh Progressive Farmer*, February 28, 1888; see also *ibid.*, October 27, 1887; *Robesonian* (Laurinburg, N.C.), October 1887.

[56] *Raleigh Progressive Farmer*, June 19, 26, 1888; *ibid.*, August 14, 21, 1888; *ibid.*, September 4, 1888; *ibid.*, October 2, 1888; *ibid.*, February 12, 19, 1889.

Montgomery County even appealed to the state membership for cash donations to tide it over:

> We are poor; if any brother feels like helping us, we will be glad to receive it. They can remit it to J. F. Crowder, President, or J. T. McAulay, Secretary.[57]

Local Actions and Merchant Counterattack

The economic appeal, the rapid growth, and the poor yeoman membership insured that the Alliance locals would follow the lead of the Mountain Creek Farmers' Club. Throughout 1887 and 1888, and into 1889, North Carolina Alliances established co-ops and trade agreements, initiated cotton and tobacco bulking plans, and developed other collective actions. The type of local action varied with the economic season, but the number of actions taken increased so rapidly that, by late 1888, they were too numerous for the Alliance papers to report individually.

The Richmond region began to copy the Mountain Creek club as early as January 1887.[58] During that year and the next, innumerable local actions of various kinds were undertaken. A great many locals negotiated discount trade agreements with their regular merchants. Others "clubbed together" and purchased certain goods, notably fertilizers, from wholesalers or manufacturers. Some subs managed to generate full-fledged cooperatives, supplying their members with the bulk of their supplies at wholesale prices. A few even managed to extend credit to their tenant members by signing joint notes. Later in the year, various locals sold their crops in unison, forcing bids from large buyers. Others established selling agents in market towns to enable the members to take advantage of city prices. Still others drew on the financial resources of the more prosperous members to make it possible to hold their crops for a higher price. And finally, some clubs established business enterprises designed to free the farmers from any participation in certain aspects of the supply system: A flour mill was built, a foundry was constructed, fertilizers and shoes were manufactured and sold, and surplus food exchanged.[59]

Many of these efforts were ineffective because of poor planning, incompetent management, or overambition. But many were modestly successful and a few were spectacular achievements. In Union County, the combined effect of cooperative buying and selling was an average $60 per year savings, a 20% increase in farmer income. Moore County clubs forced merchants to bid against each other, chose the best offers, and saved their members thousands of dollars. A cluster of clubs spanning several counties bought their fertilizer wholesale and saved $20,000. A bulk

[57] *Raleigh Progressive Farmer*, October 2, 1888.
[58] *Raleigh Progressive Farmer*, January 26, 1887.
[59] *Raleigh Progressive Farmer*, September 29, 1887; *ibid.*, November 3, 10, 17, 24, 1887; *ibid.*, January 12, 19, 1888; *ibid.*, February 2, 16, 1888; *ibid.*, March 3, 1888; *ibid.*, April 3, 10, 17, 1888; *ibid.*, May 1, 1888; *ibid.*, June 5, 1888; *ibid.*, September 18, 1888; *ibid.*, October 4, 1888; *ibid.*, November 13, 1888.

cotton selling system brought about a 25% price increase for all farmers in the Union—Anson—Stanly region to the west of Richmond.[60]

It was these successes which activated the already articulated merchant opposition. The merchants had expressed their views from the beginning, but at first they had done little.[61] An Allianceman from middle North Carolina characterized their posture in middle 1888:

> The merchants and professional men are very much opposed to our order, and are talking and working against it. They laugh at us and tell us it will fail; the first frost will kill it. . . .[62]

By the beginning of 1889, and earlier in many places, the laughs had changed into snarls. The merchants felt the squeeze and tried to respond. In one town, two merchants offered a $5000 reward for the destruction of the state organization. Other actions included refusal of credit to Alliancemen, refusal of any local merchants to sign a trade agreement, and assorted machinations to frustrate bulk selling efforts.[63] The deputy organizer of Stanly County wrote: "They would turn the very dogs of perdition loose upon us if it were possible."[64]

When these attacks began, the Alliance successfully responded. In Moore County, the refusal of local merchants to sell fertilizer at a discount simply forced the clubs to band together and buy from manufacturers.[65] Nearby, a merchant boycott of the Alliance produced bulk buying at a huge discount at the regional capital.[66] When big city cotton factors refused to boost their price, the local Alliances sold in another, more agreeable town.[67]

But when manufacturers backed up the merchants, the tide turned. Cooperative shoe buying was frustrated by the refusal of manufacturers to deal with the Alliance. A boycott failed to exert enough pressure to budge them.[68] When every manufacturer of acid refused to sell directly to the Alliance, locals simply had to capitulate or do without.[69] And finally, the biggest single success—cooperative fertilizer buying—was ended in fall 1888, when all the manufacturers boycotted the Alliance.

The Richmond County experience was not typical, but it illustrates the experience of frustration.[70] The Mountain Creek Farmers' Club had struggled through 1887

[60] *Raleigh Progressive Farmer*, October 9, 1888; *ibid.*, May 1, 1888; *ibid.*, March 13, 1888; *ibid.*, April 3, 1888; *ibid.*, November 6, 1888.

[61] *Raleigh Progressive Farmer*, April 10, 1888; *ibid.*, May 22, 29, 1888; *ibid.*, June 5, 1888; *ibid.*, July 3, 10, 1888.

[62] *Raleigh Progressive Farmer*, August 8, 1888.

[63] *Raleigh Progressive Farmer*, August 8, 1888; *ibid.*, October 2, 1888; *ibid.*, October 9, 1899; *ibid.*, March 27, 1888.

[64] *Raleigh Progressive Farmer*, September 4, 1888.

[65] *Raleigh Progressive Farmer*, May 1, 1888.

[66] *Raleigh Progressive Farmer*, August 21, 1888.

[67] *Raleigh Progressive Farmer*, April 17, 1888.

[68] *Raleigh Progressive Farmer*, November 17, 1887.

[69] *Raleigh Progressive Farmer*, February 29, 1888.

[70] This account is based upon information found in *Raleigh Progressive Farmer*, October 6, 1887; *ibid.*, November 10, 1887; *ibid.*, January 19, 26, 1888; *ibid.*, March 7, 1888; *ibid.*, August 7, 1888; *ibid.*, September 25, 1888; *Charlotte* (N.C.) *Daily Hornet*, November 3, 1887; *Rockingham* (N.C.) *Rocket*, January 1888.

and survived into 1888. It had been unable to produce the dramatic savings for a large membership which it had produced for its small membership the year before. By fall of 1887, its numbers had dwindled, and while it survived long enough cooperatively to purchase fertilizer the next spring, it died soon afterward.

In the meantime, a number of new Alliances copied the Mountain Creek strategy in 1887, with mixed success. The local merchants quickly saw the implications of farmer unity and put up resistance, and several guano wholesalers refused to deal with the Alliance. The response was a countywide purchase plan. Local business agents took orders and credit securities from their membership. They negotiated with local merchants for the entire order but signed no contract until the county agent offered the business of the entire county to Wilmington merchants. Whichever deal was better would be accepted.

The plan had mixed results. Some locals got good offers, but the Wilmington wholesalers were already beginning to feel the squeeze. Therefore, the county Alliance was unable to obtain a reasonable discount that would make the countywide co-op feasible. Without this, the local merchants were able to renege on their offers or refuse to deal with the Alliance locals the next year. Escalation defeated the cooperative movement in Richmond.

As 1888 progressed, more and more county Alliances faced the same insurmountable problem. The local merchants refused to sign trade agreements, and the wholesalers would not deal with the co-ops. One discouraged member wrote forlornly: "It seems the entire mercantile world is combined to crush the Alliance."[71]

The Struggle for the Alliance Exchange

The Texas Exchange opened in January 1887, so when Alliance organizers began their work in North Carolina the following April, they were already advertising the fabulous possibilities of this institution. In June, the *Raleigh Progressive Farmer* began to print regular news stories about the progress of the Texas Exchange,[72] and the organizers themselves constantly referred to it in their appeals.[73] But these appeals and advertisements did not lead inevitably to the formation of an Exchange; instead, its construction awaited the failure of the local actions.

In January 1888, some of the earliest Alliances were already frustrated by the local activities, and they began to agitate for an Exchange. An Anson County Allianceman wrote to the *Raliegh Progressive Farmer*, demanding immediate action. According to him, there was a "loss of confidence and interest in the organization" because "so little had yet been accomplished." A statewide business meeting and the formation of an Exchange "would be of great good to the Alliance, restore

[71] *Raleigh Progressive Farmer*, August 14, 1888; see also *ibid.*, August 21, 1888; *ibid.*, October 2, 1888; *ibid.*, November 7, 1888; *ibid.*, February 2, 1889; *Shelby* (N.C.) *New Era*, November 1888.

[72] *Raleigh Progressive Farmer*, June 9, 1887; *ibid.*, July 7, 1887; *ibid.*, September 15, 1887; *ibid.*, May 15, 1888; *ibid.*, July 17, 1888.

[73] *Raleigh Progressive Farmer*, October 6, 1887; *ibid.*, May 1, 1888.

confidence in its organization, and reanimate its members."[74] Editor Polk urged patience, comparing the youth of the North Carolina Alliance to the maturity of the Texas group, which took 8 years to develop the Exchange system.[75] However, Anson County had a solid basis for its complaint. As early as May 1886, it had organized 10 farmers' clubs. It had the first Cotton Belt county club, and it had sent 32 delegates to the January 1887 farmers' convention, second only to Wake, where the convention was held. When the Alliance arrived, it made steady progress in Anson, with 12 clubs by November, its own deputy organizer by December, and about 800 members at the start of 1888. In nearly 2 years of organizing and ferment, the farmers of Anson had won no major victories and saved little money.[76]

The demoralization in Anson was not, however, based upon the failure of co-ops and boycotts, since few such efforts had yet been undertaken. Thus, as the spring proceeded, the Anson County Alliance became involved in exposing a fraudulent cotton seed company, in establishing a trade committee, and in other local actions.[77]

It was left for Richmond County to reopen the Exchange debate, as a result of a serious rejection of local action as impractical. By spring 1888, the Richmond countywide cooperative had already been defeated by wholesalers, and the county meeting in March passed a pro-Exchange resolution:

> *Resolved, that the Richmond County Farmers' Alliance request the State Alliance to take steps to establish a N.C. State Exchange, and that we recommend what is known in Texas as the Walker County Plan.*[78]

This resolution marked the beginning of an 18-month struggle around the establishment of the Exchange. At first, the initiative lay with county organizations searching for a solution to the dilemma of escalation which would "restore confidence and reanimate members."[79] While the Exchange was not the only possibility, it quickly gained popularity because it suited the angry spirit that animated the Alliance membership. This spirit was elegantly expressed by Upton P. Gwynn, a particularly eloquent Stanly County member. He urged that the Alliance discard all pretense of sympathy for the "insatiable greed" of the mercantile class:

> *I style them enemies for they are nothing more or less, and it is the height of hypocrisy to pretend that we entertain any other feeling than loathsome hatred towards a class whom it would be sacrilege to [view] otherwise.*

"There is one radical remedy by which we can become disenthralled," Gwynn wrote, but only if

[74] *Raleigh Progressive Farmer*, February 9, 1888.

[75] *Ibid.*

[76] *Raleigh Progressive Farmer*, May 5, 19, 1886; *ibid.*, September 28, 1886; *ibid.*, February 9, 1887; *ibid.*, November 17, 1887; *ibid.*, December 1, 1887; *ibid.*, January 5, 12, 1888.

[77] *Raleigh Progressive Farmer*, March 13, 1888.

[78] *Raleigh Progressive Farmer*, April 24, 1888.

[79] *Raleigh Progressive Farmer*, February 9, 1888.

we unite with an indomitable determination to cast aside the insufferable yoke that enslaves us. It is by conducting and controlling our business, in all its ramifications, through business agencies and exchanges. . . . Such control will dispense with all intermediate manipulation, thus doing away with the hosts of jobbers, brokers, wholesalers, factors, middlemen of every description; whose commissions we can pocket ourselves. . . .

It's hard, they say, to teach an old dog new tricks, but one thing is certain, we've either got to learn new tricks or be tricked to death by the most infernal set of tricksters that ever tricked humanity.[80]

Throughout the remainder of 1888 and for most of 1889, local members, club secretaries, and county leaders expressed these same sentiments. The spirit peaked during the summer of 1888, subsided during the fall, and returned with full force that winter when the spring supply contracts were written.[81]

The Richmond region was particularly insistent in its advocacy of the Exchange. During the summer of 1888, the local clubs pressed for the plan in local newspapers and meetings.[82] When pledges were solicited, the oldest clubs responded to the call because they were the first to experience local failures. Forty-three clubs contributed over $100 to the fund, and all but 5 of these were among the earliest organized clubs. This group included 7 clubs from Robeson County and 3 from Richmond, as well as several others from the rest of the region.[83] These contributions were not the donations of rich farmers, but the excruciating dues of "one-horse farmers or renters" trying to escape debt through the Exchange;[84] and the exhortations were sometimes the first letters the authors had ever written.[85]

When these efforts did not produce the Exchange, people became impatient. One Richmond Allianceman spoke for members all over North Carolina in June 1889:

The Alliance of which I have been president for nearly two years, nearly all the members have paid in their five dollars long ago, and some of these members are scarcely worth one hundred dollars and don't own a foot of land in the world. They have made no trade arrangements with any merchant, but are simply waiting for the establishment of the State Exchange, and to do this they will pay more if necessary. We know that times are hard but it will not do to stand still so long. The order in this state, as well as elsewhere, is getting to be large, and to keep so large a body

[80] *Raleigh Progressive Farmer*, October 22, 1889.

[81] *Raleigh Progressive Farmer*, June 12, 19, 26, 1888; *ibid.*, July 3, 10, 17, 24, 31, 1888; *ibid.*, August 8, 28, 1888; *ibid.*, December 4, 1888; *ibid.*, January 29, 1889; *ibid.*, February 12, 19, 26, 1889; various issues, March–May 1889.

[82] *Robesonian*, July 8, 1888; *Raleigh Progressive Farmer*, February 9, 1888; *ibid.*, July 7, 1888.

[83] *Raleigh Progressive Farmer*, April 30, 1889; *ibid.*, May 12, 28, 1889; *ibid.*, August 17, 1889; *ibid.*, April 15, 1890; *ibid.*, June 30, 1890.

[84] *Raleigh Progressive Farmer*, August 17, 1889; *ibid.*, July 25, 1889.

[85] One Richmond correspondent wrote: "Bro. Polk, this is the first effort of my life. If you see proper to publish any part thereof, first 'view it with a critic's eye, then pass all imperfections by.'" *Raleigh Progressive Farmer*, April 2, 1889.

contented we must act together, we must give some benefit, we must impart life,
vim and interest to our work, and we must all see and feel that ours is a common
cause and as just a cause as ever enlisted the sympathy and support of any people; and
one of the things in support of this cause is not to be two or three years in raising
this fund.[86]

But things moved very slowly. In June 1888, the state leadership sent an Exchange
plan to locals, calling for monetary pledges of $5 per member to back up the Ex-
change. However, this request was not publicized, and only one article appeared
in the *Raleigh Progressive Farmer* explaining the pledges and urging support.[87] In
July, all the counties were asked to discuss the Exchange at their meetings, and
tremendous support was exhibited, including thousands of dollars in pledges; still
the state leadership did not activate the Exchange.[88]

At the state convention in August 1888, a specific program was adopted, but
the state executive committee tried to cool off the impatient membership:

Inasmuch as the members of various subordinate and county Alliances of the state
are enquiring and desiring to know something of the State Alliance Business Agency,
we deem it due them and ourselves to say that the Agency is in its infancy. You must
not expect too much of the Agency, or expect it too fast.[89]

Only cash business would be accepted "for the present." Clubs were urged to make
local buying arrangements if they could. The entire operation could not be funded
in time to "accomplish any important results for the fall trade."[90]

Even this reduced exchange failed to materialize. During September, the locals
and counties elected Exchange agents who met with the state agent on October
26. Instead of launching the Exchange, this meeting abandoned the plan entirely
for the year.[91] The problem was the fund. The state leadership felt that the Exchange could not begin business until $50,000 in secure pledges were obtained,
and despite over $30,000 in pledges during the summer, the convention felt
obliged to call for a renewal of all these before the Exchange could be established.[92]

During the winter of 1888 and for most of 1889, the North Carolina State Alliance
did nothing to collect the money necessary to fund the state agency. Nevertheless,
pledges and cash were sent in from locals and counties, along with exhortations
and plans designed to aid in the establishment process.[93] By state convention time
in August 1889, $22,414.74 in cash had been collected in addition to uncounted

---

[86] *Raleigh Progressive Farmer*, June 11, 1889.

[87] *Raleigh Progressive Farmer*, July 10, 17, 1888.

[88] *Raleigh Progressive Farmer*, various issues, July—August 1888.

[89] "Report of the Executive Committee of the N.C. Farmers' State Alliance, August 14, 1888," reprinted in *Raleigh Progressive Farmer*, August 28, 1888.

[90] *Ibid.*

[91] *Raleigh Progressive Farmer*, October 4, 30, 1888.

[92] "Report of the Executive Committee of the N.C. Farmers' State Alliance, August 14, 1888"; "Annual Report of the Secretary of the N.C. Farmers' State Alliance, August 14, 1888," reprinted in *Raleigh Progressive Farmer*, August 28, 1888; see also *ibid.*, October 2, 1888; *ibid.*, November 13, 1888.

[93] See, for example, *Raleigh Progressive Farmer*, November 27, 1888; *ibid.*, July 2, 27, 1889; *ibid.*, August 13, 1889.

thousands of dollars in pledges.[94] In November 1889, the Exchange published its first price list and began taking orders.[95]

The Exchange that emerged from this 18-month process was unlike the Texas Exchange. Individual clubs made up orders which they sent—along with cash payment—to their county business agent. These county agents sent the bulk orders to the state agent, who then negotiated a wholesale rate with suppliers. The suppliers sent the goods directly to the counties, and the state agent sent the suppliers the cash collected from the members. The state fund, which eventually exceeded $50,000, remained untouched so that it could be used to guarantee the transactions.[96] There was no credit at all, the Alliancemen had to wait while their orders were consolidated and processed, and no crops could be sold. It served only the most solvent yeomen, and few tenants. Those who needed the Exchange the most were excluded by the restriction to cash transactions.[97]

Even with such a limited scope, the North Carolina Exchange was not without effect. During the spring of 1890, it averaged over $40,000 in supply business per month, saving its customers over 40% of most items. During this same period, it sold 10,000 tons of guano from its own fertilizer factory, saving its customers $500,000, as well as producing a general price decrease. The publication of Exchange price lists created the possibility of comparison shopping and competition with local merchants. Lien contracts were altered and undermined. Before its demise in 1891, the North Carolina Exchange had had a significant effect of the agricultural supply system in North Carolina.[98]

The Alliance Exchange in North Carolina seems to have reflected both the lessons learned from Texas and the growing leadership—membership division inside the organization. Consider the following aspects of its history:

1. While the original statewide organizing in North Carolina emphasized the promise and success of the Texas Exchange, the state organization put none of its resources into developing this institution.
2. The early successes of the Texas Exchange were lavishly publicized by the North Carolina Alliance papers, but the later failures were completely suppressed.
3. As time went on, the conditions for beginning operations were constantly escalated and the potential participants repeatedly restricted, without any membership discussion of these changes.
4. Local members, subordinate clubs, and county leadership complained increasingly about the recalcitrance of the leadership, but these complaints were never answered.[99]

[94] Raleigh Progressive Farmer, August 20, 1889.

[95] Raleigh Progressive Farmer, November 12, 1889.

[96] Cincinnati Enquirer, April 10, 1890.

[97] Hicks, op. cit., p. 173.

[98] Cincinnati Enquirer, April 10, 1890; Wilmington Messenger, April 1890; Agriculture Report, pp. 435–436; Raleigh Progressive Farmer, March 11, 1890; ibid., April 15, 22, 1890; ibid., August 12, 1890; Hicks, op. cit., p. 172.

[99] For a sampling of these complaints see Raleigh Progressive Farmer, July 24, 1888; ibid., October 2, 9, 1888; ibid., January 29, 1889; ibid., June 11, 1889.

What seems to have happened is that the North Carolina leadership was inti-midated by the Texas experience. The tremendous success in Texas had created a ferocious counterattack which had destroyed the Exchange and nearly dis-credited the leadership. The North Carolina leadership was unwilling to expose itself to such personal risk, especially since the leaders themselves were prosperous farmers with little to gain from the Exchange. They therefore demanded a large fund to protect the transactions and refused to engage in any credit business. These actions guaranteed that the operation would be invulnerable to escalation. But they also guaranteed that the Exchange would serve only a small fraction of the membership, that it would be unable to meet the day-to-day needs of even these cash customers, and that it would never entirely replace the middlemen of the supply and sales systems.

The North Carolina Alliance leadership did not publicize the demise of the Texas Exchange, because it did not want to lose its membership. Many Alliance-men had been recruited because of the vision of the Exchange, and this vision became all the more urgent when local actions were defeated. Without the pro-mise of the Exchange, there would be no program to sustain membership commit-ment.

We see here a poignant example of structured ignorance created and maintained because of the internal cleavage in the Alliance. The North Carolina leadership did not inform its membership of the Texas experience, and thus it encouraged the locals to make the same mistakes that the Texas Exchange had made, while preventing membership discussion of possible alternatives. At the same time, the state leadership sabotaged and reformulated the program to protect itself. Since this reformulation deprived most Alliance members of any benefits from the Ex-change, the leadership could not clearly delineate the new plan from the begin-ning. Instead, the changes appeared over time, introduced with no membership participation or understanding. The desire of the leadership to protect its own interests led it to suppress information, suspend democratic decisionmaking, and impose a policy that benefited only a small minority.

While the Exchange struggle went on, the Alliance leadership sought to develop and maintain programs that would be less risky and more promising to them. One of these was the jute boycott, which occurred during the Exchange struggle and contributed to the membership—leadership cleavage. The final option was a massive entry into politics, which ultimately freed the state leadership from its dependency on membership.

The Jute Boycott

North Carolina was one of the earliest states to enter the boycott. As soon as the jute trust was formed in July 1888, the Alliancemen of North Carolina were apprised of its existence and dangers. The *Raleigh Progressive Farmer* provided its readers with long analytic articles about the development of the trust, and it reported all protest activities against it.[100] This coverage contrasted dramatically with the neglect of the Exchange, which was just at that time failing to accumulate the necessary pledges to begin business that year.

Certainly this attention, and the speechmaking of Alliance organizers, contributed mightily to the enthusiasm with which the local members joined the struggle. But the clubs did not follow the state leadership. In its article first exposing the trust, the *Raleigh Progressive Farmer* appealed to farmers to grow their own jute. It was left to the Montgomery County Alliance (Montgomery County is just west of the Richmond region) to propose a boycott.[101] The shape of the struggle was determined by the incremental contributions of individual clubs and county Alliances. The idea of using cotton bagging came from Fair Bluff Alliance #2 in Wake County and was soon afterward adopted at the state convention.[102] The Richmond County Alliance proposed a boycott of all guano bagged in jute, and this proposal spread across North Carolina into nearby states and was finally endorsed at the national convention that december.[103] Other local groups in the Richmond region attacked opposition newspapers, worked on the establishment of Alliance cotton bagging factories, and boycotted gins that used jute.[104] The locals threw themselves into the fight with a kind of creative vigor that projected confidence of victory. One Richmond Allianceman captured this spirit:

> *This is really our first battle against oppression and to yield an inch is to acknowledge defeat in a measure. If we are ever to arrest the oppressive blows of our tyrannical monopolies why not now?*

He advocated using cotton wraps, a strategy that would create a market for 100,000 bales of cotton; he called for a boycott of guano bagged in jute; and he urged tenants to refuse to redeem their liens if they could not obtain a jute substitute. The boycott would continue for one year or until the price of jute was returned to pretrust prices. The future of the Alliance and of the farming class was at stake:

> *Your honor as well as your manhood is involved in this fight and to waver would not only subject you to the criticism of a watchful public, but endangers our future success. We have long been told we could not unite, would not stick, etc. I, for one, am tired of such an encomium [sic]. We are men; let us demonstrate it.*[105]

Not only did the boycott succeed, it inspired a wide range of other actions spontaneously initiated by local groups during early 1889. In a single issue of the *Raleigh Progressive Farmer*, 17 different proposals appeared, ranging from a coffee

---

[100] *Raleigh Progressive Farmer*. Every issue from July 31, 1888, until January 8, 1889, carried some coverage of the struggle.

[101] *Raleigh Progressive Farmer*, July 31, 1888; *ibid.*, August 7, 1888.

[102] *Raleigh Progressive Farmer*, August 7, 28, 1888.

[103] *Raleigh Progressive Farmer*, September 4, 25, 1888; *ibid.*, October 9, 16, 23, 1888; *ibid.*, November 6, 13, 20, 27, 1888; *ibid.*, December 4, 11, 25, 1888.

[104] *Raleigh Progressive Farmer*, September 4, 11, 25, 1888; *ibid.*, October 23, 1888.

[105] *Raleigh Progressive Farmer*, September 25, 1888.

boycott to a demand that judges' salaries be cut.[106] Of particular importance was a fertilizer boycott inspired by the jute struggle and triggered by the refusal of guano manufacturers to deal with Alliance co-ops.[107] When the price of guano went up abruptly in late 1888, the movement gathered momentum. Locals bought only from manufacturers who dealt with the Alliance at 1888 wholesale prices, or they produced their own guano. Without any action or endorsement by state organizations, the boycott spread to Georgia and Virginia in March, and by May, cheap guano was again available.[108]

The successful boycotts greatly encouraged the Alliance rank and file. That fall, the local clubs adopted policies of expelling noncompliant members. The boycott of jute-bagged fertilizer was reintroduced by the Robeson County Alliance and quickly gained widespread support. Many areas saw no jute wrapping at all, while those who used jute paid pretrust prices. The boycott was a resounding success.[109]

But in 1889, the state leadership became less interested in the boycott. The *Raleigh Progressive Farmer* offered none of the analytic articles it had published the year before; it gave much less attention to the local actions; and it hardly covered some of the important national events in the struggle. At the state convention in August, neither President Alexander nor Secretary Polk even bothered to mention it, and no boycott proposals were reported in the minutes.[110]

In fact, in 1889, the North Carolina leadership was just plain depressed. While the local groups continued to be optimistic, the state president was declaring that all the previous year's political demands had failed, that co-ops "had no place within the Alliance," that the Exchange had "not proved the success we anticipated," and that:

> The financial condition of the membership has not improved since our last meeting, nor can I see any hope of improvement as long as trusts and combines fix the price on nearly everything we buy or sell.[111]

President Alexander drew no comfort from the 1888 jute boycott nor the spring fertilizer struggle because they had not eliminated the trusts. He saw little hope for change:

> The classes to which our membership belong have suffered worse than others from evil laws in all civilizations that have preceded us, and if we fail to do our duty, we cannot complain when we find "like laws produce like results."[112]

---

[106] *Raleigh Progressive Farmer*, February 5, 1889.

[107] *Raleigh Progressive Farmer*, November 20, 1888.

[108] *Raleigh Progressive Farmer*, January 1, 22, 29, 1889; *ibid.*, February 5, 12, 19, 26, 1889; *ibid.*, March 5, 12, 19, 26, 1889; *ibid.*, May 21, 1889.

[109] *Raleigh Progressive Farmer*, March 2, 19, 1889; *ibid.*, May 14, 1889; *ibid.*, June 4, 1889; *ibid.*, July 14, 1889; *ibid.*, August 10, 27, 1889; *ibid.*, September 3, 10, 17, 24, 1889; *ibid.*, October 15, 1889; *ibid.*, November 5, 1889.

[110] *Raleigh Progressive Farmer*, August 20, 1889.

[111] "Address of President S. B. Alexander, to the N.C. Farmers' State Alliance at its Third Annual Session Held at Fayetteville, N.C., August 13, 14, 15, 1889," reprinted in *Raleigh Progressive Farmer*, August 20, 1889.

[112] *Ibid.*

President Alexander had little hope for change, and he resigned his office. The new state officials were somewhat more optimistic about changing the laws, and they pressed upon the 1889 convention a resolution to work for political candidates who favored a railroad commission.[113] Thus, in the midst of the greatest success the Alliance had achieved, the North Carolina leadership abandoned the boycott tactic and embarked upon political action.

The Entry into Politics

The state leadership in North Carolina had entered the Alliance with a political orientation they had developed in the farmers' clubs. President Alexander, with the energetic support of prominent Alliancemen and Alliance newspapers, nearly captured the Democratic nomination for governor in early 1888. His convention address in August 1888 contained no economic discussion, only the political rhetoric familiar in election campaigns.[114] That fall, Alliance leaders devoted themselves to campaigning actively for the Democratic ticket. Even L. L. Polk, state secretary and soon to be national Alliance president, participated—and neglected to report this in his newspaper, the *Raleigh Progressive Farmer*.[115]

But despite this individual involvement, the leadership made no effort to bring the Alliance organizationally into electoral politics, except for the passage of state demands. Alliancemen were urged to vote *as citizens* but not to participate as local clubs. However, as their initial enthusiasm for the Exchange waned, and when they failed to establish a leadership-oriented strategy for the jute struggle, Alexander, Polk, Elias Carr, and other North Carolina officials looked with increased interest at political strategies. As early as February 1889, the *Raleigh Progressive Farmer* was giving front-page coverage to electoral activities undertaken and political resolutions adopted by some local groups. In March, President Alexander called for a major lobbying effort to redress Alliance grievances.[116]

As the year progressed, the leaders began to use the vast membership to gain entry into political circles. During a controversy over the removal of the director of the state insane asylums, local resolutions were obtained to back up leadership lobbying for his reinstatement.[117] They even negotiated with representatives of the railroads over the position the Alliance would take on the railroad commission law, with President Alexander agreeing to removal of rate setting power.[118]

The real commitment began after the August 1889 convention. During August,

[113] *Raleigh Progressive Farmer*, August 20, 1889.

[114] "Address of President S. B. Alexander, Delivered Before the North Carolina State Farmers' Alliance in Annual Convention Assembled, Raleigh, N.C., August 14, 1888," reprinted in *Raleigh Progressive Farmer*, August 21, 1888; *Raleigh Robesonian*, October 1887; *News and Observer*, March 21, 1888; *ibid.*, April 20–28, 1888; *ibid.*, June 1, 1889; Noblen, *op. cit.*, p. 229.

[115] *Raleigh News and Observer*, November 3, 1888.

[116] *Raleigh Progressive Farmer*, March 26, 1889.

[117] Josephus Daniels, *Tar Heel Editor* (Chapel Hill, 1939), p. 425.

[118] *Raleigh News and Observer*, March 23, 1889.

September, and October, the state organization devoted itself to exhorting the membership to enter politics.[119] Besides speechmaking and analyses of political issues, there was a consistent attempt to advertise the political involvement in other areas of the country.[120] When the *American Agriculturist,* a nationally read journal, urged farmers to run for office, the Alliance press reprinted the article.[121] A new Alliance paper in Cumberland County was established around the editor's advocacy of political action.[122]

By early 1890, the state organization had abandoned all interests outside political lobbying and electoral politics. In January 1890, local Alliance activities disappeared from the front page of the *Raleigh Progressive Farmer,* and the leadership pressed local groups for endorsements of national resolutions. By early March, reportage of local economic activities had dwindled dramatically, and the paper was increasingly devoted to the political activities of national and state leadership. More and more energy was put into creating an Alliance presence at the Democratic nominating conventions in May and June.

While the state organization pursued politics and exhorted its membership to do likewise, the local clubs were carried in a different direction by the dynamics of the jute struggle and the promise of the as yet undeveloped Exchange. In fact, during the summer of 1889, a movement began to prohibit the enunciation of political demands by locals, since they had accomplished so little, and a motion to this effect was passed at the convention.[123] At the same convention at which the state leadership declared all the economic projects a failure, a resolution was passed endorsing the efforts of local regions to develop cross-county cotton bulking plans.[124] While the state leadership devoted the fall to organizing its entry into statewide politics, the North Carolina rank and file raised $30,000 to help establish the Exchange. And during this same period, the local clubs organized a boycott of jute so effective that it deterred a price rise for a whole year afterward.

Successful economic action required the coordination that only the leadership could provide. When this coordination was withdrawn, and when the Exchange was revealed as a restricted operation, the local groups found their efforts were increasingly unproductive. Even so, they did not immediately pick up the political cudgel. Instead, there developed a sort of aimlessness in which different locals wandered into different activities.

In Richmond County, this aimlessness was reflected in the wide variety of activities undertaken by the subordinate Alliances. Hoffman Alliance, despite the history of escalation and in the face of President Alexander's denunciation, began work on a cooperative store. State Line Alliance, while still holding out some hope for the Exchange, began an ill-starred effort to establish a cottonseed oil

---

[119] *Raleigh Progressive Farmer,* various issues, August–October 1889; *National Economist,* October 12, 1889.
[120] For example see *Dexter Ky. Free Press,* October 1889, reprinted in *Raleigh Progressive Farmer,* November 5, 1889.
[121] *American Agriculturalist,* October 8, 1889; *Raleigh Progressive Farmer,* October 15, 1889.
[122] *Farmers' Exchange,* October 1889, reported in *National Economist,* October 12, 1889.
[123] *Raleigh Progressive Farmer,* July 30, 1889; *ibid.,* August 20, 1889.
[124] *Raleigh News and Observer,* September 15, 1889.

mill. Smyrna Alliance abandoned economic action and embarked upon a campaign against pornographic literature. Zion Alliance could find no organized activities that interested it, and wrote an article describing the countryside.[125]

As these projects met their fate, the local groups began to realize the need for statewide leadership. One member expressed this angrily and eloquently:

> *There appears to be a want of cohesion on the part of the sub-Alliances in our business operations. . . .*
>
> *Our plan of campaign must first be carefully mapped out by our most skillful Generals, and then, if necessary, our whole force must be irresistably hurled against one stronghold of oppression (trust or combine) at a time until they are all crushed. . . . How much wiser would it be if each sub-Alliance, instead of trying single-handed to redress their wrongs, would refer them to their county Alliances, and offer being considered by these, if found just, to be by them endorsed and then referred to the State Alliance, or, if urgent, to the executive committee, of the National Alliance, who, if they consider it a* casus belli, *shall instruct the President of the National Alliance to issue a proclamation to that effect, and if necessary he shall employ his whole force to redress that wrong.*
>
> *This great industrial war we are inaugurating is no child's play, and if we would have our efforts crowned with success, we must act upon the same principles as those which obtain among military bodies, which are by far the most perfect of all human organizations.*[126]

Unfortunately, the "Generals" were unwilling to command the economic war, and this left that struggle leaderless. As a consequence, many local groups became demoralized,[127] while others began to accept the necessity of following the only open path. As early as Fall 1889, some locals had begun to work on candidate endorsement,[128] and by spring 1890, the locals were increasingly involved in political issues. News of successful nominating efforts and local endorsements of national issues filled the press. Increasingly the energy of the organization, at the top and bottom, was devoted to influencing government.[129] By convention time, the Alliance had all but abandoned economic action and substituted politics. President Carr captured the essence of the new orientation when he explained his focus on national politics: "There, in the Capitol at Washington, have originated the farmers' woes and from that source alone can come the remedy."[130]

Moreover, this new focus was centered on leadership action and membership support. Whereas most of the economic activity had dependent upon the work of the rank and file, now the rank and file was a support and defense group. This

---

[125] *Raleigh Progressive Farmer*, July 30, 1889; *ibid.*, June 11, 1889; *ibid.*, August 6, 1889; *ibid.*, April 16, 1890.

[126] *Raleigh Progressive Farmer*, February 9, 1889.

[127] *Raleigh Progressive Farmer*, August 20, 1889.

[128] *National Economist*, September 28, 1889.

[129] *Raleigh Progressive Farmer*, April 8, 15, 22, 30, 1890; *ibid.*, May 6, 13, 20, 27, 1890.

[130] "Address by President Carr Before the State Alliance at Asheville," reprinted in *Raleigh Progressive Farmer*, August 19, 1890.

change is dramatically proven by the reports from the locals. In a single week in December 1890, all the local actions revolved around promises not to support any candidate who did not endorse Alliance political demands.[131] In practice, this meant three things:

1. Alliance leaders would go to prospective candidates and poll them on Alliance issues. If the candidate was acceptable, the leadership would tell their members to support him. If not, another candidate would be sought to replace him.
2. Alliance leaders would themselves become candidates.
3. Certain known public figures who publically opposed the Alliance would be attacked and unseated if possible.[132]

All these actions were rank-and-file support of one leader or another. And ironically, even that support was betrayed after its first big victory. The main target of the 1890 North Carolina campaign was Senator Zebulon Vance, a staunch opponent of the Alliance sub-treasury plan, which hoped to generate government loans for farmers at harvestime. Running on anti-Vance platforms, Alliance Democrats captured a majority of the state legislature's seats, so they could replace Vance with an Alliance supporter.[133] However, when the vote in the legislature was taken, the Alliance leadership supported Vance, despite the cries of outrage from the rank and file. An observer described what happened:

> I had talked with both Patterson and Holman [Alliance legislators]—both close friends—about how Vance could be elected without strings used to save the face of Alliance Democrats committed to the Ocala platform. It was not easy. It was made possible largely because Alliancemen had perfect faith in Holman [i.e., he could fool them], a watchdog of the Treasury . . . where he accepted the resolution, Alliance men felt they could follow where he led. It was adopted so quickly that many didn't realize what had been done until afterwards. A few extreme Alliance men were disgruntled, for they wanted to hogtie Vance, but they were not numerous.[134]

The oligarchization process had been completed. The North Carolina leadership had moved, without membership mandate, into electoral politics. The leaders had succeeded in winning the rank and file to follow them. They had set the terms of participation and selected the candidates to support. They had designated the issues that would be raised. And finally, they had betrayed their own platform and program.

---

[131] Raleigh Progressive Farmer, December 23, 1890.

[132] Noblen, op. cit., p. 240; Furnifold M. Simmons, F. M. Simmons, Statesman of the New South, (compiled and edited by J. Fred Rippy, Orham, N.C., 1936), p. 18; Raleigh Progressive Farmer, various issues, November–December 1890; Daniels, op. cit., p. 451–452.

[133] National Economist, January 3, 1890; Noblen, op. cit., p. 248.

[134] Daniels, op. cit., p. 451–452.

17

The Logic of the Shift into Politics

> *A weapon that comes down as still*
> *As snow flakes fall upon the sod,*
> *But executes a freeman's will,*
> *As lightning does the work of God;*
> *And from its force, nor doors, nor locks,*
> *Can shield you;—'tis the ballot-box.*
> [Howard F. Jones, Allianceman from Steedsville, North Carolina, *Raleigh Progressive Farmer*, May 13, 1890]

The entry of the North Carolina State Alliance into politics was similar to that of other state organizations: By 1890, the Southern Democratic Party was swamped by Alliance electoral efforts. In one sense, the Alliance's political activism was a dramatic departure from the pattern of economic protest organized as a direct attack upon the structure of cotton farm tenancy. But in another sense, it was the ultimate expression of the complex structural logic that governed the behavior of the Alliance from its inception. And even though the entry into politics destroyed the Farmers' Alliance as a protest group, it also fit perfectly into the evolving pattern of organizational change.

The defeat of the Exchanges and the discontinuation of the jute boycott left the Alliance without the promise of progress. If demoralization and disintegration were to be avoided, a new program likely to succeed was needed. The years after Clebourne had created the conditions for the entry into politics by conjoining the forces which made political activity the obvious choice. The organization has become enormous—nearly 1 million members were enrolled in 1890.[1] In most Southern states, it commanded a voting bloc of fearsome proportions. Acceptable candidates were available, either from among disgruntled planters or from the Alliance itself. The Alliance leadership was by and large eager to pursue the

---

[1] See Michael Schwartz, "The Southern Farmers' Alliance: The Organizational Forms of Radical Protest" (Ph.D. diss., Harvard University, 1971), app. II.

political activity as a plausible strategy for enacting the changes that suited its elite origins or connections. And, finally, the Exchanges and the jute boycott had provided the leadership with mass visibility and autonomy which freed it from the constraints of rank-and-file hesitations.

The entry into politics was an attempted escalation. The Alliance, which had not defeated the established structure with power generated directly by its membership, tried to get its victory by using the power of the government. Thus, we have escalation through institutionalization—a policy that was previously enforced by farmers' power would henceforth be enforced by governmental power.

The establishment of cooperatives and Exchanges, the use of boycotts and trade agreements, and the establishment of factories were all actions that depended upon the role of Alliancemen in the economic system. The use of political action depended upon the power that Alliance members could exercise in the political system. Essentially, this power had to do with their right to vote. Thus, while all policy changes required an alteration in Alliance structure, this departure required a major reconstruction, since the nature of the power to be exercised shifted along with the program. Consider the structural tension created by the shift into politics. The Alliance had a number of resources it could offer a candidate. The state group could offer money (since it came to be a central dues collection agency) and big-name lecturers (since the state organizers had become public personalities). The local groups could provide their votes as well as local political workers to canvass their friends and neighbors on the candidates' behalf. Furthermore, a well-organized and experienced local group had a certain prestige and trust which the local inhabitants might look to in choosing a candidate.

Because the statewide Alliance sought to advance the Alliance program, its endorsement was generally based upon a few specific demands. It presented a list of demands to candidates, asked for public adherence, and then provide the endorsing candidates with Alliance support. The procedure had certain predictable parameters:

1. State organizations were content with endorsement of policies and did not demand adherence to all Alliance principles.

2. The organizational resources were concentrated in marginal districts where the result of the election was in doubt. Where the endorsing candidate was an easy victor or a big loser, little effort was expended.

3. There was therefore an uneven mobilization of the local groups to support the candidates. In areas where the result was in question, the local groups were exhorted to work hard for the candidate. In other areas, little mobilization was needed and little occurred.

4. Since there was a "win" strategy, the candidate was likely to change his platform during the campaign and take positions opposed by the Alliance. Alliance members were expected to support him nevertheless and had no control over these positions. These state-endorsed candidates often opposed local actions of the Alliance. This created internal stress in the local groups.

5. Such stress had a detrimental effect on the discipline and commitment of the local membership. Support for candidates who opposed local actions meant a lessening of commitment to them or a less intense commitment to the candidate. It also resulted in membership turnover—new members entered because they liked the candidate and those who opposed him were likely to depart.

6. Active pursuit of local policies that were opposed by the candidate were bound to hurt his chances. If the local organizations adopted the election as a primary emphasis, they had to discontinue or suspend more militant or controversial actions during the campaign.

7. This kind of logic resulted in interruptions and defeat of locally oriented actions which were the major drawing cards to the local groups. Since elections came once every year at best, the postelection period was always one in which the local groups needed to rebuild themselves and reinitiate local actions.

Let us contrast this procedure with the process that obtained when candidate endorsement proceeded from the local level. In this case, the motive force tended to be frustration of local demands. The local groups might initiate a number of projects and be unsuccessful in accomplishing their goals. One method to advance their campaigns and gain new adherents was to nominate and elect candidates to state or local office. These men, who supported local policy, could take advantage of the campaign to speak to many people about Alliance principles and convince non-members of the efficacy of the programs. If elected they might be able to make some contribution to furthering whatever programs the Alliance might adopt. Given this philosophy, it is possible to point to certain parameters of locally initiated political campaigns:

1. Since the campaigns derived from local programs, they did not oppose the local programs. They therefore had the effect of strengthening, rather than weakening, the current orientation of the locals by bringing in membership much like the current membership.

2. Since the motive for election was to advance ongoing projects, there was no special emphasis on winning; the emphasis would be on winning adherents to Alliance ideas.

3. Since winning was not paramount, there was less incentive to compromise on other Alliance programs which might be less popular. There was little inclination to support a candidate who oppose significant Alliance principles. Consequently, locally initiated candidates were much more likely to be committed Alliancemen who supported most of the local programs.

4. The campaigns therefore concentrated upon winning people to ongoing projects and they were not destructive of these projects.

5. Locally initiated candidacies were less well financed and less likely to win, since they were less compromising and "political" in their nature.

6. This non-win, eclectic, local emphasis was at the expense of coordinated action around a single issue. Support was lost for any given issue, since those who strongly disapproved of some other program would not support the candidate.

Statewide organization, which was less closely tied to its followers and had a less encompassing program, was undermined by the powerful advertising of the entire local program.

These contrasting processes point to the internal tension between the state and local levels of structure. Emphasis on issue-oriented statewide projects inhibited local groups' initiative and disrupted local organizing. On the other hand, locally initiated campaigns tended to win adherents directly to the organization rather than to particular issues. This greater commitment strengthened the local chapters, but it made membership connection with the state organization tenuous. Dues collection, recruitment, and commitment to statewide policy were significantly lessened by the mediation of the more enveloping and immediate local membership.

This contradiction between state and local organization was resolvable, but only in the direction of strengthened local groups. Local degeneration was the result of subordination to the "win" strategy of the statewide program. This subordination could be circumvented only if the Alliance membership fully supported both sets of issues and could ultimately win prospective supporters to both the local and statewide programs. That is, Alliancemen had to convince prospective voters that the association of the candidate with controversial Alliance programs (which were not discontinued during the campaign) was not so bad because those policies were not so bad. This amounted to convincing voters to support Alliance programs as well as vote for a particular candidate. In this way, the subordination of the local programs—and the subsequent degeneration of the local organization—could be prevented. However, such a strategy meant that the local groups would have much extra work, since essentially two organizing campaigns were necessary and then the extra effort of reconciling apparently contradictory policies would also be required.

The ability of this strategy to succeed depended on one crucial point—the state and local campaigns had to be consonant and noncontradictory. Here we again face an underlying structural problem. If the leadership at the state level adopted policies truly contradictory to local ones, then no real reconciliation could be made, and one or the other program would be sacrificed in any campaign. And once the group became stratified according to class interests, this problem began to occur. Demands for agricultural colleges, for example, attracted the support of planters and merchants who were inalterably opposed to local cooperatives or the jute boycott. Endorsement of Democratic party candidates almost always involved the risk of canvassing for an individual who had opposed the entire array of Alliance economic projects. Thus, internal class antagonisms meant that Alliance entry into politics was bound to destroy the local and county organizations. After the failure of the jute boycott, the Alliance developed the "sub-treasury" plan which would have made the government a banker for the farmer. To get this plan enacted, the Alliance attempted extensive lobbying in many state legislatures and in Washington. When this effort failed, Alliance demands were used as a "yardstick" to measure possible nominees, and the Alliance went to conventions to get those who endorsed their demands nominated. When this tactic did not work, the Populist party was formed, and it ran candidates who represented the Alliance point of view. When the Populist party died, the Alliance movement was dead.

It is beyond the scope of this study to look at these periods and strategies in detail. However, during the period when economic action was emphasized, the Alliance engaged in political action as well. Mostly it focused upon local politics, but state-wide actions were also tried. In this section, we shall look briefly at the latter to see the strain statewide political action placed upon the structure designed for economic action and to see the implications of these actions for the Alliance's economic undertakings.

After Clebourne, almost every important Alliance convention at the state and national levels generated a set of demands. The placing of demands by itself was a political act, since the demands represented an attempt to get some governmental body to take action on behalf of the farmers. However, these demands meant little until the Alliance began to support them organizationally. Such support re-presented a positive step into electoral politics and had to be accompanied by the appropriate strategic decisions and organizational construction.

The first important political action was taken by the Texas Alliance in 1888: A legislative committee, made up of articulate and resourceful Alliance leaders, was established to lobby for Alliance demands in Austin.[2] Through pressuring elected officials and presenting the arguments for Alliance programs, this com-mittee was supposed to facilitate the passage of laws that would reflect the needs of small farmers and prevent the passage of laws that would hurt them.

The decision to go into politics and the decision to use lobbying as a tactic reflected the organizational situation at that time. The Texas Alliance, the oldest, most experienced, and best organized of all the state structures, was likely to be the first to enter the political arena—especially when resources for building the organization were so precious. But late 1888 was perhaps the time when the Texas Alliance was least in need of new tactics. It was in the middle of the effort to build the Exchange and had just completed the first year of action against the jute trust—hardly the appropriate time for the organization to set out upon a new course.

To understand this paradox, we need to look at the organizational situation in terms of internal dynamics, and we need to look at the exact nature of the effort needed to engage in lobbying. After the first year of the Exchange, and after the first real statewide action on jute, the main focus of the organizational initiative had shifted away from the local groups to be placed firmly in the state structure. Even so, the state structure was not so strong that it could easily get membership commit-ment and local action to support its programs. The significance that the state had achieved was administrative: It controlled the monetary resources, access to the membership, and the actions of the public figures in the organization. But it did

[2] Roscoe Martin, *The People's Party in Texas* (Austin, 1924), p. 25.

not control the loyalties and commitments of the membership. This control—this access to "organizational discipline"—still lay with the locals.

Thus, the state structure was in a position to develop and enact various programs, but it could not really lead the local membership. Therefore, it favored policies that did not depend upon membership activity. We can see the attractiveness of lobbying, precisely the sort of action which the state organization could handle. The legislative committee talked to legislators—a job that depended upon having a keen political sense and status in the political realm, both of which attributes the state leadership possessed. Ultimately, lobbying depended upon being able to reward and punish legislators through influence over the increasingly large Alliance vote. The legislative committee actually had to do little more than simply place demands. The lobbyists sought legislative backing for various Alliance programs. Helpful legislators were to be rewarded with Alliance votes in the next election. Unhelpful legislators would be opposed.

The effectiveness of lobbying depended upon the willingness of the membership to change their votes according to the private and semiprivate agreements between their state leaders and legislators. Naturally, such membership action was needed infrequently—a certain credibility had to be maintained—and the rest of the operation centered upon the skill and ability of the leadership. But in order to establish this credibility, the leadership had to exercise to very organizational discipline which they lacked.

Herein lay the role of the demands that the legislative committee was organized to pursue. The demands represented the already formed commitment of the local groups, and if the committee restricted itself to pursuing these, it would have little difficulty in rallying the Alliance membership behind it. It could simply act as a conveyor of information and it did not need the sort of confidence that was required to bring membership response on issues that were unclear beforehand. Thus, the organizational situation in the Alliance severely restricted the flexibility of the legislative committee. We shall return to this problem later.

We have, therefore, demonstrated why the state Alliance, with its new-found leadership of the organization, sought to engage in lobbying rather than any other political strategy. However, we have not explained why any political action was undertaken at all. The answer lies in the ferocious counterattack mounted against the Exchange in spring 1888. Even though it was initially defeated, the full implications of the Exchange were revealed, and this revelation crystalized the many latent leadership–membership divisions that had been developing.

The Alliance leadership was largely elite in origin, and this meant that their stake in the Exchange's future was different from that of the membership in five ways. First, once the Exchange proved itself capable of undermining and perhaps destroying the crop lien system, it became a threat to the planter interests within the Alliance. These interests, which had particular influence at the leadership level, benefited from the lowered prices only insofar as they did not threaten to free tenants from their control. When prices dropped 40%, this possibility loomed very large. Thus, for planter interests, the success of the Exchange was at best a mixed blessing, if not an unadulterated evil.

Second, the ferocity of the merchant—banker counterattack, including charges of malfeasance and corruption, made it apparent that the Alliance leadership would be vulnerable to public humiliation and possibly prosecution even if charges were unfounded. While local members would lose money if the Exchange fell under attack, the leaders were threatened with disgrace and imprisonment. This was danger enough to intimidate any person, but the Alliance leadership was drawn largely from among prosperous planters and politically ambitious individuals who had far to fall.

Third, the only way for the Exchange to survive was for the wealthier members to contribute to the Exchange fund, risking their own prosperity for the good of the whole organization. Thus, pursuit of the Exchange meant a greater risk for the elite members represented by the leadership than for the rank-and-file member with little money to bank with the fund.

Fourth, the politically ambitious Alliance leadership was a priori interested in pursuing political activities. Whether or not there was a structural necessity for such action, a substantial proportion of the leadership favored it to advance their own careers.[3]

Fifth, wealthy farmers had considerable stake in such political issues as agriculture colleges which were not relevant to poorer farmers. Therefore they, too, were anxious to enter politics without any immediate structural impetus.

By the summer of 1888, the state Alliance had become large enough to exert electoral pressure; the state structure was strong enough to pursue lobbying; and the class divisions within the group had begun to coincide with structural divisions. The Dallas credit boycott focused all these developments and pushed the Alliance into state politics.

Lobbying soon affected the organizational structure. Effective lobbying required the backing of voting blocs, and when lobbying began in 1888, only a few issues could command membership loyalty at the polls. To guarantee future work, the legislative committee needed to establish positive links with the rank and file. The lobbying effort itself gave the state organization influence with the membership which increased its freedom to choose state issues and to consider a wider range of political actions. Once the state leadership was well-known and favored by the membership, it could consider nominating candidates and even running for office itself. Faith in the leadership would induce members to take the advice of the leadership that even candidates not closely identified with Alliance goals had made secret agreements to enact. Alliance proposals or were personally honest. In effect, the lobbying efforts freed the Alliance leadership from reliance on lobbying. It opened the way to more extensive political action.

The transition from lobbying to the influencing of conventions was easy. Once the

---

[3] In North Carolina, even though he could not get any organizational endorsement, state Alliance President S. P. Alexander ran for governor and utilized his Alliance office as a main prop for his candidacy. *Raleigh Progressive Farmer*, various issues, spring 1888.

leadership could reach the membership with political messages, it could persuade followers to attend local conventions and to support certain candidates, as happened in 1889 and 1890 in many states.[4] An appeal from a trusted and popular leadership could result in vigorous membership activity at the local level. This structural development had great significance for the later behvior of the organization, but that is out of our range here. What is important to us is the relationship of such developments to failure in the economic realm.

The jute boycott brought the Alliance to a crossroads. The organization could not continue to build new structures. Future success depended upon a return to the primacy of local groups, renewed membership commitment, and more control and initiative at the local levels. Only this would allow the Alliance to defeat the manufacturers and cotton exchanges that had opposed the boycott. The escalation which had defeated the boycott could be countered only by strengthening the local organizations.

The failure to present this choice to the membership reveals the underlying logic of the Alliance leadership. More economic action involved unacceptable risks, while political struggle was a safer course. At the national convention in 1890, President Polk warned of two evils: "indifference or inactivity," on the one hand, and "grasping for the impracticable or unattainable," on the other. Further economic action was, in Polk's view, simply impractical.[5]

The development of the legislative committees and the beginning of political involvement at the state level had opened another alternative to the Alliance, and it set the stage for a real organizational choice in late 1889 and 1890. At that time, with both the jute boycott and the Exchanges failing to stimulate continued growth of the Alliance, the organization could go back to local organizing or it could shift to politics and maintain the locus of strength in the state structure.

The relative strengths of the two levels determined the decision. All the actions of the previous two years had placed the statewide leadership in the preeminent position if any important conflict arose. Here was a perfect case of such conflict. One policy would enhance one level, the other policy would enhance the other level of the organization. The state leadership prevailed, and the Alliance embarked upon political activity at great cost in terms of resources and membership commitment.

Our discussion of political action has demonstrated two important relationships between economic and political action.

First, political action is a substitute for economic action. It is another way to solve the same problems. Just as trade agreements and cooperatives were different tactics for lowering costs, politics differed from economic action in form, but it was another attempt to accomplish unrealized economic objectives.

The significance of this identity lies in the origin of political action. It did not

---

[4] See, for example, William D. Sheldon, *Populism in the Old Dominion: Virginia Farm Politics, 1885–1900* (Princeton, 1935), p. 64.

[5] "Message of L. L. Polk, president of the National Farmers' Alliance and Industrial Union, Ocala, Florida, December 2, 1890," reprinted in *Raleigh Progressive Farmer*, December 12, 1890.

arise as a new demand but as a way of reaching goals that had not been met by the farmers' acting directly against the economic system. Underlying this "replacement" aspect of the political arena is the difference between the kind of power exercised in the two realms. Economic power used in the economic realm was structural power that flowed from the position the members of the Alliance held in the economic system. In the political realm, the Alliancemen had no unique structural power. The power they tried to exercise was simply that possessed by all citizens—the vote. There was no natural relation between the farmers' role in the system and the changes to be made.

These alternatives generated a tremendous conflict within the organization. Endorsement of the political tactic—belief that it could work—put it in direct competition with all economic action. Any political activity could be posed as a substitute for all economic action. Moreover, it acted to inhibit the exercise of further economic power. Since political power allows the same structure to be used over and over again to protest and change many different aspects of the system, it need not be rebuilt for each further action. Thus, a political organization, which was built to act in the political realm, would constantly pose itself as an alternative preferable to any economic action.

Our second important relationship flows from the role politics played in strengthening and enhancing the power of the central organization. If the natural process of the organization stayed within the economic realm, the leadership would end up returning to the membership for initiative and increased commitment. The ability of the leadership to shift into politics sent it into a realm where such a return was not necessary—or at least not until the failure of lobbying became clear.

Entry into politics was a one-way street. As soon as politics became a possibility, it could compete with any economic action for the resources of the organization, finding its allies in the upper structure, because political activity was more suited to strengthening the central organization. Ultimately, as various economic activities were replaced by political plans, the forces shifted.

In the Farmers' Alliance, the shift into politics was the final step in a long and twisted oligarchization process conditioned and created by the multitude of tiny yet powerful influences that shaped the organization:

1. The original local boycotts and co-ops triggered escalations which could not be answered without the creation of a powerful statewide structure.

2. The initial success of the local actions had brought enough people into, or close to, the organization to provide the resources for state action and rapid expansion.

3. The organizational expansion and Exchange efforts brought into the state leadership elite elements with substantially different interests from those of the rank and file.

4. The escalation against the Exchanges and the resistance to the jute boycott affected leadership and membership very differently. The leadership—membership

structural conflict, added to the differences in interest, meant that policies that would serve one would hurt the other.

5. The steady strengthening of the state structure, including dues collection, control of newspapers, and incipient lobbying efforts, allowed the state leadership more and more freedom to initiate and control the organization's behavior.

6. When escalations could no longer be met by further development of structure, the solution lay in increasing membership commitment and local control of action. However, by the time this point was reached, leadership had come to have a very different class perspective from that of the membership. Strengthened membership control would not only reduce the degree of oligarchy but also change the direction of policy to conform more with rank-and-file interest than leadership interest.

7. Leadership groups, therefore, could not afford to strengthen membership commitment even for a policy they favored. So they initiated a transition to political activities although the membership did not participate in making this shift.

8. Ultimately, the membership could not veto the leadership's program, and the leadership pursued its own interest, dragging the membership behind it.

The Alliance formally ended in 1890, but it remained powerful until 1896. The paradox in these dates is only apparent, because in 1890, the leadership was no longer in any substantial way controlled by the rank and file. It was then that the leadership entered the political arena in full force, bringing with it the bulk of Southern farmers. The impact of Alliancemen within the Democratic party and, after that, as the most important and radical third party ever established in this country, was impressive indeed. But the organization that did this work was based upon a few leadership groups and lacked the popular base that made the Alliance the largest protest group in American history. The oligarchization of the Alliance had reached its logical conclusion: disembodied leadership groups appealing to a mass membership. The history of the "Alliance legislatures" and the Populist party is important and revealing, but they were not the products of a coherent mass-based protest organization.

Conclusion

18

The Legacy of Populism Defeated

The mortgage system is a gigantic evil which is crushing the very life blood out of the hearts of the toiling sons of soil, shedding its withering and blighting influences over every nook and corner of our land.
[*Raleigh Progressive Farmer*, April 14, 1886]

I work all week in the blazing sun
I work all week in the blazing sun
I work all week in the blazing sun
Can't buy my food, lord, when my payday come.

I ain't treated no better than a mountain goat
I ain't treated no better than a mountain goat
I ain't treated no better than a mountain goat
Boss takes my crop, and the poll tax takes my vote.
["Work all Week in the Blazing Sun," blues as sung by Josh White]

Can't you hear that train whistle blow
Can't you hear that train whistle blow, lord
Hear that train whistle blow
Oh, lord, that train is Jim Crow.
["Jim Crow Train," blues as sung by Josh White]

The proper conclusion to the history of the Southern Farmer's Alliance is not easily marked. The chronology just completed ends with the transformation of the Alliance from a mass-based activist organization into a political lobbying effort. This new Alliance was very different from its predecessor and it became even more different as lobbying turned into candidate endorsement, candidate endorsement became political campaigns, and successful campaigns produced participation in state government.

A proper history of the Alliance might end with the election and betrayal of "Alliance legislatures," but here too the demarcation would be at least a little artificial. The history of the Populist party begins with the "Alliance legislatures," since the failure of Southern Democrats to honor their promises to Alliance Demo-

281

crats was the proximate cause of the establishment of the Populist party in the South. The same leadership groups which led the Alliance into politics, augmented and modified by politicians drawn from the remnants of previous movements, sought a new organizational vehicle for its pursuit of state power. From 1892 to 1896, the Populists contested for power in every single Southern state and drew near to victory in many of them. In a sense, then, the history of the Alliance must extend into the history of the Populist party, its most important and illustrious offspring.

But even here, the end is ambiguous. In 1896, the Populist leadership, now even further transformed via the cauldron of electoral politics, divided over the endorsement of Democrat William Jennings Bryan. The history of the Alliance therefore extended back into the Democratic party at the same time that the movement continued into the early 1900s as an independent, but electorally inconsequential, left wing alternative.

This historical extension of the Southern Alliance has led most historians to mark off the history of the Farmers' Alliance from its origins in each state in the 1880s to the demise of the Populist party in the early 1900s.[1] However, the history of the Alliance and Populism does not end with the reintegration of protest movement into the Democratic party in 1896, nor does it end with the ultimate death of the Populist party in 1910. Its history is continued until the present through the changes it wrought in the fabric of Southern society. Or rather, Southern society, through the agency of its planter—merchant—industrial elite, responded to Populism by imposing changes that affect the lives of Southerners today.

Only a few Southern historians have attempted to link Populism with the later development of the South.[2] This inattention has contributed to the confused understanding of the origins of the one-party racial caste system, since the crushing of Populism was an integral part of the establishment of that system. What follows is an attempt to sketch these unattended connections and fit them together into an analysis of recent Southern history. No effort is made to document the broad outlines presented here—this must be left for another time. However, when one looks across the landscape of Southern history from the perspective provided by the Alliance experience, certain otherwise obscure features are brought into sharp relief.

The defeat of Populism resulted from a complicated combination of processes in which planters played central roles. The planter presence inside the movement diverted Alliance and Populist demands from tenancy proper to anticommercialism, while the threat of planter opposition from outside the movement further channeled movement actions. When electoral action was undertaken, the planters utilized their domination in Black Belt areas to control elections. Fraud, corruption, and coercion had allowed the planters to use Black votes in the 1880s to defeat

[1] See Chapter 1 for a brief review of the history of Southern Populism.

[2] Sheldon Hackney, *From Populism to Progressivism in Alabama* (Princeton, 1969); C. Vann Woodward, *Tom Watson, Agrarian Rebel* (Baton Rouge, 1939); William Kirwin, *Revolt of the Rednecks; Mississippi Politics, 1876–1925* (Gloucester, Mass., 1964).

corporate and commercial interests in statewide elections. When the Alliance and Populist party became an electoral threat, these same tactics were turned against them.[3]

Thus, it was the power of planters, within and outside the movement, which ultimately defeated Populism. However, this power was very fragile indeed. Alliance economic activities had demonstrated that fragility all too clearly, and the electoral threat of the Populist party was defeated only by resorting to the most explicit illegalities. Planter control of Black votes was threatened by the determination of Black tenants to struggle against their oppression, and thus this source of planter strength became a potential weakness. The desperation of the planters is amply illustrated by this editorial in the *Mobile Daily Register*:

> *We warn the colored voters that when they unite with the white Third party they invite a catastrophe from which their race cannot recover in a hundred years. The white Democracy have protected the colored race in their rights, giving them the same judges, the same juries, and the same courts as they have given the whites. We have divided the school fund rateably among the races, notwithstanding the whites have paid nearly all the taxes. We have helped their churches, employed them in business, have given them every opportunity and encouragement for progress and happiness.*
>
> *If in spite of all this, the colored voters attempt to foist upon us this Third party, who are enemies to their race and to the white Democracy, whose principles are those of the highwayman and whose logic is that of a set of stuttering idiots, we say now, clearly, pointedly and with full deliberation, and knowledge of the weight of our words, that so certain as Alabama goes for Weaver on the eight day of November, we do not intend to wait for a force law after next March to tie us hand and foot and to deliver us over to such black leaders as Wickersham, Booth and company, but the Alabama legislature meeting in November, will before a new year sets in, take negro suffrage by the throat and strangle the life out of it. The colored voters can now take their choice. If they take the side of the white Populists against the white Democracy they can expect nothing from us beyond the naked skeleton of the law. The bones will remain to meet the requirements of constitutional obligations, but the heart and soul, the flesh and blood and nerves will be dissipated into empty nothingness.*[4]

The threat that Populism represented to the continued control by the elites of the South had been grave indeed; and, even after its death, the powerholders on both sides of the rural—urban chasm could expect more problems. Just as the Alliance had risen from the ashes of the Grange, there was the obvious prospect of a new, perhaps stronger, movement arising from the ashes of burnt-out Populism.

However, no such new movement did arise; the establishment of the one-party racial caste system prevented it. In effect, a coalition was hammered out which resolved the planter—industrial conflict and this resolution created and maintained

[3] For accounts of fraud see William Rogers, *The One-Gallused Rebellion* (Baton Rouge, 1970); Hackney, *op. cit.*; Woodward, *op. cit.*

[4] *Mobile Daily Register*, October 30, 1892.

a social control apparatus capable of containing and redirecting agrarian discontent.

The consequences of such a coalition between agrarian and industrial elites have been discussed on a societywide basis by Barrington Moore.[5] According to Moore, if a rising industrial bourgeoisie breaks the power of the rural elite, a parliamentary bourgeois democracy arises; however, if the rural elite remains strong, fascist and authoritarian regimes arise. In the United States as a whole, the Civil War marked the end of the Southern aristocracy as a contender for national hegemony; the victory of the North represented the beginning of the uncontested rule of industrial capital and the creation of the firm foundation for our current two-party political system nationally.

But within the South, the slavocracy was succeeded by a new planter aristocracy which successfully contested with the relatively weak industrial interests represented there. The impulses of the national elite to destroy the planter elite were originally frustrated by their need for cotton, which the consolidating aristocracy provided, and by the ostreperous behavior of Blacks and poor whites in Reconstruction. The impulse for attack lasted until the 1890s—the last salvo was the aborted Force Act of 1892—but the threat of Populism muted it once and for all. The role of the planters in the ultimate defeat of Populism gave them the leverage they needed to force a coalition which allowed them to preserve and strengthen the tenancy system over which they presided. The system that emerged from this process resembled the authoritarian regimes that Moore studied in Japan and elsewhere.

In many ways, 1890 was a turning point in Southern history. It was the year of the zenith of the Southern Alliance and it was also the beginning of the racial caste system, signaled by the enactment of the first constitutional degradation of the Black race in Mississippi. As the 1890s progressed, the spirit of Populist rebellion was eclipsed by the spirit of racial hatred, and the early 1900s saw the final victory of segregation as a social system throughout the South.

These events were visible at the time and they have become even more visible since then. But certain less obvious features of this period have remained obscure. One of them is the disappearance of the landlord—industrialist conflicts which gave life to the two-party system in the 1870s and 1880s. The early 1900s heard much anticapitalist rhetoric, but this was never connected to the sort of programmatic thrust which existed before. Moreover, the symptoms of this conflict subsided. The scandals about legislative corruption no longer focused on railroads, and major struggles about labor laws did not occur.

A second, less obscure, development was the virtual exclusion of Blacks from the industrialization which finally began to take hold in the South. At least until World War I, Blacks were excluded from the newly developing industrial employment, while whites were attracted to such jobs in increasing numbers. This exclusion from industrial employment was a reflection of the development of the racial

---

[5] Barrington Moore, *The Social Origins of Dictatorship and Democracy* (Boston, 1966).

caste system, and it was by no means unresisted, even by white workers.[6] Nevertheless, its long-term effect was to lock Blacks into agricultural work and certain menial categories of nonagricultural labor.

This job segregation has not gone unnoticed, but its important connections to the broader system have remained unanalyzed. The exclusion of Blacks from nonagricultural labor represented the resolution of the landlord–industrial conflict. With Blacks forced into tenancy, with no hope for higher paying urban jobs, the Black Belt landlords were assured that the one weak point in the tenancy system was repaired. Debt peonage depended upon the inability of the tenant to find alternative employment. During the 1880s, the existence of, or possibility of, mining, industrial, and railroad jobs had given tenants considerable leverage over landlords and had triggered numerous struggles between landlords and industrial interests.

With the onset of job exclusion, the most powerful landlords—who already were using Black tenants or soon would acquire them—no longer had to compete with industrial and commercial employers. This removed the main reason underlying the landlord–industrial conflict, and the struggle subsided. Thus, the South emerged from the nineteenth century with the foundation laid for the racial caste system. The planter elite had emerged at the top of a tenancy system that trapped working farmers into permanent debt. To stabilize this system, planters needed an "unfree" labor market which prevented the exit of liened tenants to other jobs, and the job exclusion aspect of the segregation system guaranteed that Black workers would always be available. Industrial interests were forced to accept this arrangement because otherwise they would fall under constant attack from a planter elite which had demonstrated far too graphically its capacity both to attack and to defend the extremely vulnerable industrial development.

The consequences of this arrangement for the common citizens of the South were truly extraordinary. Had Black and white labor successfully defeated Black exclusion from the industrial work force, then the immiseration of Black tenancy would have been much more problematical, and the potential for resistance would have been greater—especially if the white–Black unity that Populism promised had been achieved. However, once Black superexploitation was accomplished, everything else followed. The lowered standards for Black tenants made it all the easier to impose upon white tenants conditions that were only a little better than those suffered by Blacks. When white tenants complained of mistreatment, landlords could threaten to bring in Blacks, who would work for even less than would poor whites. The immiseration of Black tenants led to the immiseration of white tenants.

Unlike Black tenants, whites were free to escape crop liens and move into any available industrial jobs. This option certainly gave white tenants considerable leverage over their landlords, but the extreme poverty created by tenancy and

[6] Lorenzo J. Greene and Carter G. Woodson, *The Negro Wage Earner* (Washington, D.C., 1930) especially pp. 337–345; Paul B. Worthman, "Black Workers and Labour Unions in Birmingham, Alabama, 1897–1904," in *Black Labor in America*, ed. Milton Canter (Westport, Conn., 1969), pp. 53–85.

maintained by racial competition allowed business to offer extremely low salaries yet still draw tenants away from the countryside. These conditions also made violent repression of workers' movements possible, since there were always hungry tenants to replace alienated workers.

Moreover, racial exclusion and the consequent superexploitation of Black tenants provided even further leverage over white labor. Whenever whites successfully attacked their own oppression, employers could bring in Black scabs who found even the lowest paying nonagricultural jobs an improvement over farm work. Just the threat of Black scabs became enough to inhibit white organizing.[7]

Ultimately, the Southern social system, which began with the execrable exploitation of tenants, depended upon racial exclusion to maintain a captive force of tenant labor, to control agricultural labor costs, and to prevent industrial unionization. And from this dependence arose three important features which have characterized the South since the early part of this century.

First, the intense racial ideology and social segregation of the South has two profound stabilizing functions. By preventing the alliance of whites with Blacks, it insures against the reoccurrence of a unified Black—white protest movement which could threaten that system as Populism did. By giving credence to arguments of racial competition, the racial caste system has provided nonthreatening outlets for the massive discontent generated by the oppressiveness of the social structure. Many of the most extreme forms of segregation have arisen in response to the deflected discontent of the white poor.

Second, the political anomaly of the one-party South reflects the need for extremely refined censorship of issues. The threat that renewed Populism posed to the system was magnified by the multiplicity of interests which became dependent upon the maintenance of the racial caste system. Since the entire economy was hooked into it, and its maintenance depended upon the racial disunity of rural and industrial labor, the need for careful screening of issues was heightened. Such intense monitoring of public debate was incompatible with even the rudimentary two-party system that existed before 1890, because the Populists have proven the danger of even that setup. Under prolonged attack, political participation was progressively limited, until not only all Blacks but most whites were eliminated. Political leadership rested firmly in the hands of political bosses with deep and abiding ties to the elite, thus guaranteeing a firm and constant control over issues.

Third, a reign of terror was unleashed against Blacks. White protest was effectively neutralized by the variety of mechanisms attached to the segregation system, but these mechanisms served only to intensify Blacks discontent. And, since Black tenant labor formed the cornerstone of the entire system, it could not even be allowed to disrupt the system. This necessity, combined with the day-to-day surveillance intrinsic to tenancy, translated itself into pre-emptive violence: an extremely repressive system designed to punish even the hint of resistance so that no organized opposition would arise.

[7] See Greene and Woodson, *op. cit.*

The legacy of Populism in the South was primarily a legacy of its failure. Populism demonstrated that white and Black Southern labor could generate the power to remold and reconstitute Southern society. Its defeat gave the planter elite the credibility it needed to establish its claim to permanence vis-à-vis Northern capital. From that claim there arose new labor arrangements which again incorporated racism and superexploitation into the foundation of Southern society while establishing the pattern of segregation and formalizing the role of Black labor at the bottom of American society.

Subject Index

289